The Writer's Guide to
Everyday Life in the Wild West

Praise for THE WRITER'S GUIDE TO EVERYDAY LIFE IN THE WILD WEST

"Candy Moulton has done every writer of the American West—fiction and nonfiction alike—a great service in publishing *The Writer's Guide to Everyday Life in the Wild West*. This book is an absolute must, not only for writers, but for teachers, students and armchair historians."
　　—James A. Crutchfield, author of *Mountain Men of the American West*

"A must for every (fiction) writer who uses a western setting."
　　—Carolyn Lampman, award-winning historical romance author of
　　A Window in Time

"It is every writer's task to be both accurate and interesting. Not only does Moulton give us the facts, she gives us the examples. Dates, facts, timelines, Moulton covers them all in what is more than a reference book—a writer's delight."
　　—Jerrie Hurd, president, Women Writing the West and author of *The Lady Pinkerton Gets Her Man*

"Candy Moulton has pulled off the hat trick with *The Writer's Guide to Everyday Life in the Wild West*. Rich in detail, and stuffed with information on the frontier era, her finely-crafted book will serve as an invaluable research source for those who write about the West of yesteryear. A blue-ribbon winner!"
　　—Matt Braun, author of *Wyatt Earp, Rio Grande* and *The Gamblers*

"Candy Moulton has crammed an amazing amount of material about the West into this book. I am a stickler for accuracy, and hunted the text looking for errors. I found none, and indeed, the text broadened and deepened my knowledge of the West. This splendid book is going on my reference shelf and it is going to be used frequently."
　　—Richard S. Wheeler, author of *The Buffalo Commons*

"This guide is the 'jumping off' place for anyone interested in writing about the historical American west. Well-organized and research-friendly, it also proves just plain fun to read. Every western writer should keep this volume within reach."
　　—Mike Blakely, president, Western Writers of America

"Turn here before you dive into the piles of research books; you will most likely find your answer. We consider *The Writer's Guide to Everyday Life in the Wild West* to be indispensable. It should be on every scholar's and enthusiast's desk. Nothing like it is available on the market today."
　　—W. Michael Gear and Kathleen O'Neal Gear, authors of *People of the Masks*

THE WRITER'S GUIDE TO

EVERYDAY LIFE
in the
WILD WEST

Candy Moulton

WRITER'S DIGEST BOOKS
CINCINNATI, OHIO

The Writer's Guide to Everyday Life in the Wild West. Copyright © 1999 by Candy Moulton.
Printed and bound in the United States of America. All rights reserved. No part of this
book may be reproduced in any form or by any electronic or mechanical means including
information storage and retrieval systems without permission in writing from the publisher,
except by a reviewer, who may quote brief passages in a review. Published by Writer's
Digest Books, an imprint of F&W Publications, Inc., 1507 Dana Avenue, Cincinnati, Ohio
45207. (800) 289-0963. First edition.

This hardcover edition of *The Writer's Guide to Everyday Life in the Wild West* features a "self-
jacket" that eliminates the need for a separate dust jacket. It provides sturdy protection
for your book while it saves paper, trees and energy.

Other fine Writer's Digest Books are available from your local bookstore or direct from
the publisher.

Visit our Web site at www.writersdigest.com for information on more resources for writers.

To receive a free biweekly E-mail newsletter delivering tips and updates about writing and
about Writer's Digest products, send an E-mail with "Subscribe Newsletter" in the body
of the message to newsletter-request@writersdigest.com, or register directly at our Web
site at www.writersdigest.com.

03 02 01 00 99   5 4 3 2 1

Library of Congress Cataloging-in-Publication Data

Moulton, Candy Vyvey.
    The writer's guide to everyday life in the wild west / Candy Moulton. 1st ed.
        p.   cm.
    Includes bibliographical references and index.
    ISBN 0-89879-870-1 (alk. paper)
    1. West (U.S.)—Social life and customs—Handbooks, manuals, etc. 2. Frontier and
pioneer life—West (U.S.)—Handbooks, manuals, etc. 3. Historical fiction—Authorship—Handbooks, manuals, etc. 4. Western stories—Authorship—Handbooks, manuals,
etc. I. Title.
F596.M694   1999
978—dc21   98-48127
                                                                                       CIP

Editor: David Borcherding
Production Editor: Christine K. Doyle
Production Coordinator: Kristen Dawn Heller
Designer: Sandy Kent

ACKNOWLEDGMENTS

It has been great fun researching and writing this book. Not many weeks after I first discussed it with Roseann Biederman at Writer's Digest, I started working on the book, not heading to the library, as you might suspect, but rather climbing aboard a covered wagon to travel the Mormon Trail from Winter Quarters to Salt Lake City. I spent the better part of four months on the trail, riding in a chuck wagon owned by Ben Kern and driven by Donny Marincic, a couple of my Wyoming pals. On portions of the trail I pulled a handcart with Jonathan Dew, a new friend from Utah, and I walked with Englishwoman Sue Smith.

Many on that trek wore period clothing and cooked traditional foods using nineteenth century implements. All rode wagons, walked or rode horses. I had the opportunity not only to research everyday life in the West during the 1800s but also to actually live it.

Writing this book has been quite a journey, made with encouragement and assistance from many people. I have made every effort to provide the best information about life in the Wild West from 1840 to 1900, but if I have misinterpreted the writings of others, I hope you will overlook any unintentional errors that are mine alone.

For reading the manuscript and making research suggestions I am deeply indebted to a number of writers who have studied specific areas for years. First and foremost is James A. Crutchfield, Western Writers of America Secretary-Treasurer, who vetted the entire manuscript, provided guidance and lent me research materials. I'm so fortunate to be traveling a parallel road with you, my friend. Closely behind in making a significant contribution is Glenda Riley, past president of the Western History Association, who took the time from her own work and a planned trip to Kenya to read the manuscript.

Others who read specific sections or provided details included Jacqueline Williams, food; D.L. Birchfield, Native American issues; Paula Taylor, clothing and Mexican-American War; Robert Vaughan, military; Tom Lindmier, cowboy gear; Paul Andrew Hutton, military; and Sierra Adare, Native American issues. Paula and Sierra gave me free access to their extensive personal libraries, including many rare books and documents. For providing research suggestions I'm grateful to Lucia St. Clair Robson, Pat Patterson, Earl Murray, Marcus Huff, Larry Jay Martin, James Work, John Duncklee and Rita Cleary.

In a less direct way I am indebted to the members of Western Writers of America, Women Writing the West, and the Western History Association as I have relied extensively upon their writings in preparing this book. And I could never have done it without the assistance of the University of Wyoming Information Network, which loaned me microfilm to read in the convenience of my office, and to UW-Coe Library with its liberal lending policies, which made it possible to obtain research materials for extended time periods. I also must recognize Travel Montana, the Grand Encampment Museum, Betty M. Vyvey, and Penny Walters for access to photograph artifacts, and I'm tremendously indebted to Bobby Daniels, who prepared the maps.

For encouragement and assistance through the years I thank my family, Steve, Shawn and Erin Marie, and these additional professional friends, R. Richard Perue, Gay Day Alcorn, Lori Van Pelt, Mike and Kathy Gear, Larry Brown, Mike Blakely, W.C. Jameson, M.J. Van Deventer, Shelly Ritthaler, Dan Neal, Nancy Curtis, Rob Hurless, Dan Greer, R. Eli Paul, Rick Ewig, Ann Nelson, Jean Brainerd, Chuck Coon, Sheila Bricher-Wade and Chuck Bowlus.

I am tremendously indebted to my agent, Marcy Posner, for her unfailing support, encouragement and help, and to Eric Zohn for dealing with contract issues so I could concentrate on research and writing. I appreciate my editors at Writer's Digest, Roseann Biederman and Dave Borcherding, as well as the rest of the Writer's Digest staff for their efforts on my behalf.

And finally, for forcing me to take breaks from research and writing, and being there when no one else was, I am grateful for my dearest friend, Bill Romios. The bond we have grows tighter every year. I finished this manuscript with a heavy heart as Bill and I dealt with the death of his son, Ben, taken from us at age twenty-one by an avalanche.

ABOUT THE AUTHOR

Candy Moulton is a fourth-generation westerner, who was reared on the Wyoming ranch her grandparents homesteaded. Moulton has a degree in journalism from the University of Wyoming. Since 1974 she has worked for various newspapers as an editor, reporter and photographer. She is a staff writer for *Persimmon Hill*, the official publication of the National Cowboy Hall of Fame, is the editor of *Roundup*, the magazine of Western Writers of America, and writes regularly for *American Cowboy*, *Sunset*, *Wild West*, the *Casper Star-Tribune*, the *Fence Post*, and the *Rawlins Daily Times*. Her work has also appeared in *Time* magazine, the *Denver Post*, *Adventure West*, *Travel and Leisure*, *True West*, *Western Horseman*, *Southwest Art* and other publications.

Her nonfiction books are *Steamboat: Legendary Bucking Horse* (High Plains Press, 1992, coauthored with Flossie Moulton); *Legacy of the Tetons: Homesteading in Jackson Hole* (Tamarack Books, 1994); *Roadside History of Wyoming* (Mountain Press Publishing, 1995); *Wagon Wheels: A Contemporary Journey on the Oregon Trail* (High Plains Press, 1996, coauthored with Ben Kern); *Roadside History of Nebraska* (Mountain Press Publishing, 1997); *Salt Lake City Uncovered* (Seaside Press, 1997, coauthored with Sierra S. Adare); and *The Grand Encampment: Settling the High Country* (High Plains Press, 1997).

Moulton belongs to Western Writers of America, Women Writing the West, Western History Association, the Oregon-California Trails Association, National Trust for Historic Preservation, Wyoming Writers, Wyoming Media Professionals, and the National Federation of Press Women.

Moulton makes her home near Encampment, Wyoming, with her husband, Steve, and two children, Shawn and Erin Marie.

TABLE OF CONTENTS

PART THREE:

WILD WEST SOCIETY

INTRODUCTION

This book is a guide for fiction writers who are telling stories about the West and its people during the sixty-year, primary development period. And it's designed as a resource for nonfiction writers who need ready access to details.

Because I am covering a broad region and subject, of necessity my writing is not as detailed as that of a historical scholar, who may write multiple books about the topic of any one of my chapters. I have made every effort to provide a concise overview of the various subjects, and I have included bibliographies so you will be able to find additional resource materials should my information be too sketchy. No one volume like this can even hope to be a comprehensive guide to life during an era.

With any book about a region it is essential first to define its boundaries. I used the generally accepted view of the Trans-Mississippi West as that area beyond the Mississippi River and have expanded that to include Alaska, which came under ownership of the United States in 1867. But I have not included Hawaii, known as the Sandwich Islands during the period. Although there were early cowboys, called *paniolos* in that area, much of the culture there is unlike that of "The West." Likewise, although I included the Mississippi border states such as Minnesota, Iowa, Missouri, Arkansas and Louisiana in my region, I did not expend large amounts of energy and words on them. Rather, I concentrated on the plains, prairie, mountain, southwest, northwest and coastal areas. Incidentally, people during the era referred to everything east of the Mississippi as "The States."

I recognize, however, that the West had different boundaries in different years. Consider this item from *Frank Leslie's Illustrated Newspaper* (*FLIN*) in 1876 included in a regional overview of news from throughout the United States:

> THE WEST—Dr. Linderman reported in favor of establishing the new mint at Indianapolis, Ind., . . . A successful experiment was made at Milwaukee with an apparatus designed to transmit eight telegraph messages each way at the same time. . . . Governor-Elect R. B. Hayes of Ohio, was inaugurated on the 10th. . . . The St. Louis Whisky trials will be resumed on the 20th. . . . The Chicago distillery fraud cases were called on the 11th.
> —FLIN, *January 22, 1876, 315-4*

At that time Ohio and Indiana were "The West." Not too many years before, Tennessee and Kentucky had been "The West." Writers must recognize these boundary changes and also be aware of attitudinal changes. Let me use an actual incident to illustrate my point. During a 1990s tour of the Wounded Knee battlefield as part of a program on the African-American Buffalo Soldiers' role in the 1890 massacre, one of the tour participants, an African-American reporter, had quite a confrontation with an elderly Lakota woman. The reporter, using his 1990s base of knowledge, sense of political correctness and "rainbow coalition" perceptions, questioned the Indian woman. She curtly told him *black* soldiers had joined with *white* soldiers to slaughter her *red* people at Wounded Knee. She blamed both the white and the African-American soldiers for the atrocity and didn't feel any kinship with him or other African Americans just because of their color.

While some people may attempt to align African-American soldiers more closely with Native Americans than with white military leaders and soldiers, in reality African Americans and Indians fought on opposite sides during the frontier wars. Though they may form a coalition today, they never did in the latter portion of the 1800s. Not only did the Indians see African-American soldiers as a threat, the Buffalo Soldiers themselves viewed the American Indians as the enemy.

It is as incorrect to assume that Indian people of the 1870s through the 1890s treated African-American soldiers any differently than they did white soldiers as it is to assume that the environmental attitudes of today had any relevance during the 1850s. Land in that era was a disposable commodity. It was easier to move west and carve out new homes and new fields, than to apply manure to older areas that had been overplanted and denuded of nutrients.

Of course it's also incorrect to characterize all white settlers in the West as intent only on raping and pillaging, which some revisionist historians have been inclined to do. The Anglos came for land, certainly, and the opportunity to forge a better life. Those were the very same reasons the earliest Native Americans migrated into the region some ten to twenty thousand years ago. Blackfeet, Arapahos, Comanches, Lakota and most other tribes pushed each other around almost constantly as they sought better hunting grounds and opportunities. Scholars still don't know what caused the demise of the Anasazi cultures in places like Canyon de Chelly and Chaco Canyon, though warfare and environmental changes likely played a part.

As writers we must recognize that things change. What was appropriate and accepted in 1850 or 1860 isn't now. For instance, people used the term "nigger" freely back then. It's routinely printed in newspapers and periodicals of the day and included in narratives written by former slaves themselves. That term is offensive today. Similarly, today we don't call Indian women squaws, nor Indian men braves, but those were terms commonly used by whites and the military during the period 1840-1900; therefore, we can use them if we are writing about that time and in that context. However, we must not use them in writings dealing only with Native Americans because Indian people generally did not refer to each other as squaws or braves. As writers we must be careful not to impose our modern attitudes on historic characters, be they real people or fictional folk.

Speaking of real and fictional folk, it is important to point out that space precludes full and complete discussion of life in the West for all cultural groups during the period. Although I have included information about Native Americans, Hispanics and Asians, my details are by no means complete. Instead I have concentrated my work around Anglos, who became the dominant people in the region during the period. And I have attempted to provide bibliographic references to help you further your study of other cultural groups.

I have included several timelines, which can serve fiction writers and nonfiction writers alike. In addition to the general chronology, I have timelines detailing Indian treaties, and conflicts related to the Civil War and to the Indian Wars in the West. To know what was happening in any given year it is necessary to compare all of the timelines.

In the West, the various cultures lived by different sets of rules and by different rules than people in the East. Native Americans, for example, had complex societies guided sometimes by their men and other times by their women. We often think of woman's suffrage as starting in Wyoming, which first granted women the right to vote in 1869, and Utah, where the first women actually cast ballots just weeks before the Wyoming women did. In reality, woman's suffrage started with Native Americans. Many tribes not only allowed women to have a say in tribal affairs but also some were matrilineal and actually guided by the women. Sacajawea likely was the first woman given the opportunity to vote by a white man, when she cast her vote along with the remainder of the Lewis and Clark Corps of Discovery about where to winter in 1805. Incidentally, the commanders gave York, Lewis's black servant, the right to vote on that issue as well.

Western women had an unusual amount of equality in other aspects of their lives during the period as well. They drove teams across the overland trails, they planted and harvested crops, they dug cellars or helped build houses even while they cooked, cleaned, sewed and had children. They cut off their skirts or cast them aside in favor of bloomers, divided skirts or pants, so they could better live their active lifestyles. In countless cases they carried on alone, or with the help of their children, when they divorced or their husbands died or deserted them.

Western men, meanwhile, staked homestead and mining claims, fought wars, moved cattle, harvested timber and built roads and railroads. The era 1840-1900 was America's call for Manifest Destiny as people overspread the continent in a way never imagined at the beginning of the period. That settlement forever changed the West by displacing native people, plants and animals.

My study of the West has been primarily on the ground. My forebears were among those who settled in the region during the period, living in Kansas, Nebraska and Wyoming, and coming as immigrants from Belgium to claim homesteads. My own childhood was spent on the family homestead. I still live in ranch country with neighbors who've been cowboying on the same land since the early 1880s. I've ridden in Conestoga wagons, freight wagons, chuck wagons, and a stagecoach, traveling over the Bridger, Oregon-California and Mormon trails.

Though I recognize not everyone has the opportunity to experience the West as I have, I hope my work will give you a sense of the West and its lifestyle so you can write passionately about this special era and region of the country.

PART ONE

The Land, Government and War

CHAPTER ONE

THE LAND ITSELF

nyone who writes about the region must understand the West as a place. Though it is important to make every effort to get the western elements related to a particular time, such as food, clothing and transportation, correct, it is vital to get the place correct. Reading about the West in various historic and contemporary nonfiction accounts can help give you a sense of the West as a place, as can a good topographical map, but nothing can replace actually visiting the region. You can read all you want about emigrants traveling by wagon train to Oregon or California, but only when you have actually followed their footsteps, ridden in or walked beside a covered wagon for day after day in wind, rain, sun, hail, snow, blistering heat and freezing cold, can you truly know what they endured.

Experiencing the West as it was in the period 1840 to 1900 is not totally possible; there are too many modern encroachments like roads and power lines. However, it's also not *impossible*. There are many places in the West where you can touch the land in just exactly the same way the pioneers did. You can climb aboard a covered wagon and bounce over the salt sage of the Oregon Trail. You can pull a Mormon handcart through the sand of the Sweetwater River valley. You can walk the *actual* boardwalks used by miners in Virginia City, Montana, and walk among the ancient homes of Native Americans at Acoma, or amongst their ruins at Canyon de Chelly near Chinle, Arizona, at Navajo National Monument near Kayenta, Arizona, at Bandelier National Monument near Santa Fe, New Mexico, at Mesa Verde National Park near Durango, Colorado, and at dozens of other sites, particularly in Arizona, New Mexico, Colorado and Utah.

It is possible to explore military posts at such locations as Fort Laramie National Monument near Fort Laramie, Wyoming; Fort Robinson near Crawford, Nebraska; and many other sites throughout the West. Some posts are restored from the original; others are recreations.

Mountain man trading posts such as Bent's Fort near La Junta, Colorado, and Fort Bridger in Wyoming have been recreated. The Grand Encampment Museum in Encampment, Wyoming, has original buildings including a stage station, one-room log schoolhouse, homesteader's house, tie hack cabin and various business establishments.

It is only when you cast aside your computer and your car and walk upon the land—whether that occurs in Montana or Texas, in Arizona or Oregon—that you will get to know what life was like for westerners in the settlement period, 1840-1900.

LANDSCAPE

The West's landscape has little changed in many regards since 1840. Along the Oregon Trail in central Wyoming, for example, the same types of sagebrush and greasewood still grow, and the alkali lakes continue their cycles of life. The ancient pictographs of Native Americans in the desert Southwest still mark sandstone walls, and the changes in season continue with a profuse abundance of color and vibrancy following rain storms or with a stark withdrawal of blooms as summer heat sucks the moisture from the air and the ground. There are prairies on the Great Plains that have never been plowed, just as there are timbered regions in the Rocky Mountains and the Pacific Northwest that have never experienced a saw blade. What you need to do to write about life and the land in any earlier period is to seek out such natural places, experience them, and then leave them as you find them.

Visit such locations as Monument Valley in Utah and Arizona, the lava beds of central Idaho, the badlands of western South Dakota and the virgin forests of Oregon and California. Hike in wilderness areas such as the Bob Marshall in Montana or the Bridger-Teton in Wyoming. Ride a horse through Canyon de Chelly, the backcountry of Yellowstone, across the Llano Estacado in Texas or in Montana's Bitterroot Valley. Spend a day in May or early June walking alone somewhere in "Tornado Alley"—Texas, Oklahoma, Kansas or Nebraska—and watch the dark clouds form and swirl, bringing with them severe storms including rain, hail and tornadoes.

TERRAIN/VEGETATION/WILDLIFE

For the most part the terrain of the West has not changed. The region is divided into several primary geologic types: mountains, plains and basins. Though we define the West as the region to the west of the Mississippi River, for many people of the period the true West began near the 100th meridian, where the

Stagecoaches and freight wagons carved these ruts in sandstone on the route of the Cheyenne-Deadwood Stage Route after the trail opened in 1876.

humid climate of the East gave way to the dry West. The region from Canada to Texas and east of the Continental Divide, for the most part, is known as the Great Plains and is characterized by its flat, or nearly flat, landscape and few or no trees. The Great Plains vegetation ranges from the tallgrass prairie in its eastern portion, to the short-grass prairies of the western areas with their natural covering of buffalo or grama grass that grew and matured quickly, retaining nutrients and keeping a tight hold to the soil through an extensive root network. One common element on the plains is the wind, which generally blows more often and more strongly than in other locations, partially due to the relatively flat land and the absence of trees.

Roughly dissecting the West is the Continental Divide, which ranges from a gentle rise at its southern end to towering 14,000-foot peaks in today's Colorado

Rockies and glacier-covered peaks across Wyoming and Montana. Though there were few trees on the Great Plains, a variety of species became established along watersheds, and extensive forests of juniper, piñon pine, spruce, fir and aspen blanket the slopes of the Rockies.

To the west of the Divide the terrain is widely divergent. The Pacific Northwestern area is characterized by large pine forests and lush vegetation. Much of the country has a volcanic base as, millions of years ago, lava spread across what is Oregon, Washington and Montana. The coastal areas in present California, Oregon and Washington are generally more humid than most of the rest of the West, receiving more than sixty inches of rainfall annually. By comparison much of the Great Divide basin and the desert Southwest receive less than ten inches of rain annually.

Most other areas west of the 100th meridian receive between ten and twenty inches of rainfall annually, while the region between the Mississippi and the 100th meridian generally receives between twenty and forty inches of rainfall. The area to the southeast, including southern Missouri, Arkansas and Louisiana gets from forty to sixty inches of rainfall each year.

The desert Southwest is characterized by sharp land shapes such as towering rock pinnacles, buttes, mesas, and canyons carved out of sandstone. The terrain there is shaped by the scouring action of the wind combined with the erosion by water in such places as the Rio Grande valley and Grand Canyon.

Vegetation in the West today may include the same species of plants that were present during the period 1840-1900; however, they now are likely to be found in different locations. For example, there were few trees anywhere in the Great Plains during the period; now a variety of trees grow in Nebraska, having been planted by residents as early as the 1870s. The Texas brush country is another example where differing practices, including overgrazing, have altered vegetation. Brush country is not so extensive in many locations, while it is encroaching in other areas. In southern Arizona, for example, prior to the 1853 Gadsden Purchase little grazing occurred. But when the United States obtained that section of southern Arizona, livestock owners expanded herds, leading to overgrazing, which eliminated grass. "The brush: mesquite, catclaw, white thorn, . . . began its invasion into the grassland because the periodic fires, which had once kept these woody species confined to the watercourses, couldn't burn without the grass as fuel," wrote John Duncklee in "A Sense of Place," an article in *Roundup Magazine* (April 1991, 16-17).

Besides altering the landscape through changes in use, people during the period introduced new plant species. One woman carried dandelions with her over the Oregon Trail. Russian settlers brought a red wheat with them that grew well on the Kansas and Nebraska prairies; they also brought the seeds of Russian thistles, considered a noxious weed, which spread throughout the Plains and eventually to other parts of the West. The following items appeared in *Frank Leslie's Illustrated Newspaper* (*FLIN*):

California has recently imported 5,000 chestnut trees from Japan.—FLIN, *November 5, 1870, 119-4*

The rapid growth of timber in Oregon seems to be a settled fact. Lands which twenty years ago were prairies, are now covered with a young and vigorous growth of timber.—FLIN, *April 22, 1871, 87-4*

Various animal species have different territories presently than they did in the period 1840-1900. By 1840 few beavers remained in western streams, their numbers having been significantly affected by trapping operations during the previous two decades. Grizzly bears and wolves, both of which once had ranges extending onto the Great Plains, saw their territories reduced during the period. The most significant impact on wild animals occurred with the buffalo, which numbered in the millions as the period started and less than one hundred by the end of the time. Other animal species also had changes in their range and habitat through the period.

To know which animals and plants existed in particular areas, reference materials must be consulted. Some of the best are personal accounts, journals, diaries, letters and the like. Archaeological surveys, particularly those that include botanical references, also can be particularly helpful in determining existence of certain types of flora and fauna.

RIVERS/WATER

The key to the West relates to its water resources—the rivers, streams and natural lakes and springs—partially because a large portion of the West is arid. Western rivers became the first conduits to travel, used by Native Americans and all the people who followed them into and through the region. There are hundreds of streams and small rivers, and several large ones including the Mississippi, which are the demarcation line used during the period for the beginning of "the West." The Missouri served as a major expressway for people headed into the West. Steamboats provided transportation for people and goods to the northern areas, such as present-day Montana, and to "jumping off" places for the various trails.

Hundreds of thousands of people followed trails along rivers including the North and South Platte, Gila, Rio Grande, the Grand or Colorado, Columbia, Snake and American. Some water transportation occurred on each, with the most significant river travel on bigger rivers such as the Columbia and American.

Native Americans knew where water holes were in dry regions, such as the High Plains, the Staked Plains or Llano Estacado, and the desert Southwest, which they showed to later travelers and settlers.

For people living in or traveling through the West, finding water, more importantly locating good water, was a demanding task that literally meant life or death to them.

If people did not live near streams or rivers, they might try to locate a natural spring, or lacking that they dug wells by hand. Exploration generally followed rivers, and individuals like John Wesley Powell, who was the first, in 1869, to lead an expedition down the Green/Colorado rivers through the Grand Canyon, recognized that the aridity of the West would require irrigation, or reclamation as he referred to it, to make the region productive and sustaining. By the end of the period significant irrigation projects had started throughout the West, and they were later boosted by federal reclamation projects.

For people, rivers and streams truly represented the lifeblood of the West as they sustained extensive life cycles of plants, animals and even microscopic organisms. They eroded mountains and valleys, exposing rich minerals, and for Native Americans, they represented one of the great life forces of nature.

WEATHER/NATURAL DISASTERS

The one element of the West as a place that affected all life there relates to the weather; it was so in 1840 and remained so in 1900. Conditions like droughts, blizzards, floods, cold, heat, snow and sunshine determined what people wore, how and where they lived, and whether or not they prospered. Winds that scoured the landscape affected both mental and physical attitudes and attributes.

Prairie settlers constructed storm cellars in which they could take shelter from fierce winds such as cyclones and tornadoes. They learned to watch the sky and knew that when the clouds appeared to have a greenish cast it was likely to hail, although in some cases the green color came from the millions upon millions of grasshoppers that flew as a cloud and descended upon the land. When that happened, the insects quickly devoured anything and everything in their path, from corn and wheat crops to clothing and even leather goods such as harnesses.

Devastating grasshopper infestations affected the prairie states of Kansas and Nebraska in 1873, 1874 and again in 1893. Farmers burned sulphur, hoping the smoke would drive the grasshoppers away, and they built wooden or metal grasshopper traps to capture the pests which devoured crops and fouled water supplies. The grasshoppers also burrowed into straw that farmers then burned to kill the insects.

The Osceola, Nebraska, *Homesteader,* in July 1874, reported:

> Our foreign readers must forgive us for giving so much grasshopper news. We really cannot help it. The air is filled with them, the ground is covered with them, and people think and talk of nothing else. It rains grasshoppers, and snows grasshoppers. We cannot walk the streets without being struck in the face and eyes by grasshoppers, and we cannot sleep for dreaming grasshoppers, and if

the little devils do not leave for some other clime soon, we shall go grasshopper crazy.

The *Miner's Register*, of Sept. 7th, [1864] printed at Central City, Colorado Territory, says: "The immense clouds of grasshoppers which passed over the city yesterday were a sight, we believe, has never before been witnessed in the Territory. By looking towards the sun they could be seen in a dense cloud like a swarm of bees. They appeared to be coming from the western slope and going eastward to the plains. They were very high up, probably 2,000 feet, as they were flying entirely above all the mountains about here. A few straggling ones lighted here, but the vast majority of them passed over. We should expect to see everything swept before them wherever they go."—FLIN, *November 12, 1864, 115-1*

Drought

When Stephen Long made his exploratory expedition through the West in 1819, he declared the Great Plains region that is now central and western Nebraska and Kansas "The Great American Desert." Subsequent mapmakers likewise labeled the region as such. When homesteaders started moving into that region after the 1870s, they defied Long's proclamation by plowing and planting.

A common theory preached during the period was that "rain follows the plow." Farmers and a few scientists in the region from Canada to Texas believed that plowing the ground would release moisture into the air, which would then be returned to the soil in the form of rain. They were convinced that the more they plowed under the native buffalo grass, the greater the amount of moisture the country would receive. When the theory didn't hold up in practical application, farmers turned to irrigation for their crops. Nevertheless, even that didn't ensure success because periodically drought took hold of the land; at these times there was no snow or rain and little water available for irrigation.

Particularly bad drought years on the Great Plains were 1873 and 1893, which coincided with subsequent increases in grasshoppers. But drought didn't limit itself to the Great Plains; it affected all areas of the West periodically.

California has been visited by a great storm, which terminated on the 28th of November. It did considerable damage, but the good which it accomplished more than outweighed all the loss which it ocassioned [*sic*]. Mining and agriculture operations, which had long lain stagnant on account of the drought, were speedily renewed, with the most flattering promise of success.
—FLIN, *January 21, 1865, 275-2*

Blizzards

The reverse of drought was severe storms, with floods caused by heavy rains, or blizzards, which were particularly felt in the northern and Plains regions. In many cases, such as the School Children's Blizzard of 1888 that swept from North and South Dakota across Nebraska and to Kansas, the storms struck with little or no warning and great ferocity. The 1888 blizzard occurred just as children were being released from school for the day. Many were unable to return home and, with their teachers, remained at the schools. Other students and teachers tried to get to nearby ranches but were caught in the blizzard. Some found refuge in haystacks, but some teachers and children perished.

When a blizzard struck, people sought shelter in a home, business, school, or even a stack of hay. If they needed to leave their homes, they often tied a rope to the dwelling and hung onto it, so they could find their way back. Blizzards sometimes lasted for days, killing people and animals.

The blizzard of 1886-87 became known as the Great Die-Up because hundreds of thousands of head of cattle died on ranges from Canada to Texas. The storms included heavy snow and bitterly cold temperatures followed by a short warm period that caused some of the snow to melt before another cold spell gripped the region, turning it into an ice-encrusted range. Cattle drifted with the wind and became stranded in deep drifts, in gullies and against fences, dying where they stood. John Clay, a Chicago businessman and later manager of the Swan Land and Cattle Company in Wyoming, wrote of the disaster:

> Three great streams of ill-luck, mismanagement and greed now culminated in the most appalling slaughter of animals the west had ever seen or would see again, second only to the slaughter of the buffalo.

Other accounts also point to the severity of winter storms and their effects:

> The Western papers state that the winter now happily passing away has been the severist [*sic*] felt for 18 years. They attribute the raids made by the Indians partly to the machinations of the rebels and to the destitution caused by the inclemency of the weather.
> —FLIN, *April 1, 1865, 19-3*

> The snow-storms that have prevailed along the route of the Union Pacific Railroad have seriously interrupted travels, and occasioned much discomfort to travelers unfortunate enough to be in a hurry to reach the East. The road from Ogden to Cheyenne was particularly bad. As soon as a train passed through a drift, the wind quickly filled the cuts, bestowing upon the next train the necessity for more laborous work. Some passengers were detained nearly three weeks on the road, while at one time there were collected eight

hundred freight-cars and a number of disabled engines at Cheyenne. The thermometer very inconsiderately went down to twenty-
five or thirty degrees from zero. Attempts were made to clear the
track for the mail-trains, when the laborers found themselves regarded by being snow-bound on each side.
—FLIN, *February 17, 1872, 357-4*

Tea was a dollar a cup to the snow-bound Pacific travelers.
—FLIN, *March 9, 1872, 407-4*

Prairie Fires

Equally devastating to stock raisers and to farmers were prairie fires, which
routinely occurred as prairie grasses cured (or dried) each year and then were
set ablaze by a careless hunter or outdoor cook, or by a lightning strike. Settlers
dug fire guards, plowed furrows around their homes, fields or towns and cut
grasses to reduce the risk of a prairie fire, but when one broke out it could
quickly spread across hundreds of acres.

In such cases, people fought the fires by plowing additional firebreaks,
hauling water to spread in its path, and by beating it back with wet rags, grain
sacks or other materials. Sometimes they lit their own fire—called a backfire—
to burn toward the onrushing flames, clearing the land of fuels and thereby
forcing the prairie fire to die out.

Prairie state newspapers annually published warnings and reminders to
farmers and residents to protect their property from prairie fires by preparing
firebreaks. In November 1860, the *Nebraska Advertiser* told readers:

> The horizon is now, every evening illuminated by the burning prai-
> rie—sometimes shedding more light over limited districts than the
> full moon, and rivaling the aurora borealis in beauty.
>
> We hear of numerous instances of loss from fire in various portions
> of the country. Some have lost their hay, some their corn, and
> others their fences.—The loss sustained from prairie fires is very
> great every year; and yet, *every year,* farmers neglect to protect their
> property! . . . Reader, if your hay, fences, corn, buildings, or any
> other property is unprotected from the prairie, attend to it imme-
> diately. Do not wait until tomorrow. Those who have lost the most
> property, both this year and last, were *"a-going to plow round it*
> *tomorrow,"* but they delayed it one day too late.

And the Beatrice, Nebraska, *Express* on October 24, 1872, added this:

> Prairie fires are again sweeping across the country making their
> annual havoc with the grain stacks and buildings of careless settlers
> who have neglected to provide means of safety until too late. . . .
> The results of a year's work are swept away in a flash of flame, . . .

and yet the next year finds just as many procrastinators unprepared. They know the fire is sure to come and they mean to get ready for it, but they wait until the fire is in sight, and then it is too late.

The forests in Washington Territory along Puget's Sound, are on fire. Thousands of acres of splendid timber have been destroyed.
—FLIN, *August 28, 1869, 375-4*

The losses by the fire in Virginia City, Nevada, will probably reach three-quarters of a million dollars. The insurance amounts to $350,000. Four entire blocks were burned over. The fire originated from a defective smoke-stack of a planting-mill. Many firemen were injured by falling walls or scorched by the flames.
—FLIN, *October 7, 1871, 55-4*

But not all fire was considered devastating. Indian tribes routinely burned the prairies, and even mountain country, in the spring in order to aid the growth of new grass for their ponies.

Terminology

Blizzard: A particularly harsh winter storm involving high winds, cold temperatures and snow. Common on the northern plains. The first use of the word in relation to weather came from Iowa newspaper editor O.C. Bates who on March 14, 1870, referred to a storm as blizzard. Blizzards can last from a few hours to several days.

Butte: An upraised landmass similar to a mesa but smaller. Most common in the Southwest, but also located in the Northern High Plains region. Formed when erosion wears away soil from around it.

Chinook: A warm wind usually on the east face of the Continental Divide from Montana to Colorado that causes the temperature to rise rapidly and subsequent melting of snow and ice.

Mesa: A large, upraised landmass, sometimes a mile long and half a mile wide. Common in the Southwest.

Norther: A cold wind in Texas that comes from the north, also known as a blue norther. A solid sheet of black clouds often accompanies the cold winds when the temperature may fall from 25° to 55° within a matter of an hour or so. Some northers last for three or more days.

ADDITIONAL READING

Bleed, Ann, and Charles Flowerday, eds. *An Atlas of the Sand Hills.* Lincoln: Conservation and Survey Division, Institute of Agriculture and Natural Resources, University of Nebraska, 1990.

Blouet, Brian W., and Frederick C. Luebke, eds. *The Great Plains Environment and Culture.* Lincoln: University of Nebraska Press, 1979.

Clark, Robert. *River of the West.* New York: HarperCollins West, 1995.

Dick, Everett. *Conquering the Great American Desert.* Lincoln: Nebraska State Historical Society, 1975.

O'Hara, William H. *In All Its Fury—The Great Blizzard of 1888.* Lincoln, Nebr.: J&L Lee, 1988.

Oppelt, Norman T. *Guide to Prehistoric Ruins of the Southwest, 2d ed.* Boulder, Colo.: Pruett Publishing, 1989.

Roadside Geology Series. 21 vols. Missoula, Mont.: Mountain Press Publishing Co., 1972-1998. An excellent series of books that deal with geology of the individual states.

Sandoz, Mari. *Love Song to the Plains.* New York: Harper and Row, 1961. Reprint, Lincoln: University of Nebraska Press, 1966.

Van Bruggen, Theodore. *Wildflowers, Grasses and Other Plants of the Northern Plains and Black Hills.* Interior, South Dakota: Badlands Natural History Association printing, 1992.

Webb, Walter Prescott. *The Great Plains.* Boston: Ginn & Company, 1931.

CHAPTER TWO

LAND OWNERSHIP

rior to 1803 France and Spain alternately owned or controlled much of what became the American West, but with the Louisiana Purchase a large portion of the region became the property of the United States. Spain, Mexico and Britain continued to have claims on portions of the West through the 1840s, but in that decade the United States obtained control of the entire region.

The Russians, meanwhile, claimed Alaska and the coastal areas of western Canada to near the 54th parallel. The region east of the Rio Grande was Texas. Land north of the Red River and Texas, and extending from the settled states in the East (Illinois, Arkansas, Missouri, Wisconsin) to the mountains of the Continental Divide and clear to the Pacific Ocean in the northern portion of the region was Indian Country, off limits to white settlement. Land south of the Rio Grande and west of the Continental Divide in the southern portion of the region was under Spanish control, including what would eventually become New Mexico, California and portions of Utah, Colorado and Nevada.

In December 1823 President James Monroe, concerned about the threat from Spanish efforts to control portions of today's American West, outlined his policy opposing European interference in land claims and governances of the Western Hemisphere. The Monroe Doctrine, outlined by a president for a country which certainly didn't have the military power to enforce its claims, became a crucial element to the United States's ultimate expansionist policies.

The United States allied with Britain in restricting Spain's efforts to expand its territory in the West. When Russians attempted to extend their boundary

17

south to the 51st parallel, the United States and Britain again joined together in opposition, stopping the Russian encroachment.

During the 1830s, the United States government began its Indian Removal policies, relocating tribes from lands east of the Mississippi River to regions west of the Mississippi in Indian Country. Some believed that would serve two purposes. First, it would give the Indians a place to live where they would be unaffected by white settlement. Second, it would also limit the white settlement, effectively keeping the nation from spreading too far west and becoming unmanageable. A series of treaties and policies led to Indian relocation, with the provision that the new Indian lands would not be settled by whites.

Even so, throughout the period 1825-40, American fur trappers staked claims in the West, building forts used for trading purposes. And the trappers explored the western region, making maps and determining transportation routes.

By 1840 legal white settlement in the United States was allowed only as far west as the Mississippi River; all lands beyond that were reserved, on paper at least, for Indians. The region between the Continental Divide and the Pacific Ocean, south of Russian Territory and north of Spanish Territory and California, became Oregon Country, including all or portions of what are now Oregon, Washington, Montana, Idaho and Wyoming. The United States shared a joint claim to the Oregon region with Britain.

By 1839 Oregon Societies had organized in the East with a goal of members to migrate to Oregon. On December 16, 1841, Missouri Senator Lewis Linn introduced legislation that encouraged people to undertake such migrations. Although his bill ultimately failed, interest in the Oregon Country had been aroused, and it continued as the first emigrants started toward California in 1841. In 1843 the first parties of emigrants made it to Oregon City. That started a wholesale migration to the West.

In 1842 John Charles Frémont made his first explorations of the Rocky Mountain region under the guidance of mountain man Kit Carson, and three years later Frémont again journeyed through the West seeking information for the United States. His explorations augmented earlier efforts by such men as Stephen A. Long (1819).

Editorial writer John L. O'Sullivan castigated the federal government for its hesitation in dealing with Mexico. O'Sullivan wrote in the *United States Magazine and Democratic Review* in July 1845 that it was the United States's "Manifest Destiny . . . to overspread the continent." The phrase "Manifest Destiny" became synonymous with Western expansion as a rallying cry for people seeking a new start and greater opportunity. It also ultimately led to war with Mexico and continued usurpation of Indian lands.

In the mid-1840s, significant events occurred that changed the land ownership in the West. Not only did the United States involve itself in a war with Mexico (1846) that resulted in additional lands including California and New Mexico, as well as portions of what would become Utah, Colorado and Nevada,

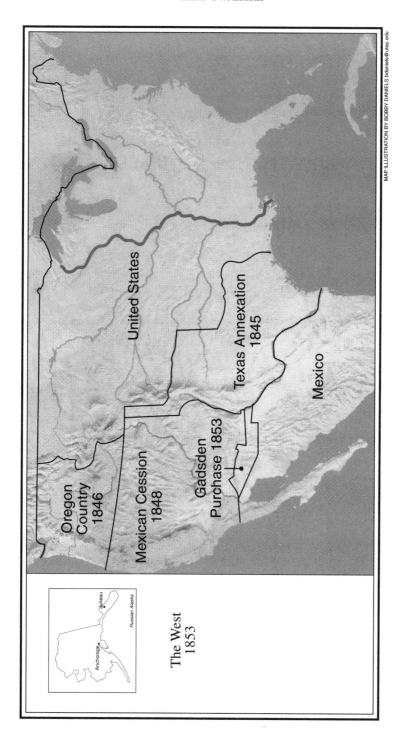

Oregon Country 1846

Mexican Cession 1848

Gadsden Purchase 1853

United States

Texas Annexation 1845

Mexico

The West 1853

Anchorage

Juneau

Russian Alaska

MAP ILLUSTRATION BY BOBBY DANIELS bdaniels@utep.edu

falling under United States's jurisdiction, but also the Republic of Texas became a part of the United States when it was annexed on October 13, 1845, and subsequently became a state on December 29, 1845.

The conclusion of the Mexican War came with the Treaty of Guadalupe Hidalgo, February 2, 1848, which transferred to the United States all lands south of Oregon Country, north of the Rio Grande and the Gila River and extending between the Pacific Ocean and the region of Texas, roughly bordered on the east by the Continental Divide. When Texas also ceded lands between the borders of the present state and the lands that had been under Mexican control, the United States had its general boundaries defined.

Additional expansion in the West occurred in 1853 with the Gadsden Purchase, which extended the southern boundary slightly south of the Gila River in present Arizona and southwestern New Mexico. The primary reason for taking that action was to acquire a region through which a railroad could easily be built. The colonization of the West during the period 1825-53 defined the United States boundaries, the northern border of which had been determined in 1846 with the fixing of the United States-Canadian border at the 49th parallel.

In 1853 the region west of the Mississippi River included the states of Texas, Louisiana, Arkansas, Missouri, Iowa and California; several territories including those of Minnesota, Oregon, Utah and New Mexico; and unorganized land located between the Missouri River and the Continental Divide and extending from Canada to Texas.

One of the greatest fights of all occurred during the early 1850s as conflict arose over Kansas and Nebraska. The issues revolved around slavery as abolitionists squared off against pro-slavery factions. Ultimately, in 1854 Congress approved the Kansas-Nebraska Act, which allowed for creation of Kansas Territory and Nebraska Territory and provided the option for each to choose whether it would enter the Union as a slave or Free State. Nebraska quickly rejected slavery status but Kansas became a battleground for opposing factions, receiving the title "Bleeding Kansas." It joined the Union in 1861 as a Free State.

By 1860 unorganized territory in the West had been divided into Indian Territory (present Oklahoma), Kansas Territory (from the Missouri River to the Continental Divide) and Nebraska Territory (the rest of the area including portions of the present states of Nebraska, Wyoming, South Dakota, North Dakota and eastern Montana). Beyond the Continental Divide, Oregon Territory had been split to form the State of Oregon, with the remainder included in Washington Territory (Washington, Idaho, and western Montana). The United States acquired Russian Alaska in 1867.

> A remarkable change of population is going forward in Missouri;
> the old secesh citizens are leaving the State, not for the South, but
> for places in the West where they are less known, and their places

are filled by emigrants from the Eastern and Southern states. There is great activity in land sales, and Missouri is already feeling the impulse of freedom.—FLIN, *April 22, 1865, 67-1*

By 1870 the West had been apportioned into the configurations of the present states with the exception of North and South Dakota which were still one unit—Dakota—although many of the areas were still territories and would not achieve statehood for decades.

Our New Arctic Possessions

It is a very pleasant thing to know that our country is growing— that, in spite of the recent threatened paralysis in its heart, the lustiness of youth is found at the extremities, where we are still adding articulation to articulation, and joint to joint. . . .

. . . The trade carried on there consists of the products of hunting and fishing, and although the value of these does not involve to one per cent. of the sum we are invited to pay, it may not unreasonably be expected that the superior enterprise of our citizens, who will flock thither, were it only for the novelty of the thing, will increase these amounts considerably.—FLIN, *April 20, 1867*

The population of the territory [Alaska] is estimated at about 61,000, of whom perhaps 6,000 are Russians, Creoles, Kodiaks, and Aleots, while the remainder are almost entirely Esquimaux. —FLIN, *April 20, 1867, 78-3*

HOMESTEAD LAW

Development of the United States under various provisions of the homestead regulations started in 1841 when Congress approved the Preemption Act, under which a settler could file on a 160-acre claim and purchase the land for $1.25 per acre after erecting a dwelling and meeting certain conditions. In 1849, Congress passed the Swamp Land Act to help states with poor land lure settlers. In 1854, Congress approved the Graduation Act, which regulated the price of land based on quality, with some parcels selling for as little as twelve and one-half cents per acre.

From 1842 to 1853, the Donation Acts encouraged settlers to claim land in remote areas such as Oregon, Washington and later New Mexico by providing it free to emigrants who moved to those regions and began farming. Those provisions led the first great waves of people to cross the continent. Among the leaders in formulating United States land-development policies was Senator Thomas Hart Benton of Missouri. He believed the United States should sell land "for a reasonable price to those who are able to pay; and give without price to those who are not."

A quarter of a century later, Representative Andrew Johnson of Tennessee

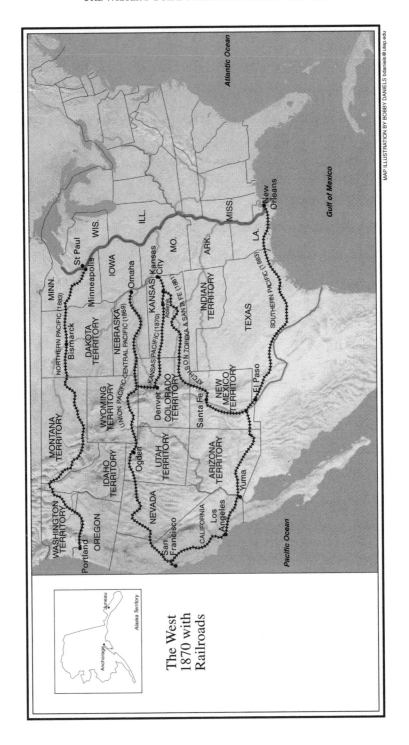

The West
1870 with
Railroads

DEVELOPMENT OF THE WEST

Alaska: Territory purchased from the Russians in 1867; became a state in January 1959.

Arizona: Annexed north of the Gila River as a result of the Mexican War, became part of New Mexico Territory in 1850, and became Arizona Territory on February 24, 1863. Became a state February 14, 1912.

Arkansas: Became a state June 15, 1836. It broke away as part of the Confederacy and was restored to the Union in 1868.

California: Was under Mexican rule until the Mexican War of 1846. Was declared an independent country in the Bear Flag Revolt, June 14, 1846, but was subsequently transferred to the United States under the Treaty of Guadalupe Hidalgo on February 2, 1848. Became a state on September 9, 1850.

Colorado: Became a territory on February 28, 1861, and achieved statehood August 1, 1876.

Idaho: Became a territory March 4, 1863, and achieved statehood July 3, 1890.

Iowa: Became a territory in 1838, and achieved statehood December 28, 1846.

Kansas: Became a territory on May 30, 1854; became a state January 21, 1861.

Louisiana: Became a state on April 30, 1812.

Minnesota: Became a territory March 3, 1849 (then encompassing most of present North Dakota), and achieved statehood May 11, 1858.

Missouri: Became a state August 10, 1821.

Montana: In 1863 western Montana, which had been part of Oregon and Washington territories, was united with eastern Montana (which had been a part of Nebraska Territory from 1854 to 1861 when it became part of Dakota Territory) to become part of Idaho Territory. Subsequently Montana Territory—involving the present state configuration—was established May 26, 1864. It became a state November 8, 1889.

Nebraska: Became a territory May 30, 1854, and achieved statehood March 1, 1867.

Nevada: On March 2, 1861, Nevada Territory was separated from Utah Territory; became a state October 31, 1864.

New Mexico: Annexed as a result of the Mexican War, it became a territory September 9, 1850, involving much of present Arizona and was reduced as a territory to present boundaries in 1862. Became a state January 6, 1912.

North Dakota: Previously part of the vast Nebraska Territory, it organized March 2, 1861, as the combined Territory of Dakota with present South Dakota. Was separated and achieved statehood on November 2, 1889.

Oklahoma: Was unorganized and then was set aside in 1834 as Indian Territory which it remained until April 22, 1889, when the ground was opened to settlement. The western half of Indian Territory became Oklahoma Territory May 2, 1890. The two territories were unified and made the 46th state November 16, 1907.

Oregon: Became a territory August 14, 1848, and achieved statehood February 14, 1859.

South Dakota: Previously part of the vast Nebraska Territory. Organized March 2, 1861, as the combined Territory of Dakota with present North Dakota. Was separated and achieved statehood November 2, 1889.

Texas: Organized a provisional government as the Republic of Texas March 2, 1836, and subsequently fought for independence from Mexico. Voted in 1836 for annexation to the United States, but that was not accepted by the United States until December 29, 1845, when Texas was admitted as a state, with slavery allowed. On February 1, 1861, Texas withdrew from the Union; it was readmitted March 30, 1870.

Utah: Mormons living in the area declared it the State of Deseret in 1849 and it also included the later state of Nevada, but the United States government did not recognize it as such and instead authorized Utah Territory in 1850. With its present boundaries it became a state January 4, 1896.

Washington: Became a territory in 1853, having earlier been a part of Oregon Territory. Became a state November 11, 1889.

Wyoming: Initially the region was a portion of many different territories including Oregon, Utah, Nebraska and Dakota. It became a territory July 25, 1868, and achieved statehood July 10, 1890.

---

backed several homestead bills. His arguments mirrored those of Benton. "Take one of these men, transplant him in the West upon 160 acres of its fat, virgin soil, and in a few years . . . you increase his ability to buy a great deal," Johnson said. As the Republican Party leader, Abraham Lincoln championed the cause; as president of the United States, he signed it into law. "I will simply say that I am for those means which give greatest good to the greatest number," Lincoln said. On May 20, 1862, Congress approved the Homestead Act, which became effective January 1, 1863.

The 1862 Homestead Act allowed men and women to claim up to 160 acres of land. Anyone who was twenty-one years old or the head of a family, who was a United States citizen or in the process of becoming one, and who had never fought in a war against the United States could claim a homestead. Up for grabs were hundreds of thousands of unappropriated public acres, primarily west of the Mississippi River. In order to prove up or gain title, an individual had to live on the claim for at least six months each year during a five-year period and make improvements. After a five-year development period, the land became the homesteader's property. For those not wanting to wait so long, title could still be obtained under the process of preemption for $1.25 per acre.

In 1873 Congress approved the Timber Culture Act, which provided for claimants to secure title to an additional 160 acres of ground if they planted and kept growing forty acres of trees for eight years. The obligation was reduced to ten acres of trees in 1878. The law didn't specify the type of trees, and home-steaders planted a variety from cottonwood to box elder, and fruit trees such as wild plum, gooseberry or chokecherry.

The Desert Land Act of 1877 also provided landholding opportunities for homesteaders. Under its provisions they could purchase or claim up to 640 acres of ground that needed irrigation before it could be cultivated. Settlers could pay $.25 per acre and occupy the land for three years, or purchase it outright for $1 per acre. A common practice was to pay the $.25-per-acre fee and use the land for grazing for three years but never make the improvements needed for permanent title.

The 1862 Homestead Law remained in effect throughout the period. It was amended under a provision by Nebraska Congressman Moses Kinkaid on June 28, 1904, to allow for people who had never taken a homestead to file on 640 acres of land, or if the individual had taken a claim of less than 640 acres, he could claim more ground up to a maximum of 640 acres. Those people who already had homesteads had first right to claim lands adjacent to their original homesteads. The Kinkaid amendment applied only to Nebraska.

> The government of the United States is the proprietor of sixteen hundred million acres of land. The direct sales by the government during the last year were about fourteen million acres. The amount appropriated to various corporations and under the bounty laws of Congress, amount, according to the report of the Commissioner of the Land Office, to something like four times that amount.
> —FLIN, *February 2, 1856, 118-3*

> The colored citizens of Arkansas are smart. They pre-empt land, and hire Chinese laborers to work it.—FLIN, *September 4, 1869, 391-4*

As territorial and state divisions spread throughout the West, development occurred at sporadic intervals. Though Congress approved several western states fairly rapidly, from the period 1867 until 1889 only one state (Colorado in 1876) was admitted to the Union. Other states failed in any efforts they launched to achieve statehood in part because of political divisions in Congress. Republicans didn't want to allow statehood for territories they thought might elect Democratic representatives, and vice versa. Only when the Republicans gained control of both houses of Congress did it become possible for territories to achieve statehood, and in 1889 and 1890 Congress admitted six states: Wash-ington, North Dakota, South Dakota, Montana, Wyoming and Idaho.

At that time a state needed a population of at least 60,000 to earn admittance to the union; Wyoming barely qualified, and some estimates are that Wyoming actually had only about 55,000 residents at the time of statehood in 1890. With statehood, residents became fully enfranchised, allowing them to cast ballots in presidential elections and for top state officials, such as Congressional representatives.

As the West developed, several factors influenced growth. Communities sought designation as the territorial or state capital as that provided them with governmental representation and jobs, and it ensured stability. Territorial or state capitals had post offices, land offices and governmental offices. Designation of county seats had similar benefits such as availability to government jobs, and road or other construction or public works contracts. Many areas of the West had severe conflicts over establishing county seats. Sometimes residents of one community went into another and took official records such as a county charter or records, then claimed county seat status for themselves. Bitter battles both on the ground and in the courts occurred over the designation of county seats, with perhaps the greatest amount of conflict in Kansas.

Also of importance to a community in showing its vitality and stability were railroads. Towns that didn't have a railroad significantly lagged behind those that did. Though some early railroad towns, like Benton and Bear River City, in present-day Wyoming, on the Union Pacific Railroad line had brief existences, most towns with railroads thrived because they had transportation services for people and freight. Many communities raised subscription money to help pay for railroad construction. To be in a community near but not on the railroad line could mean the town's days were numbered.

ADDITIONAL READING

Abbott, Carl, Stephen J. Leonard, and David McComb. *Colorado: A History of the Centennial State.* Boulder: Colorado Associated University Press, 1982.

Andreas, A.T. *History of the State of Nebraska.* Evansville, Ind.: Unigraphic, 1975.

Derig, Betty. *Roadside History of Idaho.* Missoula, Mont.: Mountain Press Publishing Co., 1996.

Fugate, Francis L. and Roberta B. Fugate. *Roadside History of New Mexico.* Missoula, Mont.: Mountain Press Publishing Co., 1989.

———. *Roadside History of Oklahoma.* Missoula, Mont.: Mountain Press Publishing Co., 1991.

Gulick, Bill. *Roadside History of Oregon.* Missoula, Mont.: Mountain Press Publishing Co., 1991.

Hasselstrom, Linda. *Roadside History of South Dakota.* Missoula, Mont.: Mountain Press Publishing Co., 1994.

Metz, Leon. *Roadside History of Texas.* Missoula, Mont.: Mountain Press Publishing Co., 1994.

Moulton, Candy. *Roadside History of Nebraska.* Missoula, Mont.: Mountain Press Publishing Co., 1997.

————. *Roadside History of Wyoming.* Missoula, Mont.: Mountain Press Publishing Co., 1995.

Olson, James C. *History of Nebraska.* Lincoln: University of Nebraska Press, 1966.

Pittman, Ruth. *Roadside History of California.* Missoula, Mont.: Mountain Press Publishing Co., 1995.

Trimble, Marshall. *Roadside History of Arizona.* Missoula, Mont.: Mountain Press Publishing Co., 1986.

Wexler, Alan. *Atlas of Westward Expansion.* New York: Facts On File, 1995. An excellent resource that provides a good overview of western land development.

CHAPTER THREE

NATIVE AMERICAN TERRITORIES, LEADERSHIP AND LIFESTYLE

N ative Americans lived on the land, and from it, raising crops or providing for themselves and their families by hunting and gathering natural products. Some tribes, particularly those in the Southwest, had agrarian societies. By 1840 all tribes had access to horses, which greatly aided them in finding food and in engaging in battles with Indian or non-Indian foes. The tribes or various Indian nations had regions or territories they used, which varied greatly depending upon the time period. Within the scope of this book it is impossible to outline all Indian territories at various periods. However, some generalities are possible.

By 1840 the Five Civilized Tribes—Cherokee, Choctaw, Chickasaw, Seminole and Creek—had been removed from their traditional homelands in the southeast United States and reestablished in Indian Territory (Oklahoma). Generally they remained in that region throughout the period.

The Plains Indians ranged in the region from Canada to the Gulf of Mexico and between the Mississippi River, the Rio Grande, and the Rocky Mountains. Southern Plains tribes included the Lipan Apache, Tonkawa, Tawakoni, Caddo, Wichita, Comanche, Quapaw, Kiowa, Kiowa-Apache, Osage, Kansa (Kaw), Otoe, Arapaho, and Jicarilla Apache, which all remained generally south of the Platte River. Northern Plains tribes, which generally stayed north of the Platte River, included the Missouri, Iowa, Omaha, Pawnee, Ponca, Cheyenne, Crow, Yankton Sioux, Santee Sioux, Yanktonai Sioux, Teton Sioux, Shoshone, Arikara, Mandan, Hidatsa, Assiniboine, Gros Ventre, Blackfeet and Plains Chippewa.

West of the Rocky Mountains and generally north of the Colorado River

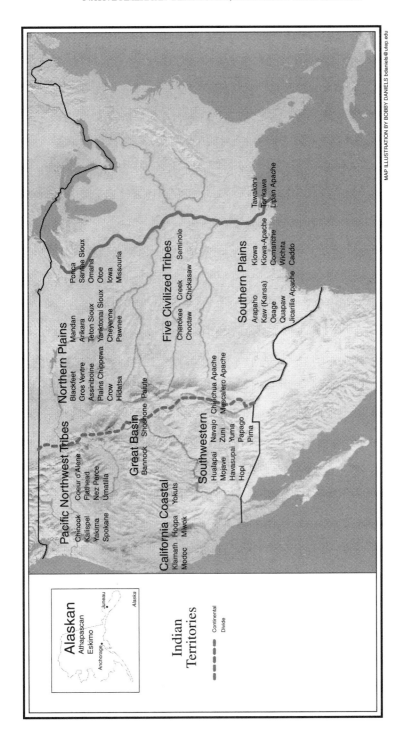

were some members of the Shoshone tribe, and other tribes including the Bannock, Paiute, Ute, Nez Perce, Modoc, and the many tribes of the California coastal region as well as the Pacific Northwest, which had been occupying the same location for decades.

In the Southwest, located generally west of the Rocky Mountains and south of the Colorado River, tribes included the Navajo, Pima, Hopi, Pueblo and various branches of the Apache.

For the most part, by 1840 the tribes had forged territories by forcing other enemy tribes out. Through the period 1840-65 the tribes found themselves increasingly confined to smaller regions as white settlers started encroaching on their territory. After the 1862 Santee Sioux uprising in Minnesota, for example, that tribe was pushed farther west to make room for white settlers, but the movement in turn displaced other tribes.

By 1850 western migration had escalated with people moving through or into the Trans-Mississippi West seeking land, wealth or religious freedom. That movement created difficulties for tribes adjacent to the great migration trails because it affected grazing opportunities for Indian horse herds and impacted wildlife, most particularly the buffalo, upon which the Plains tribes relied for food and shelter.

In spite of treaties negotiated in the 1850s that would allow access across Indian territories and construction of forts and outposts, conflicts began, as discussed in chapter five. The treaties themselves delineated tribal territories, and as subsequent conflicts occurred, these territories were changed and reduced in size, and ultimately most tribes throughout the West were moved from traditional homelands.

TRIBAL ORGANIZATION AND LEADERSHIP

Power in Indian tribes rested with either men or women, depending upon the particular tribe, though leadership was usually vested in the men. Indian tribes were either patrilineal, with possession of goods passing through the male line, as in the Sioux and Cheyenne tribes, or matrilineal, passing through the female line as in the Pawnee, Pueblo, Hopi and Cherokee tribes. Even though leadership usually fell to men, in matrilineal societies it did not pass from father to son; rather leadership generally descended from a man to a maternal nephew. In the case of the Pawnees, for example, Sun Chief, the final head-chief of the Grand Pawnees, succeeded his mother's brother, his uncle Pitalesharo, upon Pitalesharo's death in 1874.

While the United States government designated certain individual Indian leaders as chiefs, within the tribes themselves they weren't necessarily thought of in that manner. The leader of the tribe, or of a band within the tribe, earned the right to command. Not only must one be brave, an Indian leader also needed wisdom and compassion. He, or she, needed to demonstrate caring for people, through giving of gifts, and must put the needs of the people above personal wants and desires. Finally, the chief had to have a power beyond the physical world; he needed to be connected to the spiritual world. Such connection could come through dreams or vision quests and in cooperation with Indian priests or medicine men or women. While war chiefs might hold the tools necessary to declare the need to fight an enemy, such action could occur, generally, only with approval, support and guidance of the priest or medicine woman or man.

Native Americans gauged time by the moons, and each referred to the months of the Euro-American calendar by varying names. For Arapaho Indians the calendar went like this:

January: First Moon—Moon when the Snow Blows like Spirits in the Wind

February: Second Moon—Moon of Frost Sparkling on the Sun

March: Third Moon—Moon of Buffalo Dropping their Calves

April: Fourth Moon—Moon of Ice Breaking in the River

May: Fifth Moon—Moon When the Ponies Shed their Shaggy Hair

June: Sixth Moon—Moon When the Hot Weather Begins

July: Seventh Moon—Moon When the Buffalo Bellow

Late July: Eighth Moon—Moon When the Chokecherries Begin to Ripen

August: Ninth Moon—Moon When the Geese Shed their Feathers

September: Tenth Moon—Moon of Drying Grass

October: Eleventh Moon—Moon of Falling Leaves

November: Twelfth Moon—Moon When the Rivers start to Freeze

December: Thirteenth Moon—Moon of Popping Trees

The Lakota chief Crazy Horse and the Hunkpapa Sioux chief Sitting Bull are examples of chiefs strongly connected to the spiritual world. On the eve of the Battle of the Little Bighorn (1876), Sitting Bull dreamed of "soldiers falling into camp." When he told people of his vision, the Indian warriors believed they would achieve a great victory in the battle.

Often the chiefs prepared war shields, or had other accouterments they took into battle, which they believed gave them supernatural powers.

Chiefs amongst the Alaskan tribes and those in California and the Pacific Northwest strongly adhered to the belief that they showed their leadership through giving. One major demonstration of that trait occurred at potlatch, an elaborate feast sponsored by the chief during which he gave away gifts and food to tribal members.

Although certain men did achieve leadership status among tribes, for example, Crazy Horse with the Lakota (Sioux) and Mangas Coloradas, Cochise and Geronimo with the Apaches, they could not truly speak for their people either at Indian councils or in government-sponsored treaty councils. Native Americans generally believed that each person had the right to decide his or her own course of action; a chief could not bind all members of a tribe or band to a decision he alone made. In reality, however, the Indian people respected their leaders and usually complied with the decisions and agreements they made.

Within each tribe were many bands of Indians, each of which had its own chief or leader. In situations where decisions needed to be made that would affect the entire tribe, the various chiefs gathered in councils. That type of decision might revolve around such issues as whether to engage in war against enemies (other tribes, white settlers or the United States military), to move camp in order to follow migrating game herds, or to form intertribal alliances. In those cases discussion might last for hours or even days as the people allowed everyone in the council an opportunity to express an opinion. In most tribes, groups of warriors or soldier bands served as the fighting force, and in some situations as the police force for the tribe.

ADDITIONAL READING

The American Indians. Alexandria, Va: Time-Life Books Series, 1992-1995. An excellent series of books including such titles as *The Buffalo Hunters, The Way of the Warrior, Cycles of Life, War for the Plains, The Woman's Way*, and *The Reservations*.

Burch, Ernest S., Jr., *The Eskimos*. Norman: University of Oklahoma Press, 1988.

Burton, Jeffrey. *Indian Territory and the United States, 1866-1906*. Norman: University of Oklahoma Press, 1995. An excellent resource which provides a general overview of Indian tribes.

Carter, Cecile Elkins. *Caddo Indians: Where We Come From*. Norman: University of Oklahoma Press, 1995.

Catlin, George. *Letters and Notes on the Manners, Customs, and Conditions of North American Indians*, 2 vols. New York: Dover Publications, 1973. Originally published in London, 1844.

Debo, Angie. *A History of the Indians of the United States*. Norman: University of Oklahoma Press, 1970.

Eagle/Walking Turtle. *Indian America*. 4th ed. Santa Fe: John Muir Publications, 1995.

Ewers, John C. *Plains Indian History and Culture*. Norman: University of Oklahoma Press, 1997. An excellent resource.

Foreman, Grant. *The Five Civilized Tribes*. Norman: University of Oklahoma Press, 1970.

Gibson, Arrell M. *The Chickasaws*. Norman: University of Oklahoma Press, 1971.

Grinnell, George Bird. *The Cheyenne Indians*, 2 vols. New Haven, Conn.: Yale University Press, 1923. Reprint, Lincoln: University of Nebraska

Press, 1972. Excellent resources, particularly involving Cheyenne customs.

Haines, Francis. *The Nez Perces: Tribesmen of the Columbia Plateau*. Norman: University of Oklahoma Press, 1955.

Hassrick, Royal B. *The Sioux: Life and Customs of a Warrior Society*. Norman: University of Oklahoma Press, 1989.

Hays, Robert G. *A Race at Bay: New York Times Editorials on "The Indian Problem," 1860-1900*. Carbondale: Southern Illinois University Press, 1997.

Hyde, George. *Indians of the High Plains*. Norman: University of Oklahoma Press, 1959.

———. *The Pawnee Indians*. Norman: University of Oklahoma Press, 1951.

———. *Red Cloud's Folk: A History of the Oglala Sioux Indians*. Norman: University of Oklahoma Press, 1937.

Klein, Laura F., and Lillian A. Ackerman. *Women and Power in Native North America*. Norman: University of Oklahoma Press, 1995.

Mathews, John Joseph. *The Osages: Children of the Middle Waters*. Norman: University of Oklahoma Press, 1961.

Mayhall, Mildred P. *The Kiowas*. Norman: University of Oklahoma Press, 1962.

McLain, Gary. *The Indian Way: Learning to Communicate with Mother Earth*. Santa Fe: John Muir Publications, 1990.

Rawls, James J. *Indians of California: The Changing Image*. Norman: University of Oklahoma Press, 1984.

Ruby, Robert H., and John A. Brown. *A Guide to the Indian Tribes of the Pacific Northwest*. Norman: University of Oklahoma Press, 1986.

Taylor, Colin F. *The Plains Indians*. New York: Crescent Books, 1994.

Trenholm, Virginia Cole. *The Arapahoes, Our People*. Norman: University of Oklahoma Press, 1970.

Trenholm, Virginia Cole, and Maurine Carley. *The Shoshonis: Sentinels of the Rockies*. Norman: University of Oklahoma Press, 1964.

Underhill, Ruth M. *The Navajos*. Norman: University of Oklahoma Press, 1956.

Wallace, Ernest, and E. Adamson Hoebel. *The Comanches: Lords of the South Plains*. Norman: University of Oklahoma Press, 1952.

Woodward, Grace Steele. *The Cherokees*. Norman: University of Oklahoma Press, 1963.

CHAPTER FOUR

UNITED STATES/INDIAN TREATIES

lthough we are dealing with the period 1840-1900, it is necessary to outline some prior treaties between Native Americans and the United States government, since they affected Indian settlement within the West during our era of concern.

As early as the 1820s, debate started regarding Indians then living in the southeast United States who were members of the Five Civilized Tribes: Creeks, Choctaws, Chickasaws, Seminoles and Cherokees. Those tribal members had developed agrarian lifestyles and they had sophisticated tribal governments. Some, such as the Cherokees, had their own alphabet, a newspaper and courts, and they had established schools to educate their children. However, minerals found on their lands led non-Indian people to desire it, resulting in the removal policies of the 1820s and 1830s during which a number of treaties were approved requiring tribal members to relocate. Some eventually settled in Arkansas, but the majority moved into Indian Territory, which later became Oklahoma and was commonly called The Nations for the fact that eventually many Indian tribes had reservations there.

The United States treated those tribes as sovereign nations. Although they protested moving from traditional homelands, most of the tribes agreed to the removal, perhaps reluctantly accepting something they felt unable to stop. The Cherokees, however, were strongly divided with one faction agreeing to removal and the other bitterly opposed to it. The conflict within the tribe created animosities that existed for decades following the 1838 removal to Indian Territory.

Other treaty-making during the period prior to 1840 forced removal of northern tribes from traditional homelands to locations farther west. Ultimately most of the tribes had either been given small reservations east of the Mississippi River or were forced into the lands west of the Mississippi where continued treaty-making throughout the remainder of the century limited their territory. In certain cases tribes were required to share reservations, a situation required even among former enemy nations.

Within the West during the period 1840-1900, treaty conferences had some similarities. Usually more than one tribe was invited to each conference, which likely was organized by Indian Commissioners comprised of high-ranking military and governmental officials. Negotiations then took place with Indian spokesmen, often war leaders or chiefs, whom the federal officials believed spoke for their people and could make agreements. In reality the chiefs could not require their people to abide by any treaty decisions; individual bands within the same tribe also might disagree on treaty provisions that were accepted by some leaders, and each Indian had the right to make his own individual decision with regard to whether or not he would abide by treaties.

In almost all cases interpreters served a vital role in explaining the positions of both Native Americans and governmental officials. The interpreters could be Indians, mountain men, traders or anyone, male or female, who knew a common language with the officials.

In addition to delineating territories for Indian Tribes, treaties also commonly made provision for payments to traders who had advanced goods to Indians, and most treaties provided other annual allocations of supplies—or annuities—to the Indians. The annuities generally included food, clothing and other material items—particularly those which would induce the Native Americans to rely less on hunting and gathering and more on farming and stock raising. As an 1855 treaty with the Gila Apaches, Mescalero Apaches, Navajos, Capote Band of Utes, Muache Band of Utes and Jicarilla Apaches said, the Indians received lands on which they could settle to "cultivate the soil and raise flocks and herds for subsistence." Tribes commonly received plows and cows as part of their treaty settlement. Treaty provisions also generally required Indians to establish schools and to refrain from use of alcoholic beverages.

In finalizing the treaties, governmental officials presented medals and gifts to the chiefs, and usually they also distributed gifts to the hundreds or thousands of tribal members who had come to the treaty conferences with their leaders.

George W. Manypenny, Commissioner of Indian Affairs, noted in 1856 there were three kinds of treaties: "first, treaties of peace and friendship; second, treaties of acquisition, with a view of colonizing the Indians on reservations; and third, treaties of acquisition and providing for the permanent settlement of the individuals of the tribes, at once or in the future, on separate tracts of lands or homesteads, and for the gradual abolition of the tribal character."

The final period of formal treaty making occurred during the 1860s. Areas which were the most problematic for treaty makers included Utah, with its strong Mormon influence; New Mexico, with its past domination by Mexico; and Texas, which had been independent and still retained a certain amount of state autonomy thus creating difficulties in finding land upon which to place reservations. While the earliest treaties sought primarily to establish peace, by the end of the period the tribes had been confined to reservations, and most of the tribal lands had been divided and allocated to individual tribal members. In this space it is impossible to outline the hundreds of treaties negotiated in the West during the period; however, following are some of the key treaties and agreements reached regarding Indians in the Trans-Mississippi West.

TREATY TIMELINE

1851: Fort Laramie, September 17—Some 10,000 Sioux, Cheyennes, Arapahos, Crows, Arikaras, Gros Ventres, Assiniboines and Mandans surrender Indians lands for a fee of $50,000 each year for fifty years (later reduced to ten years) and establish new tribal lands at the treaty conference held on Horse Creek. The Indians agreed to limit hostilities and to make restitution in the event of wrongs committed against whites by Indians, and they recognized the right of the United States to have roads through their territory (the Oregon-California-Mormon Trail, being the primary one).

1851-52: Indian Commissioners negotiate a number of treaties with California tribes and with tribes in Oregon.

1853: Comanches, Kiowas and Apaches living south of the Arkansas River agree to treaties similar to the 1851 Fort Laramie Treaty.

1854: In treaties negotiated by Indian Commissioner George Manypenny, the Otoes, Missourias, Omahas, Delawares, Peorias, Shawnees, Piankashaws, Weas and Miamis cede all but 1.34 million of their 15 million acres, opening most of eastern Nebraska to white settlement. The reserved Indian lands meanwhile are allotted in farm-sized plots to individual Indians. Annuities ranging from $5,000 to $20,000 are to be paid for thirty-eight years with an additional $20,000 allocated to pay for the Indian removal to their new reservation lands and to purchase implements. Additionally, the government will provide for various trades including a blacksmith shop, grist mill and sawmill.

1857: September 24—Pawnees sign away the last of their land in Nebraska in the Table Rock Treaty at Nebraska City; they move to a reserve at Genoa, Nebraska.

> It is expected that a treaty will be negotiated this summer with the Yorktown [Yankton] Sioux Indians, in Minnesota, for the extensive region of country bounded by the Missouri river and the Big Sioux on the West and East, and the 45th parallel of north latitude, on

the North and South. This treaty will open up the best portion of
the territory of Dacota [*sic*] to settlement.
—FLIN, *August 8, 1857, 155-3*

1861: The Five Civilized Tribes negotiate treaties with the Confederate States
of America, which granted fee-simple ownership of the land to be held in
common "so long as grass shall grow and water run." Treaty provisions
further added that the lands would not be "included in any state or territory,
nor would a tribe, without its own consent, be organized as a territory or
state," according to Francis Prucha in *American Indian Treaties*. The Confederacy not only wanted the allegiance of the tribes during the Civil War, but
also may have coveted the Indian lands as noted by Albert Pike, who negotiated the treaties, when he wrote: "The concessions made [by] the Indians
are really far more for *our* benefit than for *theirs*, . . . *we*, a thousand times
more than they, . . . are interested to have this country . . . opened to settlement and formed into a State."

1863: February 16—Congress voids all extant treaties with the Sisseton, Wah-
peton, Mdewakanton and Wahpekute bands of Sioux as a result of pressures
exerted following the 1862 Sioux Uprising in Minnesota.

> The President, in his instruction to Indian commissioner Dole,
> who is about to proceed to the Far West, for the purpose of effect-
> ing important treaties with the red men, directs him to press upon
> these wild and roving people the importance and necessity of aban-
> doning their present savage and unsettled mode of life, and apply-
> ing themselves to industry and the habits of civilization.
> —FLIN, *July 15, 1865, 259-2*

1865: October—Cheyennes, Arapahos, Comanches, Kiowas and Kiowa-
Apaches gather on the Little Arkansas River for a treaty conference during
which the Cheyennes and Arapahos sign away their lands in Colorado in
exchange for a reservation in Kansas and Indian Territory. The Kiowa-
Apaches, Comanches and Kiowas meanwhile agreed to settle on a reservation in the Texas panhandle and in Indian Territory. But none of the agreements is ever carried out because neither Texas nor Kansas would allow the
agreed-upon reservations.

In 1867 the United States created its Indian Peace Commission, charged
with settling the Indian conflict by negotiating treaties and requiring Indians
to move to reservation lands and out of the path and settlement areas of
whites.

1867: Medicine Lodge Creek, October 21—Some 7,000 Kiowas, Comanches,
Apaches, Cheyennes and Arapahos gather for talks at Medicine Lodge

Creek, Kansas. The negotiations are held between the tribes and their leaders including Satanta, Black Kettle and Stumbling Bear, and U.S. Commissioners C.C. Augur, William S. Harney, Nathaniel G. Taylor, Samuel F. Tappan, John B. Henderson and John B. Sanborn. The Comanches and Kiowas receive reservations encompassing three million acres between the Washita and Red Rivers. Comanche leader Quanah Parker refuses to sign saying: "Tell the white chiefs that the Quohadas are warriors and will surrender when the bluecoats come and whip us."

Frank Leslie's Illustrated Newspaper reported on the Medicine Lodge talks:

> The commissioners were seated upon camp stools ranged in a semi-circle, and the head chiefs squatted upon the ground forming a circle about them. A shady bower had been erected to shelter the party from the sun. Satanta, the chief of the Kiowas, secured a camp chair for himself, and occupied a position in front of his principal warriors. Little Raven, a very corpulent chief, filled the second station of honor. Facing the Commissioners was Mrs. Virginia Adams, the interpretess for the Arapaho tribe, attired in a bright crimson gown.
>
> General Harney, who is held in the utmost veneration by the Indians on account of having outrun their fleetest warrior, occupied the position of grand chief in the council, and appeared in full-dress uniform. Upon the right of General Harney were Commissioner Tayler and Generals Auger and Terry, and upon his left, General Sandborn, Colonel Leavenworth, and McClosky who acted as the interpreter of the council.
>
> Senator John B. Henderson, made known to the Indians the stipulations of a treaty between themselves and the Government, after which several prominent chiefs gave an expression to their views, which in the main were in opposition to their being settled upon reservations.
>
> A subsequent meeting was held on the following day, at which there was a general interchange of sentiment upon the features of the proposed treaty, and on the 21st the Indians came to terms and the treaty was signed. . . .
>
> . . . It may be well to state as an evidence of good faith on the part of the Government, that the Commissioners have distributed over $150,000 worth of provisions, besides a large number of blankets, suits of uniforms, tobacco, Indian cloth, axes, bed-tickings, revolvers, and sixteen elegant silver medals valued at $250. . . .
>
> . . . On the 21st ultimo the Indian Commissioners and the chiefs of the Comanches and Kiowas signed a treaty of peace, which gives the Indians 6,000 square miles of land in the south-western corner of Indian Territory [Oklahoma]. Each Indian is to receive annually

a full suit of clothes; they are to have farming implements, a teacher, miller, physician, warehouse, etc., and $25,000 per annum, or its value in such things as they may need. In consideration of all this, the Indians are to be peaceable and let all railroads be built across the plains.—FLIN, *November 16, 1867, 135-2 &3*

Items immediately distributed to the Indians at the Medicine Creek treaty conference include pots, pans, kettles, nails, brushes, sugar, coffee, flour, guns, powder and clothing.

The issue of clothing to the Comanche Indians after they had signed the treaty of peace was one of singular oddity, as many of the Indians forsook their old clothes immediately upon the receipt of new. The clothing issued consists of blankets, coats, shawls, calico, skirts, hats, pants, plumes, cords, beads, needles, pins, thread, yarn and woolens by the bale.—FLIN, *November 23, 1867, 154-1*

1868: Spring—Peace Commissioners negotiate treaties with the Brulés (April 29), Crows (May 7), Northern Cheyennes and Northern Arapahos (May 10). Other Sioux bands, with the exception of Red Cloud's Oglala, agree to treaty conditions in late May.

1868: July 2—Hunkpapa chief Sitting Bull and his associates, including Gall, sign the Fort Laramie Treaty that sets aside the Great Sioux Reserve, and which requires the Hunkpapas to settle on the reservation lands.

1868: July 3—Shoshones and Bannocks agree to treaties which establish reservation lands for the two tribes in Wyoming and Idaho.

1868: August 3—Nez Perces agree to treaties and subsequent reservations.

1868: November 6—Red Cloud agrees to a treaty negotiated by General William Tecumseh Sherman at Fort Laramie bringing an end to "Red Cloud's War" that leads to establishment of agencies where the Sioux would receive annuities along the North Platte River; later they receive goods along the White River. Red Cloud had refused to negotiate at the treaty talks which began on April 29, 1868, demanding that troops stationed in the Powder River Basin be removed. Once the forts along the Bozeman trail—Reno, Phil Kearny and C.F. Smith—were abandoned by the military and burned by the Sioux, Red Cloud made his way to Fort Laramie. The agreement said:

From this day forward all war between the parties to this agreement shall forever cease. The government of the United States desires peace, and its honor is hereby pledged to keep it. The Indians desire peace, and they now pledge their honor to maintain it.

The 1868 treaties were the final formal treaties between the United States government and the Indian tribes, although various forms of negotiation continued throughout the next thirty years, as the following timeline shows:

1869: President Andrew Johnson establishes the Santee Sioux Reservation near Niobrara, Nebraska.

1873: The government establishes the Red Cloud and Spotted Tail Indian Agencies (located in different places) to distribute annuities to the Sioux and Cheyenne Indians.

Investigation of Fraud at the Red Cloud Agency

We found the system of keeping accounts at the Red Cloud Agency *exceedingly loose and defective, and for much of this the Indian Office is justly censurable.* It is only within the last few weeks that the Government has supplied the books to the agent *and required the adoption of a system calculated to exhibit clearly the state of his accounts.* Prior to that time the agent furnished his own books, and made all his accounts in a loose and irregular manner; *and when his agency expired, carried off all the books and papers as his private property.*
—FLIN, *November 6, 1875, 130-2*

1875: May—Sioux chiefs reject a $6 million government offer for the Black Hills.

1875: September—Thousands of members of the Sioux Nation watch as the Allison Commission fails to purchase the Black Hills.

In 1876 when Sitting Bull indicates he wants to purchase supplies from the Fort Peck Indian Agency, Montana Territory, the response to the agent is:

Inform Sitting Bull that the only condition of peace is his surrender, when he will be treated as a prisoner of war. Issue no rations except after such surrender, and when fully satisfied that the Indians can be held at the agency. Make early preparation to defend the agency stores and property. The military will co-operate as far as possible.

1879: Following the Meeker Massacre in northern Colorado, Utes relinquish their Colorado lands and move to a reservation in Utah. They had earlier relinquished some of their lands in the San Juan region.

COLORADO—The Utes, of Colorado, have agreed to give up the San Juan mining region, about which there has long been contention between miners and Indians.—FLIN *October 4, 1873, 59-4*

1879: Federal Courts affirm that Indians are "people" in *Standing Bear v Crook.*

Ponca chief Standing Bear went to court in a case where the judge ultimately ruled that an Indian is a "person" in the eyes of the law and thus is protected by constitutional guarantees of personal liberty. (Indians didn't earn citizenship rights until after World War I.) The Poncas in 1858 had negotiated a treaty with the United States and in 1876 the government ordered the Poncas under Standing Bear and other chiefs to Indian Territory.

"We got ready and started, wishing first to visit the Omaha reserve, but this was not allowed us," the Ponca chiefs said in a statement published in a Sioux City, Iowa, newspaper. "After some days we reached the country of the Osages, and looked over the country and found it stony and broken, and not a country we thought we could make a living in. We saw the Osages there, and they were without shirts, their skin burned, and their hair stood up as if it had not been combed since they were little children. We did not wish to sink so low as they seemed to be."

After the inspection trip the Ponca chiefs did not want to move to Oklahoma. They made their way home to Nebraska, where they intended to remain, but in 1877 the government ordered a forced relocation to Oklahoma, where many of the Poncas died. Unable to bear the hardships forced upon his tribe, in early 1879 Standing Bear broke away from the reservation in Oklahoma to return to Nebraska, where his people sought refuge with their friends and relatives, the Omahas.

When General George Crook ordered troops to take the Poncas into custody and return them to Oklahoma, *Omaha World-Herald* editor Thomas Tibbles, a former abolitionist crusader in Kansas, heard of the plan and vowed to fight "for exactly the same principals [sic] for which he [had] fought twenty-four years ago, *the equality of all men before the law,*" Kay Graber wrote in her introduction to *The Ponca Chiefs: An Account of the Trial of Standing Bear.*

Attorneys John L. Webster and A.J. Poppleton filed a writ of habeas corpus in behalf of Standing Bear against General Crook, which centered on the issue of whether Indian people had the same basic civil liberties as all other Americans.

Crook's troops took the Poncas into custody and placed them in the Omaha Barracks. While the Poncas were there, the Omaha tribe came to their aid, offering to share their reservation and to support the Poncas until they could provide for themselves. A letter signed by twenty members of the Omaha tribe dated April 21, 1879, spelled out the Omahas' concern for the Poncas:

> They are our brothers and our sisters, our uncles and our cousins, and although we are called savages we feel that sympathy for our persecuted brethren that should characterize Christians, we are willing to share what we possess with them if they can only be allowed to return and labor, improve and provide for themselves

where they may live in peace, enjoy good health, and the opportunity of educating their children up to a higher state of civilization.

After hearing the testimony on both sides of the case, U.S. District Judge Elmer S. Dundy on May 12, 1879, filed his opinion in the matter, writing:

> The reasoning advanced in support of my views, leads me to conclude:
>
> First. That an *Indian* is a PERSON within the meaning of the laws of the United States. . . .
>
> Second. That General George Crook . . . has the custody of the realtors under color of the authority of the United States, and in violation of the laws thereof.
>
> Third. That no rightful authority exists for removing by force any of the realtors to the Indian Territory. . . .
>
> Fourth. That the Indians possess the inherent right of expatriation as well as the more fortunate white race, and have the inalienable right to "*life, liberty* and the pursuit of happiness," so long as they obey the laws and do not trespass on forbidden ground. And
>
> Fifth. Being restrained of liberty under color of authority of the United States, and in violation of the laws thereof, the realtors must be discharged from custody, and it is so ordered.

1887: February 8—President Grover Cleveland approves the Dawes Severalty Act, named for its sponsor, Massachusetts Senator Henry Dawes. The act dissolves Indian tribes as legal entities and divides tribal lands, giving heads of Indian households 160 acres, single Indian people 80 acres, and minor Indians 40 acres. The Indians agree to farm their land and that they will not sell it to non-Indians for at least 25 years. Subsequent changes in the act weaken it.

ADDITIONAL READING

Anderson, George E., W.H. Ellison, and Robert F. Heizer. *Treaty Making and Treaty Rejection by the Federal Government in California, 1850-1852.* Socorro, N.Mex.: Ballena Press, 1978.

Brugge, David M., and J. Lee Correll. *The Story of the Navajo Treaties.* Window Rock, Ariz.: Research Section, Navajo Parks and Recreation Department, Navajo Tribe, 1971.

A Compilation of All the Treaties between the United States and the Indian Tribes Now in Force as Laws. Washington, DC: Government Printing Office, 1873.

Hill, Burton S. "The Great Indian Treaty Council of 1851," *Nebraska History* 47 (March 1966): 85-110.

Institute for the Development of Indian Law. *A Chronological List of Treaties and Agreements Made By Indian Tribes with the United States.* Washington, DC: Institute, 1973.

Jones, Douglas C. *The Treaty of Medicine Lodge: The Story of the Great Treaty Council As Told by Eyewitnesses.* Norman: University of Oklahoma Press, 1966.

Kappler, Charles J., comp. *Indian Affairs: Laws and Treaties,* Vol. 2, *Treaties.* Washington, DC: Government Printing Office, 1904. (58th Cong., 2d sess., 1904 S. Doc. 319, serial 4624.) An excellent resource.

Kickingbird, Kirke, and others. *Indian Treaties.* Washington, DC: Institute for the Development of Indian Law, 1980.

Kvasnicka, Robert M. "United States Indian Treaties and Agreements." In *Handbook of North American Indians,* Vol. 4, *History of Indian-White Relations,* ed. Wilcomb E. Washburn, 195-201. Washington, DC: Smithsonian Institution, 1988.

Prucha, Francis Paul. *American Indian Treaties: The History of a Political Anomaly.* Berkeley: University of California Press, 1994. An excellent resource.

Trafzer, Clifford E., ed. *Indians, Superintendents, and Councils: Northwestern Indian Policy, 1850-1855.* Lanham, Md.: University Press of America, 1986.

CHAPTER FIVE

WESTERN WARS

T he West had conflicts on nearly all sides throughout most of the period
1840-1900 as frontier army regular troops and volunteers engaged in
wars with Mexicans, Mormons and Indians. Many who had served together during the Mexican and Mormon wars of 1846-47 and 1857,
respectively, chose sides during the Civil War, some becoming Confederate officers or soldiers and others remaining as a part of the Union
army.

Common elements for all soldiers during all periods related to isolation, poor food, inadequate medical care and limited supplies. The few forts
in the Trans-Mississippi West in 1840 burgeoned to more than one hundred
by the peak Indian War years of the 1860s and 1870s. The troops and their
officers often worked long hours for little pay and almost always in difficult
circumstances and with inadequate or improper clothing.

FRONTIER ARMY

The United States government established military posts across the West and
throughout the period 1840-1900, with some seventy already established by the
time the Civil War started in 1861. Initially the posts had soldiers from among
the regular forces; however, during the Civil War when those regular troops
were needed to participate in battles between Union and Confederate armies,
the western region relied on volunteer forces, such as militia groups raised in
Colorado, New Mexico, Nebraska or California. Sometimes their officers—
like many of the volunteer troops—were Indian-hating zealots.

Initially many of the volunteer troops were raised to protect communication links—telegraph lines and overland trails—but before the end of the Civil War, when Regular Army troops returned to garrison the western posts, the volunteers also engaged in battles with Indians and in some cases fought in Civil War battles as well.

Soldiers who enlisted for five-year terms (later changed to three-year terms) had certain requirements to meet: They needed to be between eighteen and thirty-five years old, of good character (or a past that couldn't be traced or in which there were no severe charges outstanding), able-bodied and with no ill habits (though drunkenness was a common problem among the troops). Cavalrymen needed to be between 5'5" and 5'10", and not weigh more than 140 to 150 pounds, as horses with all their tack could only carry about 240 pounds; horsemanship was not a requirement.

Army recruits earned $13 per month for the first two years of enlistment; $14 during the third year; $15 in the fourth year; and $16 in the fifth and final year. Pay then increased to $18 each month for the next five-year enlistment followed by a $1 per month increase for each subsequent five-year enlistment. Corporals earned on the same prorated basis ranging between $15 and $20 per month while duty sergeants earned from $18 to $23 each month. First sergeants received between $25 and $30 per month, depending on years of service.

Congressional action on July 28, 1866, provided for African Americans to enter the Regular Army. The African-American regiments, including the 9th and 10th Cavalry and the 38th, 39th, 40th, and 41st Infantry, became known as Buffalo Soldiers, so-called by Indians who believed their hair resembled the shaggy mane of the buffalo, and also because the African-American soldiers often wore buffalo coats. In 1868, the four infantry regiments were consolidated into two, the 24th and 25th infantry regiments.

Military Outposts

The western outposts of the period were located in strategic places along trails, borders and the like. They had many similar characteristics, isolation being one of the primary common denominators. Each outpost, no matter where it was located, also had certain needs: fuel, water and defensible position.

Fuels ranged from wood to coal in cases where there were supplies nearby. Water might come from a stream, river or hand-dug wells. Few western forts were enclosed, though they might have a perimeter somewhat defined by the strategic location of buildings and watchtowers. Most forts also had to have livestock feed nearby.

In 1845 there were only a dozen posts and eleven forts located in the region west of the Mississippi River. During the period 1845-98 there were some 317 forts or other military outposts located in western states and territories, though not all of them were in use at the same time and during the entire period.

The most significant period of frontier military post development in the West occurred between 1868 and 1880.

The military constructed some forts in locations it considered strategic, such as those on the Bozeman Trail built in 1865-66, but others were made of earlier fur trader posts like Fort Laramie. It had started as a post of the American Fur Company in 1834 and was purchased by the United States government in 1849 as a strategic location to protect travelers on the Oregon-California-Mormon trails.

The western outposts fell into a number of categories such as forts, posts, subposts, depots, stations, stockades, blockhouses, arsenals and picket-posts, locations where guards watched to avoid being caught in a surprise attack. Some locations were called cantonments early but later were renamed as camps. Generally the term "fort" referred to a more permanent structure, while a "camp" had a shorter life, but there are exceptions; some forts lasted only a couple of years, while other camps existed for decades.

A garrison, a permanent military installation, located at an Indian agency was also called an "agency." Depots were locations where supplies were stored and from which they were distributed, while subdepots were in separate locations but under the jurisdiction of a depot.

Arsenals, barracks and batteries (groupings of military arsenal) were associated with other posts, though troops could be held at a barracks prior to assignment to various posts or forts.

Stations were located along overland mail or telegraph routes. A Spanish fort, or presidio, was a garrisoned plaza or a *castillo*, a traditional fortification similar to an American military fort. French and British forts generally served as both trading areas and frontier protection, but they were generally no longer in use after 1840.

Most U.S. military forts were named for military leaders, others received their names based on geographical location, and at least sixteen were named for Indian tribes.

Organization

Regular Army soldiers enlisting during the Indian Wars started their career at one of four recruit depots: cavalry at Jefferson Barracks, Missouri; infantry at David's Island, New York, or Columbus Barracks, Ohio, and prior to 1870 at Newport Barracks, Kentucky. Little training occurred at the barracks. There the soldiers received their uniform issue: navy-blue wool sack coat, two pairs of light blue kersey trousers, two dark blue or gray flannel shirts, two suits of underwear, a light blue wool caped overcoat, one pair of rough boots or ankle-length brogans, a kepi or forage cap, and a leather waist belt. (See chapter six for more information.) They purchased cleaning kits to maintain their uniforms.

Initially soldiers were expected to learn by watching others. They received *The Soldier's Handbook* after 1884, which helped them in their duties, if they were literate. In general they received little training or firearms practice.

The first sergeant ran the company; all men had to obtain permission from him to speak to other officers. There was a rigidly enforced officer-enlisted man caste system in place among the Regular Army from 1865 through the mid-1890s. Though the officers and the enlisted men could socialize at holidays, such as Christmas, or participate in joint sporting events, in all other situations—except actual combat—they led separate and distinct lives. During battles the separateness disappeared because both enlisted men and officers watched each other's backs.

Each Army regiment was comprised of ten or twelve companies of about eighty men each, though the companies were seldom stationed together. In most cases when new men joined a company, they were subjected to a period of hazing where fellow soldiers pulled a variety of pranks at their expense.

Lifestyle

The troops at western posts served in forts, posts, camps or barracks built of wood framing, sawed lumber, logs or adobe, depending on the location and materials available. There was little privacy; cots, with woven wire springs or wooden slats supporting bedcoverings, sat about three feet apart with an aisle between rows. Kerosene lamps or candles provided light, with heat coming from cast-iron woodstoves. The men ate together at long tables, using tin cups and plates and iron utensils until the late 1880s when dinnerware consisted of heavy white china plates and mugs. Food was notoriously poor in quality and in short supply. (See chapter seven for more information.)

For the most part, life at the western outposts was filled with "isolation, boredom, and monotony," according to Don Rickey in *Forty Miles a Day on Beans and Hay.*

Weekly activities included an inspection on Sundays, foot or mounted drills or target practice through the week, and cleanup work on Fridays and Saturdays. A high point of every day—and on nearly every post regardless of size— occurred during guard mount, when trumpeters and buglers sounded call to change the guard of the previous twenty-four-hour period. At guard mount officers inspected the guard and had them present arms and exchange passwords before a new guard began its twenty-four-hour duty.

Camp life generally involved a number of civilians, often women, who provided such duties as laundry service. Soldiers had to obtain water, wood and other necessities. Band music and dress parades often occurred when troops who had been out in the field returned to the various posts or forts.

Entertainment

Nearly everyone associated with the frontier army drank alcoholic beverages, including soldiers, officers and even chaplains. They obtained liquor by buying it from post traders or sutlers, or at post canteens; sometimes they stole supplies. In February 1877 President Rutherford B. Hayes signed a bill outlawing the sale of liquor on military reservations. That led to establishment of "hog ranches," which sprang up near most military posts. They sold alcohol and provided other entertainment ranging from gambling to the services of prostitutes. The establishments were called hog ranches perhaps because some started by actually raising hogs for pork to feed military troops. Other origins of the name could refer to the women who worked there, or the fact that each of the women had a following like "an old sow and her numerous little pigs," according to Larry Brown in *Hog Ranches of Wyoming*.

Through most of the Indian War period, soldiers received no vegetables as part of their regular rations, so the men planted gardens. Food and other supplies reached the outposts in a variety of ways. In the early portion of the period freighting companies handled the deliveries; later railroads often distributed supplies to central locations from which they were taken to individual posts.

Regular Army soldiers during the Spanish-American War used the following types of pipe tobacco: Piper Heidsick, Green Turtle and licorice-and-molasses-flavored Black Jack.

CINCHING UP

Next to the officers of an exploring expedition in the West, the packer holds the most responsible position. The art of loading pack animals with heavy burdens of miscellaneous articles so that they will carry safely, without hurting the mules, is one acquired by long experience on the frontier. A man who understands his business can literally cover an animal with cooking utensils, surveying instruments, blankets, guns, picks, and the like, in a surprisingly short space of time, and the work will be done so well that repeated stumbles and rubbing against trees will fail to loosen them. Indeed, the beast frequently rolls down a hill or tumbles into a ravine without doing much damage to his pack. . . . Packers fasten their packs to pack saddles which are sinched [*sic*] around the animals' belly, and not around his chest as is done in the East. The Western packer follows the Mexican and Spanish custom in saddling and packing.—FLIN, *September 19, 1874, 23-3*

MEXICAN WAR

Tensions between the United States and Mexico began escalating in the early 1840s due to continued disputes between Mexico and the Republic of Texas, which had formally voted for annexation to the United States in 1836. While the United States had not yet accepted the annexation, it did have a stake in Texas's future and did not want the region to fall under Mexican domination again.

A series of conflicts occurred during the early 1840s. On September 18, 1842, forces from both Mexico and Texas engaged in the Battle of Salado

Creek, east of San Antonio, and on March 25, 1843, seventeen Texans died in the "Black Bean Affair" when the Mexican general Santa Ana captured 170 Texans and ordered retaliation for a December 1842 confrontation between the Mexicans and Texans during the Mier Expedition. Santa Ana ordered ten percent of the Texans to die and determined who would be executed by conducting a lottery. He placed seventeen black beans in a jar to total 170 beans and had the men each select a bean; those who chose the black beans were executed.

Finally on March 28, 1845, Mexico broke diplomatic relations with the United States, precipitating the subsequent war. Expansionist President James K. Polk sent the first troops to Texas to guard the border with Mexico on May 28, 1845, and nearly a year later, on May 11, 1846, he declared war on Mexico. On June 3, 1846, Polk ordered Colonel Stephen Watts Kearny to take his Army of the West to New Mexico and California to take possession of the area. Kearny was promoted to General upon arrival at Las Vegas, New Mexico.

On June 14, 1846, residents staged the Bear Flag Revolt in California by raising a flag with a bear on it. John Charles Frémont participated in the Bear Flag Revolt and subsequently led the independent Republic of California, organizing the California Battalion on July 24. As Frémont made his move and while Kearny marched to Santa Fe, Commodore John Sloat headed toward California by sea, occupying Monterey on July 7 and claiming it for the United States, even as, on August 17, Commodore Robert Field Stockton seized Los Angeles, annexed California and proclaimed himself governor. Kearny took Santa Fe on August 18 without firing a shot, claiming New Mexico for the United States. Charles Bent quickly became governor of New Mexico, while Kearny continued on his march toward California.

Fighting continued through the remainder of 1846 as American forces took control of Tucson and El Paso. After Mexican rebels retook Los Angeles, American forces again captured it on January 10, 1847, under the command of General Kearny and Commodore Stockton. That marked the end of fighting in California and on January 16, 1847, Frémont became California's governor.

However, fighting involving forces from both countries continued in the region south of the present Mexican-United States border. On September 7, 1847, the Mexican government rejected an offer of peace from the United States, but just a week later (September 13-14), the Chapultepec Palace outside Mexico City fell to troops under the leadership of Major General Winfield Scott bringing the war to an end.

The subsequent Treaty of Guadalupe Hidalgo, approved February 2, 1848, transferred to the United States a large section of land including California and most of the Southwest including the present states of New Mexico, Arizona, Nevada and Utah.

> The sailors in the Mexican war held a meeting in this city [New York] last week to prepare a petition to Congress to make the same

donation to the sailors who served in the Gulf during the Mexican war as those who fought on the Pacific coast received for their services which was 100 acres of land and three months' pay.
—FLIN, *July 19, 1856, 83-1*

MORMON OR UTAH WAR OF 1857

Concerns over polygamy and general practices of Mormon leaders in Utah led the United States in the spring of 1857 to appoint Alfred Cumming as the new governor. But threats that he would not be allowed by the Mormons to take office caused the United States to organize an army and send it toward Utah with the goal of ousting the Mormon leadership and installing the new governor. There were a series of false starts on the part of the army due to changes in leadership, but by September, Albert Sidney Johnston and his army were en route to Utah.

The Mormons controlled Fort Bridger at that time and organized to delay and harass the oncoming government troops. Just east of the Green River during the night of October 4, Mormon Battalion Major Lot Smith and his guerrilla band attacked three different army provision trains, burning the wagons of two trains in a depression of land which became known as Simpson's Hollow. As the federal troops neared Fort Bridger, the Mormons continued their "scorched earth" policy when they burned the fort and retreated to Salt Lake City, building fortifications in the canyons east of the city.

> Brigham Young will 'fire the prairies' and even 'burn his own city, if necessary, before he will submit to the demands of the United States Government.'—FLIN, *November 7, 1857, 359-3*

Brigham Young announced plans to defend Salt Lake City, but he rallied his people to abandon the city and head south toward Provo, intending to burn Salt Lake City before letting government troops take it.

The federal government responded with another call for forces; as *Frank Leslie's Illustrated Newspaper* reported on December 5, 1857, "Troops from California and Oregon are to be sent to Utah." The troops under Johnston's command, meanwhile, reached Fort Bridger, where they dug in for the winter, nearly starving and freezing due to a lack of adequate provisions and supplies. Some troops headed across the Colorado mountains toward Fort Union, New Mexico Territory, to obtain supplies, nearly dying as a result of the difficult winter journey. In the spring Johnston's forces continued to Salt Lake City, where Governor Cumming was installed without bloodshed in June of 1858, and the residents of Salt Lake City, who had fled to Provo, returned to their homes.

THE MORMON BATTALION

Among the members of Kearny's Army of the West was the 600-member Mormon Battalion, a fighting force raised on the banks of the Missouri River near present-day Council Bluffs, Iowa, during the late summer of 1846. The Mormons had been en route to a new place in order to escape persecution in Illinois. When they reached the Missouri River they had no authority to cross the river and continue west nor to camp on the western bank of the river as that was Indian country, controlled by the Omaha, Otoe and other tribes.

When President Polk appealed to Mormon leader Brigham Young for troops to join United States forces en route to California for the pending war with Mexico, Young negotiated for the right to cross the Missouri and establish a temporary camp, which became Winter Quarters for the Mormons. The 600 members of the Mormon Battalion, with some camp followers, left the Missouri River and headed south to Fort Leavenworth, in present-day Kansas, then west with Kearny. They provided their own weapons and clothing, allowing the funds they received from the army for those items to go to Young and their families.

The enlistment of the Mormon Battalion not only assured the United States government that the Mormons would not fight on the side of the Mexicans in the conflict (as had been feared), but also provided the Mormon families with funding for supplies and a place to spend the winter of 1846-47.

The Mormon Battalion split before reaching Santa Fe, with a portion of the members—known as the Sick Battalion—heading northwest to winter at Pueblo, Colorado, before rejoining the main Mormon emigration headed toward Utah in the spring and summer of 1847. The Sick Battalion joined the main Mormon migration at Fort Laramie, in present-day Wyoming.

Meanwhile, the remainder of the Mormon Battalion accompanied Kearny to New Mexico and then marched to California, arriving there after the conflict had been resolved. When released from military duty, some of the battalion members headed east to the Great Salt Lake Valley and back along the Oregon Trail route—over which the Mormons were headed west—joining either Young's advance party, or the later Mormon contingent including their families and led by Mormon Parley Pratt. Some battalion members remained in California and were present at Sutter's Mill when gold was discovered there on January 24, 1848.

CIVIL WAR

Although most of the primary Civil War battles were fought east of the Mississippi River, western regions such as Louisiana, Arkansas, Missouri, Texas, Indian Territory (Oklahoma), Kansas, Nebraska Territory and New Mexico Territory had a role in the conflict, with troops from Iowa and Minnesota serving in Union forces.

The war itself started with the firing at Fort Sumter, April 12-14, 1861, and

MOUNTAIN MEADOWS MASSACRE

Although there were no lives lost as a direct result of tensions related to the Mormon War of 1857, one of the West's most tragic episodes had its genesis during the conflict.

Alexander Fancher, originally from Tennessee, later from Missouri and Arkansas, led a wagon train toward California that summer. Upon reaching Salt Lake City, Fancher turned his party toward the southwest to continue on to California. Traveling through Utah, Fancher's train received no assistance from the Mormons. This was partly due to the prewar hysteria associated with the threat from Albert Sidney Johnston and the U.S. Army then headed toward Utah, and somewhat because of long-held feelings of resentment by the Mormons toward anyone from Missouri, where the Mormons had been severely persecuted before they relocated to Utah.

Fancher's party reached Mountain Meadows in extreme southwestern Utah (northwest of St. George, Utah) by early September, where on the seventh the wagon train was attacked by a party of about 150 Paiute Indians— who had been induced to launch the attack by the Mormons. The wagons formed a defense and held off the attackers for five days. Then Mormon Indian agent John D. Lee arrived on the scene, ostensibly to negotiate a resolution to the attack. However, unbeknownst to the Fancher party, Lee and the Mormon Militia were in consort with the Paiutes and, when the wagons hitched and rolled from their defensive position, the militia and the Indians attacked, killing all but a number of children believed to be too young to remember what had happened.

Not until twenty years later did the full story of Mountain Meadows spread. John Lee was ultimately arrested, tried and convicted of mass murder, and he himself was executed at the massacre site in 1877. Mountain Meadows created great controversy and some claimed Lee became a scapegoat for the affair.

concluded with the surrender of Confederate troops, April 2-9, 1865. As the war fever escalated in the early 1860s, Texas (which had achieved statehood with legal slavery in 1845) withdrew from the Union (1861) and ultimately several important battles on the western front occurred as a result. Further, many of the later important Confederate war leaders had served together during the Mexican War or in Texas following that conflict.

> A gentleman has just arrived here from Texas, Louisiana, Mississippi, Arkansas and Tennessee. He says the feeling in the portion of Texas that he visited was more for herself than the remainder of the Southern states; that she is more anxious to secure her own independence, and become what she was sixteen years ago, than to take part in a war for the benefit of the cottonocracy. She will fight for the States rights of Texas to the last, but will not be over prominent in the balance of the conflict.—FLIN, *June 8, 1861, 51-3*

Indian Territory also played a role. Because many members of the Five Civilized Tribes, particularly the Cherokees and Choctaws, owned slaves, they were divided in their loyalties to the Union and the Confederacy. The Chickasaws and Choctaws fought for the Confederacy, and ultimately so did the Creeks and Seminoles, though some from those tribes also supported the Union. The most bitter division occurred amongst the Cherokees, some of whom supported the Union and others of whom fought for the Confederacy.

> The National force at Fort Gibson, in the Cherokee country, numbers about 5,000 men, with two batteries of six guns each. The force is divided as follows: 3,000 Indians and 2,000 whites. The Indians are formed into a brigade by themselves, under the command of Col. R. W. Furnas of Nebraska. The Cherokee nation may be considered as two-thirds loyal. John Ross, the principal chief, is astride the fence, and needs decision upon the part of the National Government to make him take sides. He is, however, under arrest by the commander. The Creek Indians are about two-thirds loyal. The Choctaws are mostly 'Secesh.'—FLIN, *September 6, 1862, 371-1*

Once the Civil War itself started, Kansas was the site of several battles, including the raid on Lawrence by Missouri raider William Clarke Quantrill. Among the members of Quantrill's raiding party were Frank and Jesse James and Cole Younger. In early Civil War skirmishes, Quantrill fought with Confederate troops; by November 1861 he had organized Quantrill's Raiders. In Kansas in 1862, they attacked Jayhawkers, antislavery guerillas who operated in Missouri and Kansas prior to and during the Civil War. The Raiders sometimes participated with Confederate troops, as at the August 1862 capture of Independence, Missouri, where Quantrill earned a promotion to captain.

Attempting to aid the Confederacy by attacking abolitionists, particularly in Kansas, most of Quantrill's wartime activities were outside the purview of the regular Confederate Army. He planned the raid on Lawrence, Kansas, targeting the community as an abolitionist base and by drawing up a "hit list" of people to be killed. Quantrill's men rode into the sleeping town on the morning of August 21, 1863, first killing the Rev. S.S. Snyder as he milked his cow. Besides attacking the remnants of a camp where the Union's 14th Cavalry had been bivouacked, Quantrill's raiders killed about 150 men in Lawrence, and they burned much of the business district and many homes. Only one of Quantrill's men (Larken Skaggs) died before the raiders rode from the Lawrence ruins.

Various other raids instigated by Quantrill took place throughout the war, called the Civil War, the War Between the States, or by some Southerners and particularly by Texans, the War of Northern Aggression.

Confederate troops and leaders eyed the West, not only to enlarge their domain, but in part because of the riches there. Gold and silver could be obtained in the West to give the South the financial credit it needed to purchase supplies—particularly guns and ammunition—from foreign countries.

And if the Confederacy controlled the ports in Louisiana, Texas and even in California, it could ensure that those foreign supplies could not only be purchased, but also delivered. Though Louisiana and Texas had already allied themselves with the Confederacy, New Mexico had not and that became the prize plum for the South. Confederate leaders knew that if they controlled New Mexico they not only obtained potential gold and silver, but they also could maintain vital supply lines.

The military actions in the West prior to the Civil War—in the Mexican War of 1846-47 and during subsequent activities such as the short-lived 1857 Mormon War—had been training ground for officers and troops who fought on both sides during the Civil War. As the first shots still echoed at Fort Sumter, Federal officers—such as Robert E. Lee, Joe Johnston, Albert Sidney Johnston and Pierre Beauregard, all of whom had been born in the South—resigned their commissions and left the Army of the West to offer their services to the Confederacy. Northern leaders had also served during the Mexican War or had been classmates of the men who led the Confederate Army.

Within the West, war sentiment was divided. In Taos, New Mexico Territory, for example, when Southern sympathizers pulled down the American Flag, Kit Carson immediately raised a new flag and stopped the southern supporters from flying a Confederate flag, noting the territory had been won for the Union during the Mexican War and adding it "will stay Union!" Carson ultimately became active in the New Mexico Volunteers and, assisted by Federal troops, held the territory for the Union. Other primary fighting in the West involved Louisiana, Arkansas and Texas, particularly near Galveston, where Union forces blockaded the port, which was retaken by a Confederate fleet of five Cottonclads (named for their bales of cotton used as protection), commanded by Major General John Magruder, on January 1, 1863. Troops from Texas, as well as Indian troops, played major roles in some Civil War battles east of the Mississippi.

Primary Civil War battles involving Western troops or locations are these:

New Mexico Campaign—July 1861-July 1862—This was the primary fighting in the Trans-Mississippi theater of the Civil War. The initial fighting occurred July 3 and 4, 1861, when Confederate troops led by Lieutenant Colonel John Baylor attacked Fort Bliss near El Paso, Texas. Other major engagements included the Battle of Valverde (New Mexico) on February 21, 1862, and the fight at Glorieta Pass, March 26-28, 1862.

The fighting in New Mexico centered on the Confederates wanting control of New Mexican trade routes and gold and silver in New Mexico and California. The initial battles included those at Fort Fillmore (New Mexico) and at San Agustin Spring, where Confederates captured U.S. regular troops. That led to creation of a Confederate Territory of Arizona with a delegate named to represent the area at Richmond, Virginia. Then Confederate Brigadier General Henry H. Sibley raised a brigade of 3,500 soldiers at Fort Thorn. From there he moved the troops north to Fort Craig on the Rio Grande near

Valverde. There on February 21, the 3,800 Union troops commanded by Colonel Edward R.S. Canby met the Confederates under Sibley in a battle to determine who controlled the Rio Grande ford. Initially Canby's Federals crossed the river and forced the Confederates to fall back, but ultimately the Confederates rallied and Canby's Union troops retreated downriver to Fort Craig. When that happened the Sibley troops had an open door to Santa Fe, which they went through, occupying first Albuquerque and then Santa Fe. Their ultimate goal was the taking of Fort Union, northeast of Santa Fe, which would provide access to Colorado with its own gold and silver resources. Also, Fort Union was a primary Federal supply depot in New Mexico.

Once they had occupied Albuquerque and Santa Fe, the Confederates needed only to cross Glorieta Pass to launch their final assault on Fort Union, and then march into Colorado. They headed that way, but Federal troops—the 1st Volunteer Colorado Infantry Regiment—under command of Colonel John P. Slough had reinforced the troops at Fort Union and on March 22, 1862, he led 1,342 men south toward Santa Fe. As the Confederates headed north and east, Slough headed south and west. His troops had been raised in barrooms and mines in Colorado, and they were tough and spoiling for a fight. Joined by Regular Union troops and New Mexicans, Slough's Colorado Infantry started toward Glorieta Pass. He sent Major John Chivington with an advance force of Colorado troops, which on March 26 met the Confederates at Apache Canyon, just west of Glorieta Pass, defeating the Southern troops in a running battle, and handing the Union its first victory in New Mexico.

By March 28, the Confederates had regrouped and been reinforced. They again headed east where they encountered Slough's Federal forces at Glorieta Pass. As the fighting got underway there between the main Confederate and Union forces, Chivington had meanwhile taken 490 troops, crossed the mountain, and destroyed a Confederate supply train. Though the Federal troops had fallen back from the fighting at Glorieta Pass, the destruction of the Confederate supply train by Chivington's forces led the Confederates to request a truce. They retreated to Santa Fe, then eventually to Mesilla and back to San Antonio, Texas. The collapse of the Sibley offensive dashed Confederate hopes to control the West. It meant the Civil War would primarily be fought on ground east of the Mississippi River, with some limited engagements west of the river. Because of the decisive role the Battle of Glorieta Pass played in the war, it became known as the Gettysburg of the West.

Northwest Arkansas—March 7-December 8, 1862—Troops fought in the area between Springfield, Missouri, and Van Buren, Arkansas, throughout the period. General Samuel R. Curtis commanded the 10,000 Federal troops who captured Springfield in February 1862. They forced the Missouri State Guard under command of Major General Sterling Price south into northwestern Arkansas where they joined with Confederate troops led by General

Ben McCulloch and Indian forces organized by Brigadier General Albert Pike. Over the course of the next several weeks the Union and Confederate forces periodically changed territories. Among the battles were those at Pea Ridge (March 7-8, 1862) and at Prairie Grove (December 7-8, 1862), and neither side won decisively either time, though after Prairie Grove, Confederates no longer had control of northwestern Arkansas or Indian Territory north of the Arkansas River. Ultimately the Confederate troops retreated, leaving Arkansas open to subsequent Union attack; however, by then leaders on both sides were more focused on areas to the east.

Lower Mississippi Valley—April 24-July 1862—Residents were involved in battles along the Mississippi River, including the surrender of New Orleans, Louisiana, April 28-May 7, and battles at Vicksburg, May 19-June 24, as both sides struggled to control the Mississippi.

Vicksburg—December 1862—The first battles at Vicksburg occurred in December 1862. Though technically not in the West, Vicksburg was a primary location as a doorway to the West. As President Abraham Lincoln put it, "Vicksburg is the key. The war can never be brought to a close until the key is in our pocket. We can take all the northern parts of the Confederacy, and they can still defy us from Vicksburg. It means . . . fresh troops from the States of the far South, and a cotton country where they can raise the staple without interference." The first attacks on Vicksburg by Federal troops were unsuccessful. Not until the second and third Vicksburg campaigns (January 8-July 4, 1863) did Federal forces manage to take Vicksburg, which gave them control of the Mississippi River.

Red River Campaign—March 10-May 22, 1864—Fighting in Louisiana involved the Battle of Mansfield, on April 8, 1864, and the Battle of Pleasant Hill on April 9, 1864. As a diversion from the Red River Campaign, Major General Frederick Steele began the Arkansas Campaign—March 1-May 22, 1864—leading 8,500 men south from Little Rock toward Confederate forces commanded by General Sterling Price. On April 18, Confederate troops in northern Arkansas decisively defeated the Federal forces, killing a large number of African Americans who had joined Union troops. At Marks' Mills on April 25, the Confederates captured and took more than 1,000 Union troops as prisoner, and they also killed large numbers of African-American soldiers. Ultimately the Federal forces withdrew to Camden, having been defeated by the Confederates.

INDIAN WARS

Indian-settler or Indian-military conflicts occurred throughout the period, but Indian tribes also fought with each other over tribal lands and for other reasons as outlined in chapter three. The primary fighting, however, and that which permanently changed how and where Indian people lived in the West, occurred between the tribes and the U.S. Army. There were some conflicts during the period 1840-65, but by far the majority of the Indian fighting in the Trans-Mississippi West occurred after the Civil War. Then the federal government, having settled the question over states rights and slavery, turned to the "Indian Question," determined to bring the matter to a close.

President Abraham Lincoln set the stage for the Indian War period of 1865-80 when he noted during the Civil War: "If we get through this war, and I live, this Indian system shall be reformed."

Of course Lincoln did not live to deal with the Indians in the Trans-Mississippi West; however, others did take the task seriously. The primary way to settle the disputes—governmental officials believed—was to confine the Indians to reservations where they could teach them farming and other skills; in short to assimilate them into white society. During the first period of fighting (1864-68), federal officials believed they could overpower the tribes with superior military abilities. During the period 1870-90, a combination of forces including government battles, the slaughter of buffalo by hide hunters, and natural environmental factors, removed the Indians' food supply by decimating the once immense buffalo herds. Military troops also attacked villages and destroyed food and supplies, believing that when the Indians became hungry enough, they would submit to federal demands that they live on reservations and become farmers.

There were different areas of conflict, some which occurred simultaneously, involving the four major cultural groups: the Pacific Northwest and Coastal tribes, the Southwestern tribes, the Plains tribes and the Five Civilized tribes.

The Five Civilized tribes, Choctaws, Chickasaws, Creeks, Cherokees and Seminoles, had no direct conflicts in the West. However, they had had encounters, not necessarily of a military nature, when they were forced by the removal policies of the early part of the 19th century (1820-40) to leave traditional homelands in the south—Florida, Georgia, Tennessee—to resettle in Indian Country (Oklahoma). There were limited conflicts between the U.S. military or settlers and the tribes of the Pacific Northwest and Coastal areas (California). The primary conflicts centered on the Southwestern tribes and the Plains tribes.

Not all fighting involved Indians against the military; in certain cases tribes allied themselves with the federal troops, particularly if they thought it would help them to defeat their own Indian enemies. And some Indians provided valuable services to the Army as interpreters and scouts. Apaches, Crows and Pawnees are among those who worked in such capacities.

INDIAN-MILITARY/INDIAN-SETTLER CONFLICTS

Pacific Northwest/California Coastal Region

1847: November 29—Cayuse Indians, believing their children (who were dying of measles) are being killed by missionary doctor Marcus Whitman,

PAWNEE SCOUTS

In 1864, General S.R. Curtis commanded the 12th and 16th Kansas Cavalry and a company of the 2nd Nebraska Cavalry when he recommended that Frank North organize a company of Indian scouts to assist in the fight against the Sioux. The Pawnees were chosen because the Sioux were their traditional enemies; they had not been involved in any major confrontations against American soldiers or settlers, and most Pawnees then lived at the Pawnee Indian Agency not too far from Columbus, Nebraska, where Frank North also lived. North not only knew many of the leading Pawnee men, he also spoke their language.

North selected seventy-seven Pawnee warriors, who agreed to provide their own horses. By October 1864, North had the scouts ready for action. They were the first Indians recruited to scout for the Army in the West. The company mobilized at Columbus, Nebraska, and proceeded to Fort Kearny, where they established winter quarters. They were promised cavalry pay and an additional payment for the use of their horses, though they never received either following the initial campaign against the Sioux.

The Pawnee Scouts served in a variety of engagements during the next dozen years. They pursued some of the Cheyennes and Sioux who were involved in the two battles at Platte Bridge, in present-day Wyoming, on July 26, 1865. They saw action in the Connor Battle later that year along the banks of the Tongue River in present-day north-central Wyoming. Frank North commanded various groups of Pawnee Scouts through the 1870s. His scouts served on patrol and guard duty during construction of the Union Pacific Railroad. In the summer of 1870, Yale University professor O.C. Marsh traveled throughout the West studying the fossil beds of the region. North, by then a major in the Army, and two of his Pawnee Scouts guided the professor to the Loup Fork River, in Nebraska, where he studied fossil beds.

Pawnee Scouts served under General Crook in the fall and winter campaign of 1876-77 and assisted the military in bringing Red Cloud to Fort Robinson and Red Cloud Agency, where he put down his arms in October 1876. They also participated in the November 1876 Dull Knife battle in Powder River country along the Bighorn Mountains in Wyoming.

attack the Whitman mission, slaying Whitman, his wife Narcissa, and a dozen other people before taking fifty-seven hostages. This begins the Cayuse War. The hostages are ransomed by Peter Skene Ogden in January 1848, but the conflict continues until 1850 when the Cayuses turn over five men known to have been involved in the attack. The five Cayuses are taken to Oregon City where they are tried, convicted and sentenced to death. They are hanged on June 3, 1850, with United States Marshal Joe Meek officiating. His daughter, Helen Mar Meek, had been at the Whitman Mission the day of the attack. Though she wasn't killed during the attack, she had the measles at the time and died due to lack of proper care. Immediately after the attack,

Meek had appealed to his "shirt-tail cousin" President James Polk, receiving territorial status for Oregon.

1866: Fighting is reported throughout the region between Indians and settlers, although most incidents involve few participants.

1867: January—Lieutenant Colonel George Crook with the 1st Cavalry fights Indians on the Malheur River in Oregon in two separate engagements.

1867: February—The 8th Cavalry and Indians battle in Nevada, and the 1st Cavalry has an engagement at Surprise Valley, California. Fighting continues throughout the year in both regions.

1872: November 28—Fighting starts between California's Modoc Indians under the leadership of Captain Jack and military troops of the 1st Cavalry commanded by Captain James Jackson when the Modocs refuse to move to the Klamath Reservation in Oregon.

1873: April 11—Captain Jack kills Brigadier General E.R.S. Canby during peace talks with the Modoc Indians; fighting continues throughout April. Some 150 of the Modocs surrender at Fairchild's Ranch, California, on May 22. Captain Jack and three other Modocs are hanged October 3, 1873, for the murder of General Canby and the Rev. Eleazer Thomas.

1877: July 11—Nez Perces, told they must leave their traditional homelands, first engage in attacks on Idaho settlers. Then the Nez Perces are attacked by General Oliver O. Howard in the Battle of the Clearwater (Idaho), which leads to their flight led by Poker Joe and later by Chief Joseph. Subsequent battles occur in Montana Territory at the Big Hole (August 9) and at the Battle of the Bear Paw Mountains (September 30), and ultimately leads to the surrender of the Nez Perces by Chief Joseph in Montana's Judith Valley just forty miles from the Canadian border (October 4-5).

Plains Region

1854: August—Lakota kill Lieutenant William Grattan and twenty-eight men near Fort Laramie, precipitating hostilities along the Oregon Trail. The conflict starts when a Miniconjou kills a cow belonging to some Mormon emigrants. The Sioux try to make restitution for the animal but are not allowed to do so. Grattan and his party then go to the camp of Conquering Bear (sometimes called The Bear) to arrest the Miniconjou. The tribe refuses to let this happen, Grattan opens fire, and subsequently his entire command is killed, as is Conquering Bear.

1855: September 3—General William S. Harney and U.S. Army troops attack Sioux under Little Thunder at Blue Water Creek in western Nebraska, avenging the Grattan deaths a year earlier. The battle is variously referred to as the Bloody Blue Water, the Battle of Blue Water or the Harney Massacre.

1862: August 18—Santee Sioux led by Little Crow stage raids in Minnesota attacking, raping, killing and capturing emigrants and settlers near New Ulm, in part because government supplies due the Indians have not arrived at the Lower Sioux Agency at Fort Ridgely. Up to 400 people die in the earliest attacks; before Little Crow and his Indian fighters are stopped in late September, 644 citizens and 757 soldiers die. About 1,500 Sioux are imprisoned at Fort Snelling, ultimately most are released; a number are pardoned by President Abraham Lincoln, and thirty-eight are hanged (December 26) at Mankato, Minnesota. One sentenced to hang is spared at the last moment.

> The 39 Sioux Indians, convicted of being engaged in the recent Minnesota enormities, were hanged at Mankato, Wis., [sic] on Friday, the 26th of Dec.—FLIN, *January 17, 1863, 201-2*

1864: Indian raids occur throughout the Plains, particularly along the route of the Overland-Oregon-California-Mormon Trails, and in Colorado.

1864: July 28—General Alfred Sully's troops attack Hunkpapa Sioux Sitting Bull's camp in the Battle of Killdeer Mountain on the Little Missouri River (western North Dakota). This is one of the first attacks by soldiers in the West on Indian women and children.

1864: November 29—Colonel John Chivington attacks Black Kettle's band of Cheyennes and a few Arapahos at Sand Creek, Colorado Territory, even though Black Kettle had been offered protection just the month before. The Sand Creek Massacre, as the raid becomes known, leads to intense and widespread fighting during 1865.

1865: A year of intense fighting referred to as the Bloody Year on the Plains, resulting in part from the Sand Creek Massacre of 1864. Raids occur along the overland routes through Nebraska and Wyoming, along the Smoky Hill Route in Colorado, and in other areas throughout the West.

1865: June 11—U.S. military forces under command of Major General G.M. Dodge begin a removal of about 2,000 Sioux from near Fort Laramie, intending to have them settle near Fort Kearny instead. Along the way Indian men are beaten and women are raped before the Indians effect an escape near Fort Mitchell, Nebraska. In making their escape, the Sioux kill four soldiers.

1865: July 25—Sioux and Cheyenne warriors attack troops at Platte Bridge Station (near present Casper, Wyoming), but an ambush by the Lakota isn't carried off as planned when the soldiers return to the post. On July 26 the Indians attack and kill all men traveling with a military wagon train returning to Platte Bridge Station. The Indians also attack a rescue party sent from the post.

1866: June 13—Talks begin at Fort Laramie (Wyoming) between the federal government and Lakota leader Red Cloud, who walks out when he sees Colonel Henry B. Carrington and 700 troops, who are on their way to establish forts along the Bozeman Trail in Wyoming's Powder River Basin and Montana's Little Bighorn Valley. Red Cloud vows to kill any white man who enters the Indian country—which had been set aside as theirs during the 1851 treaty talks.

> The Governor of Montana, in a recent call for 500 volunteers to go against the Indians, requests them to arm and equip themselves, as he can only furnish 39 Springfield rifles.
> —FLIN, *April 7, 1866, 35-2*

1866: The U.S. military establishes Fort Reno and Fort Phil Kearny in present-day Wyoming and Fort C.F. Smith, Montana Territory, to provide protection for travelers along the Bozeman Trail. Even with the forts, attacks by Indians are frequent on the route.

1866: December 17—General Patrick E. Connor issues orders to troops to kill every male Indian over the age of twelve.

1866: December 21—Lakota including Red Cloud and Crazy Horse lure Captain William J. Fetterman and the 80 troops with him from Fort Phil Kearny over Lodge Pole Ridge and into a trap set by the Indians. The entire Fetterman command dies (some perhaps by suicide). Previously, Fetterman had said with 80 men he could "ride through the whole Sioux nation." Subsequently, civilians Portugee John Phillips and William Bailey ride from Fort Kearny first to Fort Reno then to Horseshoe Station and ultimately Phillips rides to Fort Laramie with news of the battle, which becomes known as the Fetterman Massacre. Reinforcements are sent in early January 1867.

> Our troops were slaughtered in consequence of the ignorance of their officers of Indian warfare, and that they fell victims to the deep-laid stratagems of their foe.—FLIN, *April 20, 1867, 66-4*

1867: Indian fighting continues throughout the plains, from Kansas and Colorado to Wyoming and Montana.

> We illustrate the grand and solemn council, with all the circumstances of Indian etiquette, which the hostile chiefs of the Ogallalla, Brule, Sioux and Cheyennes have held with General Sherman and the Commissioners at North Platte, Nebraska. . . . Through their chosen representatives and spokesmen, Spotted Tail, Man Afraid of his Horses, Standing Elk, Pawnee Killer, Big Mouth, Star Eagle, Turkey Foot, Swift Bear, and Black Bear, have the nations spoken. . . . They were plain and straightforward. From their very hearts they cry out 'Stop those two roads—The Powder River Road

and the Smoky Hill—and then You'll have life.' Each and all sing the same song.—FLIN, *October 26, 1867, 92-1*

1867: August 1—Cheyennes led by Dull Knife and Two Moon attack a party of soldiers and civilians in a hayfield near Fort C.F. Smith, Montana Territory, in what becomes known as the Hayfield Fight.

1867: August 2—In a raid apparently timed to correspond to the Hayfield Fight, Lakota under Crazy Horse and Red Cloud attack wood trains near Fort Kearny. Soldiers commanded by Major J.W. Powell take cover in a fortification made of wagon boxes, successfully repelling the overwhelming numbers of Indians in what becomes known as the Wagon Box Fight. The soldiers use .50 caliber breech-loading Springfield rifles with Allin conversions for the first time. This makes them easier to shoot and reload, inflicting heavy casualties on the Indians who had been used to a period of time between rifle volleys during which soldiers had to reload the muzzle-loading rifles they had formerly used.

1868: July—Lakota warriors burn forts C.F. Smith, Phil Kearny, and Reno when they are abandoned by the U.S. military.

1868: September 17-25—About 500 Sioux and Cheyennes led by Roman Nose attack troops led by Major George A. Forsyth and Lieutenant Frederick Beecher in eastern Colorado. The U.S. military force manages to hold off the attackers with their rifles and Colt pistols. Two men who went for reinforcements return to find only a small body of Indians waiting and hoping the troops who had been surviving on horsemeat and wild plums would "starve out." The battle is variously called the Battle of Beecher's Island (Lieutenant Beecher died in the attack), the Battle of the Arikaree, or the "fight when Roman Nose was killed."

1867-68: Peace commissions are held at Fort Laramie, bringing an end to Red Cloud's War, or the First Sioux War, and at Medicine Lodge Creek, Kansas, bringing relative peace to the plains. Some attacks continue, but the scale of warfare is significantly less following the treaty negotiations (see chapter four for more information).

1869: General Eugene Carr leads the 5th Cavalry against Tall Bull's Cheyenne Dog Soldiers in the Battle of Summit Springs, attempting to free two women who had been taken captive in Kansas earlier. One of the women is killed, the other rescued. Tall Bull dies as well. This is one of the last major Indian battles in Colorado.

1870: Troops led by Colonel Eugene M. Baker in Montana kill some 175 Blackfeet Piegans including Chief Heavy Runner, women and children in what becomes known as the Baker Massacre.

1874: Lieutenant Colonel George A. Custer leads a scientific expedition to the Black Hills of South Dakota, during which gold is discovered. Miners subsequently move into the hills, although prohibited from doing so under provisions of the 1868 Fort Laramie Treaty.

1875: September—The Fort Laramie Treaty is officially broken when the U.S. government fails to return the Black Hills to the Sioux. As a result the Second Sioux War, or Crazy Horse's War, begins.

1876: March—General George Crook heads north to Powder River country in an offensive campaign against the Sioux and Cheyennes.

1876: March 17—Troops commanded by Colonel Joseph Reynolds, and who were an advance party under General George Crook, attack the peaceful camp of He Dog (Sioux) and Old Dog and Two Moon (Cheyenne) in Montana Territroy. Reynolds withdraws during the attack, however, and numerous Indians escape. Later warriors led by Crazy Horse recover about 800 horses that had been taken by the army in the raid.

1876: April—Troops from Fort Hartsuff, Nebraska, skirmish with the Sioux in the Battle of the Blowout.

1876: May 17—The three-pronged attack by military troops commanded by Brigadier General Alfred H. Terry, Brigadier General George Crook and Colonel John Gibbon begins. The three columns involved twelve companies, including five companies of the 7th Cavalary commanded by General George Armstrong Custer. The subsequent conflicts include the Battle on the Rosebud (June 17) involving Crook's troops and Sioux and Cheyennes led by Crazy Horse, and the Battle of the Little Bighorn (June 25) involving the five companies of the 7th Cavalry commanded by Custer against Sioux under Crazy Horse and Sitting Bull, as well as Cheyennes, Blackfeet, and Sans Arcs. Both battles occurr in southeastern Montana Territory. Custer's immediate command dies during the attack; only his horse Comanche survives. Five other companies involved in the Battle of the Little Bighorn have some deaths, but are not wiped out as is Custer's command. The Custer defeat grips the nation following widespread reports on the outcome.

1876: July 17—William F. Cody kills Yellow Hair (sometimes called Yellow Hand), claiming the "first scalp for Custer" in a skirmish on Warbonnet Creek, Nebraska.

1876: September 9—Oglala and Miniconjou Sioux, under the leadership of American Horse, engage General George Crook's troops, commanded by Captain Anson Mills, in the Battle of Slim Buttes in present-day South Dakota. American Horse dies later as a result of wounds received in the battle. The Army troops involved in this battle then continue toward Fort Robinson, Nebraska, and are forced to kill and eat their horses when they run out of supplies. The incident becomes known as the Horsemeat March or the Starvation March.

1876: October—Red Cloud is brought in to Fort Robinson. Other Sioux subsequently surrender.

1876: November 26—Pawnee Scouts participate in the Dull Knife Battle, Wyoming Territory.

1877: May 6—Crazy Horse surrenders and with about 900 men, women and children goes to Fort Robinson, Nebraska; Sitting Bull goes to Canada.

1877: May 7—The Battle of Lame Deer (or Muddy Creek) occurs in Montana between Lame Deer's Miniconjou and troops commanded by Colonel Nelson Miles.

1877: September 5—A sentry at Fort Robinson stabs and kills Lakota Chief Crazy Horse.

1878: Northern Cheyennes led by Dull Knife and Little Wolf break away from their reservation in Indian Territory and make a run for their traditional lands along the Powder and Tongue Rivers in Montana. They divide forces in Nebraska. Little Wolf's band makes it to Montana, but Dull Knife's band is captured and incarcerated at Fort Robinson.

1879: January 9—Cheyenne warriors with Dull Knife break away from Fort Robinson; they are located at a hideout January 22, and eventually surrender although sixty-four Cheyennes and eleven soldiers die before that occurs.

1879: September 29—Ute Indians at the White River Agency in northern Colorado revolt, killing agent Nathan Meeker and others at the agency and taking several captives. When troops from Fort Fred Steele in southern Wyoming respond, they are attacked by the Utes. Eventually the situation ends and the Utes are moved to a reservation in Utah; their Colorado lands are opened to settlement.

1890: December 15—Indian Police attempt to arrest Sitting Bull, who has returned to the Standing Rock Reservation, in present-day South Dakota, and in a struggle kill the chief.

1890: December 29—Colonel James Forsyth attempts to disarm Lakota at Wounded Knee in South Dakota and the incident escalates into a massacre of Indian men, women and children, the last major military-Indian conflict during the frontier period.

Southwest Region and Southern Plains

1847: January 19—Mexican and Indian malcontents from Taos Pueblo revolt, killing Governor Charles Bent and five other leading New Mexican citizens. Two weeks later United States regular and volunteer troops surround Taos Pueblo, bombarding the dissidents and eventually subduing them. Subsequently instigators of the January 19 attack are tried, found guilty and hanged.

1851-53: Apaches led by Mangas Coloradas carry out raids in Mexico, killing about 500 residents and destroying wagon supply trains. In July 1852 Mangas Coloradas reaches a peace agreement with the United States, but not with Mexico. At this time he aligns himself with his son-in-law Cochise, who ultimately has his own conflicts with the United States military. Mangas Coloradas receives severe wounds in 1852 during an ambush of army troops staged with Cochise. In January 1853 they launch a raid on prospectors led by Joseph R. Walker who are returning from California's gold fields. However, Walker meets with the 1st California Cavalry and devises a plan to capture Mangas Coloradas, taking him prisoner when he approaches the white truce flag that is raised by Walker's party. He is subsequently tortured (when soldiers hold fire-heated bayonets to his feet) before he is murdered. Although soldiers buried the chief, an army surgeon exhumes the grave and cuts off the chief's head.

1864: January 6—Colonel Kit Carson leads the New Mexico Volunteers in punitive raids against Navajos at Canyon de Chelly (Arizona). Through the year some 12,000 Navajos surrender. From January through March about 8,000 prisoners are marched 300 miles to the Bosque Redondo Reservation in New Mexico (near Fort Sumner on the Pecos River). Hundreds of them die on the march that becomes known as ''The Long Walk.'' They are held in prison camps until 1868. It is at those prison camps that Navajo women begin wearing wide-tiered skirts, often made of brightly colored velvet, because that is the style of dress worn by the other women at the fort.

1864: February 23—King S. Woolsey entices Tonto Apaches to a conference at Bloody Tanks, Arizona, telling them he is a personal representative of President Abraham Lincoln. However, once there, Woolsey feeds and kills the Indians with strychnine-laced pinole, and he kills the chief. The act occurs because of the discovery of gold on Indian lands near present-day Prescott, Arizona. There are later retaliatory raids led by the Tonto Apaches.

1864: September—Colonel Kit Carson's troops capture war leader Barboncita and some 7,000 Navajos at Canyon de Chelly, transferring them to Bosque Redondo.

1864: November 26—The New Mexico Volunteers under Kit Carson attack Kiowas at their winter camp, routing the Indians who flee to Adobe Walls, Texas, an abandoned trading post that had been constructed by William Bent about 1843. The Kiowas defend themselves from within the adobe walls of the former post, and they are reinforced by Comanches who had been camped nearby. Carson has two mountain howitzers to use in the Battle of Adobe Walls. After fighting throughout the day, the Indians withdraw in the evening, and Carson's troops return to the site of the morning camp, which they destroy before leaving the area on November 27.

1865: January 8—About 1,400 Kickapoos under Chief No-Ko-Wat attack and defeat the Texas militia at Dove Creek, not far from San Angelo, Texas.

1866: Skirmishes between military troops and various Indian tribes occur throughout the year.

1867: Fighting continues in Texas, Arizona and New Mexico between soldiers and various tribes including Apaches, Comanches and Kiowas.

1867: July 22—A ten-member detachment from the 2nd Cavalry under command of Lieutenant Lyman S. Kidder engages in a battle with Sioux led by Pawnee Killer on Beaver Creek in Kansas. All of the soldiers die in the fight that becomes known as the Kidder Massacre.

1868: November 27—Cheyenne chief Black Kettle is killed when Lieutenant Colonel George A. Custer commanding 800 men from the 7th Cavalry attacks the Cheyenne camp on the north bank of the Washita River in Indian Territory (near present Cheyenne, Oklahoma). At the time the Cheyennes are camped on reservation lands and, like before, at Sand Creek, Colorado Territory, they have been told by military authorities they are safe in their location. In a subsequent visit to the Washita battle site, Custer finds eighteen of his troops who had died. Those troops, under leadership of Custer's second-in-command Major Joel Elliott, broke away from Custer's troops during the fight, and Custer did not search for them before leaving the scene. Custer is later castigated for his actions.

1869: Sporadic raids occur throughout Kansas.

1870: Kiowa chief Kicking Bird leads his warriors in a fight with members of the 6th Cavalry commanded by Captain C.B. McLellan. Kicking Bird, earlier called a coward by his people, redeems himself by defeating McLellan's troops.

1871: April 30—A mob of Americans, Mexicans and Papago Indians under the leadership of William S. Oury attack and massacre Apaches at Camp Grant, Arizona Territory. The incident launches a fifteen-year war with the Apaches.

1871: May 5—Chiricahua Apache leader Cochise defeats a detachment of the 3rd Cavalry at Bear Springs, Arizona.

1871: May 17—Kiowa Chief Satanta leads his warriors and Comanches against the wagon train led by Nathan Long at Salt Creek, Texas, in what becomes known as the Warren Massacre.

1871: July 5—Satanta and Big Tree are sentenced to hang for their part in recent Indian raids.

1871: August—Death sentences against Satanta and Big Tree are commuted to life in prison.

1873-74: Fighting continues between the army forces and various Indian tribes in Texas and Arizona.

1874: June 27—The second battle of Adobe Walls occurs when Comanche chiefs Quanah Parker and Lone Wolf, along with about 700 Comanche and Cheyenne warriors, face off with twenty-nine buffalo hunters and one woman who are gathered in the Adobe Walls fortress. The buffalo hunters use their Sharps .50 caliber buffalo guns, known as "Big 50s," to repel the Indian attackers who had on "bulletproof" yellow body paint provided by medicine man Isatai. Parker's warriors continue to raid and attack in Texas, New Mexico, Kansas and Colorado, following the Adobe Walls fight.

1874: August 30—Colonel George Miles battles a combined force of Kiowas, Cheyennes and Comanches in the Palo Duro Canyon of Texas, launching the Red River War.

1874: September 28—Colonel Ranald MacKenzie orders the destruction of one thousand Comanche horses in Palo Duro Canyon before marching captured Indians—who had been led by Quanah Parker—two hundred miles to Fort Sill, Oklahoma.

1875: June 2—Quanah Parker and the last Comanches surrender to Colonel Ranald McKenzie at Fort Sill, Oklahoma.

1880: October 14—Mimbres Apache Victorio dies in a battle with Mexican troops south of El Paso, Texas, as the Apaches flee from United States troops led by Colonel Eugene Carr and Colonel George Buell.

1886: March—Geronimo surrenders to General George Crook, then reconsiders and flees into Mexico.

1886: September—Geronimo surrenders to General Nelson A. Miles in Skeleton Canyon near Fort Bowie, Arizona. He and many of his followers are subsequently exiled to Florida. In 1887 Geronimo moves to Alabama and in 1894 he and the imprisoned Apaches move to Fort Sill, Oklahoma, where they agree to share a reservation with the Comanches and Kiowas.

RANGE WARS

After 1870 cattlemen and women ran their herds on vast ranges, often hiring an army of men to protect the animals from natural calamity, wild animal depredation and most specifically from rustlers. As a result, conflicts arose, particularly between large-scale, open-range ranching interests and smaller operators, homesteaders and settlers. Large- and small-scale range wars erupted periodically in most regions of the West. The conflicts could involve livestock loss, fences, or range and water use and availability.

Texas ranchers I.P. "Print" Olive and his brothers enforced their range and cattle operation by using force—guns and killing—when necessary. When the Olives relocated to Nebraska, they continued their management style, eventually having a conflict with homesteaders Ami Ketchum and Luther Mitchell, who may have been rustling a few Olive cows. A shoot-out left Bob Olive dead and Print Olive gunning for Ketchum and Mitchell. Ultimately Print and some of his hands captured Ketchum and Mitchell, hung them, and someone later burned the bodies. Though Olive had enforced his brand of justice having had the cooperation of various law enforcement officers, he was ultimately tried for the hanging and sent to prison. He was later released to await a new trial, which never occurred.

In regions where sheep and cattle shared the range, conflicts arose as well. Most cattlemen hated sheep, and they destroyed herds and killed herders if they allowed the sheep to cross certain boundaries, known as dead-lines. Cattlemen also hanged rustlers or had them killed by range detectives (see chapter seventeen).

Some range wars were large-scale, military-like operations, such as the Johnson County Invasion of 1892 in Wyoming. In that incident, cattlemen from the Wyoming Stock Growers Association hired gunmen from Texas and Idaho for an invasion of Johnson County. They planned to make a fast march to the county seat in Buffalo, kill the officials there, then eliminate men whose names had been placed on a dead-list. As they rode from Casper toward Buffalo, however, the invaders—who called themselves Regulators—changed their plans and attacked a cabin where two of the men on the dead-list had holed up, or hidden. The Regulators killed Nate Champion and Nick Ray at the KC Ranch, but others on the dead-list spotted them as they surrounded the cabin and spread the word to Buffalo, where citizens gathered, armed themselves and prepared for defense and war.

After leaving the KC Ranch, the invaders made their way toward Buffalo, but people sympathetic to their cause warned them of the uproar in Buffalo, so they stopped at the TA Ranch south of town instead and they themselves were placed under siege by the townspeople. The three-day standoff ended when the Regulators managed to get a message to Wyoming Governor Amos W. Barber (who knew of the plan). He subsequently contacted Senators Francis E. Warren and Joseph M. Carey (supporters of the Wyoming Stock Growers Association), and they took word of the situation to president Benjamin Harrison. He ordered U.S. cavalry troops from Fort McKinney to ride to the TA Ranch and take the Regulators into custody. That done, the invaders were sent to Cheyenne where they were released on bail. The case never went to trial.

WEAPONS

Military Arms

In the early portion of the period, soldiers used a variety of weapons and often purchased their own guns and knives, believing they could then have better resources in battle.

By July 1866 the Army authorized use of the Allin M1866 conversion, an improvement to the Springfield rifle that used a .50/70 caliber centerfire cartridge. The real benefit was accuracy, as the Allin M1866 was considered twice as accurate as the .58 caliber rimfire Allin M1865 when shot 500 yards.

In 1873 the Army standardized weapons were the Colt .45 Single Action Army revolver, known as the Peacemaker, and the .45/70 caliber Springfield, known as the Trapdoor Springfield, with an Allin Conversion that allowed for more rapid firing.

Infantry soldiers carried their heavy metallic cartridges in service cartridge boxes, designed to hold two packages of twenty rounds each if the tin liners from the boxes were removed. Some soldiers also carried their cartridges in leather waist belts with loops that would hold up to fifty cartridges.

Frontier cavalrymen in the 1860s and 1870s generally carried side arms, most commonly the .44 caliber percussion revolver. Many soldiers carried more than one side arm. George Armstrong Custer, for example, had both a Colt Model 1860 and a .44 caliber Remington. Handgun manufacturers included Remington, Colt, Smith & Wesson, Starr and Whitney.

Some large military campaigns utilized Gatling guns and mountain howitzers, but not all commanders took them into the field due to the difficulties in transporting the large weapons, which also were of notoriously poor quality because the barrels fouled and overheated and they often jammed.

Cavalrymen had carbines, revolvers and sabers, though they often abandoned the latter (particularly during and after the 1870s) as being too cumbersome.

Soldiers used Springfield, Henry, Winchester, Sharps, Spencer and Remington metallic-cartridge, black-powder weapons, which were fairly accurate at long distances if the man shooting the gun understood and properly used the elevating-leaf rear sight and properly allowed for wind and bullet drift.

During the Spanish-American War (1898) Rough Riders used Krag-Jorgensen carbines and cartridges with smokeless powder. Regular army troops used 1873 Springfield rifles, .45/70 caliber, single-shot breechloaders using black powder. (For more information about military weapons see chapter six.)

Indian Arms

Like soldiers, Indians also had a variety of weapons. Though early in the period Indians relied on their bows and arrows, or even a well-thrown tomahawk or knife, by the 1860s many had guns. They had obtained them in a variety of ways: through legitimate trade, as plunder during previous attacks, and even as gifts from the U.S. government.

As First Infantryman James S. Hamilton noted in 1876:

> We were told that . . . Winchester rifles had previously been issued by our government to the Indians for shooting buffalo. . . . Indians had better rifles than our own men. . . . When they were disarmed at Standing Rock they had cap and ball Colts plus various kinds of rifles, but for the most part they carried good Winchester rifles.

An account published in *Frank Leslie's Illustrated Newspaper* shows how the Indians obtained some of their guns:

> Our Indian visitors of the Mineconjou tribe of the Sioux nation left New York, June 9th, after having enjoyed themselves at Gilmore's Summer Garden, at the races in Jerome Park, and at the various 'stores' in town—notably at Remington's where each Indian was presented with a rifle. If the Government would only distribute homesteads instead of rifles among Indians of every tribe, there might be some prospect of reaching, ultimately, a satisfactory solution of the Indian problem.—FLIN, *June 26, 1875, 247-3*

Though the Indians didn't always understand the weapons and how they could be more effective at long range if allowance was made for the natural fall of a bullet and effects of wind, they were generally excellent shots when firing at close distances and while riding their horses.

Civilian Arms

Civilians used a combination of weapons including rifles, pistols or revolvers, and shotguns. Between 1840 and 1865 westerners used a variety of weapons, primarily muzzle-loaders. Muzzle-loaders were fairly reliable, particularly when the task at hand was to kill game for food, and they were less expensive to purchase and operate than subsequent repeating rifles. Muzzle-loading guns used black powder, caps and balls, which were generally obtainable even in remote locations. The muzzle-loading rifles were powerful and could be depended upon to kill game and could also be used in defense against outlaws. The use of muzzle-loaders generally declined in the 1860s and was virtually eliminated by the mid-1870s.

Following the Civil War the government sold surplus military arms to civilians, such as Starr, Gallagher and Joslyn carbines, which brought $1 to $4.60 each at the Denver Arsenal in 1866. J. Miller & Company in Galveston, Texas, likewise obtained a stock of military-issue weapons including Kentucky, Sharps, Maynard, Henry and Ballard rifles and a selection of shotguns and revolvers, which it provided to general purchasers after 1867.

Other gun manufacturing companies during the period included Winchester, Browning, Marlin, Colt and Bullard.

The most popular repeating rifles in the West after 1865 and well into the 1880s were the Spencer and the Henry, used by stagecoach drivers, railroad workers and other residents. In 1866, New Haven Arms Company was reorganized into the Winchester Repeating Arms Company and began manufacturing the first Winchester, an improved Henry rifle. The Winchester Model 1873 is known as the rifle that "won the West."

Domestic sales of Winchester repeating arms started in 1867 and continued throughout the period. An advertisement in the Leavenworth *Times Conservative* on October 7, 1868 noted:

Winchester Repeating Rifles !

Firing Two Shots a Second, as a Repeater, and Twenty Shots a Minute as a Single Breach-Loader.

These powerful, accurate, and wonderfully effective weapons, carrying eighteen charges, which can be fired in nine seconds, are now ready for the market, and are sold by all responsible Gun Dealers throughout the country. For information send for circulars and pamphlets to the WINCHESTER REPEATING ARMS CO., New Haven, Conn.

Likely the most widely used rifle in the postwar West was the single-shot Sharps, which usually had a twenty-six-inch, full-octagon barrel, though some models had round or combination round/octagon barrels. The 1869 model used a .50/70 caliber cartridge, though later centerfire rounds included the ".40 Berdan Short" or .40/50 caliber, the ".44 Berdan Short" or .44/60 caliber, and the ".44 Berdan Long" or .44/77 caliber. The Sharps guns weighed between eight and twelve pounds and could be purchased with double triggers, extra-heavy barrels and globe-and-peep sights. The most famous Sharps was the .50/90 caliber, known as the "Big Fifty" or the "Poison Slinger," commonly used by buffalo hunters. Later buffalo hunters used the .44/90 "Creedmour," using 520-grain bullets they generally loaded themselves, replacing the "Big Fifty" in popularity.

Handguns in use during the period included percussion arms such as the .44 caliber Army Colt and the .36 caliber Navy Colt, derringers, pocket pistols, bulldog revolvers, and pepperboxes. Among the manufacturers were Colt, Smith & Wesson, Merwin, Hulbert & Co., Remington Arms, E.C. Meacham Arms Co., Hopkins & Allen, Forehand & Wadsworth, Harrington & Richardson, and Webley.

Men and women carried revolvers in single or double gun belts slung low around their hips, with the guns held either butt forward or butt backward; in shoulder holsters; and for small weapons, in their boots or even up their sleeves.

ADDITIONAL READING

Mexican War

Bauer, K. Jack. *The Mexican War, 1846-1848.* New York: Macmillan, 1974. Reprint, Lincoln: University of Nebraska Press, 1992.

Bergeron, Paul H. *The Presidency of James K. Polk.* Lawrence: University Press of Kansas, 1987.

Connor, Seymour V., and Odie B. Faulk. *North America Divided: The Mexican War, 1846-1848.* New York: Oxford University Press, 1971.

DeVoto, Bernard. *The Year of Decision, 1846.* Boston: Little Brown & Co., 1943. Reprint, Boston: Houghton Mifflin, 1989.

Eisenhower, John S.D. *So Far From God: The U.S. War With Mexico, 1846-1848.* New York: Random House, 1989.

Henry, Robert S. *The Story of the Mexican War.* Indianapolis: Bobbs-Merrill, 1950.

Johannsen, Robert W. *To the Halls of the Montezumas: The Mexican War in the American Imagination.* New York: Oxford University Press, 1985.

McCaffrey, James M. *Army of Manifest Destiny: The American Soldier in the Mexican War, 1846-1848.* New York: New York University Press, 1992.

Nevin, David. *The Mexican War.* Alexandria, Va.: Time-Life Books, 1978.

Singletary, Otis A. *The Mexican War.* Chicago: University of Chicago Press, 1960.

Smith, Justin H. *The War With Mexico,* 2 vols. New York: Macmillan, 1919.

Weems, John Edward. *To Conquer a Peace: The War Between the United States and Mexico.* Garden City, N.Y.: Doubleday, 1974.

Civil War

Athearn, Robert G., ed. *Soldier in the West: The Civil War Letters of Alfred Lacey Hough.* Philadelphia: University of Pennsylvania Press, 1957.

Buenger, Walter L. *Secession and the Union in Texas.* Austin: University of Texas Press, 1984.

Colton, Ray C. *The Civil War in the Western Territories.* Norman: University of Oklahoma Press, 1959.

Faust, Patricia L., ed. *Historical Times Illustrated Encyclopedia of the Civil War.* New York: Harper & Row, 1986.

Josephy, Alvin M., Jr. *The Civil War in the American West.* New York: Alfred A. Knopf, 1991. An excellent reference.

Josephy, Alvin M., Jr., and the Editors of Time-Life Books. *The Civil War: War on the Frontier, The Trans-Mississippi West.* Alexandria, Va.: Time-Life Books, 1986. An excellent series of reference books.

McPherson, James M., ed. *The Atlas of the Civil War.* New York: Macmillan, 1994. An excellent reference to readily find dates of primary battles.

Spurlin, Charles, ed. *West of the Mississippi with Waller's 13th Texas Cavalry Battalion, CSA.* Hillsboro, Texas: Hill Junior College, 1971.

Williams. R.H. *With the Border Ruffians*. Lincoln: University of Nebraska Press, 1982.

Frontier Army and Indian Wars

Brady, Cyrus Townsend. *Indian Fights and Fighters*. New York: McClure, Phillips & Co, 1904. Reprint, Lincoln: University of Nebraska Press, 1971.

Brown, Larry. *Hog Ranches of Wyoming: Liquor, Lust, and Lies Under Sagebrush Skies*. Glendo, Wyo.: High Plains Press, 1995.

Bruce, Robert. *The Fighting Norths and Pawnee Scouts*. Lincoln: Nebraska State Historical Society, 1932.

Eales, Anne Bruner. *Army Wives on the American Frontier: Living by the Bugles*. Boulder, Colo.: Johnson Books, 1996.

Emerson, William K. *Encyclopedia of United States Army Insignia and Uniforms*. Norman: University of Oklahoma Press, 1996.

Forsyth, George A. *Thrilling Days in Army Life*. New York: Harper & Brothers, 1900. Reprint, Lincoln: University of Nebraska Press, 1994.

Frazier, Robert W. *Forts of the West*. Norman: University of Oklahoma Press, 1965.

Goetzmann, William H. *Army Exploration in the American West, 1803-1863*. Austin: Texas State Historical Association, 1991.

Greene, Jerome A. *Yellowstone Command*. Lincoln: University of Nebraska Press, 1991.

Leckie, Shirley A., ed. *The Colonel's Lady on the Western Frontier: The Correspondence of Alice Kirk Grierson*. Lincoln: University of Nebraska Press, 1989.

Marcy, Randolph B. *Thirty Years of Army Life on the Border*. New York: Harper & Brothers, 1866.

Michno, Gregory. *Lakota Noon*. Missoula, Mont.: Mountain Press Publishing Co., 1997.

Miles, Nelson A. *Personal Recollections & Observations of General Nelson A. Miles Vol.1 and Vol. 2*. Chicago: Werner Brothers, 1896. Reprint, Lincoln: University of Nebraska Press, 1992.

Olson, James. C. *Red Cloud and the Sioux Problem*. Lincoln: University of Nebraska Press, 1965.

Reedstrom, E. Lisle. *Apache Wars: An Illustrated Battle History*. New York: Sterling Publishing Co., 1990.

Rickey, Don. *Forty Miles a Day on Beans and Hay*. Norman: University of Oklahoma Press, 1963. An excellent resource for information about general conditions of frontier soldiers.

Smith, Thomas T., ed. *A Dose of Frontier Soldiering: The Memoirs of Corporal E.A. Bode, Frontier Regular Infantry, 1877-1882*. Lincoln: University of Nebraska Press, 1994.

Utley, Robert. *Frontier Regulars*. New York: Macmillan, 1984. Reprint, Lincoln: University of Nebraska Press, 1984. An excellent reference book.

————. *Frontiersman in Blue.* New York: Macmillan, 1967. Reprint, Lincoln: University of Nebraska Press, 1981. An excellent reference book.

————. *Indian Frontier of the American West, 1846-1890.* Albuquerque: University of New Mexico Press, 1984.

Utley, Robert, and Wilcom E. Washburn. *Indian Wars.* New York: American Heritage, 1965.

Range Wars

Crabb, Richard. *Empire on the Platte.* Cleveland: The World Publishing Company, 1967.

Drago, Harry Sinclair. *The Great Range Wars: Violence on the Grasslands.* Lincoln: University of Nebraska Press, 1985. A good source of information about the various range wars.

Moulton, Candy. *Roadside History of Wyoming.* Missoula, Mont.: Mountain Press Publishing Co., 1995.

Weapons

Garavagli, Louis A., and Charles G. Worman. *Firearms of the American West, 1866-1894.* Albuquerque: University of New Mexico Press, 1985. Reprint, Niwot: University of Colorado, 1997. An essential reference book for anyone writing about firearms used during the era.

Rosa, Joseph G. *Age of the Gunfighter: Men and Weapons on the Frontier 1840-1900.* Norman: University of Oklahoma Press, 1995.

————. *Guns of the American West.* New York: Exeter Books, 1988.

Rosa, Joseph G., and Robin May. *An Illustrated History of Guns and Small Arms.* London: Peerage Books, 1984.

PART TWO

Everyday Life

CHAPTER SIX

CLOTHES AND ACCESSORIES

Clothing for men, women and children of the West throughout the period reflected the styles and attitudes in the East; however, western styles generally lagged behind, due in part to delays in communication and deliveries or shipments of goods.

In the early part of the period (1840-1865), most people who settled in the interior West traveled there using wagons to transport themselves and their families. They took with them what clothes they had (or could fit into the limited storage areas of wagons) and wore them until replacements could be obtained. In many cases that meant years as the new westerners established their homes and businesses. Those folks who lived near the Pacific coast, particularly in California after 1849, had access to items transported by ships. But even so, new clothing was difficult to obtain, particularly during the earliest period, due to transportation limits.

When westerners did need to replace clothing, they most often resorted to making their own. Women spun wool and used it in a variety of fabrics, or knitted it into such items as socks and sweaters. They also wove a variety of materials, ranging from wool to cotton, linen (from flax they grew) and silk (in some areas from silkworm production). The most popular material of the early period was homemade linsey-woolsey, a combination of linen and wool. Later, calico became the fabric of choice, but throughout the period wool was the standard material used.

To color homespun fabric, a variety of natural materials were used, such as goldenrod for yellow, walnut bark and sumac for dark slate or gray, and butternut hulls for "butternut brown," the color of Confederate uniforms.

Materials also included natural items such as buckskin, buffalo hides and even the canvas from wagon tops (which were turned into such things as shirts or pants, curtains or table coverings).

By far most of the clothing in the West throughout the period was home-made, although after establishment of mail order catalogs such as Montgomery Ward and Company, Carhartt, and, in 1895, Sears, Roebuck and Co., western-ers were more likely to purchase ready-made clothes. In cities, dressmakers and milliners had popular and often quite successful businesses making cloth-ing and hats for women primarily. Milliners did some work for men, but most men obtained their own hats from hatters.

When making their own clothes, women relied on patterns taken from old clothing too worn to be of further use, or they purchased patterns or took them from publications of the day. Periodicals like *Frank Leslie's Illustrated Newspaper, Godey's Lady's Book, Petersen's Magazine* and *Frank Leslie's Gazette of Fashion* sold patterns and ran regular features on clothing styles. *Harper's Bazaar* started publication on November 2, 1867, and also provided fashion information. The magazine came out weekly and cost $.10 per copy or $4 for a year's subscription. Many of the fashions depicted in those publications were geared toward eastern women, or those who had lady's maids to assist them in dressing, but western women read the magazines and sometimes copied the styles. Any new woman in a community became a source of information, particularly if she had recently been in larger cities or places in the East and thus exposed to newer trends in clothing styles.

After 1870 when railroads started extending throughout the region, it be-came easier to obtain materials and commercially produced clothing items.

NATIVE AMERICAN CLOTHING

Traditional dress for Native Americans varied from tribe to tribe and within the five cultural groups: Plains, Plateau, Southwestern, California and Northwestern Coastal. To write about any Indian tribe with accuracy it is necessary to conduct research into the *specific* tribe, for even within the cultural groups there were tribal variations in the area of dress. It is outside the scope of this book to detail the various tribal dress of those Native American groups, but some generaliza-tions can be made. Almost all Indians had blankets which they draped around themselves in various ways, to denote bachelorhood, for example.

Plains Indians wore garments fashioned primarily of materials available from animals, such as buckskin. The buffalo provided nearly everything they needed for both food and clothing.

> Ninety-six thousand Buffalo robes have been imported since the beginning of the Spring, into New York. These warm and popular coverings are invariably tanned by the women Indians, the brutal braves considering such work unworthy of them.
> —FLIN, *October 13, 1860, 325-3*

Most Indians wore moccasins, though the styles varied from tribe to tribe. Southwestern Indians and those living in regions where rattlesnakes and other potentially harmful snakes or insects were common might also wear long leather leggings. Southwestern Indians often wore garments made of cloth, which may have been cooler in their hot climate. When dancing, the Pueblo men of the Southwest wore no shirts, but they had short blankets around their waist, wore red moccasins, and had accessories such as a buckskin fringe, yarn or even squirrel tails.

According to writings from missionary teacher Mary L. Stright who had a school in Jemez, older native girls and women living in New Mexico in 1882 "often wear buckskin wrapped around their legs fold and fold from their ankles to their knees presenting the appearance in shape of a small stovepipe." Little boys often wore only a shirt, and little girls had a shirt and usually a shawl or blanket around them. Indian men in New Mexico and the Southwest usually wore pants of some type and shirts, but the latter were worn out and not tucked in as Euro-American men tended to wear theirs. Other Indian men wore leggings and breechcloths.

The natives of Alaska wore clothing made primarily of animal products such as seal, Arctic fox, bear and other furs. People living on the Aleutian Islands in 1879 wore seal skins, often with the hair trimmed and inside touching their skins; under the skin suits they seldom wore other garments. Those people also made watertight raincoats from the materials that came from the intestines of walruses and other sea mammals. They wore their clothing several sizes too large, to provide room for natural insulation from their own body heat, and tucked pants into boots that were made in the Russian style, which had come into use after the Russian occupation of the area.

MEN

During the period, the majority of men's clothing items were constructed of duck, wool, corduroy, and cotton jeaning, which became known as denim. Cowboys usually wore wool pants, while farmers and miners tended to like trousers made of jeaning or duck, a durable, tightly woven cotton material. Almost all men throughout the period routinely wore vests and coats. Styles for Anglo men weren't necessarily different than those for African Americans, though they might be of better materials. Hispanic and Asian men tended to have clothing more reflective of their ethnic background, such as tight-fitting pants and big hats for Hispanics and loose-fitting clothing with wide-brimmed hats of straw for Orientals. Since the majority of men in the region in the period were Anglos, most of these references are to their styles. Bear in mind that any man could wear these types of garments, regardless of ethnic background, and that styles differed among Euro-American groups since immigrants often had, and continued to wear, clothing styles reflective of their own homelands, such as Scottish kilts.

Emigrants/Homesteaders: Men wore red or blue flannel or cotton shirts and short coats, often of wool. Pants of woolen material had seats and legs reinforced with buckskin. Pants might also be made of jeaning or denim. The men wore long woolen socks and high boots into which they could tuck their pants. High boots were worn to protect against rattlesnakes and vegetation such as prickly pear and sticker bushes. In the winter, men often wore moccasins which were more pliable and allowed better circulation to keep feet warm.

Hide Hunters: Male buffalo hunters wore buckskin pants, cotton or buckskin shirts, and leather or buckskin jackets. The hunters carried a variety of guns, both revolvers and rifles, primarily the .50 caliber Sharps known as the "Big Fifty," and nearly all wore a wide-brimmed felt hat as well as tall leather boots or moccasins. Some wore suspenders and others wore belts used for their guns and ammunition.

Lumbermen: Loggers wore sturdy trousers, rolled into cuffs or cut short to prevent the likelihood of tangling the legs on fallen trees, and long-sleeved shirts, which usually buttoned up the front. Sometimes their shirts were underwear style. Depending on weather conditions, they also wore jackets, and almost all wore suspenders, though a few wore bib-style overalls in Oregon in the 1880s. Almost all wore a felt hat, with a brim to keep the sun out of their eyes, and leather gloves. Heavy boots were a necessity. Lumbermen placed pointed metal calks (pronounced "corks") on the soles to give added traction.

Miners: The men who prospected at various precious minerals strikes in the West could be evaluated for success in their endeavors by looking at the clothing they wore. A man working hard but barely making enough money to purchase food and other necessary supplies, likely wore a pair of overalls or britches, often patched, and usually with holes in the knees caused by kneeling on rough ground.

Almost all working miners wore some type of wide-brimmed hat or sombrero, which might have been soaked in oil to make it waterproof, and a miner often tucked his worn britches into high boots. Sometimes the tops of the boots themselves were turned down. The men almost always wore long-sleeved shirts of various colors and material patterns, buttoned high to the neck. They completed their attire with a vest either alone or in combination with a longer coat, which they buttoned at the neck, generally leaving the lower buttons undone. Many miners wore suspenders and some also wore belts into which they might tuck a revolver. Those miners who had success with their diggings often wore a ruffled shirt and tied a brightly-colored silk scarf around their neck. Because many miners were from other countries, such as Ireland or China, they often wore clothing of the style they knew in their homelands. Asian men wore "loose-fitting light-blue denim pants, blue tuniclike shirts, white stockings, skull caps and cloth shoes with paper soles. Many wore the large conical straw, or 'coolie' hats that provided some protection from sun and rain as well as storage space,'' according to Carole Nielson writing in *Wild West*.

The following items were considered essential for men headed into the Alaska gold mining region: three suits of heavy underwear, six pairs of heavy wool mittens, one dozen pairs of heavy wool socks, two pairs of heavy mackinaw trousers, two pairs of overalls, one heavy mackinaw coat, two pairs of shoes, two pairs of heavy rubber boots and an oilcloth suit.

Military

One characteristic of the frontier military was its lack of consistency. For example, during the period 1865-70 frontier soldiers all wore blue coats, but the *shade* of blue varied greatly, not only among different units but also *within* units, so the frontier army had a rainbow hue to its overall look when on parade. And because frontier soldiers for the most part received clothing allowances from surplus supplies following the Civil War, soldiers often didn't have well-fitted uniforms. Shirts, coats and britches might be too long or too short, too loose or too tight. Some soldiers had their clothing altered to fit better, but not all did so. Officers didn't receive a clothing allowance, but were required to purchase their own uniforms; subsequently, they generally had better clothing, made of better quality materials, and also tailored to fit each individual officer.

The 1st U.S. Dragoons of 1846-48 carried an 1833-model saber, two Model 1836 Flintlock horse pistols and a .54 caliber smoothbore rifle. Dragoons used .52 caliber Hall carbines during the Mexican War. Beginning in 1847, Springfield Armory started manufacturing muzzle-loading, smoothbore "musketoons." They were ineffectual as fighting weapons, particularly during subsequent conflict with Indians; however, they were the standard gun issued by the Army. During that same period (1846-48) the Dragoons rode Grimsley saddles.

An infantry second lieutenant (1846-48) wore a dark blue, single-breasted frock coat and light blue pants which had a 1½-inch-wide white stripe running down the leg seam. He wore a forage cap, carried an 1840 officer's saber, and his rank was shown on shoulder scales with a silver border lace. Infantrymen in the same period wore a light-colored uniform of single-breasted styling. Both officers and infantrymen carried cotton haversacks on which was information about their company and regiment. The haversacks were bags like knapsacks that had only one shoulder strap. The infantrymen of the period carried a variety of types of guns, such as the .54 caliber flintlock, the U.S. Model 1817 "common rifle," the Model 1841 .52 caliber percussion Hall Rifle, or the .69 caliber flintlock manufactured as a U.S. Model musket. During the period 1846-48, the men generally wore their pants over their boots.

In 1857, the military adopted a uniform with a dark blue, single-breasted wool coat. Designed to fit snugly, the unhemmed frock fell to a point midway between the hip and the knee. The coat had nine brass buttons and light blue trim on the collar. The tight fit of the coat created some problems for frontier soldiers, who could not add or remove underlayers of clothing to better protect them during cold winters or hot summers. Enlisted men and officers wore similar styles of coats; however, the officers purchased their own coats, which were therefore better fitting and made of better-quality dark blue broadcloth. Black velvet often lined the stand-up collars on officer's coats, and the buttons were larger than those used on enlisted men's uniform coats. The gilt-plated buttons had the letter *I* (for Infantry) or *C* (for Cavalry) on a shield on an eagle's breast.

In 1858 infantry soldiers started wearing a black felt hat with a six-and-one-quarter-inch-high, flat-topped crown. The left side of the brim was to be held up and pinned with an eagle insignia. But infantry soldiers who had difficulty in sighting their guns instead pinned up the right side of their hats, as was standard practice for cavalry soldiers. Also adopted in 1858 for enlisted men was an unadorned forage cap made of dark blue wool broadcloth and featuring a thin, tarred-leather visor. A chin strap could be placed over the visor as a type of hat band when not under the chin. The high crown was longer in the front than in the back and unsupported so it sloped or drooped forward. The cap was hot in summer, not warm in winter and hard to clean because the brim had pasteboard in it, and it provided little protection from sun, wind, rain and other weather-related conditions on the frontier. Though the forage cap was meant to be worn with a company insignia, there was no consistency to its use or placement on the cap.

Nearly all frontier soldiers wore a sack coat, which had been adopted as a fatigue jacket in 1858. It became the standard item among the frontier army.

By the period 1861-65 soldiers wore their pants tucked into their black boots for the most part. Cavalry boots were fourteen inches high; infantrymen wore lace-up shoes, called bootees. In both cases the footwear was black. They weren't always designed with a definite right and left foot, so soldiers almost always soaked the shoes or boots in water then wore them until they dried in order to get them to conform to their feet. Overshoes, available after 1862, helped keep feet warm but not dry, as they were short and barely covered the soldier's short bootees. Many soldiers, therefore, obtained other overshoes from commercial stores, or cavalry boots. When necessary they resorted to other means, as 18th Infantryman William Murphy noted while stationed on the Bozeman Trail in Wyoming in 1866-67: "Burlap sacks were at a premium and saved our lives. We wrapped them around our shoes to keep from freezing, for there were no overshoes or rubbers to be [found] at the fort."

During the decade immediately following the Civil War, much of the clothing used by the frontier army was leftover items from the Civil War. The general clothing during the period included dark blue shell jackets, light blue wool trousers, often with a baggy fit, and a "kepi" or forage cap with its floppy crown. Often the soldiers paid little attention to military regulations with regard to their uniforms, wearing broad-brimmed hats instead of the unpopular forage caps and buckskin pants, such as those donned by Lieutenant Colonel George Armstrong Custer. The men had white or grey flannel shirts which they wore in cold weather, often leaving them in their haversack during periods of hot weather. For underwear they had long flannel drawers, which were too hot in warm climates and not heavy enough for cold, winter conditions in the northern portion of the region. To compensate for the flannel underdrawers in hot climates, soldiers either cut them off above the knees or simply didn't wear them at all, though in such cases they had difficulty with chafing caused by the rough kersey material of their trousers. In cold climates they usually wore several layers of clothing in the winter, and many soldiers obtained outer coats made of buffalo or bear hides as well.

A man's buffalo hide coat, Grand Encampment Museum.

For accouterments during the late 1860s, soldiers had sabers hanging from the left side of their belt and they carried a .44 caliber Colt in a holster on their right side. They also carried .50 caliber Spencer carbines, often slung from a wide leather shoulder belt. The sabers were seldom used in battle and were particularly ineffectual for cavalry troops, so they often were discarded by the soldiers.

During that same period an artillery company quartermaster sergeant wore a shell jacket with a single row of buttons, and he carried an 1840-pattern saber. As a side arm he carried either a Colt percussion or a Remington .44 caliber, or any other type of gun he had available. Infantrymen carried a .58 caliber Springfield musket, Model 1861. They had a knee-length heavy greatcoat with a cape that fell just below the shoulders, and around their waists wore a belt from which they hung a percussion cap pouch, bayonet and scabbard. They carried a knapsack, a tin cup and canteen, and wore a "Bummer" cap, which provided no shade for faces or necks.

By 1872 the Army had a new regulation uniform, the greatest improvement being in the area of headgear. Mounted troops had a helmet with a horsehair plume. Infantrymen had new forage caps made of felt with an indigo blue cloth covering, lined with brown cotton, and featuring a strip of gold braid around the top and base and a flat leather visor, or they wore shakos, stiff caps with high crowns and plumes. Officers had a gold eagle insignia embroidered with "Arms of the United States," an infantry bugle branch insignia, and a plume of white cock feathers in a gilt holder. Soldiers continued to wear forage caps, and they also had a black felt folding campaign cap with a wide brim cut in an oval shape to shade the face. It had a system of hooks so the cap brim could be folded up on both sides leaving it with a point in front and back. The new uniform included a five-button, dark blue flannel fatigue blouse with a falling collar. Trousers were in sky blue kersey with the inside legs and seats reinforced with canvas for cavalry troopers. Cavalry officers had gauntlet-style buckskin gloves, sometimes with fringe, and high boots that ended just below the knees. They often wore a scarf tied around their neck. Officers wore double-breasted dress coats of dark blue broadcloth with a standing collar.

In 1872, officers who had previously worn dark blue trousers started wearing sky blue trousers, just as the enlisted men did. Another change involved the leg strips. Earlier uniforms had a narrow strip of cloth sewn to the outer legs of the trousers, but the colored welt for officers in 1872 was one and one-half inches wide. Officers disliked the wide welt. Trouser strip also had color coding, blue for infantry officers and yellow for cavalry officers.

To better serve soldiers in colder climates, the Army issued blanket-lined overcoats starting in 1871, though some members of the 7th Cavalry probably had them as early as 1868.

Enlisted men wore white dress gloves, purchasing their own until 1872 when they became a part of regular army issue. The gloves were made of "Berlin," a cotton-wool blend.

Beginning in 1872 and lasting throughout the period, the uniform for cavalrymen also included stable frocks and overalls, which the men could wear over their uniforms while grooming their horses, thus keeping uniforms clean. Many soldiers stationed in the Southwest wore the stable frocks and overalls in the field, in part because they were lighter and cooler than the standard uniform.

In spite of recommended changes in military clothing in the late 1870s, most uniforms varied little as soldiers didn't adopt new styles. The buffalo overcoats were sometimes replaced by lighter canvas overcoats—known as "Miles Overcoats"—in part due to the fact there were fewer buffalo from which to obtain hides for coats. The Miles Overcoats, however, were never popular. After 1883 a different, more refined version of the Miles Overcoat was developed and continued in use through the period.

After 1859 soldiers rode McClellan saddles, which were little more than a wooden saddle tree with a horn and a strip of leather across the seat to which stirrups could be attached.

Throughout the latter portion of the period, soldiers carried sabers and had bayonets, which could be attached to their rifles, though they found both to be ineffectual or a hindrance to free movement and often discarded them.

From 1870, frontier soldiers carried their side arms and saber in a brace yoke, a suspender-style contraption of leather straps that attached to their waist belt. They carried knapsacks, clothing bags and/or haversacks and had

MILITARY RANK

Officer rank
1865
Strips of wool bordered by gilt with an insignia between the border that denoted officer or soldier rank as follows:
Lieutenant General—three stars
Major General—two stars
Brigadier General—one star
Colonel—spread eagle
Major—gold leaves
Captain—two bars
First Lieutenant—one bar

Noncommissioned officers
Chevrons of separate one-half-inch stripes, made of worsted lace for company grades and of silk for staff sergeants. Color denoted cavalry (yellow) and infantry (sky blue). Chevrons were to be worn points down above the elbow on both overcoats and dress coats. The number of bars denoted rank as follows:
Sergeant Major—three bars surmounted by an arc of three stripes
Quartermaster Sergeant—three bars with a tie of three straight bars
Orderly or First Sergeant—three bars with a diamond cradled in the
    angle
Corporal—two bars

Soldiers also wore chevrons denoting their years of service, participation in a recognized war, or indication that they had served during peacetime.

1872
Officers wore shoulder knots made of double rows of intertwined gold braid with an oval outer end, in which the regimental number and rank was embroidered in gold. The rank was denoted as follows:
Lieutenant General—three stars
Major General—two stars
Brigadier General—one star
Colonel—silver eagle with spread wings
Lieutenant Colonel—silver leaves
Major—gold leaves
Captain—two bars
First Lieutenant—one bar
Second Lieutenant—only the unit number
Noncommissioned insignia remained the same as in 1865.

The 1872 insignia for infantry was a bugle. The 1875 infantry had an insignia of crossed rifles. The cavalry insignia during the period was crossed sabers. The insignias were generally worn on the front of infantry forage caps and on the side of cavalry headgear. Placed above the insignia was a letter or number representing a soldier's company.

cartridge boxes and pouches attached to their belts as well. Other equipment included a canteen, mess outfit (including a tin cup, plate, knife, fork and spoon), a meat can, poncho and rubber blanket.

The Rough Riders who participated in the Spanish-American War of 1898 wore khaki trousers, heavy blue flannel shirts, cotton underwear and socks, gray campaign hats and navy-blue-and-white polka-dot scarves (their real trademark), and they had canvas leggings, high-topped brogans, ponchos and blankets. Their horses were equipped with 1859 McClellan saddles, saddlebags, and rifle boots.

For further information on military firearms see chapter five.

Cowboys/Ranchers/Cattle Barons

Cowboys dressed differently in various regions of the West, though they had some common clothing articles. While a working cowboy might have only one hat, coat or slicker and a couple shirts or pairs of pants, men who owned the ranches (or foremen, who earned more than cowboys) generally had more extensive wardrobes. When working, ranchers and cattle barons wore the same styles as the men they employed, although their clothing was generally of better-quality materials and it had been made to fit them. But when traveling or in town on business, they generally wore three-piece suits and seldom wore cowboy clothing styles.

The earliest cowboys of the West were Spaniards and Mexicans who were sometimes assisted—and later replaced—by African-Americans, Indians, and mestizos, who were people of both American Indian and European ancestry. Collectively they were known as vaqueros, "the working cowboy of Mexico's missions and ranches," according to Richard Slatta in *Comparing Cowboys and Frontiers.* In California they became known as *Californios.* Common dress of the vaqueros included hats with wide brims and low crowns and a loose shirt with a colorful sash tied around the waist. As Jo Mora, author of several books about the vaqueros of Spanish California, wrote in *Californios: The Saga of the Hard-Riding Vaqueros, America's First Cowboys:*

> His short pants, reaching to his knees, buttoned up the sides, and were open for six inches or so at the bottom. Long drawers (which were once white) showed wrinkles at the knees and were folded into wrapped leather *botas* (leggings). He wore a pair of rough buckskin shoes with leather soles and low heels, to which were strapped a pair of large and rusty iron spurs. This costume was finished off by a *tirador* (a heavy, wide-at-the-hips belt) that helped him to snub with the *reata* (rawhide rope) when lassoing on foot. The ever-present long knife in its scabbard was thrust inside the garter on his right leg.

Vaqueros also generally wore a poncho or *serape*, and often their pants had a broad, brightly-colored stripe down each leg. Their saddles had large skirts made of stiff leather with coverings over the stirrups, called *tapaderas* or taps. The heavy leather saddle skirts and taps protected riders from rough brush and cactus. The vaqueros also were the first cowboys of the region to wear leg protectors, known as *chaparreras* or chaps (pronounced with a soft sound, as in "shaps").

The Spanish gentleman riders of the middle and upper class, known as *charros*, meanwhile, became the landed elite of the region that included Spanish California. They were also known as *caballeros*. The term *caballero* is Spanish for "gentleman" and is literally interpreted as "horseman." The charros or caballeros wore clothing made of silk and velvet featuring elaborate silver trim. Their saddles and bridles, likewise, were made of finer materials than those of the vaqueros, and were often adorned with silver trim.

Cowboys started rounding up herds of wild cattle that had freely roamed in Texas prior to and during the Civil War, in some cases establishing ranches and other times herding the animals to northern ranges. As a result, most of the cowboys who worked on the Northern Plains got there from someplace else. Though they may have been wearing clothing representative of Texas or the Southwest, once in the north plains country the cowboys adopted certain styles with respect to both their equipment and their clothing.

Generally, cowboying on the Northern Plains started in the early 1880s, when range herds came north from Texas, though some herds had pushed into Montana as early as the 1870s. Most of the clothing styles were similar during the entire period of the true range cowboy from 1870 to 1890.

Photographs taken of a cowboy roundup during the period show men in similar attire: They wear pants; long-sleeved, button-front shirts, which were often a pullover style; vests (called waistcoats) and/or other short jackets; and broad-brimmed felt hats shaped in myriad ways. Most have scarves or bandannas knotted around their neck. Beyond those basic clothing items, the cowboys wore a variety of accessories, ranging from belts (seldom) and boots to chaps.

Cowboys often wore sweaters and military issue overcoats with an accompanying cape or coats made of cloth with beaver collars and cuffs or of buffalo or even bear hides.

Boots: Boots used by cowboys during the period often had stovepipe uppers and generally had wide, often square, toes and low heels. Though "cowboy" boots were made during the period, many cowboys simply used standard, over-the-counter work boots and those considered government surplus which were sold in the Montgomery Ward and Company catalog for $2.75 a pair. The boots with soles held to uppers with hardwood pegs cost slightly more than those where the two parts were sewn together. Average prices ranged from about $7 to $15 per pair, with made-to-measure boots more expensive than store version ready-made styles.

The American cowboy boot with a higher heel came into use during the 1870s as narrower stirrups required a narrower boot and one that had a heel so the rider's foot wouldn't slide clear through the stirrup. At the same time, the square boot tops started giving way to other designs, such as the popular V cut and the addition of two leather loops used to pull on boots. Fancy stitching on the boot uppers began appearing in the 1880s. Boots were most often black. The vaqueros and charros wore short shoes, rather than boots.

After 1887 cowboys on the northern plains wore shaggy chaps made of long-haired angora, such as these in shotgun style, with tight, straight legs. The chaps belong to the author.

Chaps: Like slickers, cowboys used chaps (leather leg protectors which originated in Mexico, but which also had been used by mountain men and Indians) to protect themselves from the elements. The leggings came in a variety of styles and not all cowboys used them. Trail-driving cowboys moving herds north from Texas often wore bullhide chaps, which they called "leggins." On the Northern Plains, however, men tended to use straight-legged shotgun chaps, which often had pockets on each front leg. In the late 1880s batwing or wing chaps (which had wider legs) became more popular. And late in the period (after 1887) men used woolly chaps—either black or a light cream-colored version made of angora. Northern cowboys generally wore chaps for warmth when riding at night or in cold, wet weather; southern cowboys used them as protectors from brush and sharp thorns on mesquite bushes.

Coats, Vests, Outerwear: Coats of canvas, duck or denim often had blanket liners and were made and sold by such companies as Montgomery Ward and Company or Carhartt. Southwestern cowboys wore canvas or buckskin jackets that reached to their waist or hips, particularly when they were riding in rough country because the coats protected them from mesquite thorns and brush. These jackets had little ornamentation, though they might have fringe, and were tailored in the Mexican style with small lapels.

Northern cowboys sometimes had sack coats that had once been part of a store-bought suit of clothes, often made of wool, and after 1890 some wore a wide-waled corduroy coat known as a "Sweetor."

Though a gum-rubber fabric had been developed by Charles Goodyear in 1844, not until November 1881 did Abner J. Tower develop rain gear for cowboys. That year he started selling his Fish Brand Pommel Slicker. It came in black or a yellow mustard color and had a long slit in the back so it would fit over a horse and saddle. Other companies quickly followed Tower's lead and began making and selling their own version of the yellow slicker. To waterproof slickers, cowboys treated them with linseed oil. The slickers had red flannel lining inside the collar prior to 1910 and cost about $3.50. The slickers—referred to as a Fish, a Fishbrand or a Tower—became so popular that many cowboys didn't even own coats, though almost all wore vests.

Like coats, vests often had been part of a store-bought suit of clothes. They were particularly useful when they had four small pockets, to hold tobacco and cigarette makings, a tally book and perhaps a watch. The vests were warm, but lacking sleeves, they gave cowboys freedom of arm movement needed when roping, riding or doing other chores such as branding or doctoring cattle. Some Texas cowboys wore vests of antelope or deer skin in the 1880s and they also liked laced leather vests; calfskin vests became popular in the 1890s.

Light linen coats known as dusters were little used by cowboys. They were designed solely to keep clothing from becoming dusty while traveling and didn't have features designed for warmth or to keep a cowboy dry in inclement weather. (Stagecoach companies, however, often provided dusters to male and female passengers to keep them from getting their clothes dirty.)

If they weren't actively working with livestock or at other ranch chores, ranch owners often wore three-piece suits, and in winter they may have added an overcoat of raccoon, which cost as much as $50, therefore placing it out of the pocketbook for most cowboys who earned only $30 to $40 per month. Cowboys did wear blanket coats, often white with bright red, yellow or blue stripes, and they also wore "sourdough" coats made of canvas or duck, lined with blankets or flannel and painted to make them waterproof and wind resistant.

Northern cowboys also sometimes acquired buffalo coats that reached nearly to their ankles and had wide collars that could be turned up to protect necks and ears from wind-driven snow and the cold. The buffalo coats were big, bulky and heavy. They fastened with toggle fasteners, or sometimes with buttons, and kept cowboys warm during cold winters. The alternative was to wear numerous layers of clothes, as reported by Teddy Blue Abbott in *We Pointed 'em North* when writing about the Montana winter of 1886-87:

> I wore two pairs of wool socks, a pair of moccasins, a pair of Dutch
> socks that came up to the knees, a pair of government overshoes,

two suits of heavy underwear, pants, overalls, chaps and a big heavy
shirt. I got a pair of woman's stockings and cut the feet out and
made sleeves. I wore wool gloves, and great big heavy mittens, a
blanket-lined sourdough overcoat and a great big sealskin cap.

—*Teddy Blue Abbott, Montana cowboy, winter 1886-87*

Gloves and Gauntlets: Cowboys wore gloves to protect their hands from cold
weather and rough work. Few wore gauntlets, which were leather extensions
sewn directly to the gloves, though many wore leather cuffs to protect their
shirts. The cuffs generally had some type of ornamentation provided either
by stamping the leather or by adding small silver pieces such as conchas or
studs in a design. They were about eight inches long and fit tight at the
wrist, tapering toward the elbow.

Guns: Almost all cowboys wore side arms, usually carrying the .44 caliber
Colt Single Action Army revolver known as the Peacemaker, though few
range cowboys carried two revolvers. They did often carry two guns—one
revolver and one rifle in a leather scabbard hanging from their saddle. (For
more information about cowboy weapons and gear see chapters five and
thirteen.)

Hats, Scarves and Bandannas: Though most wore broad-brimmed hats, depending on the season, cowboys also wore wool or fur caps in a variety of
styles. Cowboys in the northern plains region had hats with narrower brims,
while those in the Southwest and California had wide brims for protection
from sun.

John B. Stetson gets credit for making the first true cowboy hat. While
living in Colorado in 1865, Stetson, the son of a hatter in Philadelphia,
developed his first western hat, known as the "Boss of the Plains," which
had a four-inch brim and four-inch crown. Made of two ounces of felt, the
hats cost $5. Some hats sold for as much as $10 or $20. By 1900 Sears, Roe-
buck and Co. offered a new styled "Boss of the Plains" made with six ounces
of felt and sold it for $4.50. The important feature on Stetson's hat was its
brim size, which was much smaller than the wide sombrero hat brims of
California and the Southwest though it still shed water and shaded cowboys
from the sun.

The shape of the hat depended somewhat upon the wearer. Many men
creased their hats forward and back, but a good-sized majority had the front
brim tipped back from their faces. That meant the sun hit their noses, but
it may have given them a better view of the range. The crown shape ranged
from the Montana peak (all four sides pushed in to a single peak in the
center) to no crease at all with the hat simply left in its original rounded
shape. Cowboys in Texas were more likely to leave the hat uncreased, as
were Indian cowboys.

During the period 1870-90 hat crowns tended to be short—four to four and one-half inches. The "ten-gallon" style didn't come into play until after 1900.

Many cowboys had bands made of leather or braided horsehair placed around the crown of the hat. These may have been held in place or ornamented with buckles, tacks or silver conchas, which were shell-shaped ornaments, or small oval or round metal disks. The band not only gave the hat some ornamentation, it also helped it hold its shape when wet. Cowboys in the 1880s sometimes also added braided leather or horsehair strings which they could knot under their chin to keep their hat in place when riding fast or in windy conditions, and vaqueros held their hats in place with a chin strap, or *barbiquejo*. Often cowboys let the strings fall behind their head and down their back.

> I wore a black plush hat which had a row of small stars around the
> rim, with buck-skin strings to tie and hold on my head.
> —*J.L. McCaleb, late 1860s, Abilene, Kansas*

Hats kept sun and rain or snow off a cowboy's head, and they were used as signals to other riders, as water containers, as fans to make a campfire flame, and by waving them, as something with which to haze livestock or get animals to move in a certain direction.

Cowboys wore scarves or bandannas around their neck, which could be pulled up over their nose when riding behind herds that raised dust clouds, or in cold weather. They also tied the scarf or bandanna over their hat to hold it in place and keep their ears warm. Most cowboy clothing was dark, but bandannas and scarves were often brightly colored.

Pants: Cowboys liked pants of wool, and they wore California pants made with tight waists and loose legs in colors ranging from light buckskin to gray and often of an interwoven plaid design. They were made primarily by the Oregon City Woolen Mills, and a pair cost as much as twelve dollars, according to an account by Teddy Blue Abbott who wrote in *We Pointed 'em North*, "we had . . . striped or checked California pants made in Oregon City, the best pants ever made to ride in."

By 1874 Montgomery Ward and Company sold trousers made of canvas, duck or denim, but the most important addition to the cowboy clothing line occurred in 1873 when Levi Strauss started manufacturing pants of denim. Strauss had been making and selling pants of brown canvas used primarily by miners since 1853. When he started using denim, he dyed the pants indigo blue and made the seams with orange thread. In 1873 Strauss added a back pocket and patented rivets at the pockets and along seams to provide strength. Cowboys did not immediately start wearing the new jeans, since known as Levis. They considered them "poor man's wear, or more likely the sort of clothes a 'pilgrim' farmer would wear,'' according to Don Rickey in *$10 Horse, $40 Saddle*.

In 1890 Strauss introduced his 501 jeans with straight legs, made so they would "shrink to fit" and then cowboys started wearing them regularly. Few pants had any belt loops until after 1890. Waists were generally tight so pants stayed in place without the need for a belt, which was seldom worn during the period, except among the vaqueros. Some men used suspenders, and they often wore a gun belt.

Shirts: Most cowboys wore homemade shirts with an opening in the front that extended partway down the shirt. They drew the shirts over their heads and closed the opening, or placket, with three or four buttons, or perhaps with leather lacing. Most shirts were gray, blue or black. Cowboys also wore dark blue army shirts of wool twill either obtained through trade with soldiers or from post stores. Other shirts were of dark flannel or wool, striped silk (which had a tight weave that kept the wind out) and a black sateen-type material (popular during the 1880s). Montana cowboys working on the DHS Ranch in the 1880s participated in roundups wearing white shirts (and became known as the white shirt brigade) as they attempted to garner attention from the daughters of ranch owner Granville Stuart. All ready-made shirts had little variation in sleeve length, so cowboys wore arm garters to keep their cuffs in the proper place.

Spurs: Spurs used by California, Texas and southwestern cowboys and vaqueros had large rowels, two or more inches in diameter, and the spurs themselves often had ornate carving. The rowels are the round metal pieces attached to the back of the spurs which rotate and can be used to give a signal to the horse that the rider wants a certain action, such as a faster gait or speed, or a turn in a different direction. Spurs also may have had two small metal pieces (sometimes called clinkers) attached near the rowel that jingled as the cowboys walked, giving them the name jinglers or jingle bobs. Northern cowboys had spurs with two-inch or smaller rowels, and they were seldom as ornate or fancy as those of southern and California cowboys. Ornamentation increased after the 1880s.

Men's Accessories

Belts: Not commonly used during the period.

Coats/Outerwear: Men wore vests and coats on an almost routine basis. Animal skins such as buffalo, raccoon and bear were used for heavy coats.

Glasses: Men wore eye protectors of solid materials, often wood, with slits cut into them to protect against snow blindness. And if they wore spectacles they generally were wire-framed and round or oval-shaped.

Hair and Beards: Men for the most part had mustaches or full beards. Asian men shaved their heads but retained their long pigtail or queue, which hung down their backs. Manchu dictators forbade Chinese men from returning to China without a queue, so retaining one was a necessity for those who planned to visit China.

Handkerchiefs: Though some men's handkerchiefs were of linen with fancy border stitching, men also carried heavy brocade silk handkerchiefs in black, white and solid colors, and heavy twilled silk handkerchiefs in both white and solid colors.

Hats: Men wore flat-brimmed straw hats made of braided strands of straw, or wool felt hats in a variety of styles such as top hat, derby, or low-crowned and flat-brimmed. They also wore hats made of animal hides such as coyote, wolf, buffalo or even skunk.

> **The California Hat**—The soft and really comfortable hat, now known as 'the felt,' first came into fashion after the commencement of the Mexican war at Palo Alto. It is little singular that the religious newspapers are adopting these 'rowdy castors' as emblems not only of comfort but piety. A late number of the *Central Presbyterian,* speaking of the subject says:
>
> Indeed, the soft felt is the only sensible hat now worn. Instead of the shiny, hard and stiff fur or silk hat, so lately universal—a perpetual annoyance to the owner; in his way in every conveyance and in every crowd; never protecting him from sun or rain, but keeping him anxiously trying to protect it; very much in the shape and about as pleasant to the head as a section of stove-pipe would be; always getting blown off, or mashed, or weather-stained; instead of all this, we now have the broad-brimmed, flexible-bodied, easy-fitting hat, without fur on it or stiffening in it, never binding the brow or causing headache, never injured by rough handling; always in shape, if shape it might be called, which shape has none, always shading the face from sun and sheltering it from storm; and last, though not least, the prettiest hat, if beauty is associated with utility and the fitness of things. This is the hat which constitutes one of the most to be lauded inventions of the present day—one which should universally supplant its absurd predecessor, and be worn by all classes, clergymen included.
> —FLIN, *January 24, 1857, 115-3*

Scarves: Used by cowboys and miners.

Suspenders: Commonly used by lumbermen, miners, homesteaders/emigrants and sometimes by cowboys.

Undergarments: Men wore waist-high drawers of cotton, wool flannel, silk or combinations of those materials during the period 1860 to about 1880. The drawers had three or four buttons and a tie-string used to hold them in place; some had tie-strings near the ankles, while others had knitted or elastic gatherings at the bottom. Montgomery Ward and Company advertised "Scarlet Knit Drawers" and "matching undershirts" in the late 1870s, but the one-piece union suit wasn't available until the mid-1890s. In 1897 men could purchase silk finish, merino or wool underwear with separate shirts or drawers in a variety of weights and costing from $.45 to $1.25 from Sears, Roebuck and Co.

WOMEN

Many western women wore silks and satins in styles as fashionable as their eastern counterparts, and they also forged a style of their own, abandoning numerous petticoats, hoop skirts or, for that matter, any kind of skirt, for more practical items. They sewed metal bars or lead shot into their skirt hems to keep them closer to the ground in windstorms, and they wore bloomer pants when walking west with wagon trains. The women who lived out-of-doors helping establish western ranches and homesteads were more likely to wear shorter skirts and divided skirts that made walking and riding horseback both easier and safer. Women miners in California, Alaska and other locations wore pants and flannel shirts. Their adoption of such styles showed their independence and gave them a freedom of action eastern women didn't have.

Though women of the region attempted to have clothing in the style of the day, many women who emigrated into the West had clothing they brought with them, and they may not have replaced it for years. Therefore, it would not be unusual to see a woman in the West wearing clothes representative of styles that had been popular a decade or more earlier. That was particularly so in rural areas and among the women who lived on the land, working alongside their husbands on homesteads and ranches or in mines. Women did, however, remake their dresses into new garments more reflective of up-to-date styles, and if they didn't have silk or brocade, they might use gingham and calico to fashion "ball gowns" complete with multiple flounces, bustles and trains, depending upon the popular style at the time.

Hispanic and Asian women wore clothing representative of their cultures, such as the heavy, ornately trimmed dresses worn by upper- or middle-class Spanish or Mexican women and the loose-fitting blouses and skirts of Hispanic peasants. Asian women wore tight-fitting kimonos, and both Hispanic and Asian women also wore a combination of cultural and Euro-American styles. For most women of all ethnic groups fashion was dictated by necessity.

In almost all cases, the women tried to reserve at least one dress "for good" or use as a "best" dress. Such a dress might be of fine silk, representing a more prosperous time in a woman's life. Because most of the women worked hard to build a new home, they often set aside many of the conventional attitudes of the day. Women in urban areas or the East might wear from six to ten petticoats, but western women likely wore only one or two. They had neither the materials for more nor the time to keep them clean. For a woman who hauled water by hand, heated it over a fire, then scrubbed clothing one piece at a time, it was unnecessary and impractical to wear half a dozen petticoats, particularly when she might go for weeks without seeing anyone outside her immediate family.

The women did appreciate fine fashion, and they always dressed in their best—including more than one petticoat if they had it—when going to town, to church, to weddings and funerals or to the annual Fourth of July picnic.

Women washed clothes in wash tubs and on wash boards, or using washing machines such as this model with a hand-cranked wringer. This one is located in the W.T. Peryam House at the Grand Encampment Museum.

Because many women of the West brought clothing with them from elsewhere, some were highly fashionable. After the 1870s, communities might look more like they'd been literally picked up from Germany, England or some other foreign location as immigrants poured across the Atlantic and into the West. The community of Victoria, Kansas, is such an example. Settled by wealthy English aristocrats, the families had gold and silver, crystal and china; they wore silk and satin and participated in soirees or cricket games. Contrast that to some homesteader areas where men, women and children dressed in homemade clothing made from feed sacks, and ate off of tin plates placed upon a homemade wooden table.

Common materials used for women's clothing included linsey-woolsey, calico, silk, plaid, muslin, printed cotton, wool challis (a soft, lightweight fabric), dimity (a corded cotton material with stripes or checks worked into the plain weave) and grosgrain-striped silk taffeta with its pattern woven to include crosswise cotton ribs. Ornamentation and design elements included handmade lace collars and wool braid placed around the hem. Most dresses had a pocket sewn into the right side seam. Women used a fluting iron to place, and keep, ruffles in their calicos. The heavy metal fluting iron had **V**-shaped indentations on two separate sides of the iron. Women placed the ruffles of their dresses on the heated iron, then rolled the top portion over the bottom portion to press in the ruffles, similar to the way a waffle iron makes indentations in batter.

If women were fortunate enough to have more than one dress, they were all generally made in the same style, though one might be of calico, another of sturdy linsey-woolsey, often called the "heavy dress," and the "best" dress could even be of silk. The difference in the dresses, apart from the materials used for making them, lay in the trim placed on each. If they had the opportunity, women wore their best dress over a crinoline or hoops and later over a bustle. That let neighbors know they were aware of fashion trends and styles.

Women's dresses during the period 1840 through 1865 tended to have long, full skirts that were sometimes attached to the bodice, and at other times were not, even though the outfit appeared as if it were one piece. Necklines in the 1840s were high and round. From about 1850 on, women wore more two-piece outfits with the top separate from the skirt, but not until the 1890s did the true shirtwaist (blouse), or waist as women referred to them, evolve.

A dress made during the period 1840-65, with its full skirt, required ten yards of calico or about fourteen yards of silk. The calico came on a wider bolt than did silk, which was only about twenty-two inches wide.

The "bloomer style" came into being in the early 1850s. It had trousers beneath a tunic-style dress. Though it never became widely popular—except as a subject for jokes and caricature—some women did wear the bloomers. *Frank Leslie's Illustrated Newspaper* reported on September 6, 1856, "Miss Amelia Bloomer denies being the originator of the celebrated Bloomer costume, and gives the credit (!) to Mrs. Miller, daughter of Gerrit Smith. She says Mrs. M. had been wearing the breeches two or three months before herself, and others were induced to adopt the style."

Though women in the East may have hesitated to wear bloomer outfits, they had a practical appeal for women in the West as is evidenced by this comment from Miriam Davis Colt, who lived with her husband in Kansas in 1856:

> Am wearing the Bloomer dresses now; find they are well suited to a wild life like mine. Can bound over the prairies like an antelope, and am not in so much danger of setting my clothes on fire while cooking when these prairie winds blow.

In San Francisco the style attracted attention when a ladies dress store owner, Mrs. Cole, not only attired a store display figure in a bloomer costume but also wore one herself consisting of flowing pink satin trousers that were tight at the ankles beneath a green merino dress. And the San Francisco *Alta* wrote on July 14, 1851, of other San Francisco woman wearing "flowing red satin trousers" beneath a black satin skirt.

Some called the bloomers knickerbockers because they were similar to the loose britches worn by young boys and eastern men. The bloomers generally reached only to the top of a woman's boots and she often wore a knee-length skirt overtop. For women traveling to California via the Panama area, who went partway on horse- or mule-back (riding astride and not on a sidesaddle), bloomers became an essential clothing item.

Mormon leader Brigham Young endorsed bloomers for overland travelers to Utah. Once the women had reached Utah, however, Young decreed they should wear the "Deseret Costume," an outfit similar to the bloomer design but with a loose overlayer that had little shape.

> A Cincinnati paper complains of respectable young ladies dressed
> in male attire promenading the streets of the city. The stories of
> girl soldiers have made them crazy for breeches.
> —FLIN, *November 28, 1863, 146-3*

Women tended to set aside the tight-corseted styles of the day and dressed in simple garments that fit more loosely. Any woman traveling west during the period who wore a silk dress was quickly labeled as a prostitute, though in some cases respectable women did wear fine dresses, finding it necessary to do so because their plainer garments were worn out and useless.

When traveling on stagecoaches or trains, women wore linen dusters over their clothes to keep them somewhat clean from blowing dirt or coal dust and ash. The dusters were light garments designed to protect clothing, but not meant for warmth or to keep a traveler dry in inclement weather.

Chinese women, who were used to wearing lose kimonos, and Hispanic women, who had worn loose-fitting garments as well, had quite an adjustment when they started to wear the clothes of Anglo women: a corset or brassiere; hip pads; long skirt; tight-fitting, high-necked blouse; and a large hat. Corsets, considered necessary by Anglo women in more urban areas, often made it nearly impossible for the wearer to breathe, and at times the woman had to seek privacy where her husband or another woman could loosen the corset strings. Mary A. Maverick wrote in *Memoirs*:

> A belle of the ball in San Antonio purchased a new silk dress that
> fit so tightly she had to wear corsets for the first time in her life.
> She was several times compelled to escape to her bedroom to take
> off the corset and "catch her breath."

Some women at home and with little likelihood of company took their hoops off and hung them in the kitchen while they worked.

In May 1857 *Frank Leslie's Illustrated Newspaper* reported, "A bevy of principal fashionable ladies in Cincinnati appeared on promenade a few days since without hoops, and with robes descending 'classically' straight."

In January 1859 the crinoline was introduced in Washington, DC. It had an underskirt or hoop structure made of whalebone or wire that held skirts out in a bell-like shape. As *Frank Leslie's Illustrated Newspaper* noted on February 25, 1860, "(The) crinoline is not without it's [*sic*] uses. It saved the lives of two young ladies, Miss Temple and Miss Williams, some few days since. They were crossing the Mississippi at Dubuque, Iowa, when they sunk through a spot of spongy ice. Their crinoline, however, spread out and held them up until assistance arrived."

In the late 1860s the bustle replaced the crinoline, and it was widely in use in time for the Centennial Exposition in 1876 in Philadelphia. Made of a horsehair cushion, a pillow, wire, wicker or even whalebone, the bustle attached to the waistband and supported the voluminous folds of material which were then concentrated at the back of the dress. Materials used in making bustles included muslin, calico or silk taffeta, often stuffed with wadding, cork or straw. Dresses might be brightly colored silk or have plain waists with rows of silk ribbon on the skirt.

The use of a bustle didn't last long. Even as some women began wearing bustles, others abandoned their crinolines and went directly to simpler styles:

> IOWA—Des Moines has initiated a dress reform. The platform announces moderately short walking-dresses for the street; skirts lightened of their burden of trimmings and suspended from the shoulders; corsets to be loosened or widened; the extremities warmly clothed, and superfluous finery to be discarded on church costume.—FLIN, *September 20, 1873, 27-4*

Woman's Dress

> This is what Mary Kyle Dallas says about it: 'Take a man and pin three or four large table cloths about him, fastened back with elastic and looped up with ribbons; drag all his own hair to the middle of his head and tie it tight, and hairpin on about five pounds of other hair and a big bow of ribbon. Keep the front locks on pins all night and let them tickle his eyes all day; pinch his waist into a corset, and give him gloves a size too small and shoes ditto, and a hat that will not stay on without a torturing elastic, and a frill to tickle his chin, and a little lace vail to blind his eyes whenever he goes out to walk, and he will know what woman's dress is.
> —FLIN, *June 19, 1875, 233-4, 234-1*

Mother Hubbard dresses, characterized by their fitted neckline but long, flowing style, became popular in the 1880s, and many women found them unconfining and therefore practical when living an active lifestyle. But the Mother Hubbard had its drawback and Pendleton, Oregon, town officials (all male) took action to force women to use a belt to hold them in because the loose dresses could "scare horses, cause accidents, and ruin business." The *Sedalia Bozo* in Missouri, likewise, advocated the use of belts by women wearing Mother Hubbard dresses.

Erin Moulton wears the two-piece dress that belonged to her great-great grandmother, Margaret Kepner Fisher of Effingham, Kansas, and later of Encampment, Wyoming. The dress, circa 1895, has a tightly fitted, fully-lined bodice with long sleeves and lace trim at the wrists and also around the collar/bib. The dress belongs to the author.

In 1882 some stores sold ready-made clothes for women and men. Dress styles had narrower waists and straighter lines by the 1890s.

Cowgirls/Ranchwomen: Cowgirls worked the range as well as men, adapting clothing designed for men. The women often wore split riding skirts, particularly after 1890, but sometimes they used a pair of men's pants instead. Like the men, women wore hats, gloves, chaps, bandannas, slickers and boots.

Riding-Dress

There is no place where a woman appears to better advantage than upon horseback. We will take it for granted that our lady has acquired properly the art of riding. Next, she must be provided with a suitable habit. Her habit should fit perfectly without being tight. The skirt should be full and long enough to cover the feet, while it is best to omit the extreme length, which subjects the dress to mud spatterings and may prove a serious entanglement in case of accident.

Waterproof is the most serviceable for a riding costume. Something lighter may be worn in summer. In the lighter costume a row or two of shot should be stitched in the bottom of the breadths to keep the skirt from blowing up in the wind.

The riding-dress should be made to fit the waist closely and buttoned nearly to the throat.

Coat sleeves should come to the wrist, with linen cuffs beneath them.

It is well to have the waist attached to a skirt of the usual length and the long skirt fastened over it, so that if any mishap obliges the lady to dismount she may easily remove the long overskirt and still be properly dressed.

The shape of the hat will vary with the fashion, but it should always be plainly trimmed; and if feathers are worn, they must be fashioned so that the wind cannot possibly blow them over the wearer's eyes.

All ruffling, puffing or bows in the trimming of a riding-dress is out of place. If trimming is used it should be put on in perfectly flat bands or be of braiding.

The hair must be put up compactly, neither curls nor veil should be allowed to stream in the wind. No jewelry except what is absolutely required to fasten the dress, and that of the plainest kind, is allowable.—Decorum, *1877*

Emigrants/Homesteaders: Women following the western trails often cut several inches off the bottom of their dresses to make walking easier. To keep them from blowing in the wind, they sewed small pockets of lead shot into the hem. The use of lead shot or strips sewn into skirt hems likely originated with George Armstrong Custer who saw the wind catch his wife Elizabeth's dress one day. To preserve her modesty (and prevent soldiers from seeing her undergarments), Custer had Elizabeth sew the weights into the skirt hem. Such a practice became popular with women, and particularly amongst those living in windy climates, as it made it less of a chore to keep billowing skirts down around their ankles and not flying up above their heads.

Besides the problem of keeping skirts down in the wind, women had to deal with holding them up when the weather turned wet. Then they struggled to keep the voluminous skirts out of the mud, water and manure. In December 1874 the *Leavenworth Daily Times* advertised a new invention, costing seventy-five cents, to help women in that regard: "You can raise your skirt while passing a muddy place and then let if fall, or you can keep it raised with the elevator. It keeps the skirt from filth. It can be changed from one dress to another in less than two minutes.''

Olmstead & Co, in Chicago, sold Dewey's Invisible Dress Elevator in 1880 for $1.25 claiming it is "one of the most convenient, useful and economical appendages that can [possibly] be attached to a lady's dress for the purpose of holding it up any desired height, and releasing it instantly (without trouble or inconvenience to the wearer) . . . . It is attached by toilet pins with ease, and may be changed and worn on any dress.''

The emigrant woman's dress generally had no hoops, but was a simple calico frock, perhaps made of gingham or linsey-woolsey. The bodice was often lined with canvas for strength or warmth, though most dress bodices, or waists (as blouses of the latter period were called), could also be lined with linen or other fabric. Though they started out long, emigrant women's dresses were often inches shorter by the time they reached the end of the trail, having been torn at the bottom when they snagged on brush.

Military: Women with the military troops, primarily officers' wives, wore general styles of the period, though they often were slightly out of date, due to the delay in getting new garments or patterns. In cold climates the women bundled into buffalo boots, furs, cloaks with beaver hoods and shawls. Anna Blanche Sokalski had a riding habit made of wolfskin; the tails dragged on the floor and other tails hanged from her hat when she fought a court-martial with her husband, George, at Post Cottonwood (later Fort McPherson, Nebraska Territory).

Women's Accessories

Aprons: An essential part of a woman's wardrobe, aprons represented just one of the many layers of clothing deemed necessary during the period. The most common apron was white, made of homespun, cotton, linen or other materials. Some women, having nothing else, used bleached feed sacks for their aprons. Apron styles varied from those with a waistband to those with suspender straps and others with a full bodice. Most aprons were long and reached the lower skirt hem, but women also wore shorter aprons, often made of sheer black material and known as "tea aprons.''

Boots: Usually women's boots had sharply pointed toes and high lace tops. They were most often black. Though some women's boots laced, others buttoned and the women used buttonhooks to properly close their boots.

Coats/Outerwear: Women wore capes, often those which they themselves made. The capes could be short, reaching to a woman's elbow, or longer, falling to below the waist or even to near the hemline, although the full-length cloak was less common after the 1840s. Coats and jackets weren't common in the 1840s; those that did exist were short and fitted. Coats or jackets matching dresses became more popular in the 1850s and even more so in the 1860s. Like shawls, mantles were popular throughout the period. Mantles were often round or pointed at the back. Some were similar to a cape and others carefully fitted to the figure. Mantles came in various lengths from three-quarter to full length. In 1897 Sears, Roebuck and Co. sold ladies' capes and jackets made of twilled cloth and featuring ribbon or merino trim.

Fans: Women used fans more often in urban areas and in warmer climates, often hanging them from their waist. They were particularly popular with upper- and middle-class Hispanic women.

Gloves: Gloves made of kid leather were always in style; their appropriate length changed through the years with short gloves for evening wear out of style by 1865. During the late 1860s evening gloves lengthened until by 1870 they reached near the elbow. Gloves for daytime use also lengthened during the period. Only urban women and those from the wealthiest families wore gloves routinely as a fashion statement; rural women did wear gloves for warmth and to protect their hands when working at outdoor activities. Materials for gloves included suede, cotton, wool and silk. "Silk gloves have long ceased to be fashionable though thousands of women wear them," reported *Women's World,* in 1888. Though woolen gloves weren't fashionable, they were popular among western women and children, in part because the women themselves could make the gloves by knitting them using homespun wool.

Hair and Cosmetics: Hairpieces ranging from a chatelaine twist or braid, tuck-up switch or pompadour were available but not widely used by western women, except among Anglo women in urban areas. Wearing cosmetics was something "proper" women didn't do. A woman carefully shielded her face from the sun to prevent freckles, and she had various remedies to use in an effort to lessen those freckles she might have. A woman might pinch her cheeks until they had a pink tinge, but no proper white woman wore cosmetics.

Using Paints

We cannot but allude to the practice of using paints, a habit strongly to be condemned. If for no other reason than that poison lurks beneath every layer, inducing paralytic affections and premature death, they should be discarded—but they are a disguise which deceives no one, even at a distance; there is a ghastly deathliness in the appearance of the skin after it has been painted, which is far removed from the natural hue of health. —Decorum

Handkerchiefs: Women carried linen handkerchiefs, often with fancy stitching around the hem.

Women kept their handkerchiefs in boxes and men stored neckties in their own boxes, such as this matching set, which belonged to Margaret Kepner Fisher and Joseph W. Fisher. Both are from the author's collection.

Hats: Sunbonnets were constructed with casing and thin slats of wood or cardboard to make the bonnet portion protrude to protect a woman's face from the harsh sun of the open country. Almost every woman in the West during the period had at least one sunbonnet. Those of the early portion of the period were much larger than those of later years; nevertheless, the primary purpose was to shield a woman's face from the sun. The traditional sunbonnet had a wide brim and a long piece of material, known as a *bravolet* or curtain, that extended down on the sides and back. The bravolet could be anywhere from two to fourteen inches in length. The poke bonnet was much smaller and sat farther back on a woman's head.

Women called any type of hat a bonnet, making them of such materials as calico, silk taffeta, chambray, checkered gingham, muslin, velvet, sateen and wool brilliantine. Some were of straw and some had lace and feathers on them. The women generally had a winter bonnet (or hat) and a summer bonnet.

As *Frank Leslie's Illustrated Newspaper* reported on April 22, 1865:

> The new half handkerchief style of bonnet is thus described in an exchange
>
> *A sort of cup to catch the hair*
> *Leaving the head to 'go it bare'*
> *A striking example of 'nothing to wear'*
> *Is this bonnet abomination*

Again:

> *It makes a woman look brazen & bold*
> *Assists her in catching nothing but cold*
> *It is bad on the young, absurd on the old*
> *And deforms what it ought to deck*

Muffs: Women used muffs made of various materials. Those made of tanned animal skins could be used to keep hands warm when traveling or walking in cold climates.

Ribbons: Nearly every Anglo woman wore some bit of ribbon at all times, on her dress, pinned at her neck or in her hair.

Scarves: The lightweight woolen hand-crocheted shawl known as a fascinator served as a popular head covering as well as something to wrap around shoulders.

Shawls: Appearing in public in 1865 without a "scarf, shawl, or mantilla" was tantamount to not being a lady, according to *Godey's Lady's Book*, the "bible" of proper dress and decorum. *The* shawl to have was a paisley, patterned after the handwoven Kashmir shawls from India, the majority of which were made in Paisley, Scotland, and imported to America. However true paisley shawls came at high cost. According to Betty Mills in *Calico Chronicle*, prices were as much as $500 direct from Scotland, and $275 from Lord & Taylor in New York City even as late as the 1880s. Fortunately there were cheaper alternatives, such as a $2.50 shawl sold by Montgomery Ward and Company. Women liked shawls for a variety of reasons, not the least of which was the convenience in wearing one over the voluminous dresses popular during the period.

Though the paisley shawl was a symbol of prosperity and style, most shawls served a more utilitarian purpose, that of keeping women warm. Many were crocheted and others were handmade from a variety of materials ranging from wool to silk. Women took a square of material, folded it into a triangle, added a fringe to the edges and used it as an outer wrap. Most women had mourning shawls in drab colors, such as brown. Hispanic women particularly used mantillas and would not go out in public without one to place over their head and shoulders.

Women wore a variety of shoe styles, including high, lace-up black books with sharply pointed toes and heels. These are at the Grand Encampment Museum.

Shoes: Women wore what they had; calfskin shoes were precious and worn only in cold weather. Many times women went barefoot to save their shoes, or they wore rubbers to go outside.

Spectacles: If they wore any type of glasses or spectacles, women generally had those with wire frames and either round or oval in shape.

Undergarments: Undergarments evolved through the decades. In the 1840s women wore a long, loose garment called a chemise, which at that time was semi-fitted. By mid-century it became a loose bodice with an attached petticoat that fell below the knees. Embroidery and other fancy work was an essential part of each chemise, or "shimmy" as they were known. Beneath the chemise, women wore pantaloons or pantalets, which had wide legs and lace and ruffles at the lower edge. Skirts in the 1840s were shorter and the pantaloons with their ruffles at the hemline kept a woman's legs from showing. By the 1860s skirts were longer and fuller, making it unlikely a woman's legs could ever be seen, so pantaloons became less necessary as an undergarment after that time.

Women sometimes wore vests of merino wool (or later silk) next to their skin, and they also may have worn drawers beneath their pantaloons.

Throughout the period women wore long petticoats. In the 1870s women generally wore only one petticoat, as that is all that would fit beneath their dresses. The petticoats were made of whatever materials were available; After 1860 almost all women had a red flannel petticoat (for warmth), and others were quilted, also for warmth. Petticoats were generally the same shape as the dress under which they were worn.

The petticoats were worn over the top of a woman's chemise, as was a corset, "shaped with gussets at the breast and hips and stiffened with boning, cane or whalebone," according to Betty J. Mills in *Calico Chronicle*. Western women didn't always wear a corset; however, in situations where they wore their finest dresses they generally used a corset, in part to constrict their waist to the tiny measurements considered fashionable. Various companies made and sold corsets. In 1886 Bloomingdale Brothers advertised in its mail-order catalog Madam Clark's Hygeian corset or Roth's Patent double-bone corset at $1.25 each, or Dr. Warner's Coraline Corset for $1. Various other corsets sold for prices ranging from $.50 to $3.75.

In the latter part of the century the chemise or corset cover was shortened and became known as a camisole. By 1886 Bloomingdale Brothers sold them to mail-order customers for prices ranging from $.21 to $1.13. Most camisoles in the 1886 Bloomingdale catalog featured a square neckline, though some had high round necks; all had lace and embroidery trim.

When the crinoline came into use in the 1870s, women started wearing fewer petticoats. Some Texas women, not having money to purchase a crinoline, "set tucks in the underpetticoats and ran mustang grapevines through them, creating an effect almost as good as the commercial hoops," Mills reported in *Calico Chronicle.*

"Someone had said that the real pioneer in Kansas didn't wear any underwear, but this was not true of the Ellis County pioneer, and the clothes lines with undergarments advertising I.M. Yost's High Patent Flour were the best evidence," according to a report by Joanna Stratton, in *Pioneer Women: Voices from the Kansas Frontier.*

By 1897 women could buy one-piece union suits from Sears, Roebuck and Co., with the Princess selling for $.43, the Empress or Oneita for $.50 or the Snow White Venus selling for $.75.

CHILDREN

Children wore clothing similar to that of their parents in many respects. Little girls wore aprons, collars and cuffs as well as petticoats, though their dresses tended to be shorter than those of older girls and women. Boys and girls under age five wore similar garments. Children seldom wore shoes. By 1897 children's union suits were available from Sears, Roebuck and Co., at a cost of $.48 each.

ADDITIONAL READING

Abbott, Edward C., and Helena Huntington Smith. *We Pointed 'em North.* New York: Farrar and Rhinehart, 1939. Provides excellent information about cowboy work and gear in the 1880s.

Bloomingdale Brothers, with an introduction by Nancy Villa Bryk. *Bloomingdale's Illustrated 1886 Catalog.* New York: Dover Publications, 1988. Excellent visual reference and detailed descriptions about clothing, accessories and household items.

Blum, Stella, ed. *Fashions and Costumes from Godey's Lady's Book.* New York: Dover Publications, 1985. Good visual reference.

———. *Victorian Fashions and Costumes from Harper's Bazaar.* New York: Dover Publications, 1974. Excellent visual reference.

Brown, Dee. *The Gentle Tamers.* Lincoln: University of Nebraska Press, 1958. An excellent general reference to Anglo women's lives in the West throughout the period.

Bryk, Nancy Villa. *American Dress Pattern Catalogs, 1873-1909.* New York: Dover Publications, 1988. Good visual reference.

Buck, Anne. *Victorian Costume.* Bedford, England: Ruth Bean Publishers, 1984. Good visual reference.

Dalrymple, Priscilla Harris. *American Victorian Costume in Early Photographs.* New York: Dover Publications, 1991. An excellent visual reference for clothing of men, women and children.

Decorum: A Practical Treatise on Etiquette and Dress of the Best American Society.

New York: Union Publishing House, 1880. An excellent reference to ettiquette during the era. Out-of-print, but available in rare book collections of many libraries.

Dolan, Maryanne. *Vintage Clothing 1880-1980: Identification and Guide.* Florence, Ala.: Books Americana, 1995.

Gernsheim, Alison. *Victorian and Edwardian Fashion: A Photograph Survey.* New York: Dover Publications, 1963.

Gorsline, Douglas. *What People Wore.* New York: Bonanza Books, 1952.

Hall, Carrie A. *From Hoopskirts to Nudity: A Review of the Follies and Foibles of Fashion 1866-1936.* Caldwell, Idaho: Caxton Printers, Ltd., 1938.

Harris, Kristina. *Victorian and Edwardian Fashions for Women 1840-1919.* Atglen, Pa.: Schiffer Publishing Ltd., 1995.

Israel, Fred L. *1897 Sears Roebuck Catalogue.* New York: Chelsea House Publishers, 1968.

Lindmier, Tom, and Steve Mount. *I See By Your Outfit: Historic Cowboy Gear of the Northern Plains.* Glendo, Wyo.: High Plains Press, 1996. Excellent reference for cowboy gear.

Maverick, Mary A. *Memoirs.* San Antonio: n.p., 1921.

McChristian, Douglas C. *The U.S. Army in the West, 1870-1880.* Oklahoma City: University of Oklahoma Press, 1995. Excellent reference for military gear, though only limited detail for the period before 1870 and after 1880.

Mills, Betty J. *Calico Chronicle.* Lubbock: Texas Tech University Press, 1985.

Niederman, Sharon. *A Quilt of Words.* Boulder, Colo.: Johnson Books, 1993. A good source about Hispanic and Native American women.

Nielson, Carole. "Unlike Most Chinese Immigrants of his Time, Gin Lin Found Respect and A Mountain of Gold." *Wild West* (April 1998): 14.

Peacock, John. *Costume 1066-1966.* New York: Thames and Hudson, 1986.

Quartermaster General of the Army. *U.S. Army Uniforms and Equipment, 1889.* Lincoln: University of Nebraska Press, 1986.

Reedstrom, Ernest Lisle. *Historic Dress of The Old West.* London: Blandford Press, 1986. A good source, primarily deals with men's clothing.

Rickey, Don, Jr. *$10 Horse, $40 Saddle: Cowboy Clothing, Arms, Tools and Horse Gear of the 1880s.* Fort Collins, Colo.: The Old Army Press, 1976. Out of print, but available in rare book rooms at research centers; good information about cowboy gear.

Slatta, Richard W. *Comparing Cowboys and Frontiers.* Norman: University of Oklahoma Press, 1997. A good source for detail about Hispanic cowboys.

Stratton, Joanna L. *Pioneer Women: Voices from the Kansas Frontier.* New York: Simon and Schuster, 1981. An excellent reference about women's lives during the period, primary sources related to clothing, food, schools.

Willett, C., and Phillis Cunnington. *The History of Underclothes.* New York: Dover Publications, 1992. An excellent reference.

CHAPTER SEVEN

FOOD AND DRINK

The diet for rural westerners involved a lot of pork, bread, butter, corn and potatoes. Foods during the period were most often fried, and cooks often used the grease for gravies or sauces, further adding to the fat content of the diet. The potential ill effects of high-fat foods, however, were somewhat offset because people had active lifestyles. Some people living in rural areas, such as farmers, may have had as many as five meals each day including one prior to milking, another at midmorning, one at noon, and another one or two in the afternoon and/or early evening. Westerners called the midday meal dinner and the evening meal supper; they generally made no reference to lunch.

Pork was the meat of choice in part because it was cheap; hogs could be raised easily and butchering wasn't as big a chore as with larger animals. Pork also could be easily preserved by smoking or salting. Beef often was more expensive and therefore not as popular until late in the period. Even ranchers who raised cattle didn't always eat beef because they considered it a cash crop, worth more at market than on the table. Few cooks used many seasonings such as herbs and spices, although they did use nutmeg, salt and pepper when available. If they used spices, it commonly was done to cure the rank taste of older meat. Corn became a staple in all climates where it could be raised and was used in a variety of ways.

Through 1870 the primary food supply on the Great Plains was a walking pantry: the American Bison. Used for generations to sustain Native Americans, the buffalo likewise provided for other western residents. For their part, Indians made use of absolutely every part of a buffalo. Later settlers weren't, perhaps, quite so effective in utilizing the huge range animals; nevertheless, they took advantage of the meat, the fat and certainly the hides. Wherever they were available, game animals such as deer, elk, antelope, rabbit and bear provided a steady supply of food, particularly in the earliest years of settlement as people struggled to establish homes and gardens or other crops. In the Northwest, Indians and later settlers used salmon as a staple food item, as well as deer and other wild game.

Because most rural residents raised or produced their own food, they had a greater variety in their diet than many urban dwellers, particularly those who didn't have resources to purchase a variety of foods. All westerners had fresh fruits and vegetables only on a seasonal basis until late in the period, and urban dwellers had less access to fresh milk than did rural residents. Once refrigerated railroad cars were developed in 1870, the food supply for city dwellers became more varied and included more fresh fruits and vegetables.

Prior to refrigeration ice boxes were used to cool foods with ice blocks placed into a compartment, at the left, and food stored on shelves, at right. This restored ice box belongs to Penny Walters.

Winter diets in all areas tended to be more restrictive than those of other seasons, particularly in early years when it was necessary to "live off the land." When high-protein wild game wasn't available, settlers in the Pacific Northwest used such staples as huckleberries, crabapples and salmon.

Dairy products such as milk, cheese and butter were available if people had a cow, and many rural women made and sold or bartered dairy products for other goods they couldn't produce themselves. The greatest difficulty with dairy products was storage, particularly in warmer, southern climates. After 1865 condensed milk was available in cans and refrigeration methods—the use of iceboxes primarily—had improved as well, milk was more readily available throughout the region. Even so, it often was difficult to obtain ice for use through much of the West until very late in the period.

Few residents had fruit trees early in the period as it took some time to establish nurseries and orchards. But pioneer settlers planted such trees as soon as they could, so that by the end of the period, fresh fruits were widely available in some areas, particularly the Pacific Northwest. Asian residents had a diet of rice with fresh vegetables and fruits, if available. The Hispanic diet generally included use of peppers, ranging from spicy jalapenos to more mild versions.

Water supplies were seldom pure, so most people in the period—including infants and children—drank alcoholic beverages such as beer, ale, whiskey or wine. Usually the beer had a low alcoholic content—enough to make it impossible for waterborne diseases to survive but not too much for young children to handle. Tea and coffee were popular drinks throughout the period, with coffee the preferred drink after 1830, though many frontier people made it of a variety of grains and not necessarily from coffee beans. Some people drank a chocolate drink made by mixing cocoa in milk, though it wasn't widely available until late in the period. Asians who drank tea, boiling water to prepare it, had fewer problems with waterborne illnesses.

The most common sweetener in the West was sorghum, though molasses (a by-product of the sugar industry) was also popular and brown sugar was cheap.

Western cooks called recipes "receipts" and they exchanged them with each other or obtained them from periodicals distributed throughout the region. Such publications as *Dr. Chase's Recipes; or, Information for Everybody; an Invaluable Collection of About Eight Hundred Practical Recipes*, written and published by A.W. Chase, M.D., in Ann Arbor, Michigan, in 1866, provided recipes for everything of use by "Merchants, Grocers, Saloon-keepers, Physicians, Druggists, Tanners, Shoe Makers, Harness Makers, Painters, Jewelers, Blacksmiths, Tinners, Gunsmiths, Farriers, Barbers, Bakers, Dyers, Renovators, Farmers, and Families Generally."

NATIVE AMERICAN FOODS

Native American diet depended on what was available, and the people generally had either an abundance of food or very little. Most tribes had regular hunts,

SOME EARLY RECEIPTS FROM
DR. CHASE'S RECIPES, 1866

Potato Pudding

Rub through a cullender 6 large or 12 middle sized potatoes; beat 4 eggs, mix with 1 pt. of good milk; stir in the potatoes, sugar and seasoning to taste; butter the dish; bake ½ hour.

This recipe is simple and economical, as it is made of what is wasted in many families, namely, cold potatoes; which may be kept two or three days, until a sufficient quantity is collected. To be eaten with butter.

Fried Apples—Extra Nice

Take any nice sour cooking apples, and, after wiping them, cut into slices about one fourth of an inch thick; have a frying-pan ready, in which there is a small amount of lard, say ½ or ¾ of an inch in depth. The lard must be hot before the slices of apples are put in. Let one side of them fry until brown; then turn, and put a small quantity of sugar on the browned side of each slice. By the time the other side is browned, the sugar will be melted and spread over the whole surface.

Serve them up hot, and you will have a dish good enough for kings and queens, or any poor man's breakfast; and I think that even the President would not refuse a few slices, if properly cooked.

Cake, Nice, Without Eggs or Milk

A very nice cake is made as follows, and it will keep well also:

Flour 3½ lbs.; sugar 1¼ lb.; butter 1 lb.; water ½ pint having 1 tea-spoon of saleratus [sodium bicarbonate, commonly known now as baking soda] dissolved in it. Roll thin and bake on tin sheets.

---

particularly for buffalo on the plains. They killed the large animals in a variety of ways. Sometimes they drove them over cliffs or buffalo jumps (called pishkuns), where they died from the fall, or if not, they could be shot with bows and arrows. By the 1840s most tribes had guns and horses, making it much easier to hunt buffalo and other game animals, so they relied less on driving them over jumps.

With any type of game taken, Indians utilized every part of the animal, from the meat to bones (marrow was a particularly sought-after food item), sinew, hide and horns. All parts of the animals were used in a variety of ways—if not put into the cook pot, then they became clothing, shelter or utensils.

Much of the meat was dried by hanging it on cottonwood racks, and Indians also made pemmican by drying meat then pounding it into a powder and mixing it with fat and dried berries. Some tribes—such as the Pawnees, Cherokees, Creeks, Chickasaws and various Southwestern native people—were more agrarian. They planted corn and other crops and harvested natural foods as well, such as roots, bulbs and berries. Nez Perce Indians relied heavily on camas roots, and the Digger Indians got their name because of their reliance on roots and other ground plants.

"The food consists of bread made from acorns, which are first buried, then roasted, then pulverized, and lastly, mixed up with water and baked," the Santa Rosa, California, *Times* reported about the Diggers in 1875.

Native Americans—primarily the women—often roasted fresh meat in large pits by alternating layers of meat and brush over heated stones with the entire pit filled and then covered with dirt. The meat was then allowed to roast for two or more hours before the pit was uncovered and the meat eaten. When butchering freshly killed game, Indians often ate choice parts raw, such as the small intestine and the liver.

Osage Indians boiled sweet corn in buffalo grease while Pawnees routinely ate a variety of vegetables such as corn, pumpkins, beans and *pommes blanche*, a root similar to a sweet potato. Many tribes ate grasshoppers and various other insects—dried and ground into meal.

IN THE MOUNTAINS

The era of the mountain man, which began in about 1810, had nearly passed by 1840 due to declining numbers of beaver and less interest in beaver hats. The final great rendezvous took place in the late 1830s though smaller gatherings occurred as late as 1843. Some frontiersmen remained in the mountains, however, living primarily from the "fat of the land."

Like Native Americans, mountain men made pemmican. The food kept well and could be easily carried in a small rawhide bag known as a parfleche.

The mountain men ate a meat diet. They particularly liked buffalo, elk and deer, but also ate cougar, beaver (primarily the liver and tail), bear, mountain sheep, prairie dog, fish, waterfowl, horse, rabbit or dog. George Ruxton in *Life in the Far West*, noted that dog had a flavor like pork, "but far surpasses it in richness and delicacy."

When their supplies of deer, elk or bear dwindled, mountain men resorted to other food types, and one old trapper left a recipe for cake: "Take what flour you have, mix with water, shorten with coon oil and fry in coon fat."

Boudins were made from the small intestine of an animal and resembled a sausage in looks and substance. They were usually cooked in hot fat, though sometimes both Native Americans and mountain men ate them raw. Like buffalo hump and beaver tail, boudins were considered a delicacy. Because some boudins had in them plant materials, they may have had the added advantage of providing vitamin C, which prevented scurvy. If cooked thoroughly, though, the value of the vitamins was diminished or negated entirely.

ON THE TRAIL

Essential items on the trail included wheat flour; bacon or pork which was dried, smoked or salted; hard crackers and hard bread known as pilot bread, ships biscuits or hardtack; plus sugar, salt, beans, rice, lard, coffee, dried fruit and whiskey or brandy.

Typical meals for trail travelers were fried or broiled bacon, biscuits or hard crackers and coffee for breakfast; and oatmeal, a stew of dried apples, fried bacon and pilot bread for dinner and supper. In the early part of any overland journey, travelers also may have had rice, beans, potatoes or barley, but as supplies dwindled, so did the variety in menus.

There were few provisioning points, but at Fort Laramie, travelers could obtain eggs, milk, butter and cheese. In Salt Lake City they might be able to purchase peas, coffee, milk, butter, bacon, beans, preserves and bread (sometimes freshly baked). The types of products available at such provisioning points, however, varied each year and depended upon supplies.

The six-month supply of food recommended for each family of four trail travelers included the following:

800 pounds of flour
200 pounds of lard
200 pounds of beans
700 pounds of bacon
100 pounds of dried fruit
75 pounds of coffee
25 pounds of salt and pepper

Emigrants also needed cooking utensils, guns and ammunition, eating utensils, clothing and personal items and furniture. In no case should the supplies weigh more than 2,400 pounds, because animals could not pull wagons weighing more than that over a prolonged period of time.

Elder Parley P. Pratt recommended the following supplies for Mormons headed west in 1846, with the amount based on a family of five: one wagon, three yoke of oxen, three sheep, two beef cattle, two milking cows, 1,000 pounds of flour, twenty pounds of sugar, two pounds of tea, five pounds of coffee, one rifle with ammunition, a tent and poles and a keg of alcohol for each two families.

Mormon handcart pioneers traveling to Utah between 1856 and 1860 had a weekly diet prescribed by Mormon officials that included three and one-half pounds of bread; one pound of flour; a pound and a half each of oatmeal, rice and peas; two pounds of potatoes; a pound of pork; one pound of sugar; a pound and a quarter of beef; two ounces each of salt and tea; and a small amount of brandy, the latter to be used for "medical comforts," though it was seldom administered.

Supplies for a man headed to California in 1849 included between 300 and 500 pounds of food costing around $175 per person. By the late 1850s and 1860s wagon travelers had canned goods, though those were most available after the Civil War having been fairly widely used during that period in order to feed troops on the battlefield.

Travelers on the California Trail were instructed by those already at Sutter's Fort to take dried fruit and rice: "To each man 80 pounds of rice, and three quarters of a bushel of apple or peach fruit, at least are necessary, being easily cooked, they are always convenient. Now, if the emigrant will use as little side bacon, and also very little hot lard and saleratus biscuits, and more of the other articles, as above mentioned, I will warrant him to come through unscathed with scurvy," Walker D. Wyman wrote in "California Emigrant Letters" (*California Historical Society, Quarterly*, XXIV, 1945).

When traveling down the trail, women learned to put cream into a jar or bucket and tie it to the bottom or place in the back of the wagon. The rocking, bouncing motion of the wagon churned the cream into butter. And they mixed bread on the trail as well, letting it rise as they traveled so that when they reached camp it was ready to bake. In some areas on the trail, mosquitoes created quite a nuisance, and one cook noted the biting insects often swarmed while she attempted to knead her bread dough, getting into the dough. "There is nothing you can do about this," she calmly advised.

Wagon trains generally started early in the morning, with people arising at five and leaving camp by seven. Depending upon the train, sometimes the women had dinner already cooked so at noon it wasn't necessary to build fires; they could simply serve the food, making it possible to take only an hour break in the middle of the day. At other times, though, they did start a small fire to cook a pot of oatmeal, and some wagon trains took a break of several hours during the middle of the day when it was hot. This gave people a chance to rest and animals an opportunity to rest and graze.

Emigrants near Independence Rock, in present-day Wyoming, visited alkali lakes and gathered buckets full of saleratus (sodium bicarbonate commonly known now as baking soda), which they used in making bread. Mormon women reported it gave the bread a "suspiciously green cast." Mormon Thomas Bullock, on June 21, 1847, wrote, "About four miles east of Independence Rock is a small saleratus lake on the left of the road, where I would advise you to gather one or two hundred pounds weight for family use; this stuff is what you will rise your bread with, and the soda in the same lake is excellent to wash with. Remember this."

Some trail travelers hauled cookstoves with them, but often they abandoned the stoves along the trail when they found them too heavy to haul in the wagons. Most overland trail cooking took place over open fires. On days when strong winds blew, fires couldn't be started for fear they would burn into the prairie grass and start a wildfire. The travelers served their meals in tin plates with forks and knives, often spreading an oilcloth on the ground to serve as a "table."

Traveling to Kansas in April 1856, Miriam Colt wrote:

> MAY 15TH—Have a fire out of doors to cook by; two crotches
> driven into the ground, with a round pole laid thereon, on which
> to hang our kettles and camp pails, stones laid up at the ends and

back to make it as much as it can be in the form of a fireplace, so as to keep our fire, ashes and all, from blowing high and dry, when these fierce prairie winds blow. It is not very agreeable work, cooking out of doors in this windy, rainy weather, or when the scorching sun shines. The bottoms of our dresses are burnt full of holes now, and they will soon be burnt off.

ON THE WATER/IN THE MINING CAMPS

A significant number of people who were headed to the West Coast, and particularly to California's gold fields between 1849 and 1852—the years of peak California emigration—traveled by ship around Cape Horn. The 1,900-nautical-mile trip took between five and eight months to complete, allowing plenty of time for provisions to spoil. A lesser number of people took the water route to Panama, then crossed the Isthmus of Panama overland to the Pacific Ocean where they obtained other water transportation to such ports as San Francisco.

The food on some of those ships consisted of "wormy bread, putrid jerked beef, musty rice, and miserable tea" according to *Rushing for Gold*, edited by John Walton Caughey. Other ships, however, had better—though expensive—provisions, purchased when they docked at various ports.

Once in California a miner's meal might consist of a "cup of coffee strong enough to float a millstone, two small pieces of fat pork, fried and burned, and a pancake apiece, made of flour and water, fried in pork fat, and about as heavy as its size in lead," Enos Christman wrote in *One Man's Gold*.

The miners called pancakes flippers or slapjacks. They were usually fried in pork fat and made from wheat flour.

ON THE HOMESTEAD

Having the "luxury" of a permanent home meant pioneer cooks could establish routines. They had a table or other work space, some type of cupboards or storage areas, often a pantry, and many times the convenience of a root cellar, smokehouse and springhouse.

Their food items, however, remained basic: meat (likely wild game); potatoes, corn and other vegetables they were able to raise in garden plots; flour; coffee (or some version of the drink); and a sweetener such as sugar, but more likely sorghum or molasses. Few people liked vegetables, in part because cooks usually boiled or creamed them to the stage where they had very little flavor.

Some women had no breadboard or even a rolling pin, so they spread newspaper on a board or table and rolled biscuits on it. Picnic items might include fried chicken or prairie chicken, boiled ham, pickles and relishes. Cooks were innovative. They made vinegar from melon juice and syrup from the sap of box elder trees. Depending on circumstances and availability of ingredients, women made cakes and pies (custard, vinegar, pumpkin, and fruit from dried fruit first allowed to reconstitute by soaking it overnight), and cookies such as gingersnaps.

MILITARY FARE

Those people associated with military forts generally had better food supplies than did homesteaders, although soldiers in the field often had far less. A second lieutenant's wife at Fort Peck, Montana, for example, served the following for Christmas dinner: soup, salmon croquettes with egg sauce, raw oysters, potatoes, roast beef, prairie chicken, sweetbreads, currant jelly, asparagus salad, cheese and crackers, sherbet, cake and candies.

Enlisted men (and their wives) had bacon, beef, beans and hardtack every day, almost without variation. When Margaret Carrington and Frances Grummond traveled the Bozeman Trail with their husbands (Colonel Henry B. Carrington and Lieutenant George Grummond) in 1866, they had with them boxes of canned fruits, live turkeys, chickens and hogs.

Military wife Martha Summerhays, meanwhile, wrote:

> Towards evening, a soldier came for orders for beef, and I learned how to manage that. I was told that we bought our meat direct from the contractor; I had to state how much and what cuts I wished. Another soldier came to bring us milk, and I asked Jack who was the milkman, and he said, blessed if he knew; I learned, afterwards, that the soldiers roped some of the wild Texas cows that were kept in one of the Government corrals, and tied them securely to keep them from kicking; then milked them, and the milk was divided up among the officers' families, according to rank. We received about a pint every night. I declared it was not enough; but I soon discovered that however much education, position and money might count in civil life, *rank* seemed to be the one and only thing in the army, and Jack had not much of that just then.

The daily ration allowed for soldiers between 1802 and 1850 included three-quarters of a pound of pork or bacon, a pound and a half of fresh or salted beef, eighteen ounces of flour bread or twelve ounces of hard bread or cornmeal, and a gill (five ounces) of whiskey, rum or brandy, although after 1832 they had coffee and sugar in place of the whiskey. For each one hundred rations, frontier soldiers also received four pounds of soap, a pound and a half of candles, two quarts of vinegar and eight quarts of peas or beans (which could be replaced with ten pounds of rice).

Other supplies were available from the post sutler, such as cheese, raisins, tobacco or liquor (until 1877 when liquor sales on military posts were outlawed, leading to establishment of nearby off-post businesses known as hog ranches).

Marcus L. Hansen in *Old Fort Snelling, 1819-58,* provided this soup recipe:

Put into the vessel at the rate of five pints of water to a pound of fresh meat; apply a quick heat to make boil promptly, skim off foam, then moderate the fire; salt is then put in, according to the palate. Add the vegetables of the season [after] one or two hours; sliced bread [should be added] some minutes before the simmering is ended.

Soldiers on field campaigns routinely had limited food supplies, so they killed available game (ranging from prairie dogs to elk), raided bee trees, caught fish in streams and rivers, and gathered mesquite "beans" in regions where the mesquite bushes grew, eventually grinding the beans and making a bread or pudding with them. They also bought supplies ranging from butter, eggs and milk, to cheese, onions and potatoes in areas where there were settlers with such products. During the Mexican War (1846) they had only limited food. As soldier Jacob Robinson recorded in his journal, "We have no pork or bacon; no coffee, sugar, or molasses."

In the Southwest they ate corn tortillas and chilies, often remarking on the spiciness of the latter. They used the roots of wild cherry trees for tea, and made coffee from "dry steams of last year's weeds found unburnt on the creek bank," wrote William Connelley in "Journals of the Santa Fe Trail" (*Mississippi Valley Historical Review XII,* September 1926.)

In some situations soldiers ate wild roots, dogs, horses and frogs, and they even boiled buffalo hides and parfleches for the nourishment they might contain. Parfleches were leather bags made of varying sizes and used to carry supplies.

> The cook-books were maddening to us for a casual glance at any of them proves how necessary eggs, butter and cream are to every recipe. In those days, when the army lived beyond the railroad, it would have been a boon if some clever army woman could have prepared a little manual for the use of house-keepers stranded on the frontier, and if she had also realized that we had no mothers to ask, and consequently had omitted the tormenting advice to "use your own judgment."—*Elizabeth Custer in* Following the Guidon

Many officers hired enlisted men to cook for them. Known as a "striker," the enlisted man received certain privileges, such as the opportunity for better food and better quarters. He also earned an extra $5 each month as a result of his cooking duties. The use of strikers was popular in the frontier army until 1881, when army regulations placed restrictions on such arrangements.

ON THE CATTLE TRAILS

A cook using a chuck wagon prepared meals for cowboys on the various cattle trails leading from Texas to railheads and northern ranges. The foods, known as chuck, grub or chow, were similar to those of overland trail travelers and might include beef, beans, bacon, cornmeal, wheat flour, sugar, syrup or molasses, rice, dried or canned fruit (such as apples, peaches or apricots), coffee and whiskey (usually reserved for medicinal purposes).

The cook prepared most of the dishes in a Dutch oven, a deep cast-iron pot with a wire handle and a cast-iron lid with a deep lip. When hot coals are placed on the lid and the pot is set on more hot coals, the Dutch oven provides even heating for making almost anything from stews and roast to pie. Other dishes included bacon or beef, dumplings, sourdough biscuits, stew, slumgullion (a bread pudding made using cold biscuits, raisins and sugar or a stew of meat, potatoes, onions and other vegetables), and desserts using caramelized (canned) milk. The use of sourdough came from male cooks, and all cooks on the major cattle trails were male.

Cowboy cook Oliver Nelson in *The Cowman's Southwest* provided a list of provisions needed on one trail drive:

> I took an inventory of the load: forty pounds Climax Plug, twenty pounds Bull Durham, and several caddies and packs of smoking tobacco; a dozen .45 Colt single-action pistols and twenty boxes of cartridges; a roll of half-inch rope; ten gallons of kerosene and a caddy of matches; one hundred pounds of sugar; one 160-pound sack of green coffee, five hundred pounds of salt pork, twenty sacks of flour, two hundred pounds beans, fifty pounds country dried apples, a box of soda, and a sack of salt. There were bows on the wagon, a grub box on the rear end, a kerosene can cut in half for sour dough, two sixteen-inch ovens five inches deep, a coffee-grinder nailed on the side of the grub box, six bull's-eye lanterns for night herd.

IN THE BOARDINGHOUSE

Operators of road ranches, boardinghouses, stage stations and hotels served a variety of foods, depending in part on the season and availability of supplies. At boardinghouses most guests ate together, family style. Huge platters of food found their way to the center of the table where people served themselves, perfecting their "boardinghouse reach" to get the choice cuts of meat or a full serving of vegetables.

The category of individuals most likely to eat at boardinghouses or restaurants were miners, particularly those in the gold and silver fields, in part because they had the funds to do so and also they may have preferred to mine rather than to use their time in obtaining food and preparing it.

Boardinghouse owners enticed their paying customers with good food, but some, like Malachi Dillon in southern Wyoming, gave added incentives. He offered free meals so long as his customers did their drinking in his saloon.

Though Dillon didn't offer gambling on an organized basis, many boarding-houses did have gaming tables for such activities as monte or faro.

Some boardinghouses were large, frame structures, but Mary Ballou operated such a business at Negro Bar, California, in 1852 that had four posts covered with factory cloth. She had a floor in the dining area and cloth on the ground in her sleeping area, but she had nothing on the ground in the kitchen.

OBTAINING FOOD

Gardens: Gardens were essential to pioneer diet, and women raised whatever crops they could. Depending on the region they might raise cabbage, celery, corn and potatoes. When grasshoppers invaded Kansas in 1874, settlers fought valiantly to preserve their garden crops. Kansas homesteader's daughter Lille Marcks recalled, "Father said, 'Go get your shawls, heavy dresses and quilts. We will cover the cabbage and celery beds. Perhaps we can save that much.' "

Potatoes had anti-scurvy properties, which made them an essential and valuable food product throughout the West. Westerners carefully watched climatic conditions to determine when to plant. In southern areas crops could be planted earlier in the year, while in northern areas residents had a shorter growing season. Gardeners also paid attention to the moon—and to the *Old Farmer's Almanac*—when making decisions about planting. They planted crops such as beans, peas, corn and squash when the new moon was developing or waxing, and they planted root crops like turnips and potatoes when it was waning. They believed that root crops grew better when the moon went down and that, as the moon ascended, plants which also ascended (grew above ground) would do better. People liked root vegetables because they were easily stored for winter use.

> Brigham Young raised in his garden of two and a half acres, last year, 750 bushels of peaches, 400 ditto apples, 22 ditto plums, 25 ditto strawberries, 2 ditto pears, 25 pounds of cherries, 1875 ditto of grapes, with gooseberries, raspberries, and currents in abundance.—FLIN, *April 28, 1866*

Hunting: Beyond a doubt, hunting was the primary way rural people provided meat for their families throughout the period, and even those living in towns and cities relied on hunting—or on game taken by hunters who sold or traded it to stores. All types of wild game reached the table: buffalo, bear, deer, elk, antelope, mountain sheep, rabbit and wild boar.

In the 1870s buffalo hunting took on a new twist as men such as William F. "Buffalo Bill" Cody began killing the animals for the railroad. Govern-

A large tree stump could be converted into a meat chopping block such as this one at the Grand Encampment Museum.

mental officials wanted Indians to move to reservations and, by restricting food supplies, they believed the Indians would more willingly relocate. Although there is evidence to suggest the numbers of buffalo were in decline prior to the extermination policies of the 1870s, the killing during that period further descimated the herds—which were the primary food source for native people. Initial buffalo hunting under the extermination policies involved use of the meat, but later the animals were killed solely for their hides and the meat was left to rot on the plains. Native Americans also had sometimes killed buffalo primarily for the hides, though generally they used most or all portions of the animals. At the beginning of the period (1840) there were some sixty million buffalo on the western plains; by 1900 virtually all of them had been killed or had died through loss of habitat and changes in climatic conditions that restricted grazing opportunities. Only a few animals survived the slaughter, having been captured by breeders in Texas and Wyoming.

Livestock: Westerners obtained meat by raising their own hogs, cattle, sheep and chickens. After 1870 meat markets operated in many towns and cities.

Orchards: People harvested wild fruit such as berries, grapes and apples and nuts whenever they were found. Settlers planted fruit trees, but it took several years for them to reach production stage.

Stores: Craigue and Morn's Grocery Store in Topeka, Kansas, had a typical selection of food items: baskets of eggs, jars of butter, barrels of flour, meal or buckwheat flour, vinegar, salt pork, New Orleans molasses, bags of potatoes, cabbage, pumpkins, squash, turnips, boxes of soda crackers, strings of red peppers, crocks of honey, green Rio or Mocha coffee, tea, starch, bottles of soda, cayenne pepper, catsup, and cream of tartar, which was used instead of baking powder. Meat items included hams, bacon, fresh meat, pigs feet and beef liver.

Stores also sold a variety of other goods ranging from peppermint candy sticks and horehound candy drops to milk crocks, wooden tubs, steel knives and forks, pewter spoons, dishes, pails, brooms, hoes, axes, shovels, clothing goods and all kinds of other items.

In a time when people had little actual money, they often obtained needed supplies by bartering. The W.B. Hugus Company, which had trading posts and general stores throughout southern Wyoming and northern Colorado, owned the store Guy Nichols operated at Swan, Wyoming, in the 1880s. Merchandise came in from Fort Steele and the store served a wide trading area. The store took eggs, butter, beef and potatoes from ranchers in trade for merchandise and also accepted fresh-killed wild meat. The Hugus Company store liked elk the best and didn't buy antelope at all.

Market Scene in San Antonio, Texas

The vendors of chickens and red peppers, sweet potatoes and red peppers, butter and red peppers, cabbage and red peppers, and even the man who sells nothing but red peppers, pay ten cents for about ten feet of ground [in the Military Plaza] for every time they occupy it.—FLIN, *August 26, 1876, 412-1*

Food Preservation/Storage

To preserve meat, westerners cut it into thin strips, salted it heavily, and let it dry by hanging it on outdoor racks, in a smokehouse or by the fireplace. Both salt and pepper liberally sprinkled on fresh meat helped preserve it for a couple of days. To keep fresh meat for several days, cooks wrapped it in a vinegar-soaked cloth. If they had no smokehouse in which to cure hams, they wrapped them in heavy brown paper or cloth and then packed the hams in ashes.

Cooks also dried fruit. In some cases they sliced it thin and let it dry similar to the way they did meat. Other times they cooked it until it became a thin paste, then forced it through a sieve before spreading it on flat pans where they let it dry to a consistency of leather. The fruit leather could then be stored on a shelf or hung from the ceiling to be used as needed by boiling it in water, sometimes adding a bit of sweetener.

The root cellar served as the primary food storage location, though some locales had storage sheds or rooms attached to homes. Each fall, pioneer settlers filled the cellar or storage room with products ranging from large barrels of buttermilk to "wine, malt, spirits, sauerkraut, jerked deer and buffalo tongue, bear bacon, and a thousand other things," according to Virginia H. Asbury and Albert N. Doerschuk, in "The Boone, Hays and Berry Families of Jackson County" (*Missouri Historical Review*, XXIII, 1929).

After 1849, canning methods were becoming more widespread with meat, seafood, vegetables and fruit available in cans after 1850. Condensed milk was not readily available in a can until the Civil War, and use of canned goods became more prevalent and popular after that war.

An impediment to canning involved the lack of containers for the foods prior to development of the Mason jar in 1859. Its porcelain-lined lid made it possible for home canners to properly preserve food in a way that would be safe. The development of the pressure cooker for use in canning in 1874 further revolutionized home canning, but until very late in the period, home canning continued to be a risky proposition as people had difficulty learning how to seal in flavor and keep out bacteria.

After 1865, canned fruit, condensed milk, tomatoes and other products were available at stage stations, giving some variety to meals served there.

Health Problems and Diet

Among the biggest concerns for westerners was variety in the diet to prevent scurvy, called black canker by Mormons who camped at Winter Quarters in 1846. Mountain men ate boudins, sausage made from the intestines of animals, digesting the grasses already eaten and partially digested by the animals, and likely saved themselves from the illness of scurvy. Lime juice, potatoes soaked in vinegar, and wild greens provided antiscorbutic properties as did "good orange marmalade, and . . . strawberry . . . jam," according to William Ogilvie's *Klondike Official Guide.*

Bread: The essential item for all western diets, bread was often obtained as hard crackers called hardtack, ships biscuit or pilot bread. Bread was often made of wheat flour and was included with every meal if it was available.

> In an article in the *United States Service Magazine* the following hard-tack story is told: 'It appears the boxes in which the 'tack' is packed always bear the brand of the baker or maker, and a lot which arrived in the camp of the 5th New York Excelsiors, with the mark 'B.C., 603,' caused much speculation among the 'boys' as to what it meant. It was finally agreed unanimously that it must be the date when the crackers were made—603 years before Christ.
> —FLIN, *February 18, 1865, 33-3*

Travelers, frontiersmen and others cooking over open campfires sometimes baked their bread on a stick. As Isaac Van Dorsey Mossman said while he was on a military expedition in Oregon, "The dough is made up in the mouth of the flour sack, then rolled around a stick, which is stuck in the ground near the fire, and the bread is left to bake, the stick being turned as often as required."

Butter: A versatile product, butter not only found its way onto the table of western residents, it also became a primary bartering tool. Western women who made butter—known as "country made"—sold or traded it to nearby general stores in exchange for coffee, sugar or other products that couldn't be raised or produced at home. Homemade fresh butter, known as "dashed" butter because a wooden paddle, or dasher, was used to work it after churning in order to remove buttermilk and mix in salt, was preferred over that shipped to the West in wooden casks, known as firkins. The "firkin" butter often had a bitter and salty taste. Asians did not eat butter.

Liquids ranging from vinegar to whiskey could be stored in crockery jugs such as this one (left), while westerners converted cream into butter using a variety of churns such as this barrel churn (right). These items are on display at the Lake Creek Stage Station at the Grand Encampment Museum.

A coffee grinder such as this could be used to turn coffee beans, or other grains into grounds for a drink mix. This is part of the Grand Encampment Museum collection.

Cheese: Milk products were made into cheese. Hard, round cheeses kept well for long periods of time. Some cooks also made cottage cheese and soft cheeses.

Coffee: One of the main drinks in the West, and the drink of choice after 1830, coffee was made of a variety of items such as parched corn with sorghum sweetening, rye, wheat first toasted then ground, or even beans. In Kentucky, the pods from stump trees replaced coffee beans. In places where Rio, Mocha or Java coffee was available, it came as raw beans which had to be parched and ground. The name reflected the origin of the beans, which came in forty- or fifty-pound bags. Westerners preferred to grind their own beans so they could be sure they were getting unadulterated coffee. Some companies that sold ground coffee mixed in other ingredients, primarily peas. It also was difficult to preserve the flavor in roasted beans. In 1869 the brothers John and Charles Arbuckle patented their roasting method in which they sealed the coffee flavor by coating beans with a mixture of sugar and egg white. Their efforts paid off and Arbuckle's Ariosa Coffee soon became a standard brand in western kitchens.

Not everyone could afford (or obtain) Rio, Mocha or Java coffee beans— or Arbuckle's coffee—so they resorted to other ingredients such as parched peas, barley, wheat, rye or bran. Some westerners gathered dandelion roots in the fall, which they chopped into small pieces, roasted until brown, then crushed to a powder, which could then be used in making coffee.

The first ground coffee sold in a can came from Caleb Chase and James

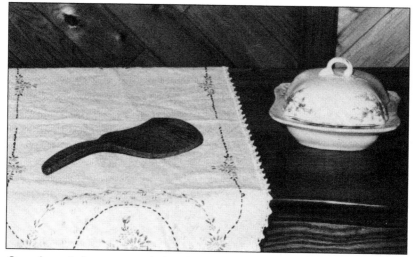

Once churned, butter was worked with a wooden paddle then placed in crocks for storage, or put into a butter dish such as this one of china. Both items belong to the author.

Sanborn in 1878, but vacuum cans weren't introduced until 1898.

When making coffee, cooks put crushed eggshells or a fish skin into the pot in order to clear the brew of grounds. When not in the pot, fish skins were kept in boxes or paper bags after having been washed, dried and cut into pieces.

Dairy: Families often had milk cows so they had dairy products such as butter, cheese, milk, and cream for their coffee.

Eggs: Chickens served an essential production role on homesteads, ranches and even in towns where they were raised for meat and for eggs.

> This day the first four chickens in the 'Great Salt Lake City' were hatched by a hen belonging to Stephen H. Goddard.
> —*Thomas Bullock, Sunday, August 16, 1847*

Fish: Mackerel, oysters and codfish were available and many families purchased kegs of mackerel each fall. Canned oysters were one of the West's most popular foods because so many migrants had come from New England and were familiar with them.

> I made a bold attempt at oyster patties. With the confidence of youth and inexperience, I made the pastry, and it was a success; I took a can of Baltimore oysters, and did them up in a fashion that astonished myself, and when, after the soup, each guest was served with a hot oyster patty, one of the cavalry officers fairly gasped.

'Oyster patty, if I'm alive! Where on earth—bless my stars! And this at Camp Apache.'—*Martha Summerhays in* Vanished Arizona

Fowl: Wild ducks, geese, turkeys and other birds were used by cooks; many pioneer women raised chickens both for eggs and meat. Chicken "fixens"— a meal made of fried or boiled chicken with side dishes such as potatoes, noodles, dumplings and gravy—were considered some of the best food items offered at many western homes throughout the period. Chicken fixens were particularly popular for picnics.

Fruits: Wild berries, grapes, apples, gooseberries, chokecherries, pawpaws, crab apples and the like found their way into the diets of all westerners. The type of berry or fruit used depended upon the location and climate. Camas root was widely used in the Northwest as a staple part of Native American diet. Some early settlers may have tasted it, but they didn't use it routinely. "It resembles an onion in shape and color. When cooked it is very sweet and tastes like a fig," Narcissa Whitman wrote in her diary.

Because most fruit was kept by drying it, cooks had to reconstitute it before use. *The Washington Standard* in 1874 published this recipe: "Take nice [dried] apples, soak them over night in rather more than enough water to cover them; In the morning boil them til soft, then add about as much sugar in bulk as there was of the apples before soaking, and cook until they look clear; season with lemon, or add a few raisins when you do the sugar." To turn the fruit into pies, the paper advised, "Strain through a colander, sweeten, season with lemon and bake with two crusts."

Many types of fruit, such as apples, pears, peaches and quinces, were obtained in a dried state. Prickly pear was a common food. "A very pleasant fruit to eat, after they are disrobed of their Coat of Pricks," wrote Thomas Bullock in his journal on September 27, 1847. "They are troublesome to get; as my hands were stuck pretty full with their needles & getting many in my lips, tongue, mouth &c is a drawback to eating this fruit, but still I gathered sufficient to satisfy my hunger as did other bretheren."

Grains: Wheat, barley, rye, oats and corn were the most common grains raised. In 1862 the *Nebraska Farmer* suggested thirty-three ways to cook corn, including hasty pudding (cornmeal mush), corn on the cob, apple cornbread, hominy, Virginia corn dodgers, pumpkin Indian loaf, corn muffins, griddle cakes, baked Indian pudding, boiled Indian pudding, maize and white pot (milk, eggs, corn meal, sugar and molasses). As bread, grits and mush, corn was on the menu almost daily in regions where corn was a staple crop. With potatoes and wheat, corn was one of the most basic food items on the plains.

Herbs: Herbs were used more by Native Americans than by Euro-Americans living in the West during the period, although some Anglo women did use herbs, utilizing information they had learned from Native Americans.

Honey: Used as a sweetener and taken from the hives of wild bees, honey was often collected from "bee trees" where the bees gathered and produced their honey. Frontier soldiers often took a small jar of honey with them when headed out on field campaigns.

> A swarm of bees and a bountiful store of wild honey were recently found in a tree by woodchoppers on the west side of the Sierra Nevada Mountains. The incident is recorded as the first discovery of the kind on the Pacific Slope. There were no wild bees beyond the Sierras when that portion of the country was first occupied by emigrants from the Atlantic seaboard. It was soon discovered that bees imported from the States thrived well, and several persons who engaged early in the business acquired large fortunes from the production of honey for the markets.
> —FLIN, *May 22, 1869, 158-2*

Meats/Game: Wild game was a common staple in most western homes and, depending upon the location, the fare could include grouse (blue or other species), prairie hen, elk, antelope, deer, buffalo, wild turkey, quail, pheasant, squirrel, raccoon or bear. But not all of those species were available in all regions throughout the period. For example, pheasant was not introduced into Calfiornia until 1857 and didn't reach Oregon until the 1880s. A grizzly bear provided food that would sustain a man (or woman) for nearly a year, and perhaps ten gallons of bear oil worth about $75 if sold in St. Louis. Every part of the animal found its way into the cook pot, from the choicest steaks or roasts, to heart, liver, tongue, brains and tripe. Hogs were butchered for bacon, salt pork and ham. Most meat was served boiled, though some cooks baked chickens, beef or pork roasts or hams. And much meat was dried or salted. When preparing previously salted meat, cooks first soaked it in water to remove the salt.

Nuts: Hickory, hazel and piñon were among the nuts used routinely.

Pie: Pie was a regular, and for many cooks, essential, part of nearly every dinner. A molasses pie recipe from *The Washington Standard* on July 11, 1874, reads as follows: "One and one-half cups of molasses, one half cup vinegar, one egg, two tablespoons of flour, one cup raisins, season with lemon or nutmeg; this makes two pies; bake with two crusts."

One of the more popular pies was made of mincemeat, which was particularly common around Thanksgiving and Christmas, though some overland travelers reported having mince pies on the trail. The following recipe may have been used by western cooks, though likely they substituted some ingredients because they may not have had a quart of Madeira or four pounds of raisins.

Family Mince Pies—Boil 3 lbs. of lean beef til tender, and when cold, chop it fine. Chop 2 lbs. of clear beef suet and mix with meat, sprinkling in a table-spoonful of salt. Pare, core, and chop fine, 6 lbs. of good apples; stone 4 lbs. of raisins and chop them; wash and dry 2 lbs. of currants; and mix them all well with the meat. Season with powdered cinnamon, 1 spoonful, a powdered nutmeg, a little mace, and a few cloves pounded; and 1 lb. of brown sugar. Add a quart of Madeira wine, and 8 oz. of citron, cut into small bits. This mixture, put down in a stone jar and closely covered will keep several weeks. It makes a right pie for Thanksgiving and Christmas.—Mrs. Hale's New Cook Book, *1857*

Pudding: Pudding was a common food item on most tables during the period. Some pioneers referred to pudding as "duff." Most traditional recipes involved mixing flour, shortening, dried fruit, water and saleratus then steaming the mixture in a cloth bag. "Poverty pudding" was made by soaking bread in milk overnight then layering bread and apples in a baking dish and baking it for an hour.

I made a wonderful pudding, for which I had saved eggs and cream for days, and dried and stoned cherries supplied the place of currants. I made a bowl of custard for sauce, which the men said was 'splendid'; also a rolled pudding, with molasses; and we had venison steak and potatoes, but for tea we were obliged to use the tea leaves of the morning again.—*Isabella Bird*

Salads: Until residents raised their own gardens, salads were seldom on the menu, though wild greens such as Indian lettuce and portulaca (which had crunchy seeds) were used.

Seasonings/Sweeteners: Cakes were sweetened with sorghum. Other sweetening products included the juice of boiled corncobs mixed with watermelon centers, wild honey, and molasses, which had a distinctive odor. Cooks generally stored the molasses in barrels, keeping with a small pitcher full for regular use.

Sugar: Sugar was available in both white and brown varieties, though sometimes difficult to obtain.

Tea: Tea was a popular drink during the period. Horsemint, wild cherry bark and catnip were used for teas, and many herbal teas were used as a beverage or for medicinal purposes.

Dandelion Tea—The tender leaves can serve as greens. For tea, dry the roots then grind to a powder. This can be added to boiling water for a refreshing hot tea.—*Anonymous early recipe*

Mr. Samuel Bowles mentions as an excellent feature of banquets at San Francisco, the serving of hot beef tea, with just a smack of claret in it, as a constant refreshment during the evening.
—FLIN, *January 13, 1866, 259-3*

Vegetables: Available vegetables included those raised in home gardens. Particularly used were corn and potatoes, the latter necessary during early years to ward off scurvy. Onions also were popular. They were known as skunk eggs to lumberjacks.

Vinegar: An important item in all western areas, vinegar was used to preserve foods ranging from cucumbers to pumpkins, to freshen water and as a cure or aid in the treatment of scurvy. Travelers on ships en route from New York to San Francisco in 1853 received a weekly vinegar allowance. Throughout the region, people reported drinking undiluted vinegar.

Water: Water was an essential element, to be sure, but not always easily obtained. Finding good sources of water was a significant consideration through most of the early period. Waterborne diseases such as cholera and typhoid reached epidemic portions during various years and in widespread locations. Many settlers hauled water from nearby streams or rivers using hand-carved yokes that fit over their shoulders, and from which they could hang (and haul) two buckets filled with water. In certain instances the water was hauled in barrels and sold. In Kansas one pioneer recalled paying forty cents for a barrel of water. Alkali water had to be boiled before use to remove some of the mineral salts and bacteria, but the taste remained bitter, so travelers or settlers used citrate or lemon juice (if available) to make it palatable. *Practical Housekeeping* advocated filtering well water, giving this method of doing so:

> Take a large flower pot, and insert a sponge in the hole in the bottom, fill the pot with alternate layers of sand, charcoal, and small pebbles. The flower pot thus filled up may then be placed on a jar or other convenient vessel, into which the water can be received as it filters through.

Other water purification methods including taking alum, a substance of aluminum sulfate, and placing it on a stick, which was then moved through water. The alum removed some of the scum from water supplies. Some people bored holes in barrels which were filled with grass. The water was somewhat purified by the process of dripping through the grass. Other people simply poured water through a cloth before drinking or using it. Until late in the period few of them realized the safest and easiest way to purify water was to boil it. Asians, however, who routinely drank hot tea had little trouble with impure water.

On the overland trails, travelers (and their animals) often drank alkali water directly from stagnant pools where bacteria could breed. When drinking tainted water resulted in stomach cramps, or possibly diarrhea or vomiting which could lead to dehydration, bacon grease or vinegar was ingested to clean out the stomach of the person or animal, easing the pain.

Many early settlers piped water to their homes from springs using lead pipes. The *Washington Standard* on July 26, 1873, suggested, "it should always be allowed to run a few moments before using, as this will insure safety from lead poisoning. Old lead pipes are safer as they become incrusted with a scale that is innocuous."

Residents used a variety of containers to store water, ranging from buckets and pans to pitchers and crocks. Some cookstoves had a water reservoir, which could be filled so homemakers had a ready supply of warm water for use in baking or washing. Lacking such a stove, women heated water in pans on open fires or stoves in order to have an adequate supply for washing bodies, clothes or dishes.

If homes had a sink at all, it may have been a dry sink, with no running water, but simply a place to work. In such cases the settlers caught the runoff water in buckets and put it to other uses, such as on gardens.

Yeast: Women tried to keep a supply of yeast, adding a bit of charred bread to it if it became bitter. They used sourdough, which they stored in a crock knowing it would turn green if kept in a tin container. If a cook had no yeast or sourdough, the alternatives were to use baking powder (known as Sally Ann), soda, or saleratus, a raw form of baking soda that often had a bitter taste and a green cast to it.

The Kentucky Housewife, published in 1839, provided this recipe for Salt-Rising, or Yeast:

> Make a quart of water lukewarm, stir into it a table-spoonful of salt, and make it a tolerably thin batter with flour; mix it well, sprinkle on the top a handful of dry flour, and set it in a warm place to rise, but be sure you do not let it get hot, or it would spoil it. Turn it round ocassionally, and in a few hours it will be light, and the top covered with bubbles; then make up your bread.

In 1854 baking powder or yeast powder was available. Sourdough was a mixture of yeast, flour, sugar and water. It was particularly popular because, if a cook carefully replenished the concoction, he or she always had a supply on hand.

"All you had to do was to leave a fistful of the malt in the bottom of the bucket when you had kneaded the dough then you just added the flour and a drop of water each time and you could keep on making loaves til Doomsday in this fashion," wrote Michael McGowan in *The Hard Road to Klondike.*

Sourdough could also be used for pancakes or biscuits, and in Alaska the miners themselves became known as sourdoughs.

FOOD PREPARATION

Most cooking during the period occurred over open fires, in fireplaces and on stoves; therefore, many of the cooking utensils were of cast iron and other heavy metals that could withstand high temperatures and direct flame. Cooks used kettles suspended over the fireplace, boiling most items. They baked in Dutch ovens, sometimes four or more inches deep with lids onto which hot coals could be placed for even heating.

SALOONS/DRINKS

Among the names for alcoholic drinks were firewater, bug juice, cactus juice, forty rod, gut warmer, Kansas sheep dip, lightning, tarantula juice, strychnine, sudden death, Taos lightning, brave maker, redeye, sheepherder's delight, tonsil varnish, white mule, tangleleg, corn, dust cutter, wild mare's milk, applejack, corpse reviver, blackstrap (a mix of rum and molasses) and metheglin (a drink of diluted alcohol and honey). Most of the redeye whiskeys had in them a little water, some pure alcohol, molasses, tobacco juice, chilies or red pepper, and, perhaps, strychnine.

> The Legislature of Ohio has just passed an act making it a penal offense to use strychnine in the manufacture of liquors.
> —FLIN, *June 6, 1857, 3-2*

> A new use has been found for the Chinese sugar cane. It makes first-rate whiskey, without the aid of strychnine. It is said, too, that an invention has been made for crystallizing the syrup by a simple and perfect process, and that the production of sugar from the cane will be greatly facilitated.—FLIN, *September 12, 1857, 230-1*

Overland trail travelers sometimes mixed a "cocktail" of whiskey, lemon and the water found at natural soda springs. Germans living in the West drank a mix of rum, steeped fruit and sugar, known as *rumtopf.*

Beer was first produced in California in 1837 by Willy the Brewer McGlover; the William Bull Brewery served Californians after 1850. Breweries in Cincinnati, Milwaukee and St. Louis bottled beer in corked bottles, which were distributed throughout the West. Several western towns had breweries of their own such as the Golden Eagle Brewery in Tombstone, Arizona, and the Virginia City Brewery in Montana. In most areas of the Southwest, beer was served warm, there being no refrigeration and limited amounts of ice, though some places imported ice from northern regions. Northern saloons could serve cold beer as long as they had ice cut during winter ice harvests on frozen lakes or rivers. Beer in Bisbee, Arizona, in 1867 cost ten to twelve cents a glass.

Making Apple Whiskey

Apple whiskey is made from apples. . . . The fruit is placed in an immense trough, and mashed into pulp by a revolving wheel. Then the liquor which results is subject to distillation. The product is called the 'firsting,' in the language of the distiller. It also requires distillation, and when the second process is finished, 'apple-jack' is the remainder. The liquor improves as the years go by, and is valuable in an exact proportion to its age. A remarkable change in its color also takes place. At first it is of the hue of gin, but, as it grows older, it takes an amber-blush: and it is this particular tint which settles its merits in the minds of connoisseurs.
—FLIN, *November 1, 1873, 127-2*

Whiskey sold straight at $.25 a drink and Madam Cliquot was $5 a pint in Hays, Kansas, in 1867. Turley's Mill in New Mexico is one of the earliest locations in the West to manufacture whiskey, having started the process in the 1830s.

A Yankee in Kansas sells liquor in a gun-barrel instead of a glass, to evade the law and make it appear beyond dispute that he is selling by the barrel.—FLIN, *August 26, 1865, 355-2*

An Oregon paper says enough liquor has been sent across the mountains to keep every man in Montana drunk all winter.
—FLIN, *March 17, 1866, 403-2*

The *New York Tribune* calculates that there are in New Orleans one grog shop to every twenty-nine inhabitants. A resolution to prohibit the Sunday traffic in liquors was carried before the board of Aldermen by a vote of six yeas to five nays.
—FLIN, *January 12, 1856, 3*

To cure a hangover, people ate canned tomatoes.

Besides beer and whiskey or some other version of red-eye or rotgut, saloons dispensed cigars and tobacco, sold food ranging from Limburger and Swiss cheese to rye bread, crackers, pickled eggs or fish, and a variety of soup, stew, sausage or ham. Saloon patrons also could gamble, get a haircut, make town decisions, hear a honky-tonk piano player, dance (or do other things) with a woman, and sometimes even attend court or church services in a saloon. Next to the general merchandise store, the saloon was the primary social/cultural/business place of most western towns.

Backbars were ornate and made of cherry, walnut, oak or mahogany, often with elaborate carving and mirrors. A primary builder of western backbars was the Brunswick Company of Chicago, selling its product for about $500 with the counter costing another $300 to $400. Spittoons on the floor served as a drawing spot for tobacco juice, but only a target, as many simply spit on the floor, which might be wood but just as often was dirt or covered in sawdust. Towels hung from the front of the bar for use by patrons to wipe the foam (or tobacco spit) from their faces, mustaches or beards. Few bars had stools; patrons simply stood at the counter.

Wall art generally included paintings of nude women, but in 1896 the Anheuser & Busch Brewing Company distributed to saloons 150,000 copies of a color lithograph by F. Otto Becker that was based on the painting "Custer's Last Fight" by Cassily Adams. The rendition soon found a spot on saloon walls.

Some saloons had swinging—batwing—doors, but often they were located in a vestibule and not directly on the street; most saloons had regular doors.

ADDITIONAL READING

American Heritage. *The American Heritage Cookbook and Illustrated History of America*. New York: American Heritage Publishing Co., 1964.

Asbury, Virginia H., and Albert N. Doerschuk. "The Boone, Hays and Berry Families of Jackson County." *Missouri Historical Review*, XXIII, 1929, 537.

Bagley, Will, ed. *The Pioneer Camp of the Saints: Mormon Trail Journals of Thomas Bullock, 1846-1847*. Glendale, Calif.: Arthur H. Clark & Co., 1997.

Brown, Dee. *The Gentle Tamers*. Lincoln: University of Nebraska Press, 1958.

Bryan, Lettice. *The Kentucky Housewife*. 1839. Reprint, Columbia, S.C.: University of South Carolina Press, 1991.

Caughey, John Walton, ed. *Rushing for Gold*. Berkeley: University of California Press, 1949.

Chalmers, Irena. *The Great American Food Almanac*. New York: Harper & Row, 1986.

Chase, A.W. *Dr. Chase's Recipes; or Information for Everybody: An Invaluable Collection of About Eight Hundred Practical Recipes*. Ann Arbor, Mich.: Published by the Author, 1866. Out of print, but a comprehensive source for the era.

Christman, Enos. *One Man's Gold*. New York: McGraw Hill, 1930.

Colt, Miriam Davis. *Went to Kansas*. L. Ingalls & Co., 1862. Reprint, Readex Microprint Corporation, 1966.

Connelley, William C. "Journals of the Santa Fe Trail." *Mississippi Valley Historical Review*, XII, September 1926, 80.

Custer, Elizabeth. *Following the Guidon*. New York: Harper & Brothers, 1890.

Doerper, John. *Eating Well: A Guide to the Foods of the Pacific Northwest*. Seattle: Pacific Search Press, 1984.

Grierson, Alice Kirk. *An Army Wife's Cookbook With Household Hints and Home Remedies.* Compiled and edited by Mary L. Williams. Tucson, Ariz.: Southwest Parks and Monuments Association, 1972.

Hale, Sarah J. *Mrs. Hale's New Cook Book.* Philadelphia: T.B. Peterson and Brothers, 1857. Out of print, but a good source that can be found in library rare book rooms.

Hansen, Marcus L. *Old Fort Snelling, 1819-58.* Iowa City: State Historical Society, 1908.

Holston, William Edward. *American Diet in the Trans-Mississippi West, 1803-1870.* Diss., University of Southern California, 1962.

Johnson Byron A., and Sharon Peregrine Johnson. *Wild West Bartenders' Bible.* Austin: Texas Monthly Press, 1986.

Luchetti, Cathy. *Home on the Range: A Culinary History of the American West.* New York: Villard Books, 1993. An excellent reference.

Mariana, John. *The Dictionary of American Food and Drink.* New Haven: Ticknor & Fields, 1984.

McIntosh, Elaine N. *American Food Habits in Historical Perspective.* Westport, Conn.: Praeger Publishers, 1995.

Nelson, Oliver. *The Cowman's Southwest, Being the Reminiscenses of Oliver Nelson, Freighter, Camp Cook, Cowboy, Frontiersman in Kansas, Indian Territory, Texas and Oklahoma, 1878-1893.* Glendale, Calif.: Arthur H. Clark Company, 1953.

Root, Waverly, and Richard de Rochemont. *Eating in America.* New York: Morrow, 1976. Reprint, New York: The Ecco Press, 1981. An excellent reference but not solely about the West.

Ruxton, George Frederick. *Life in the Far West.* London: Blackwell & Sons, 1849.

Stegner, Wallace. *The Gathering of Zion.* Lincoln: University of Nebraska Press, 1992.

Stratton, Joanna L. *Pioneer Women: Voices from the Kansas Frontier.* New York: Simon & Schuster, 1981.

Whitman, Narcissa. Diary. Oregon Pioneer Association, 19th Annual Reunion, *Transactions.* Portland, 1891.

Wilcox, Estelle Woods, ed. *Practical Housekeeping: A Careful Compilation of Tried and Approved Recipes.* Minneapolis: Buckeye Publishing Co., 1883.

Williams, Jacqueline. *Wagon Wheel Kitchens: Food on the Oregon Trail.* Lawrence, Kans., University Press of Kansas, 1993. An excellent reference for detail about cooking along the western trail.

———. *The Way We Ate: Pacific Northwest Cooking, 1843-1890.* Pullman, Wash.: Washington State University Press, 1996. An excellent reference.

Wyman, Walker D. "California Emigrant Letters." *California Historical Society, Quarterly, XXIV,* 1945, 133.

CHAPTER EIGHT

ARCHITECTURE

estern architecture generally depended upon available materials. If an area had timber, structures often were built of log or sawn lumber; where stones were plentiful, builders used them; and in areas without stone or timber, people used a mixture of clay, sand and straw to prepare adobe bricks. On the prairies and high plains with their tight grass mat, settlers cut blocks of sod, or they dug homes into the earth itself.

The pitch of a roof depended partly on materials available and also on general climate. If the area received heavy snows in the winter, roofs had steep pitches so the snow would slide off, otherwise it lay upon the roof and could become too heavy for the structure resulting in a collapsed roof. Generally, windows were small or nonexistent in the early part of the period; after the 1870s, when railroads could transport manufactured goods, windows became more popular, although often they were covered with cloth or even hides and glass continued to be a luxury item until late in the period.

While settlers relied on the building materials that were generally available, architectural styles revolved somewhat around the people themselves. In the Southwest and California most structures had Spanish architectural features because of the Spanish occupation and early settlement. As immigrants moved into the West primarily after 1862, towns and buildings took on the look of the homelands of those who settled. Some communities appeared to be directly from Germany, Italy, Scandinavia, England, Ireland, France, Bohemia, Norway, Poland and other countries as settlers used building materials and techniques with which they were familiar.

Gothic styling, such as the arched window above the entrance door of this church in Bannack, Montana, became popular in the 1870s. This church was constructed in 1877.

> The cottages are scattered prettily. . . . [Castroville, Texas] might sit for the portrait of one of the poorer villages of the upper Rhone Valley.—*Frederick Law Olmstead,* A Journey Through Texas

Greek or Classic Revival style was in use during the 1840s and 1850s. After 1880 elements of Queen Anne style became popular with brick, stone and frame walls, turrets, gables and bay windows common, particularly in rapidly growing cities and in areas of considerable wealth, such as mining communities. During that same period, Romanesque Revival style also found its way into western architecture. In many cases the entire house was covered in shingles often applied in radial patterns.

After 1850, federal buildings in Texas used cast iron and masonry to support local industries. Metal and glass facades were in use during the 1870s and 1880s throughout the region. They provided for better natural interior lighting due to the use of large plate glass windows.

The Gothic Revival style spread through the West from 1850 to 1890 and was most commonly used on churches. Affluent westerners also utilized Gothic Revival artistic design in their homes at the end of the period and continuing into the early 1900s. It is distinguished by arched or pointed windows and doorways, steeply gabled roofs and wood-frame construction with shiplap or board-and-batten siding.

Public buildings constructed of stone, brick or wood siding with stone or marble ornamentation became popular from 1855 to 1890 in an Italianate style of construction, characterized by tall windows that often had arches. Roofs were low-pitched and often flat, particularly on businesses.

Between 1850 and 1870 Americans introduced style changes in New Mexico by adding woodwork—often painted white, though sometimes brown—to adobe structures. Buildings had double-hung casement windows and occasionally picket fences after that period. Homes also evolved from basic square or rectangular structures to those in the shapes of a U or an L. Southwestern roofs were generally flat. After 1860 some people used brick for construction. After 1870 stucco became more popular as did interior wallpaper and the use of oil-based paint, items which had not been widely available earlier.

Most early buildings in mining boomtowns were of lumber, which was readily available in many of the areas where miners made strikes. The use of lumber for buildings had a significant effect: Fire was a common enemy in frontier towns. Many communities saw all or portions of their business and residential districts destroyed by fire at least once during the period. On the high plains the common occurrence of grass fires created a similar hazard for towns or homes. Settlers who built on prairie sites would plow two or three furrows around the house to serve as a firebreak in the event a prairie blaze raced through the vicinity of the home.

Many areas of Alaska had a Russian architectural influence due to ownership of the region by the Russians from the time Vitus Bering first saw it in 1741 until sale of the area to the United States in 1867. One of the most significant Russian influences in Alaska during the period was the construction of Russian Orthodox churches with their distinctive three-part plans and onion domes.

HOUSING

Adobe Houses: Adobe walls were sometimes two or three feet thick, set on foundations of river rocks or uncut stone. Hand-peeled poles or hand-split cedar placed close together and covered with straw and dirt formed the roof. Usually the walls were covered with a mud plaster and *jaspe*, a homemade whitewash, although sometimes it was tinted red. Often the doors and windows were framed with wood painted blue. Adobes were popular in areas where trees were scarce. A mixture of lime, sand and gravel called *tipichil* covered the homes. Each home had a corner fireplace and hard-packed dirt floors. The homes often had covered porches. The rooms were usually square or rectangular with high ceilings. Sometimes the houses had two or three stories. Early Spanish style homes had roofs made of *latillas* and *vigas*. The latillas were laid across the walls about two feet apart, and then the vigas, lighter poles, were placed over them as a latticework. They were then painted red, green or blue. As Rowland F. Dickey put it in *New Mexico Village Arts*:

> Beginning with a single room, the house grew like a game of dominoes. As each son brought home his bride, he added a room to one end of the paternal dwelling. Every room had its own outside door and the system solved the in-law problem by giving privacy to the married couples of the family.

The southwestern adobe houses—such as those at Indian pueblos—had a ladder leading to the second and third stories, which could be pulled into the house in situations when invaders threatened.

Asian Structures: Asian residents often lived in ghetto-shacks, flimsily built structures made of a basic frame and covered with tar paper or sometimes with canvas or even cardboard. Chinese residents often had their own section of town, known as Chinatown, which was sometimes constructed underground, as in Pendleton, Oregon.

Brick Houses: Use of lime concrete was popular in some areas, such as Seguin, Texas, where construction with such materials began after 1848. Large brick homes were particularly popular in more urban areas and in communities where residents had added wealth due to business enterprises such as gold or silver mining.

Dugouts: Such habitations were literally dug out of the ground, often into a hillside, with a roof of boards or logs covered with sod at ground level. They were popular on the high plains and prairies where there were few other building materials available. Some were full dugouts, completely in the earth; others were half-dugouts and were partially above ground. Many had portions of the interior lined with stone. Cooking often took place at open fires out of doors, so the dugout mainly served as a place to get in out of the weather, a place in which to sleep, and a place for storing supplies and what limited possessions early residents had with them. Dugouts were dirty, generally filled with bugs and insects, and often enticing to rodents and rattlesnakes.

Frame Houses: From the 1840s on, settlers employed the Classic or Greek Revival style for their homes. Such buildings had columned porches, double-hung sash windows and often featured twelve panes of glass (six panes in the upper sash and six panes in the lower), as well as thin board siding, which was usually painted white. Use of Eastlake-style elements, such as latticework, cutouts, rows of spindles and knobs, coincided with stick construction techniques involving buildings with asymmetrical composition, steeply pitched multiple gable roofs and shiplap siding. Those styles became popular in the late 1870s and through the 1890s. The Queen Anne Style in vogue during the period 1880-1900, featured diverse window shapes—some with arched tops and others with flat tops—and a combination of roof types on the same home, and utilized sawn wood as a building material, though it often had a stucco exterior.

Homesteader Shacks: By law a homesteader under the 1862 Homestead Act was required to build a residence and occupy it for a minimum of five years to obtain title to the land. Homesteaders fulfilled the requirement by using a variety of building tools and methods to build housing ranging from sod houses and dugouts to log homes or even frame structures. In most cases the house was at least twelve feet by twelve feet, but some homesteader shacks were as small as eight feet by eight feet. In many cases the frame houses had stacks of sod around the exterior, not only for insulation purposes but also to provide additional support to the often flimsy structures.

Most early homestead shacks were small and homesteaders generally built a bigger, better home as soon as they had the resources to do so. In that event the first homestead house was often converted to another use, such as a bunkhouse for ranch hands or as a shed for livestock.

Homesteaders met the law's requirements in inventive ways. They constructed cabins that could be moved, so when the requirement of proving up on the ground was completed in one location, the cabin could be moved to a new site. To "prove up" a homesteader had to live on the property and make improvements. (See chapter two for more information on homestead requirements.) Some homesteaders built across property boundaries and shared a house that met the law's regulations for both sections.

Many homesteads involved claims by various family members: parents, sons, daughters, sisters or brothers all in contiguous parcels. In such situations the individual homestead claimants built a residence on their claims, but often the houses sat in a cluster near the adjoining corners of the various property sections. That way family members could help each other with work and visit together more frequently. Generally the family members shared labor on each other's land, and women who claimed homesteads might do so to add to their family's holdings. In some cases older sisters filed claims, which they ultimately gave or sold to younger brothers who weren't able to file due to their age. Women also took claims adjacent to a boyfriend, again to provide a larger parcel of ground for their family once they married, and many remained single and proved up—or made improvements—on their own.

Hotels: As early as 1850 hotels operated in San Francisco and other California gold-rush communities. Though some were crudely built of wood with canvas sides and roofs, it didn't take long for lavish buildings to replace them. Urban areas and wealthy communities, including those affected by mineral strikes, had fashionable hotels with spacious lobbies, high ceilings and furnishings such as marble-topped tables. Such fine establishments had expanded into rural areas by the latter part of the period. The hotels promoted by railroads—and often situated in areas where there were hot mineral springs—catered to affluent guests.

Log Cabins/Log Houses: Log home construction throughout the West generally occurred in stages. The first home built was likely a shanty, rough cabin

Squared timbers, glass windows and shake shingle make it clear that this Bannack, Montana, home was built by someone with means.

Early homes in the West might include log structures, such as this Montana structure that features a board roof covered with sod and a window with no glass or screen.

or a log pen. Then as settlers became more prosperous—and had more time—they built a hand-hewn house with either one or two rooms. Even later they built a frame house of sawn wood. Some log houses had stone foundations; others had the logs placed directly on the ground.

In Texas the earliest homes were "dog-run" or "dog-trot" homes that had two rooms separated by an open space or breezeway. The dogs slept there—and so did any guests who couldn't fit into the house. The breezeway also served as a storage area for excess furniture, a place to hang the laundry or as an open porch. During hot summer months the open area had many uses because it was cooler than the interior of the home.

Another popular house style involved a combination of logs and stone in equal proportions. Logs were of the timber available locally—pine, cypress, cedar, pecan, elm and the like—with chinking placed between each. The chinking, a filler placed between each log to reduce air drafts and seal the structure from moisture, could be of varied materials such as willow sticks, small logs or boards, plaster, adobe, Spanish moss, clay or another mud mixed with grass, and in some cases people used cow manure to chink their log structures.

Log cabins generally were of all round logs, which were difficult to chink, while log houses often had timbers of log squared on one or more sides. Cabins generally were only one room, while houses could be larger. The two types of dwellings, however, had many common characteristics, such as rectangular shape, notched and fitted corner joints (with many styles of notching such as saddle notch, V, square, full or half dovetail, double, butt joint and lap joint), a chimney or smoke hole, and a low-pitched roof. In areas where there was heavy winter snow, the roof pitch could be fairly steep to enable the snow to slide from the roof. Log structures generally had small windows and often only a single door.

The spaces between logs had to be closed, or chinked. That was done with a variety of materials ranging from sticks to plaster, mud and even manure.

Tools used in log home construction included a broad ax, with the strokes usually visible on the logs; a draw knife, to shape and peel logs; an adze, to shape or cope the notches; a maul, to split logs; an auger, to drill holes in order to pin logs together; and a frow (or froe), used in splitting shingles and sometimes in shaping the logs. Some early log homes had only wooden pins or pegs to hold the logs in place, but later-period homes had nails and other hardware. In the Northwest high humidity affected log homes in various ways such as causing logs to split or rot. Log home builders in Washington and Oregon prized virgin timber because those trees had matured slowly so that they had small, tightly compacted growth rings, making it difficult for moisture to enter the cut ends of logs and to begin the rotting process. Native Americans in the region also relied on timber with various tribes such as the Coast Salish, Nootka and Chinook using logs for construction of buildings in permanent winter villages. They generally used cedar planks for the roofs, as did early settlers.

When Americans moved into Alaska, they first built log structures and gradually they improved their dwellings by constructing wood-frame buildings and cottages. In all cases the dwellings had little or no ornamentation. Because of a lack of materials, few Alaskan buildings were constructed of brick or stone.

Missions: Most of the missions of the Southwest were built prior to 1840 and all reflect the Spanish influence on the area with arches, bell towers and colonnaded porticos. Most are of adobe. Many of the missions are preserved and can be viewed today. For a photographic account of the missions see *The Architecture of the Southwest* by Trent Elwood Sanford.

Log construction involved a variety of notches such as these double dove-tail joints.

The builder of this log structure used squ[...] joints.

Native Alaskan Structures: In Alaska, native people constructed homes using locally available materials. Tlingits constructed villages near water with single or double rows of houses. Each village had from just a few houses to as many as sixty with up to fifty people from the same family living in each household. (The person with the most status had his place in the household at the back of the home; those with the least amount of status were nearer the door.) The houses were of wood construction, usually spruce, with hemlock used for thinner inner walls and featuring planks split from logs and held together by wooden pegs.

Alaskan Eskimos built a variety of home styles ranging from large, skin-covered dwellings with plank walls, to dwellings built of stone, and those dug into the ground and covered with grass. During the summer these latter dwellings appeared as grassy mounds; in the winter snow covered them. They had a tunnel entrance with a trapdoor, enabling the residents to enter during the cold season without loss of interior heat. The igloo, or snow hut, was seldom used by Alaskan natives.

Eskimos built large ceremonial houses—called *kashims* by the Koniags and *barabaras* by the Aleuts. The entrance to the barabara was through a hole in the roof; people climbed down a notched pole to the floor. The house had a post-and-beam frame and was covered with sod. It served as a home for several families with a communal area in the center and individual family cubicles at the edges of the large structure. Entrance to the kashims was through a side door. There was a common area in the center and between two and four separate rooms for individual families. Each common area had a fireplace.

Athapascan Indians built structures based on their hunter-gatherer lifestyle, often having skin-covered dwellings and sometimes constructing subterranean houses.

Native American Structures: American Indians had a variety of housing styles ranging from the adobe structures and cliff houses of the Pueblo Indians, to the multi-sided hogans of the Navajos, the wickiups (dome-shaped brush structures) of various tribes, and the conical tipis of the northern Plains Indians. The tipis were usually made of buffalo hides stretched around a framework of lodgepole pine poles. The Indians preferred lodgepole pine for tipi poles because it grew straight, tall and wasn't too large in diameter. The type of timber received its name based on its primary use for Native structures.

The villages of the native people in present New Mexico were built around a central plaza. Homes were constructed of adobe, which had the advantage of being cool in summer and warm in winter. The houses of the villages were connected, growing outward from the plaza with all doors facing inward, allowing the exterior walls to form a fortresslike structure. Many of the historic pueblos, such as Taos Pueblo and Acoma, known as The Sky City, both in New Mexico, have been continuously lived in for hundreds of years, as have the homes on the Hopi mesas in Arizona. In those communities the homes pass from generation to generation. The homes are simple in design with little ornamentation. For the best traditional view of the Hopi, visit Walpi on First Mesa, where a few families continue to live without modern conveniences such as running water or electricity.

Digger Indians in California lived in wigwams.

> Their wigwams are built throughout of red-wood bark, and are round in shape, which can better be explained by saying that they are the shape of a bowl upside down with a small one placed also upside down on top. There are no windows, and aside from the aperture for entrance, which is about two feet square, and a small opening at the top to allow the smoke to escape, there is no opening in this conical shaped inclosure. To enter one of these huts it becomes necessary to get down and crawl in. . . . They sleep in a circule in hollow places in the ground, with feet to the centre.
>
> —FLIN, *August 7, 1875, 386-3, from a report in the Santa Rosa, California,* Times

Ranch Houses: Ranch homes during the period generally were rectangular and many had flat roofs, although some had steeply pitched roofs covered with hand-split shakes of cypress or cedar. They could be made of many types of materials ranging from logs and lumber to bricks and adobe or stucco.

Sod Houses: Common on the plains and prairie where there were no trees and only limited supplies of stone or other building materials, sod houses were constructed by cutting long strips of native sod with a breaking plow called a grasshopper plow or "grasshoppers," and then stacking the sod blocks like bricks. Sod houses had thick walls—perhaps up to two or even three feet deep. Though most sod homes were small structures with a single door and small windows, some plains residents built two-story structures. The sod houses were often plastered on the inside to reduce problems with dirt and bugs, particularly fleas, which were a common problem for residents of both sod houses—soddies—and dugouts. In Nebraska where sod was a primary building material, it became known as Nebraska marble.

> Sod was stripped from the prairie with the walking plow, cut into pieces $4'' \times 12'' \times 24''$ and then stacked like bricks to enclose the $12' \times 14'$ house. A wood roof and floor was installed and wood-framed interior walls carried wallpaper and an essential shelf or two.—*Mary Ann Murray*

Tents: Tents with frame walls and canvas sides and roofs were popular in mining boom towns and among the construction workers of railroads because those communities often were temporary. They became known as "Hell-on-Wheels" towns. By using tents, residents and business owners could quickly move from one location to the next.

ARCHITECTURAL APPURTENANCES

Bridges: Truss bridges were the most common, but some areas had suspension bridges and covered bridges. Cable bridges weren't in place in the region until very late during the period. Early settlers often built bridges by lashing logs together. Nebraska City, Nebraska, had a pontoon bridge built across the Missouri River that zigzagged over the water. A hundred or more flatboats made up the bridge, which had a main span 894 feet long. There was an 1,100-foot-long approach on the east side of the twenty-four-foot-wide bridge. A round trip cost $.40 for a double team, or a quarter for a horse and rider, $.05 for cattle or people on foot, $.10 for horses, and $.02 for hogs. The bridge was only in place for one year, in 1888.

Chimneys: These were made of available materials such as stone or, in some cases, wood covered with mud.

A log structure with a false front and sod roof, Bannack, Montana.

False Fronts: False fronts are a western phenomenon, in use from Canada to Mexico and developed in towns by business owners intent on presenting a prosperous image. The false fronts generally had a massive cornice and cheap windows, and they became a place for merchants to advertise their business and wares. They were common throughout the West and on nearly every business in California gold-mining towns. In Arizona, false fronts made of shiplap lumber covered adobe structures.

Floors: Many floors were hard-packed dirt, but as people had time and money, they installed wood floors. Puncheon floors were of logs hewn smooth on one side and laid with the smooth side up. The puncheons would roll unless they were pegged together. Linoleum was available after the 1870s, but its use depended upon the location of the settler. Those in remote areas may not have had linoleum until late in the period, while urban residents and even ranchers or farmers who were near railroad lines could obtain such floor coverings more easily.

Foundations: Often foundations didn't exist; structures were built directly on the ground in the earliest part of the period. Later builders used rocks or stones as foundations.

Heat: Steam heat became common in public buildings and large houses in the 1880s. Most homes had wood heat through much of the period, provided by open fireplaces or stoves, though some also relied on buffalo or cow chips (dried manure), coal, twisted grass or hay, or corncobs, depending on availability of fuel sources.

Porches: Areas with hot climates, such as the Southwest or Texas, had homes and buildings with wide porches where people could eat, sleep and do work such as laundry or sewing. Western towns also had porches or awnings on most businesses that provided shade or protection from the weather for people either walking along the sidewalks or sitting on benches or chairs in front of the stores.

Roofs: Mansard roofs came into use throughout the region following the gold-mining-boom period in California, Arizona and Montana. The style was in vogue during the period 1865-80. Roof materials ranged from hand-cut wood shingles of locally available materials, such as cypress or cedar, to logs placed close together with a layer of sod over the top. Other roofs were of tin (particularly during the later period), or boards sometimes covered with paper or tin.

Sidewalks: Communities sometimes built sidewalks, usually of boards, but often only in business districts. Some concrete, rock or brick sidewalks were used in the latter portion of the period. Hitching rails and metal rings placed on posts along the sidewalks were used to tie horses.

Siding: Siding came in two types: horizontal wood such as shiplap, clapboard or drop siding and vertical siding such as plank or board-and-batten, where narrow battens covered joints between boards to weatherproof the walls.

Stairs: Two-story structures, particularly public buildings and businesses, usually had exterior stairways providing access to the second floor. The outdoor stairways not only provided private access to the upper floor, they

Three different roof styles are reflected on these buildings in Bannack, Montana. From left are a roof of shake shingles, then one of board-and-bat and finally the earliest type of roof style, one of sod. All three buildings have false fronts, a western style element that may have been implemented to give buildings a more imposing look.

Board siding and shutters are used on this Bannack, Montana, building, circa 1870, which also has shake shingles. The block foundation was probably added in more recent years.

were cheaper to build and didn't intrude on the space in a lower-floor room.

Streets: Most streets were dirt or mud (depending on weather conditions). Communities with brick works sometimes had streets paved with brick and examples of such work are visible in places like Missoula, Montana. In towns along the Gulf Coast, such as Galveston, Texas, residents paved streets with shells and the native hardwood bois d'arc was used for a time to cover some Texas streets, though the wood absorbed moisture and many felt it unsanitary in a period when most of the traffic involved horses.

Windows: In the Southwest, windows were often covered with *rejas* (grilles) made of wood or iron, though many cabins throughout the West had no windows at all. Window coverings included as hides, cloth like muslin, remnants of old clothes, or burlap or flour sacks.

Fences

Town fences might be built of wrought iron or wood, particularly in the latter portion of the period—after 1875. The use of—and need for—fences became apparent in the West subsequent to homesteading. When most of the land was free range, cattle ranchers didn't particularly need or want fences to control their stock. They had cowboys who could gather and sort animals as needed. But when homesteaders started claiming sections across the region, they planted crops and some started raising cattle herds with blooded stock rather than range animals. Therefore, they needed some type of fences to control animal movement—keeping livestock out of fields of corn or grain, for instance, or keeping livestock from straying. Settlers and homesteaders used a variety of fencing methods and materials during the early period. With the production and patent of barbed wire in 1874, the fencing practices in the West changed significantly as nearly everyone used the new material. It quickly became the controlling element of the West, changing the region in many ways but particularly serving as a restrictive barrier where previously there had been few effective types of fences. Some popular fences were the following:

Barbed Wire: Joseph Glidden experimented with wire fencing for some time before coming up with "The Winner," which was patented November 24, 1874. Glidden's partner in the venture was Isaac Ellwood. The men lived in the DeKalb, Illinois, area at the time. Glidden's wire fence replaced other types of fencing for its practicality. Glidden experimented with various materials in developing his wire. He first twisted his wife's hairpins around smooth wire and later used a coffee mill to make uniform barbs, which he twisted around smooth wire. To keep the barbs in place along the smooth wire, he attached two strands of wire to a tree and hooked the other ends to a grindstone wheel. He then turned the wheel, twisting the smooth wire strands together and placing barbs at periodic intervals. Glidden applied for his patent on October 27, 1873, but Jacob Haish filed for a patent on a similar design at about the same time and there was an eighteen-year-long court fight to determine ownership of the patent, even though Glidden received his patent in November 1874.

In spite of Haish's continued fight over the barbed wire design, Glidden and Elwood started production under the company name The Barb Fence Company. They began marketing their product. In the first year of production Glidden's wire sold for $20 per 100-pound roll. In 1882-83 the company sold $1.3 million worth of barbed wire, with the bulk of the business occurring in Texas. Other names for barbed wire are thorny hedges, sticker fencing, wire with prickers, pronged wire, barbwire and bob wire. Other versions of barbed wire developed such as J. Brinkerhoff's wide, twisted wire with a large hexagon-shaped barb patented in 1879, and a design by C.A. Hodge in 1887 that had two woven strands of wire with a 10-point spur fastened to the wire. In all 700 varieties of barbed wire were patented.

A test for barbed wire occurred in San Antonio, Texas, where Glidden salesman John Gates constructed a fence and then remarked to cowmen: "This is the finest fence in the world. It's light as air, stronger than whiskey and cheaper than dirt. It's all steel and miles long. The cattle ain't been born that can get through it. Bring on your steers, gentlemen!" The cattlemen put a herd of twenty-five to sixty-five head of Texas Longhorns behind the fence and tried to make them escape—but the fence held. After that sales started in earnest.

Large Texas ranches such as the XIT and the Frying Pan started enclosing their range, leading to a change in livestock operations throughout the West. Some ranchers who ran cattle on open range resisted fences of any type and routinely cut wire fences to allow animals to freely roam. Fences helped homesteaders and farmers keep livestock out of their crops, and they helped ranchers control movement of their animals by allowing them to be placed in different pastures at various times of the year. Though barbed wire provided a management tool for ranchers and farmers, it also created some difficulties. Cattle not accustomed to the barbed fences ran into them and often incurred injuries that led to infection and screwworm as a result. During periods of harsh weather the fences stopped animals from drifting, and that sometimes resulted in death loss. The cattle piled up against each other in fence corners and died from suffocation or injuries resulting from the crush of other animals against them.

Buck and Rail: Although used in areas where timber was available, such fencing was not common in much of the West. It was expensive to buy lumber and much of the West was open plains or desertlike and had no ready source of building materials.

Osage Orange: A hedge grown throughout the plains states and used as a fencing material, it was effective because it had sharp barbs that deterred animals from crossing it.

Rose Hedge: Like Osage Orange, a rose hedge was used as a natural fencing barrier. A common hedge was Cherokee Rose, but it took too long for the hedges to grow to a size that would keep animals in to be widely effective.

Stone: In locations where it was available, residents used limestone for fences. Sometimes they stacked it three or four feet high to serve as a barrier, and at other times they used limestone slabs as fence posts, stringing various kinds of wire from one post to another.

Wire: Used for twenty years before the development of barbed wire in 1874, galvanized wire was never particularly effective. It stretched in the heat and became brittle and broke in the cold. It also failed to deter animals from moving into areas in which they weren't supposed to be.

Outbuildings

Barns: Built of wood or stone and as large as was necessary to house livestock, barns were an essential element on any farm or ranch. Stables provided shelter for other animals.

All barns had feed stalls—the number depending upon the size of the operation and the need for space to house livestock—and they featured upper-story haymows. Though most barns were rectangular or box-like, some were octagonal or even round. Many ranchers and farmers started with a box-style building and only later added a peaked, pitched, gambrel or other roof. An example of a stone barn is the Elijah Filley stone barn near Holmesville, Nebraska. Constructed in 1874, the rectangular barn is a three-story limestone structure classified as a bank barn because it has a ground-level entrance at the lower east end and also an entrance on the second level on the

---

A FENCING DISPUTE

Some ranchers fenced land they didn't own, resulting in widespread disagreements and in some cases leading to court battles as occurred in Nebraska in 1899. Bartlett Richards purchased the Spade Ranch in Nebraska's panhandle in August 1888. He operated it with his brother Jarvis and John J. Cairnes, and they expanded the ranch holdings by taking additional homestead claims.

When Cairnes sold out in 1899, Richards obtained new partners, including Will Comstock, to form the Nebraska Land and Feeding Company. The new company had about 500,000 acres enclosed by 292 miles of fence; it ran some 25,000 to 40,000 head of cattle, and the Spade served as the "home ranch."

Richards fenced a good portion of range even though he didn't own all of the land. Authorities ordered Richards and Comstock to remove the fences, which they refused to do. They ultimately faced misdemeanor charges and in 1905 pleaded guilty to fencing 212,000 acres of public land. Each man was fined $300 and sentenced to six hours in the custody of a U.S. marshal (which was actually served in the custody of their attorney). Subsequently, President Theodore Roosevelt and the public demanded additional action against the Nebraska ranchers. When they went to court on new felony charges, Richards and Comstock were convicted, sentenced to a year in federal prison and ordered to pay a $1,500 fine.

---

higher west end. The Filley barn, like many others made of stone or other materials, had an area where hay could be stored, and the door to its upper story was wide and tall enough to allow teams pulling hay wagons to enter the barn.

Corrals and other buildings for livestock such as chicken houses and hog pens were added as needed and generally were built of low-grade materials, either lumber left from another project or logs cut specifically for the new facility. On the Northern Plains and throughout the mountain regions, corrals often were made of poles placed a few feet apart on a horizontal plane. In the Southwest and Texas, corrals often were made of smaller sticks placed upright and close together.

Carriage House: Carriage houses were early-day garages for carriages, wagons, buggies and the like, and were used primarily in urban areas.

Cellar: Necessary for storage of items such as potatoes and other vegetables. Women and children often dug the cellar.

Icehouse: Individual residents, particuarly those living in northern, cold climates had icehouses. Ice harvest was common in the winter with residents cutting large chunks of ice from frozen streams, rivers and lakes. They packed the ice in sawdust and placed it in the icehouses, which had thick walls and no windows to add insulation to the structure. Carefully packed ice could be preserved for use throughout most of the summer. As early as 1866 San Antonio, Texas, had an ice factory, and Jefferson, Texas, produced ice commercially by 1868. *Frank Leslie's Illustrated Newspaper* in its February 4, 1871, edition provided this description of an ice harvest using an ice plow:

> This is not very unlike an ordinary plow; for the solitary pointed blade are substituted several long, sharp prongs or teeth which act saw-fashion, and are so adjusted that the ice is cut but half through. The furrows are opened in parallel lines, giving a surface dimension to the blocks of two and a half feet by two feet. As the plow passes over a small area, the men furnished with long poles terminating in strong iron hooks for the purpose, haul the blocks to the source of the canal, where, after twenty-five or thirty blocks are collected, attachments are made, and another patient horse draws the whole to the shore. Men stand along the edge, directing with their hooked poles the course of the pieces until they reach the ice houses.

Outhouse: Also called ordinaries or privies, outhouses were common in the West and particularly in rural areas throughout the period. Though most outhouses were small with one or at the most two seats (or holes cut into a board), some areas of the West had two-story outhouses. Those larger outhouses were particularly necessary in regions where deep snow fell in the winter. When drifts of snow covered the lower door, the second level could be used without the need to shovel a pathway to the outhouse. Then the seats in the lower level were lifted or removed allowing sewage from the upper level to fall into the pit dug below the outhouse. Some Texas communities and other cities had sewage systems by the late 1870s and early 1880s; however, most rural areas and many urban locations continued to use outhouses throughout the period.

Smokehouse: Most rural residents had some version of a smokehouse, necessary to cure meat in the era before refrigeration. In Tlingit villages in Alaska, the smokehouses had two or three fireplaces and the Tlingits placed fish on horizontal boards so they could be properly smoked. Athapascan people in Alaska had similar smokehouses; they put the fish on platforms near the ceiling of the smokehouse and preserved large quantities of salmon. The smoke served a secondary purpose of deterring mosquitoes.

Springhouse: A small, usually wooden structure, the springhouse was built over a spring and used as a cooling area for butter, milk and other items that needed cooling in the period prior to refrigeration.

ARCHITECTURAL TERMS

Classic Revival: A style similar to Greek Revival with double-hung sash windows and thin board siding.

Eastlake Style: Asymmetrical composition with steep, multiple-gable roofs, shiplap siding and featuring latticework, cutouts and rows of spindles and knobs.

Gothic Revival: A style featuring arched or pointed windows and doorways, steeply gabled roofs and often of wood-frame construction with shiplap or board-and-batten siding.

Greek Revival: A style also sometimes called Classic Revival, featuring colonnaded porches and double-hung sash windows.

Italianate Style: Features tall windows and low-pitched, often flat, roofs.

Romanesque Revival: Features rounded arches on buildings often made of concrete, terra-cotta or fired bricks.

ADDITIONAL READING

Campen, Richard N. *Architecture of the Western Reserve.* Logan: University of Utah Press, 1987.

Carter, Thomas, and Peter Goss. *Utah's Historic Architecture 1847-1940.* Salt Lake City: University of Utah Press, 1988.

Clark, Rosalind. *Architecture Oregon Style.* Portland: Professional Book Center, Inc., 1983. An excellent reference with information that applies generally to other areas of the West.

Florin, Lambert. *Victorian West.* Seattle: Superior Publishing Co., 1978. Numerous photos but little text related to Victorian-style architecture.

Hoagland, Alison K. *Buildings of Alaska.* New York: Oxford University Press, 1993. An excellent reference.

Moulton, Candy. "Glidden Ancestor Developed Wire that Tamed the West." Rawlins, Wyo. *Daily Times Fair Edition,* (August 8, 1987): 8A, 9A.

———. *Roadside History of Nebraska.* Missoula, Mont.: Mountain Press Publishing, 1997.

Murray, Mary Ann. "The Murray Place: A Bicentennial Sketch of Sod Houses, Settlers, and Prairie Trails." *North Dakota Outdoors,* (November 1976): 22.

Olmstead, Frederick Law. *A Journey Through Texas.* Austin: University of Texas Press, 1978.

Robinson, Willard B. *Gone From Texas.* College Station: Texas A&M University Press, 1981. A good reference to southwestern and Texas architectural styles.

Sanford, Trent Elwood. *The Architecture of the Southwest.* Westport, Conn.: Greenwood Press Publishers, 1971. An excellent reference to southwestern style architecture.

Spears, Beverley. *American Adobes.* Albuquerque: University of New Mexico Press, 1986. Good information about adobe structures.

CHAPTER NINE

FURNISHING A HOME

The earliest homes of westerners provided only the barest amount of space necessary to shelter the family, and the interior furnishings were often as sparse and plain as the building itself. Furnishings included a table, some type of bed, perhaps a chair or two, and likely a chest or trunk in which goods had been hauled west. Boards nailed directly into log walls served as shelves and cupboards. If there were window openings, chances are no glass kept out wind, rain, snow or bugs, so the openings were covered with whatever materials available: cloth, paper or hides. An open fireplace served as a cooking area and a source of heat in early homes; later homes had some type of stove which again often doubled for cooking and heating.

In all areas of the West, people made a house into a home by adding touches such as a brightly pieced quilt on a bed or used as a wall hanging. A Bible, family pictures or a treasured piece of china might be displayed on a small shelf. The necessities of life often hung from nails in the wall: pots and frying pans, guns, traps, strings of chilies or garlic, and clothing. Early western homes had one common characteristic: They were small. Into a space perhaps only eight or ten feet square went everything a family might have, and the family, too.

By the end of the period, housing styles and amenities had improved considerably throughout the West. People not only lived in bigger, better homes, they also had nicer furnishings.

WALL, WINDOW, DOOR AND FLOOR COVERINGS

A variety of materials were used as floor coverings. In areas of the Pacific Northwest some early settlers used old sail cloth as a type of carpeting, and in the 1850s the *New York Post* advertised three different weights of oilcloth that could be used as floor covering. The use of oilcloth was popular until the 1870s when linoleum was invented and replaced it as the floor covering of choice (if it was available). As with many household items, use of a particular material depended upon location and finances. Some homeowners who may have had the money to purchase an eighteen- or twenty-four-foot wide piece of oilcloth long enough to cover their floors, couldn't obtain it in their particular location. So they made do with what was available. Though many early homes had dirt floors, most homeowners eventually (as soon as they were able) installed wood floors. By the 1870s it was not only possible to purchase linoleum, but hardwood flooring was also generally available.

In nearly all situations, residents created some type of floor covering. Any sturdy material could be used as carpeting: army blankets or burlap sacks sewn together or rags braided into rugs. Sometimes westerners used tanned hides or bearskins as rugs. In situations when the residents used hides with the hair still on them, they pointed the hair toward the door to make sweeping easier. Adobe house floors in the Southwest were dirt, sometimes covered with a *jerga*, a homespun wool carpeting, and occasionally covered with thin stone slabs. Many homes had only dirt floors and in areas with a damp climate, women sometimes found mushrooms growing from the floor each morning, which they swept away, or perhaps if it was a good variety, picked to cook.

Sweeping the floor was a never-ending chore for many western homeowners. Dirt filtered through walls, around windows and doors, and down from roofs and ceilings, not to mention the dirt tracked in by occupants. Brooms were often homemade, constructed of broom straw, rye grass, peeled willows or other natural materials.

Rugs had to be cleaned regularly. To do that tiresome job women hauled them outside where they shook them, swept them and then hung them over a clothesline where they used carpet beaters to remove the dirt.

> A carpet-sweeping machine has been invented, which consists of a small box, in which there is a revolving fan that sucks up all dust and dirt; and carries it into a small compartment containing water. The woollen fibres [*sic*] and larger particles are deposited in a drawer. The sweeping is done by pushing the box along over the surface of the carpet by handles.—FLIN, *May 2, 1857, 335-3*

Residents of adobe homes tacked mantas of cotton cloth to the ceiling and walls to keep dirt from filtering down, and strings of dried fruit, herbs and chilies hung from ceiling beams. Occupants of sod dwellings, and sometimes those who had dirt or sod roofs, also tacked material to the ceiling to keep dirt from filtering downward.

Wallpaper was available after the1850s, though not necessarily in all areas of the West, and again its use was predicated by a family's financial situation.

Walls were often papered with newspapers that had already been gleaned for any information they might contain.

In some hotels and lodging establishments, sleeping quarters were divided only with panels of cloth such as muslin. As Flora Spiegelberg traveled the Santa Fe Trail with her husband in 1875, she stayed in such a place, noting, " the bed-chambers were merely cubby-holes partitioned off with thin, all revealing muslin."

A blanket with stones or other weights tied or sewn into the bottom could be tacked to an open doorway to serve as an interim door. This at least reduced some of the drafts that would enter a structure if nothing blocked the entrance. Most doors were built of lumber and had a hole through which a latchstring could be placed outside. If the string was hanging outside, anyone could open the door from either an interior or exterior position, but when the latchstring was on the inside, only someone within the building could open the door, leading to the saying "leave the latchstring out," meaning "I hope I'm welcome at any time."

Homestead houses often started out small, but as settlers were able they constructed newer, bigger homes, such as this two room log homestead house built in the 1880s by the W.T. Peryam family in southern Wyoming. The house had log timbers in its construction with a board roof covered by sod. Heating came from a stove such as this Colonial model. This house is part of the Grand Encampment Museum complex.

Curtains were made from worn clothing. Some homes had panes of glass in window openings; others didn't. The financial condition of the family generally predicated whether or not windows had glass in them, though location affected the availability of such items. One woman in a California mining camp placed glass jars in the window opening to form a glass window of sorts. Women placed potted plants such as geraniums or cactus, and the aloe vera plant, which could be used as a salve on a burn, in their windows. Sometimes they built window boxes for plants.

Keeping flies, mosquitoes and other insects out of the house was a difficult task. After the 1870s manufactured screen was available to be placed over doors and windows, but like other goods, it became available in the West in stages,

Early cooks used open fireplaces, or even outdoor fire pits, but westerners obtained stoves. This stove was made by Chief National Excelsior Stove & Mfg. Co. in Quincy, Illinois, with a cast iron kettle, used to heat water for drinks or for washing, and with flat irons on the right (two with handles attached.) This stove is located in Virginia City, Montana.

with larger communities and areas near commercial centers having access to the materials before people in more rural locations.

Stoves/Fireplaces/Chimneys: Early settlers in Oregon continued to use outdoor fire pits or indoor open fireplaces for cooking from their arrival in the early 1840s until the early to mid-1850s, when they had the resources to purchase a stove for the house. During that period starting a fire didn't mean placing some shavings and sticks on a piece of paper and then lighting a match. It meant striking flint and steel together to throw a spark into the fire tinder. Matches, called "Lucifers," didn't always flame (particularly if they had gotten damp) and sometimes they'd explode spontaneously when handled roughly. Lucifers also cost a lot, roughly $.25 for a dozen. After the Civil War, safety matches, which would light only when struck on the box in which they came, became available, but not until late in the period were inexpensive matches widely available. Chinese matches also were available, at generally lower cost than Lucifers.

Because of the difficulty in starting a fire by throwing a spark from flint and steel, residents usually covered—or banked—the fire each evening in hopes there would still be enough coals the next day to set a new fire.

Lighting came from oil or kerosene lanterns such as these, or from candles. These lanterns belong to the author.

Common fuels were wood, if it was available, or corncobs, sunflower stalks, hay or grass and the hardened droppings of buffalo or cattle—called chips or the anthracite (coal) of the plains. In some areas settlers burned coal, which they dug from open seams in the ground. Cow chips burned hot, but quickly. It was necessary to constantly add fuel to the fire. As one Nebraska boy recalled the process: "Stoke the stove, get out the flour sack, stoke the stove, wash your hands, cut out the biscuits with the top of the baking-powder can, stoke the stove, wash your hands, put the pan of biscuits in the oven, keep on stoking the stove until the biscuits are done."

Cast-iron Franklin stoves, featuring a piece of sheet iron formed into a stove pipe and stuck through the roof, were common throughout the West. Some homes also had open fireplaces where cooking could be done, though most women preferred a stove, which they obtained as soon as they had resources to do so. The stove served the auxiliary purpose of heating the home in the winter. Since the stove made the home hot in the summer, cooking then was sometimes done outdoors over an open fire. Southwestern homes had a *horno*, a dome-shaped oven used for baking, located in front of the structure. Chimneys were often made of stones or rocks held together with mud as mortar.

Lighting: Candles were the most common type of lighting throughout the West during most of the period, though people used kerosene lamps and some had gas lamps during the latter part of the period. By very late in the period some urban areas had electricity.

Early beds often were little more than a few boards nailed together into a frame with ropes or rawhide stretched from side to side to form a place on which a bed tick and blankets could be placed. The coverings for this tie hack's bed include a patchwork quilt and a cowhide. They are part of the tie hack collection at the Grand Encampment Museum.

FURNISHINGS

Beds: In adobe houses of the Southwest mattresses made of wool and straw were folded and put against the wall for seating during the day; they were pulled out to be used as beds at night. Throughout the West some homes had beds comprised only of animal hides placed on the floor and a blanket to use as a covering. Chinese women and girls, particularly those who were slaves to either Chinese or American men, slept on rush mats. The number of people who shared a bed depended entirely upon how many beds were present and how many people needed a place to sleep. In Kansas in 1856, for instance, Miriam Davis Colt wrote they "fill the one bed lengthwise and crosswise" as the host family used a trundle bed and other guests "rolled in Indian blankets like silk worms in cocoons."

Many beds were roughly built of lumber, covered with a blanket and one pillow. Some later had bed ticks filled with straw, hay, wild grasses or, in rare instances, with feathers or down. The bed tick was often made of various kinds and colors of materials, scraps available from worn clothing or other items. Some people simply wrapped in blankets, quilts or comforters and lay upon the floor. Many families had one or two beds and an additional trundle bed, which could be slid under the main bed during the daytime to conserve space. In Palmyra, Utah, in 1856 settler Priscilla Evans had a bed made of timber with rawhide strips stretched across the frame onto which she placed bedding. In 1887 homesteader Howard Reude made a bed of hay. Concerns by some women that their children's ears or noses would freeze often led them to arise several times each night to be certain blankets covered all extremities of their youngsters. Beds often doubled as couches or chairs, particularly if a family had guests.

A rustic chair used by tie hacks, simply made with boards and few pegs or nails. From the tie hack collection of the Grand Encampment Museum.

Benches: Almost all Southwestern homes had benches, and they were often used in other areas of the West, too, because they could seat many people and were easily moved.

Chairs: Furniture could include wooden chairs with seats of rawhide. Many chairs were made of locally available wood such as hardwoods or pine, and sometimes they had rawhide stretched and woven for seats. This style was particularly popular in the Southwest. Simple chairs consisted of two interconnected flat boards roughly formed into an X with one upper portion of the X flattened to form a seat.

Chests and trunks: Used to haul items across the country to a new home in the West, chests became important items of furniture. They served as storage areas for clothing and other items and could be used as seats or chairs for visitors.

Cooking implements: Cast-iron pots, frying pans, Dutch ovens and spiders (pots with three short legs) were the most common types of cookware used in most parts of the West. They had been used by women and men when crossing the country on overland treks because the heavy metal held up well when used over open cookfires. Women could bake nearly anything in a Dutch oven, placing the oven on a bed of hot coals and putting more coals on top of the oven lid, which was specially designed with a heavy rim so the coals could be heaped over it providing more even heating within the Dutch oven. Once they'd set up housekeeping in a more permanent location, many women obtained a tin kitchen or reflector oven. It had a tin cylinder with an open back and shelves inside on which could be placed items to cook. A door could be opened to put food into the oven or to check for doneness.

Eventually most homes had stoves. Though the Franklin was one of

the most popular brands, stoves came from many different manufacturers. In 1859 a cooking stove could be obtained from C. Crosby and Company in Tumwater, Oregon, for $25. Women saw a change in cooking once they obtained a cookstove. Although cast-iron frying pans and even Dutch ovens could be used on stoves, most women started obtaining pots and pans specifically designed for use on stoves. Cast iron with an enameled coating, tinware varnished with a brilliant coating, and graniteware became more popular.

A small wood stove used for heating and limited cooking, part of the collection at the Grand Encampment Museum.

Couches: Few early residents had couches since there wasn't room for a large couch in a wagon headed West. But once railroads or ships started deliveries, residents obtained couches, often Victorian in style.

Cupboards: *Alacenas* (niches or cupboards) were used to store household articles such as clothes and dishes in adobe houses of the Southwest. In other areas open shelves, often built directly on the wall, served as cupboards. Women tacked scraps of material to the fronts of the shelves to hide the contents from view. Open shelves had sides, fronts and backs added to them as time and resources became available. Depending on circumstances, cupboards could also be freestanding so they could be placed anywhere in a home to provide storage for dishes and supplies.

Decorations: Japanese women decorated their homes carefully, placing Oriental vases, fans and jars in locations that had social or religious significance, but many American women in port cities used such items as Victorian bric-a-brac, placing the vases, jars or fans throughout their homes, not knowing or caring that placement of such items had any significance to Japanese people.

In small homes with poor lighting, a bit of color added much to a woman's life. "The gay colored quilts, which came across in a big chest, and which had been used as wrapping for a few cherished dishes and other treasures, were unpacked," wrote Lenore Gale Barette upon arrival in Oregon.

> Other bits from the old home three thousand miles away were placed on the crude shelves: a picture of grandmother's parents, a few books, the family Bible, the little treasures which had slipped between the bedding in an old chest and queer looking trunk lined with bright flowered paper.
>
> —Women's Voices From the Oregon Trail, *125.*

Dishes and Utensils: Like most other items, the kind and number of dishes varied greatly throughout the West. Most women had some pieces of fine china, often given to them by mothers or grandmothers, which they packed carefully when traveling and which often received honored places in new homes. When Bethenia Owens married in 1854, she had a few tin dishes, steel knives, two-tined forks, a cream jug, sugar bowl and a set of German silver teaspoons. She wrote:

> My cooking utensils were a pot, tea-kettle and bake oven (all iron), a frying pan and coffee pot, a churn, six milk pans, a wash tub and board, a large twenty or thirty gallon iron pot for washing purposes, etc., and a water bucket and tin dipper.

In 1877 homesteader Howard Ruede built himself a dugout in Kansas, and he put together the items he needed for keeping house. They included two iron pots, a tea kettle, two spiders (three-legged pots), three bread pans, two tin plates, a coffee pot, stove, tin wash boiler, coal oil can, three griddles, four tin cups, a steamer, a wash basin and a pepper box. Hooks near the fireplace served as a place to hang kettles, frying pans and other utensils.

Catharine E. Beecher and Harriet Beecher Stowe, in *The American Woman's Home or Principles of Domestic Science,* provide advice for homemakers on types of cookware. Necessary items included the following:

> Crockery—Brown earthen pans are said to be best for milk and for cooking. . . . Tall earthen jars, with covers, are good to hold butter, salt, lard, etc. . . .
>
> Iron Ware—A nest of iron pots, of different sizes, an iron hook with a handle used to lift pots from the crane; a Dutch oven; . . . two skillets, of different sizes, and a spider.
>
> Tin Ware—Bread-pans, large and small patty-pans; cake-pans, with a center tube to insure their baking well; pie-dishes . . . a covered butter-kettle; covered kettles to hold berries; two sauce pans; . . . an apple-corer, an apple-roaster; an egg-boiler; two sugar-scoops, and flour and meal-scoop; . . . a milk-strainer; a

gravy-strainer; a colander; a dredging-box; a pepper-box; a large and small grater. . . .

Wooden Ware—A nest of tubs; a set of pails and bowls; a large and small sieve; a beetle for mashing potatoes; a spade or stick for stirring butter and sugar; a bread-board for moulding bread and making pie-crust; . . . an egg-beater; a ladle for working butter; a bread-trough, . . . flour buckets with lids, to hold sifted flour and Indian meal.

Cooks used pie safes to store food (and cool pies). Butter churns and a clock sit atop this pie safe, with a large crockery jug beside it. This pie safe is in the W.T. Peryam homestead house at the Grand Encampment Museum.

Pie Safes: Materials from packing crates and other wooden boxes and pieces of tin were joined to form a pie safe. Builders often punched holes forming designs into the tin, which served an artistic purpose in homes usually devoid of much art. The holes also allowed air to circulate through the cabinet while at the same time preventing bugs and flies from reaching food items stored within. Often the legs of a pie safe sat in small containers of kerosene or water, which kept ants from getting into the safe, though the liquid soaked into the wooden legs.

Shelves: The first storage area for many western homes was often a set of open shelves, generally made of crates in which posessions had been moved. Onto them women placed their fine china, which often consisted of only a few pieces.

Tables: Packing boxes covered with printed material or muslin served as small dressing tables. Tables used for preparing or serving food were often handmade and usually included a small drawer for storage of utensils. Oregon housewife Jane Pattison made her table by boring holes into the floor boards "in which we fixed two upright sticks cut from the woods; on these I put some boards, letting one end extend out through a crack between the logs [of the wall, with the board extending to the outside edge of the wall] and so we had a table."

SANITATION/PRIVACY AND BATHING HABITS

Outdoor toilets, called privies, were common throughout the West and throughout the period. In homes that generally had no running water, bathing itself was a luxury, often accomplished only once a week by dragging a round or sometimes an oblong tin tub into the kitchen and filling it with heated water. Generally the entire family used the same bath water, adding some between individuals to keep it adequately warm.

Alaskan natives took fire baths where they sat in rooms filled with dry, hot air; the Russians introduced to natives the practice of taking a steam bath by splashing water on hot rocks to create steam.

Families that lived in one-room houses had little privacy, though often a blanket or sheet would be draped across a corner to separate sleeping areas. Children and even adolescents generally shared whatever bed was available, and often an entire family used the same bed.

At boardinghouses and stage stations people generally slept wherever they could find a place; strangers of the same sex often shared beds, wrapping themselves separately in blankets.

ADDITIONAL READING

Barlow, Ronald S. *Victorian Houseware: Hardware and Kitchenware*. El Cajon, Calif.: Windmill Publishing Company, 1992. An excellent reference.

Bosomworth, Dorothy. *The Victorian Catalogue of Household Goods*. New York: Portland House, 1991. Originally published as *The Illustrated Catalogue of Furniture and Household Requisites*, Silber and Flemming, 1883.

Brown, William L., III. *The Army Called It Home: Military Interiors of the 19th Century*. Gettysburg, Pa.: Thomas Publications, 1992. A good reference.

Ferrero, Pat, Elaine Hedges, and Julie Silber. *Hearts and Hands: The Influence of Women & Quilts on American Society*. San Francisco: The Quilt Digest Press, 1987.

Luchetti, Cathy, and Carol Olwell. *Women of the West*. New York: Orion Books, 1982. An excellent reference.

Miller, N., E. Langsdorf, and R. Richmond. *Kansas: A Pictorial History*. Kansas State Historical Society, 1961.

Neiderman, Sharon. *A Quilt of Words*. Boulder, Colo.: Johnson Publishing, 1988.

Root, Waverly, and Richard de Rochemont. *Eating in America: A History*. New York: The Ecco Press, 1976.

Seymour, John. *Forgotten Household Crafts: A Portrait of the Way We Once Lived*. New York: Alfred A. Knopf, 1987.

Williams, Jacqueline B. *The Way We Ate: Pacific Northwest Cooking 1843-1900*. Pullman: Washington State University Press, 1996.

CHAPTER TEN

MARRIAGE AND FAMILY

T he limited number of women in the West during the early part of the period had a profound effect on courtship and marriage as values that were traditional in more settled areas became less important than finding a mate and companionship. The first Euro-American men who moved into the region came as explorers and trappers, and they often established relations with Native American women, sometimes taking the women as their wives in Indian ceremonies. Miners who emigrated to the region found few women with whom they could share a relationship. In some cases the men returned to their former home area, met a woman and married, then again went to the West; other times they obtained a mate by writing letters to women whose photos they had seen passed around by friends and neighbors.

For men, finding a woman was difficult; for women, finding a man was something about which they could be very choosy, because there were a great many more men than women in the West, which may have contributed to a high divorce rate there throughout the period.

COURTING

Customs for courting in the West varied somewhat between cultures. Native American courtship had much ritual associated with it and greatly varied from tribe to tribe, so when writing about Indian courting, it is necessary to research the *specific* tribe.

Hispanic courtship revolved around the practices of the Catholic church in large part and around the long-standing traditions of the people themselves. Often young Hispanic women attended social functions with chaperones or their parents. There a man might show his interest in a woman by placing his hat on her head during a dance. If she wore the hat, she showed her mutual interest in him, or she could toss it aside to let him know she wasn't interested. Such activities took place at fandangos, which were social gatherings involving dancing, music and food, and at weddings, or at other social events.

In general, courting in the West occurred when girls were likely older than those courting in the East; many didn't marry until they were in their early twenties. Public displays of affection, while not overly demonstrative, were allowed, such as kissing at cornhusking bees. Courting had a few different twists in the West, particularly during the early part of the period when men far outnumbered women.

> Massachusetts has 37,000 more females than males, while California has 67,000 more males than females, and Illinois 92,000 more males than females.—FLIN, *January 17, 1863, 259-2*

> Everybody knows what a capital paper the California *Farmer* is— who would have thought its editor could be so hard up! 'A Rare Opportunity—Col. Warren, of the *Farmer*, says he will divide the emoluments of his paper with any capable lady who will take a permanent seat in his sanctum and "do up" the scissoring department of that journal. The Colonel is a trifle over twenty-four years of age, wears spectacles solely for the preservation of his eyes, neither squints nor uses tobacco, admires flowers, 'tater patches, ladies and large pumpkins, and is the owner of a double-edged rapier and a military uniform with two rows of buttons on each side.'—FLIN, *March 5, 1859, 209-1*

Mail-Order/Picture Brides

One way for men to meet women was through subscriptions to heart-and-hand clubs. The men received newspapers with information, and sometimes photographs, about women, with whom they corresponded. Eventually, a man might convince a woman to join him in the West, and in matrimony. In such cases he often sent a railroad ticket to the woman so she could make the journey, and they married without ever really having spent any time together. Other men found mates as picture brides. Perhaps they saw the photo of a friend's sister or cousin and then invited the girl to join them in marriage. Picture-bride practices were especially popular among Asian and Greek men who wanted to marry someone from their own culture.

Eliza W. Farnham organized the California Association of American Women in 1849, in an effort to encourage women to travel to California where they could meet men and marry. Her efforts, which had only limited success as only two women accompanied her to the region, preceded those of Asa Mercer, who organized two different trips to convey women to Washington where they could become brides to the men living there. On his second trip Mercer married one of the approximately one hundred women who accompanied him. The need for women to move into the West is evidenced by these reports from *Frank Leslie's Illustrated Newspaper.*

> There is a great demand for wives in Washington Territory. On the 28th of February there was to be a meeting of bachelors to devise ways and means to supply the matrimonial market with a supply of those lively, affectionate, and industrious serving machines called women.—*April 14, 1860, 305-3*

> Three-fifths of the adult white population of California are men without wives. Four out of every five white men are bachelors, and from necessity; for while there are 183,856 men in the state there are only 48,149 white women.—*August 20, 1864, 338-4*

> Young men in Lawrence, Kansas, have to marry to get shelter from the weather, the landladies there take none but married people. The unfortunate youths say it is a consparcy [*sic*] between the young ladies and the boarding-house keepers.—*November 4, 1865, 99-1*

> They are badly off for unmarried women 'out West.' At Sioux City, Iowa, fifteen hundred of them are 'wanted' immediately to serve in the double capacity of 'wives and mothers.'—*August 7, 1869, 327-4*

Throughout the period when a man pledged his love to, and his interest in, a woman, he was expected to carry through and marry her as these references from *Frank Leslie's Illustrated Newspapers* show:

> Broken love pledges are rising in value, and if juries continue to look upon the matter in the light they do at present, faithless lovers will cease to exist. Miss Frances Hobson of Cincinnati, recently received $3,300 from Asa H. Cone for breach of promise. —*March 17, 1860, 245-3*

> The daughter of a well-known commission merchant of Chicago has initiated a suit against a prominent physician for breach of promise of marriage—damages $25,000. Another young lady in Chardon, Wis., has just received a healing plaster for her broken heart in the shape of a verdict of $10,000 damages against the gay deceiver.—*January 9, 1864, 243-3*

> In Texas men in love are justified in stealing horses. A jury in Texas lately acquitted a man on the charge of horse stealing, although the crime was clearly proven against him, simply because he stole the horse to elope with his sweetheart, who was present in the court during the trial, and waiting to marry him if acquitted. —*March 24, 1860, 257-3*

MARRIAGE

Women in the West tended to court and marry at a later age than did those in the eastern and southern parts of the country. Though Victorian influences spread into the West, couples engaged in premarital sex, particularly during the latter portion of the period. Many did marry once a woman was pregnant, particularly among conservative Euro-American people, even though often the baby came within just a few months (or hours) of the marriage ceremony.

> A couple came from Ohio, arriving in Leavenworth a few days since, and were married about noon. At 8 o'clock in the evening a bouncing boy weighing ten and a half pounds, was born to the blooming bride of less than ten hours.
> —Sumner County Press, *Wellington, Kansas, January 8, 1874*

In a large number of cases, particularly early in the period, men and women never even met personally until the time of the wedding, due to their making arrangements through the mail. Among Spanish-speaking people, Jewish people, European immigrants and some Native American tribes, marriages were arranged by parents or guardians, often betrothing a girl at about age thirteen, or when she reached puberty.

> He was married a short time to a girl only 13 years old. It is against the law for girls to marry under 15, but her age was given older and then the priest will marry them if they pay extra. The young man had to pay $15.—*New Mexican settler Mary L. Stright*

> A Texas couple eloped on horseback, accompanied by a clergyman. They were pursued by the bride's father, and the minister performed the marriage ceremony at full gallop.
> —FLIN, *July 23, 1870, 295-4*

Once they were married, a couple retired for the night at an inn, hotel or other lodging property, or perhaps at their own home or the home of one of their families. When they'd settled for the night, friends paid them a call in a chivaree. Both men and women participated in chivaree parties by clanging bells, banging drums or pans and generally creating a racket. At the couple's place of abode for the night, the chivaree party pounded on the door and demanded to be let in to celebrate. Sometimes a bridegroom could give the crowd money and entice the revelers to celebrate elsewhere, but often they captured him and "kidnapped" him away for the evening. Some chivarees had violence associated with them as visitors shot holes through windows, broke down the door and ripped open feather mattresses.

Following a wedding in Kansas Territory, the couple, according to the White Cloud *Chief* on September 10, 1857, was "saluted with yelling, screaming, and hammering on all manner of tin pans and buckets. In the night a crowd proceeded to the house where the happy young pair was roosting, after they had

POLYGAMY

In 1847 when members of the Church of Jesus Christ of Latter-day Saints (the Mormons) emigrated from Nauvoo, Illinois, to establish a new Zion in the Great Salt Lake Valley, some members already engaged in the practice of polygamy—the taking of more than one wife—though they did so rather discreetly at that time. The practice of polygamy started April 5, 1841, when Mormon Church founder, Joseph Smith, took as his second wife Louisa Beaman. Formal written notice of polygamy came on July 12, 1843, when Smith privately dictated a sanction for church members to engage in polygamy. Although most church members initially opposed polygamy, the leaders, believing it was necessary to their salvation, followed Smith's dictate and started to engage in the practice. Their actions became open after 1852 when polygamy was recognized by Mormon leader Brigham Young in Great Salt Lake City.

During the period 1841 to 1852, the Mormons used the terms "spiritual wife" and "spiritual wife system" to refer to polygamous marriages. After 1852 they replaced the term with "celestial marriage." The two terms referred to the same practice. Throughout the period Mormon women believed they had to allow and engage in polygamous marriages to ensure their own salvation and in some cases to preserve their marriages. The 1882 Edmunds Act was the first time action was taken against polygamists. Polygamy continued openly until March 3, 1887, when Congress passed the Edmunds-Tucker Act outlawing the practice and placing other sanctions on the Mormons; even then the LDS Church did not have any opposition to polygamy. On October 6, 1890, the Mormon president announced at General Conference that henceforth polygamy would neither be condoned nor practiced by the church. Some individuals, however, continued the practice.

A sampling of articles from *Frank Leslie's Illustrated Newspaper* highlights some of the details provided to the nation regarding polygamy during the period.

> Considerable commotion exists in Utah, in consequence of an attempt to abduct a saint's wife, that is to say, take a young girl from a hoary villain by the power of the law, and at the request of her mother. Although Judge Drake decided the case against the Mormon scamp, the wretched girl was so lost in her sin, that she refused to obey the mandate, and was carried off by her seducer amid the triumphant cheers of the populace. The Cincinnati *Times* says, when Jeff Davis and rebellion are put down, the same wholesome process must be adopted to Brigham Young and polygamy.—*June 13, 1863, 178-4*

> A company of 43 women recently attempted to flee from the bonds of Mormonism in Utah, but they were overtaken and carried back to their lords and masters.—*February 25, 1865, 355-3*

A Salt Lake letter states that the Mormon leaders proclaim that they will sustain polygamy by force of arms, and defy openly the authority of the Federal Government. The Hon. Schuyler Colfax, in a recent letter in Chicago, said he was at a loss how to deal with the evils of Mormonism. He spoke of United States officials, even, in the territory of the Mormons who had several wives.
—*December 2, 1865, 63-2*

The Salt Lake *Vidette* says; 'We have information from good authority, that Brigham Young recently announced, in grand council, his unalterable determination to stand or fall by polygamy. It was ordered that all church officials should forthwith be instructed to promulgate this fact, and urge by every means the entrance in plurality at once of all persons who desire to hold good standing in the church. Immediate compliance was to be required, and those who failed or refused were to be informed that the church disowned them—all must become polygamists, or be no longer recognized as among the faithful.
—*April 14, 1866, 51-1*

Eighteen indictments were found by the Grand Jury of Utah for Polygamy.—*September 7, 1874, 133-4*

stowed themselves away for the night. They entered the house, seized the bridegroom, and dragged him out amid the firing of guns and the yelling of the crowd. They were taking him in chemise to a creek nearby to duck him, but were bought off by the promise of a treat on the morrow."

Early in the period slaves living in Texas, Arkansas and Indian Territory married freemen or freewomen, or other slaves if allowed by their owners. Many slave marriages took place by having the couple jump over a broomstick together.

Mormons living first in Illinois and later in Utah practiced different forms of marriage, including celestial marriage and plural marriage or polygamy. The Church of Jesus Christ of Latter-day Saints assumed controls over marriages, with church elders handling both marriage and divorce proceedings at a time when other areas of the West abandoned the principle of "reading the banns" and issued marriage licenses instead. Wrote Arizona resident Mary Annetta Coleman Pomeroy:

In September 1884, we decided to enter into the order of celestial marriage and started to St. George. Lucretia Phelps was the woman my husband chose. It was a great trial to me. Nobody but one who is in it knows the many heartaches which one goes through while living that order.

In the LDS church, a marriage could be recognized by approval of church officials, and individuals could be "sealed" to each other so that their marriage kept them together not only in life, but also after death. Such "sealing" occurred during ceremonies conducted in church temples. Mormons also endorsed polygamy believing they would reach a higher level of Heaven if they had more dependents on earth. The Reorganized Church of Jesus Christ of Latter-Day Saints, a splinter group of the main church, never condoned polygamy.

> Tax on Matrimony—The Commissioner of Internal Revenue has decided that all marriage certificates must bear a 10 cent stamp in order to be valid. He does not tell us who is to pay it, the 'happy man' or the parson. The Mormons have their women 'sealed' to them, Under the Boutwell dispensation they must be 'stamped.'
> —FLIN, *November 15, 1862, 115-1*

DIVORCE

In part due to the fact that the West had a disproportionate number of men and women, marriages were often dissolved by women when they felt abused, or were physically or verbally abused by their husbands. Native Americans had liberal attitudes regarding divorce. If a man and a woman didn't get along with each other, they divorced and went their own ways without recrimination from each other or from other tribal members. A woman could either leave her husband's lodge and return to her parent's home, or in matrilineal societies, where the couple lived with her family, a woman could simply place her husband's belongings outside the door indicating their marriage was over and that he needed to find another place to live. In some tribes the Indian man had to find a new husband for her if he divorced his wife.

Euro-Americans in the West, for the most part, also allowed divorce without much difficulty, though Spanish-speaking people and those who were of the Catholic faith generally didn't endorse absolute divorce. As a result of liberal attitudes there were far more divorces in the West than in other regions of the country during the period from 1870 to 1900.

Mormons, who practiced polygamy, also believed they could allow divorces, and Mormon leaders routinely dissolved marriages (most of them polygamous in the first place) when men and women failed to resolve differences. Often a church leader released a man or woman from marriage and soon thereafter united the same man or woman in marriage to someone else. An 1852 Utah territorial law allowed courts to grant divorces as well. The law included as grounds for divorce adultery, impotence, habitual drunkenness, inhuman treatment, willful desertion for a one-year period and a clause noting that a marriage could be dissolved if "the parties cannot live in peace and union together." The Utah divorce law was so liberal it was possible for people to apply for, and receive, a divorce in one day's time.

Judge McKean of Utah ordered Brigham Young to pay Eliza Ann Young $3,000 attorney fees and $9,500 alimony pending her suit for divorce.—FLIN, *March 13, 1875, 7-4*

In Sacramento recently a woman procured the release of her husband from jail, and that night ran off with another fellow. Her object in procuring her husband's release was to leave somebody with the children.—FLIN, *October 31, 1865, 67-3*

Among the bills recently passed by the Missouri Legislature are these: Providing that any person whose husband or wife has been engaged in the rebellion against the United States shall be entitled to a divorce on proper application to the courts. —FLIN, *March 11, 1865, 387-2*

Getting a divorce under false pretenses has caused an Illinois minister to be reduced to the ranks.—FLIN, *June 25, 1870, 235-4*

Indiana has nearly cleared off her state debt by means of divorce fees.—FLIN, *August 20, 1870, 359-4*

BIRTH

Western Euro-American families during the period tended to be large, or at least involve the births of large numbers of children. It wasn't uncommon for any western, and particularly rural, family to have six or eight children even though national averages showed only 5.42 births by 1850, and 4.24 births by 1880. There are several reasons why western families had so many children: A lack of widespread information about and use of birth control, high infant mortality rates and the need for workers to help with farm and household labor. Though a woman may give birth to many children, chances were several of them would die of disease or accidents before they became adults. Mormons had large families believing it to be their responsibility to have children and thus give spiritual beings an earthly body.

Birth-control methods during the period were limited. Women used such methods as douching, a contraceptive sponge, and a pessary made of wood, cotton or sponge and known colloquially as a "pisser." Placement of a rubber cap over the uterus was also used. Condoms made of sheep or pig intestines were used, but they tended to be expensive ($1 each) so men washed them for repeated uses. In the last portion of the period, rubber condoms costing as little as $.06 to $.12 became available. Likely the most common form of birth control and, besides abstinence, the only morally acceptable choice during the period, was the rhythm method. Women also used abortifacient powders and folk remedies such as pulverized ergot, tansy root, rue root, and water made of rusty nails and aloe. Other abortifacients—some effective, some not—were hot water douches, alcohol or sulfate of zinc, ice water and even cocoa butter.

Most births occurred at home with a midwife in attendance, although often the father or an older child assisted. Sometimes women had no help in bearing their children, a case particularly true amongst some Native American tribes. Doctors generally were called only in difficult births and often after it was too late to save the baby and the mother.

Women noted their husbands might allow a pregnant cow to graze in a pasture for a month prior to giving birth, giving the cow a chance to rest, while she was expected to cook, clean and take care of her family and hired hands up until the moment of birth, resuming her activities sometimes within hours, and almost certainly within days, of the birth.

Many families during the period did not immediately name a new baby, rather they often waited weeks or even months to do so. Native American children received several names. Their first name was given when they were small, but as they grew they received new names, often reflecting a trait they had or some incident in their lives.

DEATH

Deaths were common among all age groups due to a number of factors ranging from illness to accident. The death rate for children was particularly high throughout most of the period. The leading causes of death on the overland trails were illnesses such as cholera and accidents, particularly those with guns and other weapons, although people also died following accidents with wagons, especially children who fell under wagon wheels.

When a death occurred, the body was generally bathed, dressed and placed in a cool room with the windows opened to cool the body. Burial might take place in a town or area cemetery, but just as likely interment was on the property of the deceased. In the case of travelers on the various overland trails, burial was often in the trail itself and wagons were driven over the grave to conceal its presence from marauding Indians and wolves, both of which were known to dig up a grave. As Susan Magoffin reported on the Santa Fe Trail:

> The grave is dug very deep, the corpse rolled in a blanket, lowered and stones put over it, the earth and sod replaced and well beat down after a corral is made over it to make the earth still more firm by the tromping of the stock. The Mexicans always place a cross on the grave.
> —*Dr. Thomas B. Hall,* Medicine on the Santa Fe Trail, *106*

In other situations when there wasn't a hearse available, the body in its coffin would be transported to the graveyard in a lumber wagon or other type of wagon. At times the lines from the team's harness were used to lower the coffin into the grave.

> Of the one hundred and seventy-five deaths that occurred in St. Louis last week, one hundred and twenty-five were those of children under five years. What a community on the misery regime.
> —FLIN, *September 29, 1860, 293-1*

> The Deseret *News* announces the death of Peeteenet, chief of the Utah Indians, on the 23d of January, and adds: 'No horses were killed on the occasion, as is generally the case when an Indian of distinction dies, but a novel and brutal ceremony, by his express order, was instituted instead, and that was the killing of his wife, who was despatched by beating out her brains with an axe, a squaw being the executioner. The chief was buried after the manner of Indian sepulture [*sic*] in the mountains adjacent, and his murdered wife in the valley beneath.'—FLIN, *March 1, 1852, 231-1*

ADDITIONAL READING

Foster, Lawrence. *Women, Family and Utopia: Communal Experiments of the Shakers, the Oneida Community, and the Mormons.* Syracuse: Syracuse University Press, 1991. Good information on Mormon family life, particularly the polygamous pratices.

Hall, Dr. Thomas B. *Medicine on the Santa Fe Trail.* Dayton, Ohio: Morningside Bookshop, 1971.

Long, Francis A. *A Prairie Doctor of the Eighties.* Norfolk, Nebr.: Huse Publishing Company, 1937. Out of print, but generally available in libraries.

Luchetti, Cathy. *I Do! Courtship, Love and Marriage on the American Frontier.* New York: Crown Trade Paperbacks, 1996. An excellent resource including diaries, journals and photographs and covering the time period 1715-1915.

Riley, Glenda. *Building and Breaking Families In the American West.* Albuquerque: University of New Mexico Press, 1996. An excellent resource.

———. *Divorce: An American Tradition.* New York: Oxford University Press, 1991. An excellent resource with detailed statistics.

CHAPTER ELEVEN

DOCTORS, DENTISTS AND MEDICINE

ome of the earliest Euro-American doctors in the West were missionary doctors such as Dr. Marcus Whitman (1836), Dr. Elijah White (1841), and Father Anthony Ravelli, who first performed mouth-to-mouth resuscitation on an Indian woman in 1857 at St. Mary's Mission in present-day Montana.

Following the missionary doctors were military doctors and those who accompanied exploring parties. Lewis and Clark had no doctor with them on their journey through the West in 1804 through 1806; however, they themselves had been schooled in homeopathic medicine techniques. Later expeditions did routinely have a doctor as a member of the party.

Military doctors accompanied various troop movements in the West and were stationed at forts throughout the region as well. Though their primary function was to see to the medical needs of the men of the frontier army, military doctors also treated soldiers' and officers' wives, other civilians and Indians. Military doctors had the use of field ambulances after 1859, though the conveyances most often were in use as pleasure vehicles for officers and their families. When a military unit moved from one location to another, the officers' wives most often made the trip inside a military ambulance.

Though there were some trained physicians in the West, much of the area relied on the knowledge and common sense of individuals who had no formal training. They had learned by doing or by watching someone else practice medicine. In the West a person could be a doctor if he or she said so; whether or not he or she had any training was irrelevant. California had a medical practice law in 1866 and Texas was the first state to establish a board of medical examiners, doing so in 1873.

Western medical schools included the Medical Department of the University of the Pacific, founded in 1859 and which became the Cooper Medical School and ultimately Stanford University School of Medicine. The Toland Medical school opened in San Francisco in 1864 (forerunner to the University of California Medical School). The Medical Department of Willamette University in Salem, Oregon, started in 1867.

Some areas of the West had provisions for doctors to register with local county clerks before establishing a practice, but such regulations weren't uniformly enforced until late in the period. Doctors established a practice by settling in an area, opening an office (sometimes in a pharmacy or drug store also owned by the doctor) and hanging up a sign or putting an advertisement in the local newspaper. Doctors carried leather satchels or placed their medical supplies in saddlebags. After the Civil War their medical kits often were army surplus instruments in velvet-lined field cases.

The doctors who did settle in the West were generally well regarded by other residents, and the doctors had many responsibilities in most communities. They held public office and owned and operated businesses ranging from transportation or freighting companies to banks and stores. They were able to become so involved in part because they sometimes had better educations than did the average western citizen and therefore were held in high esteem.

Doctors received pay in a variety of ways. Sometimes they received cash, but often as not it came in the form of traded labor, or goods ranging from chickens, pigs, cows or horses to garden produce, hay or other items.

During the period there were four types of medicine as Robert Karolevitz puts it in *Doctors of the Old West:* "The homeopaths administered their tiny doses; the allopaths purged their patients drastically; the hydropaths bathed and dunked; and the eclectics borrowed a little from each."

All four types of medicine were practiced by "horse and buggy" doctors, the men and women who took their talents to outlying homes and ranches, often traveling in blizzards or other inclement weather in order to treat a patient. Some early doctors rode horses to make their calls, but as soon as they were able, most obtained a cart, buggy or wagon because in it they could carry more supplies and travel also was a bit more comfortable. In most cases the doctors had with them their medical supplies and a lantern, and perhaps a shovel (for digging through snowdrifts) and a hammer and wire cutters (for getting through fences). In later years some doctors used bicycles to make town calls, figuring they could reach their patients more quickly if they didn't have to first harness a team. The male doctors of the 1880s and 1890s generally wore side-whiskers and dressed well, wearing Prince Albert coats.

Summoning the doctor was a process all its own. Generally, someone either ran or rode a horse to the doctor's house to tell him he was needed at a certain location. During the latter half of the period some doctors had telephone service, but that was generally restricted to urban areas. There was a well-established prairie grapevine, however, so word generally traveled fairly quickly by word of mouth or signals such as flags, lighted lanterns or pieces of cloth hung outside.

Though the military had ambulances, such conveyances were seldom available in most parts of the West during the early portion of the period. By the latter half of the era, however, ambulances might be used in cities which also had hospitals. In other areas the undertaker generally provided such services, driving a wagon pulled by white horses for ambulance calls and black horses for funerals.

Probably the longest trip ever taken by a ambulance/hearse was the one Dr. William Keil arranged for his son Willie. The doctor's nineteen-year-old son died shortly before Dr. Keil led a party of people across the Oregon Trail to settle in a communal community at Aurora, Oregon, in 1855. Dr. Keil had promised Willie he would go to Oregon, and go he did, in a lead-lined, whiskey-filled casket placed in an ambulance wagon/hearse specially made for the trip.

During the 1880s the Odd Fellows had a provision in their bylaws requiring members to "sit up" with other members who were ill.

MEDICINES

Dr. Francis A. Long in his Madison, Nebraska, practice in 1882 used these twelve remedies: bismuth, Dover's Powder, morphine, podophyllin, mercury with chalk, compound cathartic pills, bromide of potassium, tincture aconite, calomel, fluid extract of ergot, tincture belladonna and tincture hydrastis. He had a pocket case of instruments, obstetric forceps, a fever thermometer, a pony to ride and a pair of saddlebags in which he carried his supplies.

A common practice for curing ills during the latter portion of the period involved taking baths in mineral hot springs. Such springs were located throughout the West and they advertised cure-alls from soaking in, and sometimes from drinking, the waters. An advertisement for Utah Hot Springs, eight miles north of Ogden, claimed: "These waters have proven a perfect specific for Rheumatism, Cataarh, Syphilis, Leading, Diabetes or any urinary affection, and the treatment of many Female diseases, has proven the efficacy of these thermal waters from the vast amount of iron they contain."

> About sixty miles from Houston, in Texas, . . . is a small lake, whose diameter may be counted by rods, the waters of which are so sour that it is almost impossible to drink them. A number of wells have been dug in the immediate vicinity, and the waters of these contain iron, alum, magnesium and sulphuric acid. . . . Large numbers of invalids go there from Southern States to drink the water of the wells and bathe in the lake and they experience immediate and remarkable benefit. The effect of the baths is sedative, and persons who have not slept comfortably for weeks, after taking a bath in the lake in the evening enjoy a refreshing night's rest.
> —FLIN, *October 12, 1867, 51-4*

DENTISTS

Few dentists practiced in the West during the period, so people who had need of a tooth extraction or other dental work often went to the doctor, or even to the druggist, for such services. One of the better known dentists was Doc Holliday, though he is generally recalled because of his association with the Earps during their days in Tombstone, Arizona, and the subsequent gun battle they fought there at the OK Corral, than he is for dealing with dental problems. However, Holliday did work at his profession in various locations in the West. Throughout most of the period there was little thought to treating a sore tooth in any way other than removing it.

> TEETH—EXTRACTING WITH LITTLE OR NO PAIN—Tincture of aconite, choloroform, and alcohol of each 1 oz.; morphine, 6 [grams]. Mix. MANNER OF APPLICATION.—Moisten two pledgets of cotton with the liquid and apply to the gums on each side of the tooth to be extracted, holding them to their place with pliers or some other convenient instrument for 5 to 15 minutes rubbing the gum freely inside and out.—*A.W. Chase,* Dr. Chase's Recipes, *187*

MIDWIVES

Doctors were not available in all situations, so often the "doctoring" fell to someone, likely a woman, who had some practical knowledge. Midwives attended many childbirths throughout the period, and in rural areas neighbor women assisted at births or fathers or older children handled the necessary duties. Infant mortality was high throughout most of the period. Western women in their writings make few references to childbirth, and when they do so, the comments are generally vague. Of the birth of her daughter in 1890, Arizona settler Mary Annetta Coleman Pomeroy wrote, "A wee little lady came to take her abode with us."

Women traveling the overland trails to California, Oregon, Utah and other areas walked or rode in the wagons up until the time they gave birth, then they soon resumed their journey. Sometimes the wagons halted for a day when a baby was born, but that wasn't always the case.

PRIMARY DISEASES/TREATMENTS

Ague (Malaria or Chills): Treated with quinine, Dr. Sappington's Anti-Malarial Pills or Dover's Powders.

Antiseptic: Products included carbolic acid (introduced by Joseph Lister in 1867). Dr. R.P.R. Gordon in Montana used turpentine as an antiseptic.

Asthma: Treated with buttercup tea.

Bleeding: Home remedies called for using wood ashes or cobwebs to staunch the flow of blood. People also put gunpowder or flour on cuts to staunch bleeding.

Blood Letting: In common use throughout the period as doctors believed the way to cure a patient was to purge, blister and bleed. If blood couldn't be produced directly because a patient was too weak, doctors might apply a blood-sucking leech instead and leeches were regularly sold at drugstores.

Blood Impurities: Treated with sulphur and molasses.

Boils: "Ripened" by using bacon rind, or poultices of bread and milk; warm, fresh cow manure; or mashed potatoes.

Bowels, Inflammation of: Treated with opiate to reduce pain; enemas and "salts" such as magnesium sulfate given hourly until the bowels moved.

Bruises or Sprains: Treated with the dried flower heads of arnica.

Burns: Treated with a poultice of slippery elm and Indian meal; a salve of turpentine, sweet oil, and beeswax; the natural salve from the aloe vera plant; a salve made from chamomile, sweet clover and the inner bark of sweet elder trees, mixed with mutton tallow and beeswax; or a mixture made from the white of an egg and lard.

Childbirth: Doctors in Nebraska in the 1880s were taught to wash their hands with soap and water prior to delivering a child, and they lubricated the examining hand with soap, petroleum jelly or unsalted lard. The standard price for an infant delivery (confinement) in Madison, Nebraska, in 1880 was $10, with a $1 fee for a doctor's visit in town either day or night.

Cholera and Asiatic Cholera: Outbreaks occurred in several different years with the most serious ones in 1849 and 1852. Treated with red pepper in whiskey or brandy, or burning barrels of pine tar beneath open windows (though that had no real effect.) In 1849 on the Santa Fe Trail, Dr. Burchard gave pills compounded of camphor, cayenne pepper, opium and calomel or rectal injections of a medicine made from sugar of lead, laudanum and gum arabica. A cholera tincture involved the mixture of pulverized cinnamon bark, cloves and gum guaiac with brandy and then taken in teaspoon or tablespoon dosages every one to four hours. Nature's cholera medicine, according to Dr. A.W. Chase, was a mixture of equal amounts of laudanum, spirits of camphor and tincture of rhubarb given in one tablespoon doses every fifteen to thirty minutes. In 1883 it became known that the disease was waterborne and could be controlled through purification of water.

Cholera Infantum: One of the most fatal diseases affecting infants. Causes diarrhea and vomiting.

Colds: Treated with mullein plant made into candy.

Consumption: The commonly used name for tuberculosis during the period. A disease affecting many people who moved to the West believing the drier climate would help them. For treatment Dr. A.W. Chase recommended use of a syrup made from tamarack bark, spikenard root, dandelion root, hops, honey and brandy. Dr. Chase wrote:

> I shall now throw in a few thoughts of my own, and from the experience of many others in the profession, which I hope may benefit all, needing light on the subject.
>
> First, then—Do not go South, to smother and die; but go North, for cool, fresh air, hunt, fish, and eat freely of the roasted game; cast away care. . . . Take a healthy, faithful friend with you, to lean upon when needed, in your rambles. . . .
>
> For females who have families and cannot leave them, gardening will be the best substitute for the travel. . . .
>
> Lastly, those who are already far down the consumptive track, and confined at home, will derive much benefit by using, at each meal, half a pint of rich, fresh cream. In *all* cases it is ahead of Cod-Liver Oil, with *none* of its disagreeableness. And if it can be borne, a table-spoon of the best brandy may be added.

Contagious Diseases: Dr. Francis A. Long in Nebraska wore a linen duster to the homes of patients with contagious diseases. At his own home he had a closet in the barn where he kept a "special basin, sublimate tablets, carbolic acid, and soap and towels." In the barn he removed his linen duster and carefully washed in order to limit the spread of disease.

Cough: Treated with onion syrup or paregoric (a mixture of opium and camphor). To promote expectoration doctors used carbonate of ammonia or muriate. They also used a mixture of equal parts of linseed oil, honey and Jamaica rum.

Croup: Treated with skunk grease.

Cuts: Stitched together with a household needle and fiddle string or some other type of thread.

Diarrhea: Treated with a cordial mixture of pulverized rhubarb root, peppermint leaf and capsicum allowed to steep in boiling water then strained and mixed with bicarbonate of potash, essence of cinnamon, brandy or good whiskey and sugar. Another cure for chronic diarrhea involved a mixture of new milk, slippery elm, sweet oil, molasses, salt and laudanum to be injected directly into the bowels. Some people used paregoric.

Diphtheria: Also called Putrid Sore Throat. There was no antitoxin throughout the period so a severe case usually resulted in death. Epidemics broke out nearly every year, usually in late fall and early winter. Doctors applied a solution of nitrate of silver to the throat or swabbed it with tincture of iodine. They also had patients gargle or spray their throats with chlorate of potassium or with hydrogen peroxide. They boiled pine tar in water and patients inhaled the fumes and steam. To deodorize and disinfect, doctors used chloride of lime in water placed under the patient's bed. They boiled sulphur or powdered brimstone in limewater and dropped it into a patient's nostrils with a quill. Folk medicine involved the use of mashed snails and earthworms in water. Dr. Phonney of Boston recommended a "remedy" of black snakeroot used as a gargle and as a rub on ailing patients. In 1883 Klebs discovered the diphtheria bacillus; in 1884 Löffler demonstrated it was the cause of diphtheria. In 1889 Von Behring and Roux developed a diphtheria antitoxin which became widely available after 1894. The first antitoxin was used in north Nebraska in 1895.

> Diphtheria is a very troublesome and dangerous disease. A very easy remedy has been found for it that will effect a speedy relief. Take a common tobacco-pipe, place a live coal in the bowl, drop a little tar upon the coal, draw the smoke into the mouth, and discharge it through the nostrils.—FLIN, *September 2, 1865, 371-3*

Fevers: Doctors used coal tar derivatives as sleep producers. People also treated fevers with sassafras tea and used aconite to control them. Dr. A.W. Chase in 1866 recommended a liniment mixture of sulphuric ether, aqua ammonia, and muriate of ammonia, "Wet the scalp and all painful parts every 2 or 3 hours, or until the pain abates."

Gangrene: Amputation.

Grippe: Also known as influenza. Symptoms treated with pain, fever or other remedies.

Gunshots: A common problem in the West resulting from foul play and accidents. Gunshots were a leading cause of injury on the Oregon and California trails primarily caused by people unfamiliar with handling weapons.

> Pulverized Gunpowder for Wounds—Many a man has bled to death upon the battle-field whose life might have been saved by a handful of flour bound upon the wound. Many soldiers do not know that gunpowder is one of the very best styptics. Reduce the grains to dust, scrape a little lint from some garment and fill it with this fine powder and apply it to the wound, binding or holding it fast.—FLIN, *December 13, 1862, 190-2*

Headache: Sick headache might be caused from "overloading the stomach," according to Dr. A.W. Chase. Other headaches, he said, could be cured by soaking feet in hot water while drinking herb teas such as pennyroyal, catnip or mint, then covering up with blankets until the person sweats for about an hour "by which time relief will have been obtained." Other headache remedies included a couple teaspoons of charcoal dissolved in water and then drunk, or a tonic created by mixing a small amount of castor, gentian, and valerian roots with laudanum, sulphuric ether and alcohol. The mixture needed to stand about ten days before use; the dosage was "A tea-spoon as often as required or 2 or three times daily."

Hydrotherapy: Used by doctors in the 1880s and later. They hung wet sheets in homes and sick rooms to put humidity into the air and wrapped people with high fevers in wet sheets to reduce their temperature.

Influenza: Often called grippe.

Insects and Mosquitoes: A common problem for travelers and settlers, particularly in areas near water. People wrapped themselves in blankets, burned fires to create smoke, used mosquito netting and traveled at night to avoid flying insects that moved, and bit, during the daylight hours.

Malaria: Treated with quinine and Dr. Sappington's Anti-Malarial Pills.

Mountain Fever: Mountain fever affected many newcomers to the West. It may have been a form of altitude sickness as it didn't strike until people reached higher elevations, or it could have been a variation of Rocky Mountain Spotted Fever or some other tick fever. Symptoms included blinding headaches, high fever, and severe pains in joints and the spine, sometimes followed by delirium.

Pain: Treated with opium, laudanum or paregoric. Frontiersmen used tea made from willow tree bark. The tea was made by boiling the willow bark, then pulverizing the bark and making a tea using a portion of the powder residue.

Pneumonia: Treated with a bromide mixture, moist heat, flax seed meal poultices, corn meal poultices, oiled silk used as a chest dressing, or the wearing of quilted pneumonia jackets.

Powders: Doctors used a variety of powders such as Dover's Powder, morphine, calomel and bismuth. They cut a newspaper into pieces and put portions of the powders onto the paper which they then folded around it. Late in the period physicians could purchase powder papers in packages of a thousand.

Scalping: Often, but not always, fatal. A four-year-old Nebraska boy had his scalp reattached by a doctor using thirty-five sutures. The doctor then put a wet skullcap on the head which was kept wet with a solution of boric acid. The child recovered.

At the recent attack made by the Indians upon the railroad at plum creek, a man named Thompson, who was sent before to repair the

182

telegraph, while engaged at the work, was surprised by the Indians, shot and scalped, but lay quiet and finally escaped, bringing his scalp, which he had picked up from the ground where the Indians had dropped it, in his hand. It is expected that he will recover.
—FLIN, *August 31, 1867, 371-3*

Scarlet Fever: Often fatal, the most serious form of the disease was known as "Black Scarlet Fever." Symptoms were treated with bacon rind, carbonized petroleum jelly, calomel, and aconite to control fever.

Scurvy: Common disease throughout the West, particularly early in the period. Treated with vegetables, potatoes, vinegar, local greenery. Residents of the Southwest ate *pommes de terre* (Jerusalem artichokes), red and green peppers, melons, squash and wild onions to combat scurvy. By 1849 travelers to California were well aware of the causes of scurvy so they utilized such foods as lamb's-quarters, poke leaves, watercress and curly dock, in addition to vinegar and potatoes. (See also chapter seven.)

Smallpox: Vaccinations were available though many people feared them. The disease was particularly deadly to Native Americans and many tribes lost up to half their members from outbreaks in the early part of the 1800s. To prevent pitting the face, Dr. A.W. Chase recommended a discovery made by the "Surgeon of the English Army in China":

> When, in small pox, the preceding fever is at its height, and just before the eruption appears, the chest is thoroughly rubbed with Croton Oil and Tartaremetic Ointment. This causes the whole of the eruption to appear on that part of the body to the relief of the rest.—*Chase, 191*

> At Omaha a red flag was placed in front of a house used for small-pox patients. A large crowd was attracted by it, who wondered when 'the auction was going to begin.' When informed of the real state of the case they 'broke out' pretty quickly.
> —FLIN, *February 24, 1872, 379-4*

Snakebite: Raw beef slabs or chicken flesh were used to draw out poison as was "vinegar mixed with gunpowder" according to *Frank Leslie's Illustrated Newspaper*, August 29, 1857. Some would cauterize the bite with nitrate of silver then give the patient ammonia and whiskey. When a rattlesnake bit Dr. Samuel W. Woodhouse on the finger, the doctor utilized every type of treatment he could to cure himself including brandy, whiskey, ammonia water, flaxseed poultice, Dover's Powders, extract of collocynth, tincture of iodine, magnesia calci, Seidlitz powders, potassium iodide and peppermint water. He recovered. When a rattlesnake bit a mule on the Santa Fe Trail, men scraped the wound then applied rattlesnake weed and hartshorn (a solution of ammonia). New Mexicans applied spurge to snakebites, and most men drank whiskey or poured it on the bite. Dr. A.W. Chase recommended animals bitten on the legs or near the feet be taken to a mudhole and made to stand there for several hours. "If upon the nose, bind the mud upon the place in such a manner as not to interfere with their breathing. And I am perfectly satisfied that soft clay mud would be an excellent application to snake bites on persons, for I know it to draw out the poisoning from ivy, and have been assured that it has done the same for snake bites, of persons as well as for cattle," Dr. Chase wrote.

Snow blindness: Men daubed charcoal beneath their eyes to lessen the glare of the bright snow. They also wore blue or green glasses or goggles with small slits cut in them to limit the light entering their eyes. Women wore a dark see-through veil for the same purpose.

Wyoming resident Fenimore C. Chatterton wrote of his own snow blindness:

> One April morning in 1879, Mr. Hugus asked me to go to a ranch near Elk Mountain and return with 20 head of horses. The country was covered with a foot of snow and the sun was bright. I faced the sun riding east that morning, and faced west in the afternoon on my return trip. As a result of the sun's rays being reflected by the snow, I became snowblind shortly after, and was confined to bed. After three days, Lieutenant Gurlack, who had been with the General Johnson [Albert Sidney Johnston] expedition at Grand Encampment [in 1857 when a number of soldiers suffered snow blindness], . . . came to my room. After inspecting me, he said that he could cure me in a few minutes with a remedy he used on the Encampment snowblind soldiers. He got a bottle of Perry Davis Pain Killer from the store and told me to wink my eyes when he put a a few drops of the pain killer in them. It was like fire, but it served the purpose and within an hour, I was at work, after three days of excruciating eye pain.—Yesterday's Wyoming, *22-23*

Sore Throat: When people had a sore throat they used several treatments. They wrapped the throat in red flannel, wrapped it with a kerosene-soaked rag or placed a poultice of fried onions around the neck. Dr. A.W. Chase recommended a liniment made of gum camphor, castile soap, turpentine, oil of origanum, alcohol and opium. "Smoking dried mullein leaves in a pipe not having been used is said to have cured many cases of Laryngitis," according to Dr. Chase.

Stomach worms: Treated with boiled pumpkin seed tea.

Tuberculosis: The people who had tuberculosis were known as "lungers." Tuberculosis was nearly always a "death sentence." It was most commonly called consumption. Treatments included removal to a dry climate, living an outdoor life, travel under favorable conditions and such medications as cod liver oil, phosphate of lime, quinine, and a diet of meat, milk and vegetables. Tuberculosis bacillus was discovered in 1882 which helped doctors realize it was a contagious disease. Thereafter they treated patients with isolation, bed rest during the active stage, sunlight, fresh air and nutritious foods. Minnie Elliott moved to Arizona when her doctor in the East told her she had tuberculosis and just six months to live. Taking her two children, a young son and an infant daughter, she traveled by train to Tempe, a town built of adobe huts and shacks. When her health didn't improve, and that of her children also was affected (the daughter contracted typhoid fever), Minnie moved farther into the desert. She there prepared meals of rabbits or quail killed by her son and ate such items as milk obtained from a local rancher and wheat ground in a coffee meal and cooked into a mush. Minnie quit wearing her corset and started to wear loose-fitting garments. As her health and stamina improved, she got more exercise and developed an improved appetite, gaining weight and losing her cough.

Typhoid: A waterborne illness prevalent throughout the period. Symptoms were diarrhea and a brown or black tongue that was dry in the center and glossy at the edges. The only known method of prevention was boiling water, but people seldom would do that. Treatments included calomel, dilution of mineral acids or sulphuric acids, cold sponging, and quinine to reduce fever and as a general tonic. One Texas woman, whose husband contracted typhoid, "poured peach tree leaf tea down him." In 1898 during the Spanish-American War, doctors and others realized flies might transmit the disease. An antityphoid serum was available after 1897.

Venereal Diseases: Common among soldiers, particularly after they had paid a visit to a hog ranch. (See chapter five for more information on hog ranches.) Also common among Indian tribes, though the diseases were introduced initially by non-Native people. Gonorrhea was treated with Balsam copaiba, and with Ephedra Antisiphilitica, an evergreen shrub native to Texas and New Mexico. Dr. John Fox Hammond in 1852 at Socorro, New Mexico, reported that Ephedra, "Is used in gonorrhea, it and local baths with water from the warm springs, are the only remedies resorted to in that disease. A pint of the infusion may be drunk during the day."

Vomiting: To induce vomiting, a youngster was held upside down while someone tickled his throat with a feather soaked in goose grease.

Whooping Cough: Doctors used a syrup made from onions and garlic sliced and stewed in sweet oil then strained and mixed with honey, paregoric and spirits of camphor. Dr. A.W. Chase recommended:

Dailey's Whooping Cough Syrup.—Take the strongest West India rum, 1 pt.; anise oil 2 ozs.; honey 1 pt.; lemon juice 4 ozs.; mix.

Dose—For adults 1 table-spoon 3 or 4 times a day,—children, 1 tea-spoon, with as much sugar and water.

Wounds: Women used knitting needles to probe a wound, a razor as a lance and embroidery scissors to remove torn skin or even fingers nearly severed in an accident.

X-ray: Discovered in 1895 but not widely available in the West until the end of the period.

Yellow Fever: Characterized by chills, high temperatures, headaches, delirium and swollen joints. Treatment of "Yellowjack" (so named because of the colored flag used to identify its presence in quarantined areas) included doses of quinine, sulphate of magneis and calomel, which were only partially effective and fatal relapses were common.

Some Common Remedies

Asafetida: A gum resin that was hung around the neck to prevent contagious diseases and colds, and for use as a stimulant.

Belladonna: Made from the leaves and roots of nightshade (a deadly plant) and used as a stimulant or to decrease bodily secretions with the exception of urine.

Blue Mass: Made from rubbing mercury on licorice and used as a laxative.

Calomel: Mercurous chloride; used as a laxative.

Digitalis: A heart stimulant made from the dried leaves of a foxglove plant.

Dover's Powder: A mixture of opium, ipecac and sugar of milk and used to cause sweating or as a sedative.

Ergot: Made from a fungus that grew in the flower of common rye grass and used as a stimulant in uterine contractions, to effect an abortion or to treat hemorrhages.

Ipecac: Made from dried roots of a South American plant and used as an emetic.

Pain Killers: Laudanum (tincture of opium), morphine (chief alkaloid of opium), willow bark tea, or a mixture of alcohol, gum guaiac, gums myrrh and camphor, and pulverized cayenne pepper.

Quinine: Made from the Peruvian bark of a Cinchona tree and used to treat malaria.

Seidlitz Powder: An effervescent anti-acid made from bitartrate of sodium and potassium, bicarbonate of sodium and tartaric acid.

Stimulants: Nux vomica (beans from an East Indian tree which contain strychnine), belladonna, digitalis and asafetida.

Tonics and Patent Medicines

During the latter part of the period a wide variety of tonics and potions were on the market to cure a variety of ills, though there is little evidence any of them actually worked as their makers and sellers claimed. Some of the common remedies included Hostetter's Celebrated Stomach Bitters, Peruna, Parker's Tonic, Lydia E. Pinkham's Vegetable Compound, Hooflands "entirely vegetable" German Bitters, Old Sachem Bitters, The Home Stomach Bitters and Colden's Liquid Beef Tonic. All had a high alcoholic content. There were dozens of patent medicines available, most not exactly helpful but certainly not harmful, and a few that could be downright dangerous if used improperly. Bitters was a generic term for liquor since most contained from five percent to fifty-five percent alcohol.

> Chinese physicians in San Francisco use medicines that one would naturally prefer to take in homeopathic doses. Hundreds of packages containing dried lizards and venomous serpents are imported from China and consigned to Chinese doctors, who use them in their practice.—FLIN, *September 14, 1872, 11-4*

NATIVE AMERICAN MEDICINES

The traditional healer in Indian cultures was the medicine man or woman. The position was passed down from one generation to the next as healers taught their skills to a younger person, perhaps a grandson or granddaughter, though females could not practice medicine until after menopause because Native Americans feared menstruation. They wouldn't allow menstruating women near them or to be involved with bodily processes. Medicine healers carried their supplies in a medicine bag. The supplies themselves included roots, bark, animal substances, fetishes, charms and herbs. Medicine healers relied on prayers and chants in conducting their healing ceremonies, but traditional Indian medicine men and women also effectively used herbs and plants. Indian healers were paid honorariums of horses, beads, clothes, skins or feathers. Many westerners adopted Native American remedies.

> Medicine Lodge Creek [Kansas] owes its name to the superstition of the Indians, who have long considered it a favorable location to *make medicine.* But do not imagine that the medicine of the Indians is a potion to be swallowed, or a salve to be applied. It is rather a charm to propitiate the spirits, good and bad, and its composition is as varied as the lively imagination of the priests or medicine-makers can invest. A great medicine lodge [is described by *Frank Leslie's Illustrated Newspaper* illustrator J.E. Taylor]:

THE GREAT MEDICINE LODGE

is delightfully situated in an open prairie half a mile from the creek. It is a circular structure, composed of limbs piled up against a rude frame-work. Within are the offerings of passing Indians—such as trinkets, arrows, beads, wampum, gourds, and feathers; and the interior of the lodge presents a strange sight indeed, with those articles strewn around, some hanging high up, and others on the floor. There is also a buffalo skull, fantastically decorated.

—FLIN, *November 23, 1867, 154-1*

Some Native American remedies included these, many of which were adopted or adapted by Euro-Americans:

Abdominal pains: Wild mint or wild verbena.

Bleeding: Cauterize by placing a stem of yarrow into the wound and setting it on fire; then pack the wound with eagle down, puff balls, sumac or scrapings from animal hides.

Bruises and Sores: Skunk cabbage or charred honeysuckle vine in bear grease (Pacific Northwest); white fir or pinion pine pitch (Shoshone and Washoe); milkweed latex (Paiutes); white oak, used as a poultice, particularly effective on foot sores caused from wearing wet moccasins.

Cuts and Wounds: Sutured with sinew sewn with bone needles.

Diarrhea: Sagebrush tea (Blackfeet).

Dropsical legs: Wild tobacco leaves placed on them.

Fever: Rest, purging, sweating, restricted diet.

Headache: Smoke mixture with root of the devil's walking stick (Cherokee). Tea made from willow tree bark.

Listlessness: Raw buffalo liver (Crow).

Nausea: Willow bark tea (Dakota), or the abdomen was scarified and powdered ragweed spread upon it.

Pain: Peyote bean or willow tree bark tea.

Snakebite: Chewed rhizomes of snakeroot with the cut then placed on the bite (Cherokee).

Sore eyes: Lotion made from wild tansy (Cherokee).

Tonic: A general tonic of the inner bark of boiled slippery elm (Omaha).

ADDITIONAL READING

Baker, Jim. *Frontier Doctor.* Marlton, N.J.: Heartland House, 1966. Of limited value as a reference.

Chase, A.W. *Dr. Chase's Recipes; or Information for Everybody: An Invaluable Collection of About Eight Hundred Practical Recipes.* Ann Arbor, Mich.: Published by the author, 1866. Out of print, but often available at research libraries. An invaluable resource for actual recipes of medicinal remedies in use during the period.

Chatterton, Fenimore C. *Yesterday's Wyoming.* Aurora, Colo.: Powder River Publishers and Booksellers, 1957.

Hall, Dr. Thomas B. *Medicine on the Santa Fe Trail.* Dayton, Ohio: Morningside Bookshop, 1971. A good reference.

Karolevitz, Robert F. *Doctors of the Old West.* Seattle: Superior Publishing Company, 1967. This is an excellent reference with photographs of early doctors, their equipment, drugstores and the like. It also has extensive listings of medicines and remedies.

Long, Francis A. *A Prairie Doctor of the Eighties.* Norfolk, Nebr.: Huse Publishing Company, 1937. Out of print, but a good reference that is often available at research libraries.

Loomis, F.A., ed. *As Long As Life: The Memoirs of a Frontier Woman Physician Mary Canaga Rowland, 1873-1966.* Seattle, Wash.: Storm Peak Press, 1994. A good reference, though most of the detail is for the period after 1900.

Smith, Elmer L. *Early American Home Remedies.* Lebanon, Pa.: Applied Arts Publishers, 1968. A good reference.

PART THREE

Wild West Society

CHAPTER TWELVE

EDUCATION

In an era when many adults themselves couldn't read, education was haphazard at best and particularly so during the first half of the period. After about 1870 organized school districts helped improve educational opportunities throughout the West. School sessions were dependent upon availability of a location, and most particularly upon the vagaries of weather and the need for students to help at home, particularly in farming regions. During the early settlement period the schoolhouse also served as a community center. It became a place not only for children to learn reading and writing, but also one where community events could be held ranging from elections and public meetings to dances and other social functions.

The earliest schools in what eventually became Oklahoma were Indian schools organized, taught and operated by members from the Cherokee, Choctaw, Creek, Chickasaw and Seminole tribes. The Cherokees had had schools prior to their relocation to Indian Territory in the 1830s, and they not only established rural schools in Indian Territory, but also built and operated male and female seminaries to provide advanced courses for tribal members. The Choctaws established schools shortly after their own relocation to Indian Territory and had nine boarding schools in operation by 1848.

The Creeks, Chickasaws and Seminoles also had schools, although their educational opportunities were not as broad-based as those of the Cherokees and Choctaws. The Indian school courses involved instruction in English, Latin, spelling, arithmetic, history, reading and vocation topics such as agriculture, carpentry, mechanical arts, cooking, sewing and child care. The tribes also created facilities for individuals suffering disabilities such as hearing loss, blindness and mental illness. After other tribes settled on reservations, schools were established for their children, with some classes offered on the reservation; other children were sent to boarding schools in other regions, the most well known of which was the Carlisle Indian School in Pennsylvania. Much of the education in that period was aimed at assimilating the Indian children into white society.

SCHOOLHOUSES

Early frontier schools started in homes or crude cabins using whatever educational materials could be obtained. The Bible was often the only text available for women or men to use in teaching their children to read. The classroom likely had a dirt floor, which served as the blackboard, and the teacher—who might also be the children's mother or a neighbor who knew how to read—would scratch the letters of the alphabet or simple mathematical problems into the floor using a sharply pointed stick.

Furnishings might include a flour barrel as a teacher's desk, and various packing crates, boxes or the dining table served as student desks. In the earliest portion of the period, the building of a schoolhouse and the hiring of a teacher depended upon the financial and in-kind contributions of area residents. Some donated land for the school, others helped construct it.

Often the schoolhouse itself was developed from an abandoned cabin or, in many cases on the plains, an abandoned dugout. One Kansas dugout school had unplastered walls, two small windows, a dirt floor and was heated with a small fireplace. The students sat on small split logs that were supported by pegs and attached to the dugout walls. The teacher had neither desk nor chair, and there was no blackboard. But education took place as the teacher shared knowledge.

Often in early classrooms the littlest children sat on seats so high their legs dangled all day. In the wintertime schoolhouses were heated with wood stoves. Students seated close to the stoves might become too hot, while those farther away were cold. Sometimes the students nearest the fire had to turn around when one side of them became too warm and the other side too cold. Students might not have maps, charts, pictures or many books, but they did usually have a spelling book and the teacher might have a few other texts to use in instruction. The most common texts included *McGuffey's Readers* and copies of *Youth's Companion*. Other helpful books included dictionaries and almanacs.

Students generally supplied their own other miscellaneous books, slates, pencils, tablets and rulers. They reached the schoolhouse either by walking, riding a horse or perhaps driving a team and wagon. Seldom did adults take children to school each day. The schoolhouses generally were centrally located in a settlement area so children could reach them each day. In almost all cases the children took their own lunches with them, carrying the meal in a tin bucket.

The schoolhouse was a center for the community throughout most of the period. It often doubled as a location for church services, public meetings, entertainment, elections and even for weddings or funerals, at least in the period before a community had a church.

Schools often were segregated, as in California where African-American children either were not allowed to attend schools dominated by white children, or were required to have classes in a separate room of the school. Likewise, Asian and Mexican children often were restricted from attending Anglo schools. Such segregation wasn't always enforced, however; some rural areas included children of different ethnic backgrounds in the same classes.

TEACHERS

The earliest teachers often were parents (generally mothers) of children. The hiring of a teacher occurred only when enough families settled in a general location to justify such an expense. In most cases early in the period the teacher's salary was provided by the parents themselves, who paid a certain amount for each child to attend classes. The "subscription" costs generally ranged from $1 to $2 each month per pupil. The teacher most often "boarded around" by living with one family for a period, then moving in with another family.

Such living arrangements often created difficulties for the teachers as they became embroiled in family squabbles and disputes. That very thing affected school teacher Glendolene Kimmell who taught at the Iron Mountain School in southern Wyoming in the late 1890s and early 1900s. When a dispute arose between the Miller family (with whom she lived) and the Nickell family over use of range lands by sheep (which the Nickells had and which the Millers disliked), Kimmell overheard discussions about planned attacks by the Millers on the Nickells. When fourteen-year-old Willie Nickell was ambushed and killed in early 1901, Kimmell became involved in the case. Her involvement had a third element, however, as she felt a romantic attachment to Tom Horn, who was eventually convicted and hanged for the murder.

Teaching was one of the "accepted" professions for women during the period, and throughout the time young women supported themselves or assisted their family with expenses by teaching. Many of the West's teachers were young women, some of them only sixteen or seventeen years old, who had completed some schooling themselves and who had demonstrated the ability to teach other youngsters (who often were older or bigger than the instructor herself). The earliest teachers received the endorsement of the local citizens who had organized the school; the teachers didn't necessarily have any formal instruction in how to teach nor did they have any certificate of approval from a state or county education association.

Later in the period, as school boards organized and state or territorial standards were established, the teachers had to show proficiency in education before they obtained a job. Teaching provided a young woman the opportunity to work, but her position generally lasted only until she decided to marry. Attitudes of the day predicated women who married to quit teaching so they could remain at home to take care of their homes and families.

> The San Francisco Board of Education has voted to discharge any female teacher who may commit the crime of marriage.
> —FLIN, *June 16, 1870, 215-4*

> The marriage of Miss Alice Tomilson reminds us that our premium school teachers are being gathered into the matrimonial net by men who place self above the public welfare. Suppose all the marriageable female teachers in the world were to be married tomorrow, the country would go to rack and ruin.
> —*Grand Island, Nebraska,* Times, *September 15, 1883*

Teachers generally determined what types of courses they would teach, but reading, writing, spelling and grammar were always included in the curriculum and other courses such as arithmetic, geography, geometry and history were taught when books could be obtained. To teach mathematical geography one Kansas teacher used an apple and a ball in place of a suspension globe, which she did not have available. Another teacher visited a nearby bed of gypsum where she collected clay, which students then shaped into flat maps and relief maps. Texts included copies of popular magazines such as *Harper's Young People* or *Chatterbox.* Teacher pay generally ranged around $15 to $20 per month, though in California's gold rush, teacher pay in certain areas was considerably higher.

Teachers provided a variety of services to schools. As Iowa teacher Anna Johnson put it: "I not only taught, but was also an administrator, mother, doctor, nurse, judge and jury, artist, cook, librarian, custodian or janitor, carpenter or fixer, advisor, psychologist, disciplinarian, and humanitarian. . . . In this rural community I was very close to the children and all the parents and many others in the area. Their problems often became my problems, which sometimes made my task even harder."

> A school-teacher named Akers was tried at Bloomington, Ill., last week, for cruelly punishing one of his pupils. The evidence showed that he had inflicted eighty-three lashes with a double switch of osage and orange.—FLIN, *January 22, 1870, 319-4*

During the latter portion of the period local school districts formed. Most regions of the West established school boards and had county school superintendents, who helped set the curriculum and supervise instructors. That helped standardize schools and opened educational opportunities to all children, not just those whose parents had resources to pay subscription costs.

SCHOOL TERMS

School terms ranged from a few weeks to a few months and were largely dependent upon weather and other conditions. School was not held during periods when children were needed to help at home—such as during the spring planting and summer and fall harvesting. Classes also could not be held during periods of severe inclement weather, because then it was either too dangerous or even impossible for students to reach the schoolhouse each day.

Education beyond primary or secondary grades was limited early in the period. After approval of the Morrill Land Grant Act in 1862, states established colleges to provide technical and agricultural education. In 1890 the Act was amended to provide funding for schools serving white and African-American scholars, which particularly affected educational opportunities for African-American students wanting higher education. The 1890 amendment also made it more possible for women to attend colleges, something they had found difficult during the earlier period.

ADDITIONAL READING

Cordier, Mary Hurlbut. *Schoolwomen of the Prairies and Plains: Personal Narratives from Iowa, Kansas, and Nebraska, 1860s-1920s.* Albuquerque: University of New Mexico Press, 1992. An excellent resource.

Fuller, Wayne E. *The Old Country School: The Story of Rural Education in the Middle West.* Chicago: University of Chicago Press, 1982.

Hobbs, Catherine, ed. *Nineteenth-Century Women Learn to Write.* Charlottesville, Va.: University Press of Virginia, 1995.

Johnson, Anna Johnson. "Recollections of a Country School Teacher." *Annals of Iowa 42.* (Winter 1975): 491-92.

Johnson, Clifton. *Old-Time Schools and School-Books.* New York: Dover, 1963.

Smallwood, James, ed. *And Gladly Teach: Reminiscences of Teachers from Frontier Dugout to Modern Module.* Norman: University of Oklahoma Press, 1976. An excellent resource.

CHAPTER THIRTEEN

EMPLOYMENT

T he earliest permanent Euro-American settlers in the West were primarily an agrarian society, as were many of the Native Americans who had called the region home for centuries. Anglo, Native American and Hispanic residents established farms and ranches, producing most of the products they needed for survival on their own land. But as the West began developing in the late 1840s, mining became a primary occupation of many workers, including those of all ethnic backgrounds. Starting with the gold discovery at Sutter's Mill on the South Fork of the American River in present-day California in January 1848 and continuing throughout the period, mining was a main industry in the West.

The mining activity spawned towns and cities, which led to other employment opportunities ranging from storekeeping to boardinghouse proprietorship and from doctoring and lawyering to publishing.

Although individuals had some livestock for personal use prior to the Civil War, not until after that conflict did widespread stock raising become a dominant industry in the West. Beginning in the late 1860s and continuing throughout the period, cattle raising escalated with stock moving north from Texas where huge herds had run unchecked during the earlier period. The stock operators soon spread to northern ranges in the present states of Montana, Wyoming, Idaho, Nebraska and Colorado, and herds moved freely to other regions as well. During that same period homesteading expanded throughout the West giving rise to additional communities and agrarian industries and movements.

A need for railroad ties to construct first the Union Pacific and Central

Pacific Railroads, and then other rail lines, supported the timber industry. Men wielded broad axes in making ties for the lines and also in chopping timbers for various mining ventures or house construction.

The West had few industrial centers such as steel mills; however, it did have occasional locations where workers produced bricks, cement or other products. And throughout the region workers engaged in various trades ranging from blacksmithing to wagon building and harness making.

MINING

On a cold January morning in 1848, James Marshall, who was building a millrace in the South Fork of the American River for use at John Sutter's lumber mill, found the first flakes and nuggets of gold that launched the California Gold Rush. He and several companions kept the strike to themselves for a limited time, but eventually word spread and the West's first gold rush started.

Marshall wasn't even certain what he had found was gold. He later recalled, "I picked up one or two pieces and examined them attentively. I then tried it between two rocks and found that it could be beaten into a different shape but not broken." Several different methods of testing the metal occurred. Some was hammered on an anvil; if it was fool's gold it would fracture, but the real stuff it simply molded into a different shape.

Marshall gave one nugget—it was about the size and shape of a chewed stick of gum—to camp cook Jenny Wimmer, who threw it into the soap kettle and boiled it in baking soda and lye. When the metal didn't change as a result, Marshall, Wimmer, John Sutter and the other employees of the mill operation knew with certainty it was gold.

Mormon Henry Bigler, who'd marched with the Mormon Battalion to California and who was working for Sutter, wrote in his journal: "Monday 24th this day some kind of mettle [*sic*] was found in the tail race that looks like goald [*sic*] first discovered by James Martial [*sic*] the Boss of the Mill."

On March 15, 1848, the San Francisco *Californian* reported:

> GOLD MINE FOUND—In the newly made race-way of the sawmill recently erected by Captain Sutter, on the American fork, gold has been found in considerable quantities. One person brought thirty dollars-worth to New Helvetia, gathered there in a short time. California, no doubt, is rich.

Not until early May did the gold fever begin in earnest. Mormon Elder Sam Brannan, who led a group of his fellow believers via ship to California at the same time Brigham Young was taking other Mormons to Utah, became an ardent California supporter. He became a California newspaper publisher and entrepreneur. His *Star* had downplayed the gold strike, but Brannan (who'd seen the gold himself) boisterously spread the word, and his declaration was one of many that led to the subsequent rush to California.

The first thing that happened was a desertion of San Francisco, which until December 1846 had been known as Yerba Buena ("good herb"), by nearly everyone as they headed toward New Helvetia, the American River and Sutter's Mill. As San Francisco became a near ghost town—both the *Star* and the *Californian* ceased publication—Sutter's Mill, farms and property became overrun with gold seekers.

In 1848, new miners dug about a quarter of a million dollars worth of gold in California. And the fever spread to the Sandwich Islands [Hawaii], Mexico, Peru, Chile and throughout the United States.

As with all mineral booms, schemers and dreamers immediately started figuring out ways they could cash in on the boom. Brannan bought every tin pan he could find in San Francisco, paying as little as $.20 each for pans he later sold in his store for anywhere from $8 to $16.

The American influx to California's goldfields started in 1849 when thousands of Argonauts—as the miners were called—made their way west, traveling by three primary means and determined to get there before all the gold was gone.

By far the majority of the American '49ers—as those gold-crazed men and women became known—went by sea, traveling 13,000 miles from the Atlantic seaboard around Cape Horn and then through the Pacific to San Francisco. The six- to eight-month journey was tiresome and fraught with danger, poor food and high cost.

A lesser number of people traveled by both sea and land, taking ships to the Caribbean side of Central America, then traveling with native inhabitants in long dugout canoes, known as bungos, partway across the Isthmus of Panama before switching to mules or proceeding on foot to the Pacific. There they again returned to the sea, traveling on any oceangoing vessel they could find that was headed to San Francisco. The Panama passage became the most popular route for those who could afford it.

Various overland routes led to the gold diggings as well, including those across the Southwest from Missouri, Arkansas or Texas to Santa Fe and then over the Old Spanish Trail or along the Gila River to southern California. Perhaps 9,000 gold seekers took those routes. Most overlanders—about 22,500 in 1849—followed the existing Oregon-Mormon Trail from Independence, St. Joseph or Council Bluffs.

Those wagon-bound Argonauts traveled as fast as their animals could go, some wagon trains reaching California within 100 days (as compared with the 111 days it took Brigham Young and his pioneering party of Saints to go from Winter Quarters [Omaha, Nebraska] to Salt Lake City in 1847).

Once there the digging proceeded at a furious pace. The greatest number of newcomers reached California in 1852, and that year they scraped and dug $81 million in gold from the earth, the largest amount recovered in any one year of the gold rush. By 1853 the yield had dropped to $67 million and it continued to decline thereafter. Even so, in the 25 years immediately following

Ore cars such as these were used to transport minerals from mining areas, particularly in underground mining situations. These cars are located in Bannack, Montana.

James Marshall's discovery of gold in the millrace on January 24, 1848, Argonauts retrieved $978 million from California's goldfields. All other mineral discoveries in the West followed the great California Gold Rush, with miners drawn from one strike to the next and communities living or dying as quickly as the strikes started and ended. When mining activities switched from surface to underground operations, miners used different techniques.

Underground or hardrock miners blasted ore from tunnels and removed it by loading it into ore cars that traveled on track systems. In some cases they took horses or mules underground to assist with the work. If the animals were kept in the darkness too long, though, they went blind. The darkness had no long-term effects on the men because they ascended from the mine each day, while the mules often remained below ground for weeks, months or even years.

Hardrock or underground miners utilized heavy air-powered tools, picks, shovels and blasting, using dynamite or nitroglycerin, to remove ore. (When blasting they yelled "fire in the hole" to warn other workers.) The ore was then placed into carts propelled along underground tracks for movement to aboveground processing areas. Some mining techniques involved use of smelters, where the minerals were separated through a series of processes often involving crushing or heating.

One common thing for underground miners, regardless of nationality, was their belief in the existence of small people living in the mining regions. German miners called those little people *Kobalds*, Mexicans referred to them as *duendes,* and the British miners knew them as "tommy-knockers." The little people were credited with (or blamed for) removing tools from mining areas and in some cases even with helping miners in trouble.

Placer miners—those who worked in open streams or by washing ore with water—used a variety of tools including a shallow pan made of iron or tin in which they placed dirt. They swirled the pan of dirt underwater allowing the dirt to wash away leaving the heavier gold nuggets, dust or flakes in the bottom of the pan. Other placer-mining methods included use of a cradle or rocker, long tom or sluice, all of which used similar techniques of putting dirt into a container and then filtering it with water to separate the dirt from the gold.

Hydraulic mining, introduced in California in 1853, involved use of giant iron fire hoses to blast water against the hills, eroding the rock and soil and thereby exposing the gold deposits.

In 1859 miners discovered the Comstock Lode silver deposits near what quickly became Virginia City, Nevada, causing a rush of miners from California's fields.

> Silver bars from Nevada containing a little gold, are arriving at New York in quantity, brought from California through England. A bar weighs about seventy-five to one-hundred and twenty pounds, contains some one-four hundredth part of gold, and is worth $1400. They pack them in ordinary looking satchels.
> —FLIN, *January 21, 1871, 307-4*

Simultaneous with the Comstock Lode discovery was the Pikes Peak Gold Rush. It occurred in 1859 on the east slope of the Rocky Mountains near what became Denver and in mining communities such as Leadville, Central City and Cripple Creek. Subsequently Colorado miners also located silver and developed extensive mines.

> A very valuable silver mine has been discovered about 50 miles south of Denver City.—FLIN, *July 29, 1865, 291-3*

Miners found gold in Idaho in September 1860.

> Portland (Oregon) papers are filled with exciting mining intelligence, principally from Boise river. Trains of provisions from Salt Lake began to arrive at those diggings on the 1st Feb. The principal mines worked are about 40 miles west of Fort Boise, extending over an area 20 miles square. There is every reason to believe the surrounding country is also rich. About 4,000 people are now there, and large numbers are arriving daily.
> —FLIN, *March 14, 1863, 387-2*

Mineral development started on Grasshopper Creek near what became Bannack, Montana, in 1863, and quickly shifted to the Alder Gulch region in 1864, leading to establishment of Virginia City, Montana Territory. Development continued there for about a year before better sources were found farther north in Last Chance Gulch, which became the city of Helena, Montana, established in the fall of 1864, where activities centered for several years.

> A dispatch from St. Paul states that Capt. Fish's expedition, which left last summer to ascertain the best northern route to the gold diggings, has been heard from as late as the 1st [of] October. They were digging gold at Grasshopper Creek, Idaho Territory, getting half a million per week. They say the diggings are the richest ever opened.—FLIN, *December 5, 1863, 162-4*

In 1874 prospectors located a rich copper vein at Butte, Montana, which operated throughout the remainder of the century and into the 1900s as well under the auspices of the Anaconda Copper Mining Company.

Miners located gold deposits on South Pass, in present-day Wyoming, as early as 1841, but development didn't get underway until 1867 when a party of miners returning disappointed from California prospected and found placer gold. Within two years hundreds of claims and thousands of miners were in the region, spawning the growth of South Pass City and Atlantic City, both in Wyoming Territory. The boom played out quickly so that by 1872 most of the miners had departed the area and the towns became near ghosts.

Elsewhere in Wyoming, beginning in 1897, there was a big boom in copper production in the Sierra Madre. The Grand Encampment Copper District grew quickly, launched the town of Grand Encampment and led to the employment of thousands of miners. That boom extended into the early 1900s, lasting just a decade.

Another type of mineral development occurred in Wyoming Territory when the Union Pacific Railroad developed coal resources along its line. The first mines and town on the UP line in that area opened in the wake of the railroad construction in 1868 at Carbon, where underground mining operations continued throughout the period. Additional mining was conducted near Rock Springs and Evanston, where Chinese miners worked in the underground production areas. Conflicts with the Chinese broke out at the Rock Springs mines in 1883 leading to an attack upon them and the subsequent death of many of the Chinese miners. Other attacks on Chinese miners occurred in Idaho.

Discovery of silver in the area near the border between Arizona Territory and Mexico caused a boom there and gave birth to the town of Tombstone. The town is most often remembered as the site of the deadly October 1881 fight involving Wyatt, Virgil and Morgan Earp and their friend Doc Holliday against Billy and Ike Clanton and Frank and Tom McLaury near the OK Corral. The gunfight actually occurred in a vacant lot near the back gate of the OK Corral. But the rise and fall of Tombstone related to mineral development. And like others, the Earps engaged in mining ventures.

The new Gadsden Purchase, or Arizona as it is called, is reported to be rich in silver.—FLIN, *August 1, 1857, 142-3*

Early Spanish explorers may have enslaved Native Americans and forced them to mine for gold in the Uintah Mountains of present-day Utah. It was reportedly Brigham Young who learned of treasure that had been buried by the Indians, having been told the story by Ute Chief Walkara. The Ute told Young he would give the gold to the Mormon Church. Thomas Rhodes, an assistant to Mormon leader Brigham Young, first understood the implications of the Spanish mining venture, and he had the job of transporting the wealth to Salt Lake City.

Reports suggest Rhodes spent two weeks at the Spanish mine and had sixty pounds of gold when he returned to Salt Lake City. He continued to mine for other gold, all of which went to the church. In 1887 he located more gold and he continued to bring the precious mineral to the church. As Rhodes hauled treasure into Salt Lake, other people came to recognize that the so-called "church mine" was much more than a single, isolated gold source. Mining activity expanded throughout the Uintah Mountains, and the biggest strike occurred when soldiers from Fort Douglas found silver in the region. Other miners found copper, which led to a huge operation just to the southwest of Salt Lake City.

Many of Utah's miners were from Greece. They came because America's mines and railroads needed a steady infusion of labor that could be acquired cheaper than the workers already in the United States. Labor agents traveled to Greek villages, recruiting young Greek men.

In 1874 a military expedition led by Lieutenant Colonel George Armstrong Custer explored the Black Hills of present South Dakota. *Frank Leslie's Illustrated Newspaper* reported on August 29, 1874, "The Custer expedition reached the Black Hills, without meeting any opposition from the Indians. Rich gold and silver mines have been found, both placer and quartz diggings, and the immense section of country now visited by white men for the first time, now promises fully to repay the visit."

Although the area had been set aside for Native Americans, miners immediately started moving into the Black Hills and subsequent action opened it to white settlement.

The final great mineral boom of the period occurred in Canada's Yukon in 1896-97, although some earlier exploration had been done. The Klondike Gold Rush attracted miners from the United States. The miners in the Klondike had particularly difficult geographic conditions with which to deal. Those who crossed Alaska to reach Dawson City in the interior did so on the Dyea Trail over Chilkoot Pass, or they traveled to Skagway over White Pass, carrying their supplies on their backs in a tortuous journey. When miners began deserting Dawson City, some found gold on the Alaska beaches at Nome in 1899 and a rush to that location started. There miners couldn't stake claims as in other regions, so they generally worked a site during the day and abandoned it when the tide came in at night. The following morning the beach had an undisturbed look to it, created by the sweeping tide.

In most mining regions, miners did stake claims, doing so in a number of ways. One common manner of marking a claim in California involved miners simply leaving their tools on the site. A notice written on any type of paper and left at a claim site—which was delineated by four wooden stakes driven to mark the boundaries—also constituted a proper claim filing. Each miner generally could make only one claim; however, people circumvented that provision by working claims as partners or by financially backing, or grubstaking, other miners.

BUSINESSES

In every region of the West residents established towns to serve as social and business centers. In them men and women launched into professions ranging from doctors and lawyers, to store- or saloonkeepers, printers and newspaper publishers. A store- or saloonkeeper needed little training or experience to get started, just a place and some supplies. Uncle Dick Wootton, for example, was an explorer/mountain man before he became a trader in Taos, New Mexico, and in Denver City. He arrived in Denver City on Christmas Eve 1858 intending to do some trading for furs. But he had a couple of barrels of Taos Lightning, which the residents wanted, and he promptly began to dispense the brew, launching the first saloon in the area.

Doctors, as already related, may or may not have had any formal training to practice, and lawyers also may or may not have learned their profession in a formal setting. Generally anyone could be a lawyer so long as he or she was twenty-one-years-old, of good moral character and able to pass an examination administered by a judge. Most lawyers did work as an apprentice by studying under the direction of an established attorney, though that wasn't required. Lawyers generally commanded a place of status in a community because they may have had more education than other folks, and they generally earned more, up to $1,000 a month. Routine work for frontier lawyers related to settling mine or land claims. Women engaged in jobs as milliners or dressmakers. They worked as domestic servants, governesses, teachers and in other business occupations.

> The Commissioner of Internal Revenue has decided that dressmaking is a manufacture, and as such, if carried on to an extent exceeding $1,000 per year, including price of goods, requires a license. The dressmaker is required to make monthly returns, and to pay a tax of three per cent on the whole value of her manufactures.
> —FLIN, *January 10, 1863, 243-1*

NEWSPAPERS

All towns with any hope of long-term survival had a newspaper, and larger cities often had several. The editors of those "rags," as they were called, sometimes had learned their trade at colleges, but often they learned on the job, starting as a printer's devil at a young age by running errands and doing small chores around the office. Newspapers throughout the region started quickly, and many ceased publication just as quickly as the printer-editor-owner left one boomtown area for another. Some newspapers provided not only information but also stability for communities. The *Rocky Mountain News* in Denver, for example, began publication shortly after the first mineral strike in the region and remains in print today. Newspaper editors/writers became intensely involved with their communities, often as the most indefatigable promoters of all, and sometimes as civic leaders. Sometimes they stepped beyond printing to take an active role in the community's well-being. William Byers, editor of the *Rocky Mountain News*, for example, endorsed, and likely participated in, a vigilante group organized in 1860.

The papers of the West were printed on whatever kind of paper could be obtained, from standard newsprint to brown paper bags, or even in rare instances on pieces of wallpaper or linoleum. The printers set type by hand using wooden or metal type, locking it in type forms, and then printing it, in most cases, on a Washington Hand Press. With the invention and availability of the linotype, where strings of words were set in hot metal and then placed in forms for printing, the printing process became somewhat easier. The first linotypes sold in the West by the Mergenthaler Linotype Company went to the *Daily Journal* in Helena, Montana, in November 1891, and to the Houston *Post*, and Denver *Times* in 1892.

Legal advertising such as land notices made up a large share of the revenues received by newspaper publishers, who by 1895 paid reporters as much as $10 per week, while paying skilled printers up to $8, women typesetters $4 and printer's devils $2.50 each week. Though some payments for advertising came in the form of goods, publishers preferred—and in some cases demanded—cash. Newspaper publishers also generally ran sideline printing businesses, known as job shops, where they prepared handbills, and other materials.

HOMESTEADING/FARMING

The U.S. Government transferred more than 270 million acres to private ownership under provisions in the Homestead Law (see chapter two for more information on the Homestead Law). That land went to men and women who intended to forge a new home. Montana had the greatest number of homesteads claimed: more than 150,000. North Dakota had between 115,000 and 120,000, while Nebraska had about 105,000 claims.

In all cases homesteaders established residences and began working the

Potatoes were a primary crop for westerners. Though they could be dug with a potato fork, some farmers used a potato digger such as this to harvest the root crop each year. This potato digger is located in Bannack, Montana.

land, turning it into cropland or in some cases using it for livestock grazing. For the most part, homesteaders and farmers were self-reliant. They built their own homes and outbuildings (out of logs, sod or lumber), they hauled water from nearby streams or dug their own wells, they tilled the soil, planted crops and harvested them, raising almost everything they needed for survival with the exception of a few items like tobacco or sugar.

LOGGING/TIE HACKING

Timber workers made their debut in the southern Wyoming mountains in the 1860s as the Union Pacific Railroad made its way across the land. The railroad needed ties for track beds, and timber resources on Elk Mountain, Medicine Bow Peak and above the Medicine Bow River provided a supply. The demand for railroad materials continued for decades as tie camps spread throughout the Snowy Range and eventually to the Sierra Madre.

In 1867, three companies contracted with the Union Pacific to cut ties in the Laramie Mountains, including Gilman and Carter, Paxton and Turner, and Sprague, Davis and Company. Gilman and Carter negotiated a contract in 1868 to provide ties for construction of the Cheyenne to Denver link of the Denver Pacific Railway.

The workers hacked ties from lodgepole pine ranging from eleven to fourteen inches in diameter, and they also cut at least seventy-five thousand cords of wood needed to fire steam engines operating on the Union Pacific line.

Initially Coe and Carter paid between $.35 and $.60 per tie, while they earned from $1 to $1.30 for each tie from the Union Pacific. After initial construction, payments dropped to about $.50 per tie. The company did a tremendous business, however, supplying ties for use in Wyoming, western Nebraska and parts of Colorado. At the time, no rules or regulations were in place to manage the tie-cutting operations in Wyoming Territory, although in 1871 the United States General Land Office attempted to regulate the industry, apparently with little cooperation from the large tie companies and therefore with little success.

During the period 1870-80, timber workers harvested an estimated 2.5 million ties and an additional 400,000 mine props from the region that is now encompassed by the Medicine Bow National Forest in southern Wyoming.

The workers cut ties during the winter and stacked them in decks along the various mountain streams. By spring they had hundreds of thousands of ties ready to drive down rivers to railroad loading points. When spring snowmelt swelled creeks and rivers, the tie hacks released the ties, floating them downstream. Men stood on the floating ties, pushing them apart with pike poles when they became entangled. Sometimes the ties spread out over fields as water flowed over their banks; on other occasions they jammed together and the men used their pike poles to push them apart and get them moving downstream again.

Cutting and driving ties represented hard, dangerous, sometimes deadly,

Tie hack tools included, from top, saws, a broad ax, chopping ax, pickaroon, and a tie peeler. These items are from the Grand Encampment Museum collection.

work. Among the accidents reported were trees falling on loggers and incidents when tie drivers drowned while trying to break jams in the rivers.

Logging became a major industry in the Pacific Northwest, that had large forest reserves and massive-sized trees as compared with those which grew in the Rocky Mountain region. Loggers utilized a variety of hand-powered and eventually motor-driven tools to harvest timber. In most regions use of power-driven saws became popular after the 1860s, and by the 1870s double circular saws were used to turn massive trees into varying sizes of planks and other lumber. A breaking-down saw was developed in the 1870s to help lumbermen deal with production of huge redwood trees, but not until the 1880s and development of the band saw did timbermen really have a way to handle the gigantic trees, many of which were at least ten or more feet in diameter.

Tools of the Trade

Broadax: An ax with a long, wide blade used to square logs into railroad ties or timbers for house and other construction.

Bucking Saw: Designed for use by one or two loggers and used to saw trees into lengths once they had been felled. Gullets tended to be less pronounced than those of falling saws.

Donkey Engine: A power engine used to move downed timber. A steel cable, called a choker, was attached to the tree and then attached to the donkey engine, which pulled it toward the engine, similar to reeling in a fish.

Falling Ax: Used by all loggers to chop trees down. Each falling ax had a long, narrow blade and a long handle or haft often up to four feet long so loggers could cut into the heart of trees, some of which were eight feet in diameter, particularly in the Pacific Northwest.

Falling Saw: A long saw, sometimes up to ten feet, used to cut down trees and most often operated by a team of two loggers. The falling saws had deep gullets between the teeth in order to take a bigger bite out of the tree on each pass.

Millrace: A series of wooden sluice gates used to release water and allow floating of timber for lumber mills.

Pickaroon: A long-handled tool with a sharply pointed head used to move logs.

> He and a fellow workman were using picaroons when he was struck just below the knee cap in the right leg, the point penetrating the bone for a depth of one and one half inches, making a very ugly wound.—Grand Encampment Herald, *June 9, 1905*

Tie hacks used a variety of tools including the tie peelers, top left; a tie caliper to measure the side of each tie, center; a scoring ax (the head only is shown at right) and a broad ax (the head only is shown at left). The small round snowshoes were used on horses when freighting in deep snow country. These items are in the Grand Encampment Museum collection.

Pike Pole or Cant Hook: A five-foot-long pole with a knotched metal hook on the end used to grab and roll logs on land or in rivers as they were floated to railroad or mill landings.

Skid Road: The trail over which logs were skidded. The skid road from logging areas to waiting ships near Portland, Oregon, became a pathway for loggers to go to town. Eventually entrepreneurs built brothels, gambling halls and saloons along the road to serve the loggers. The words "skid road" were corrupted to "skid row," a place where saloons and brothels served vagrants and alcoholics.

Skids: Wooden pieces placed over the road where trees needed to be pulled for loading onto wagons or other conveyances or to sawmills established in the mountains. The trees were skidded over the road with the use of teams of oxen or mules handled by bull whackers or mule skinners. A skid greaser went ahead of the trees being pulled and, using a broom, swept a coating of grease onto the skids. The grease might be animal fat, rancid butter or even fish oil.

Wedges: Made of metal or wood, wedges of varying width were driven into a cut in a tree to keep it open so the saw blades wouldn't pinch. They were also used to control the direction in which the tree should fall.

Positions of the Trade

Buckers: Loggers who sliced downed trees into usable lengths, ranging from sixteen to forty feet.

Choker Setters: The loggers who attached cables around trees so they could be moved with the power from a donkey engine.

Fallers: The loggers who worked with long crosscut saws to cut down trees.

Flume Herders: The workers who spread out alongside flumes—often v-shaped so logs and timbers didn't get stuck in them—to keep the wood moving at a steady pace and to make any necessary repairs.

Peelers: The loggers who stripped bark from downed trees by using sharp peeling bars. Peelers worked primarily on redwoods, which had thick bark, and rarely on spruce or fir, which had thinner bark.

COWBOYS/RANCHERS

Cowmen, cattlemen or women, or cattle barons owned ranches; cowboys worked with cattle. Some early emigrants, and certainly the Spanish land-grant families in the Southwest and California, had cattle, often in vast numbers. The trail-driving era of the cowboys started after the Civil War. Men in Texas started rounding up wild herds and began driving them north either to railheads where they could be shipped to eastern markets, or to ranges on the north plains in the present-day states of Montana, Wyoming, Colorado, Nebraska and South Dakota.

> A Texas letter writer says: 'Any man in this State who does not own 400 head of cattle and 70 or 100 horses and mules is worse than worthless. Beef sells here at 5 cents a pound, horses and mules from $15 to $30 for round lots, and are within 200 miles of a good market. As far as the eye can reach in every direction, and as far as you may go the country is alive with stock. The whole markets

of the United States might be supplied here, and there would not be any apparent decrease.'—FLIN, *November 4, 1865, 98-4*

Immense droves of cattle are already in motion in Kansas going northward, the laws of Kansas permitting the passage of Texas Cattle from December 1 to March 1.—FLIN, *January 8, 1870, 283-4*

The cowboy's "high season" lasted only about twenty years, from about 1865 until the late 1880s, although cattle ranching continued throughout the century and had existed prior to 1865 as well in certain locales.

Cowboys can be classified by their jobs (moving and caring for cattle) and their clothes (rough pants, high boots and wide hats). Most cowboys were young, in some cases barely in their teens, though quite a number had fought in the Civil War and were older, perhaps a bit jaded. Cowboys were of many ethnic heritages. Not only were they of Spanish or Mexican descent, they also were Anglo, Native American, and African American.

They bragged and swore a lot, liked pretty girls and enjoyed music both to soothe themselves and their herds.

Though cowboys have a romantic image, the fact is they worked hard, often riding hours or days at a time with only a horse as a companion; they did their jobs in all kinds of weather from blistering heat to freezing cold. To a cowboy, and to a cattle owner, the most important thing was taking care of the stock, and many a hand (a term referring to a cowboy) suffered frostbite or even death in order to do that job. The creed of the cowboy was loyalty, and for most of them the important thing in life was "riding for the brand," or being responsible to his employer.

Cowboys worked for huge ranches like the XIT, the Matador, and the King Ranches of Texas, or the Swan Land and Cattle Company in Wyoming. Though many cowboys dreamed of having their own ranches, and they might have roped and branded a few stray animals in order to achieve that goal, for the most part ranches were in the hands of wealthy ranchers. Many of them after 1870 were from Britain or Scotland when the nobility and the British remittance men found their way to the West, likely first on hunting expeditions, and later as landowners when they established cattle kingdoms. The remittance men were individuals who received regular payments from their families, sometimes in order to keep them from returning home. Such men as Moreton Frewen in Wyoming's Powder River Basin established huge ranches marked with ostentatious habitations such as Frewen's Castle.

In the earliest years after the Civil War, ranchers could establish their own empires, as did Charles Goodnight, who is remembered for having forged a trail to take cattle to northern ranges and markets. Ranchers were both male and female, often operating ranches as partnerships between husbands and wives or fathers and daughters.

The basic equipment needed by all cowboys was, first, a horse, likely a mustang captured wild on the prairie and broken to ride. Each cowboy had a string of horses to use, which were rotated to give all an opportunity to work part of the time and to rest part of the time. Though some cowboys owned their own horses, for the most part the animals belonged to the ranches. Cowboys also had to have a saddle, comprised in some manner of a wooden framework called a "tree," over which a saddlemaker placed leather to form skirts, seats and the fenders to which cowboys attached stirrups.

Saddles could be either single- or double-rigged, a term that related to the number of cinches used to hold it in place. Texans liked double-rigged saddles,

particularly for roping, because they stayed firmly in place on the horse's back; Mexican vaqueros preferred a Spanish rig, which went by the name rimfire, that had the cinch passing over the front of the horse's belly. A three-quarter rig had a single cinch positioned farther back on the saddle (and subsequently on the horse) than a Spanish rig, and the centerfire rig placed the cinch directly in the middle of the saddle (and the horse's belly). This was the most common type of western saddle rig. The earliest California saddles of the 1830s had large leather saddle skirts and hollow stirrups covered with equally large pieces of leather called

Women rode horseback throughout the West, sometimes astride as men rode, but often using side saddles. This saddle is at the Grand Encampment Museum.

tapaderas or taps. By 1850 Texans used saddles with few embellishments—little more than a saddle tree with a horn or pommel, a leather-covered cantle (at the back of the seat) and stirrups with narrow fenders. By 1870 saddles had a longer seat and the saddle tree was completely covered with leather, but the saddles weighed about forty pounds and therefore were heavier than the earlier Texas saddles and the later California saddles. The 1880 California saddle weighed about ten pounds less than the Denver saddle, and it often featured fancy tooling on the leather parts. Some cowboys believed the tooling actually helped them stay in the saddle more easily.

Cowboys guided their horses with a variety of bridles made of leather, braided rawhide or braided horsehair. Though they sometimes used a hackamore (which had no bit), particularly when breaking a young horse, more likely they rode with a bit in the horse's mouth. There were many types of bits such as the spade, curb, ring or half-breed (which had characteristics of both the curb and spade versions).

Almost all cowboys carried ropes or *riatas* to use in catching cows and calves or horses and for tying them when branding or doctoring. Spanish vaqueros used rawhide braided riatas up to sixty feet long. Most western cowboys used grass ropes that could be easily knotted to form a small loop, or honda or hondo, through which the rope passed to make a larger loop needed for catching animals.

Roping cattle was a primary job of any cowboy and how to accomplish this task became a contest of skill for the riders. Texas cowboys tied their rope hard and fast to the saddle horn, while California cowboys tended to dally rope, or simply wrap their rope around the horn. Northern cowboys—many who came from Texas—generally tied hard and fast.

Besides moving cattle from one range to another, cowboys also marked animals with the owner's brand. Brands and earmarks helped cattle ranchers determine ownership; standard practice was to consider any unbranded calf to be the property of the ranch whose cow the calf suckled. Brands could be placed on the right or left side, hip, shoulder or jaw. When moving cattle from Texas to northern ranges, a "road brand" was used. When the cattle reached their new range, they were rebranded. The L brand used by Alexander Swan in Wyoming for a road brand on a herd taken to Rock Creek in the 1870s was reversed upon arrival to make a 7, and the ranch became the Ell Seven (L7).

Cowboys heated branding irons, such as these, in fires until they were red hot before applying them to the side of an animal during branding. These branding irons are in the Grand Encampment Museum collection.

Many brands were made from letters taken from a rancher's name; some were plays on words, such as the Bar YY brand of rancher J.H. Barwise. A large number were single letters positioned in myriad ways (tumbling right K, reverse K [backward], crazy K [upside down], crazy reverse K, lazy K [lying on its back], etc.), and even more were symbols such as the pitchfork, diamond, half diamond, double diamond, key, anchor, broken heart, arrow, circle or goose egg. Ranchers had their own irons, which they heated in wood fires until they were red hot before pressing them to the animal's hide for branding. When branding they singed the hair and lightly scarred the animal's hide. Burning too deeply into the hide damaged it, so the man doing the branding was careful not to apply too much pressure.

Rustlers who stole cattle from legitimate ranchers often used a cinch ring or a "running" iron to modify brands. A rustler, for instance, might turn a K brand into a K Bar simply by adding a new brand (a single long mark) behind the existing one then keep the animal out of public view until the new brand healed. There were so many brands on the open range during the period 1870-90 that cowboys and cattlemen carried brand books issued by livestock associations in order to know which animals belonged to which ranches. Ranches also routinely published their brands in newspapers.

There were more than two hundred variations of ear notches, also used to identify animals, ranging from a simple split to a "steeple fork" or "hack." Some cattle owners also sliced the skin under an animal's neck, forming a "dewlap," which helped with identification, particularly at longer distances.

Trail-driving cowboys riding night herd—checking on the animals on night bed grounds—sang to keep the herds quiet, and they told time by watching the Big Dipper's movements around the North Star. At 10 P.M., the Big Dipper might be perpendicular with the handle up and the dipper down and to the northwest of the North Star. At 4 A.M. the dipper had rotated to horizontal and was located to the south and west of the North Star. In flat, treeless regions the North Star also served as a directional guide for the cook (who generally preceded the herd so he could establish camp and prepare meals before the cowboys arrived). Each evening, when traveling on flat terrain, the cook waited for the North Star to appear, then carefully pointed the wagon tongue toward it so he'd be able to plot his direction in the morning.

SALOON GIRLS/PROSTITUTION

Prostitutes found work throughout the West and went by names ranging from "prostitute" and "whore" to "sporting woman," "painted cat," "girl of the night," "lady of the half-world" or "*demimondaine*," "fallen woman," "calico queen," "*nymphe du prairie*" ("prairie nymph") or "*nymphe du pave*" ("street nymph"), "inmate," or "soiled dove."

There generally were four "classes" of such women and the houses where they worked. At the top of the social scale was the parlor house, which had the most beautiful girls, the finest foods and liquors, the most elegant decor and, of course, the highest prices, perhaps $100 for a visit. Often wealthy men, prominent businessmen and politicians patronized such parlor houses, and in some cases they were behind-the-scenes owners of the establishments. Next in line were the houses operated by a "madam." These were of lower quality than the fine parlor houses. Such houses charged from $2 to $100 and had a few girls, but the surroundings and provisions weren't quite so good as parlor houses. Even lower on the scale were the one- or two-room shacks, known as "cribs," where a prostitute lived and worked alone, although sometimes she had a man who helped her find clients. She earned little, perhaps only $.50 per client, but could refuse clients. At the lowest end of the scale were the dives where women had no choice in partners, and where the profession was at its most sordid, taking place in a dingy, tiny back bedroom of a saloon. Charges there generally were about $1 and $2.

The names for the various houses included: "palaces of sinful pleasure," "wine rooms," "gilded palaces of shame," "parlor houses," "cribs," "mansions," "cottages" and "female boarding houses."

Concentrations of "sporting houses" occurred in "red-light districts," which were most common in mining and cattle towns but not unheard of in any size and type of community in the West. The origin of the term "red-light district" is uncertain. It could have come from the Red Light, a sporting house in Dodge City, Kansas, which had blood-red glass in the front door windows, or from railroad trainmen who left their red signal lights outside such houses when they went in for a diversion from work.

Prostitution was not allowed on military installations; however, soldiers and women of the frontier forts routinely broke the rules. Laundresses hired by the military to assist with chores on military posts most often were prostitutes who did more for the men than wash their shirts, trousers and underwear. Though there were regulations limiting women with venereal diseases from being with troops, in most cases they were not enforced. In 1878 Congress ceased providing funding for laundress positions at frontier military posts. That didn't mean the women weren't available for various activities; they simply weren't on the posts, but instead relocated to the hog ranches. (See chapter five for more information on hog ranches.)

In *My Early Travels and Adventures in America and Asia,* Henry Stanley wrote of a visit to the Hell-on-Wheels town of Julesburg, Colorado Territory, in 1867.

> These women are expensive articles, and come in for a large share of the money wasted. In broad daylight they may be seen gliding through the sandy streets in Black Crook dresses, carrying fancy derringers slung to their waists, with which tools they are dangerously expert. Should they get into a fuss, western chivalry will not allow them to be abused by any man whom they may have robbed.

Although many girls and women engaged in prostitution for a variety of reasons, such as a way to support themselves and even in a few instances because they truly enjoyed sex, by far the majority found themselves forced into the occupation. Prostitutes generally had unhappy lives. Suicide rates were high among those engaged in the profession, as was the use of drugs and alcohol. Among those forced into prostitution were Chinese girls, many of whom were sold by their families, and others who were obtained through kidnapping and coercion. Chinese prostitutes, most of whom also were slaves, became known as "Daughters of Joy" or "Celestial females."

> CALIFORNIA—At an auction sale of Chinese girls on the 28th, ult., 22 were disposed of, the youngest bringing $450 each, while middle-aged women commanded only $100. . . . The authorities of San Francisco have discovered a Secret society which furnishes and protects houses of prostitution.—FLIN, *August 16, 1873, 367-4*

Prostitutes in Helena, Montana, in 1880 earned an average monthly income of $233, as compared with $125 earned by bank clerks, or the $90 to $100 earned each week by carpenters, bricklayers or stonemasons. And if a prostitute truly wanted to establish a new life, she could save her money from working in one town, buy respectable clothes, board a train and step off the train in another city as a "respectable widow." Some madams provided economic support to towns by lending money to businessmen, so they actually helped develop some communities.

GENERAL INDUSTRY

Flour milling became an important part of the Nebraska economy after the 1860s, but the earliest grist mill operated at Fort Atkinson in 1821. That mill used draft animals for power and could grind up to 150 bushels of grain each day. Most of Nebraska's earliest mills—those developed between 1860 and 1890—used waterpower. Very few used traditional upright waterwheels; most had a horizontal wheel or turbine. In many cases mill owners constructed a dam to provide the power, but waterpower wasn't totally reliable. In drought years streams dwindled, and sometimes there wasn't adequate water to produce the power needed for mill operations. On other occasions the millpond washed out, and work had to be suspended until a new dam and pond could be established. Some mills used wind power.

In the earliest days of plains and prairie settlement, flour mills were few and far between, requiring farmers to haul their grain many miles for processing. Some had to travel a hundred miles or more to a mill, where they would either wait to have their wheat ground or exchange it for flour from wheat the miller had previously received and ground. The earliest operations involved millstones for grinding, but in the 1880s most mills converted to more efficient steel rollers. These rollers processed wheat more finely, making it possible for millers to better use the wheat brought in by farmers.

Communities with a mill enjoyed many advantages over those without one. Not only would businesses prosper when farmers from outlying areas came to town bringing their wheat, but many early mills produced excess power, providing their communities with electricity. Another side benefit was the millpond, which served as a recreation center for the town.

A variety of other industries existed in the West during the period as well:

> During the year 1856, 14,800,000 bricks were manufactured in the Sacramento vicinity. The various yards gave employment to 141 men, and used 4,875 cords of wood.—FLIN, *March 21, 1857, 239-1*

> A silk manufactory is to be established at San Jose, California. Twenty-five acres of ground have been given to the proprietors, upon which they propose at once to erect buildings for the manufactory and for workmen. These will be mostly German and French. The California papers urge the raising of mulberry trees and cocoons.—FLIN, *December 15, 1866, 195-3*

The Mormons of Utah have turned their attention to the production of gloves that rival those of Paris in delicacy and workmanship. The gloves are made from genuine kid, raised in the vicinity of Salt Lake.—FLIN, *July 23, 1870, 295-4*

The California and Lake Tahoe Artificial Fish-culture Company, has a fish ranche [*sic*] four miles from Truckee, with six ponds, . . . containing 2,000 trout three years old, 14,000 two years old, and 110,000 one year old and younger, all born in a hatchery house. —FLIN, *February 4, 1871, 351-4*

CALIFORNIA—During the month of August the San Juan woolen mill manufactured and finished 6,250 yards of cashmere, 11,400 yards of plain, and 844 yards of heavy comb flannel, and 110 pair of white, 28 pair of brown, and 523 pair of gray blankets. —FLIN, *September 13, 1873, 11-4*

ADDITIONAL READING

Altherton, Lewis. *The Cattle Kings.* Lincoln: University of Nebraska Press, 1961.

Barney, Libeus. *Letters of the Pike's Peak Gold Rush.* San Jose: Talisman Press, 1959.

Butler, Anne. *Daughters of Joy, Sisters of Misery: Prostitutes in the American West, 1865-1890.* Urbana: University of Illinois, 1985. An excellent resource.

Clay, John. *My Life on the Range.* Chicago: n.p., 1924.

Dary, David. *Cowboy Culture: A Saga of Five Centuries.* New York: Alfred Knopf, 1981. Reprint, Lawrence: Univeristy Press of Kansas, 1989. An excellent resource.

———. *Entrepreneurs of the Old West.* New York: Alfred Knopf, 1986. An excellent resource.

———. *Red Blood & Black Ink: Journalism in the Old West.* New York: Alfred Knopf, 1998. An excellent resource.

Forbis, William H., and the Editors of Time-Life Books. *The Cowboys.* Alexandria, Va.: Time-Life Books, 1973.

Hafen, LeRoy R. *Pike's Peak Gold Rush Guidebooks of 1859.* Glendale, Calif.: Arthur H. Clark, 1941.

Johnson, William Weber, and the Editors of Time-Life Books. *The Forty-Niners.* Alexandria, Va.: Time-Life Books, 1974.

Karolevitz, Robert F. *Newspapering in the Old West.* New York: Bonanza Books, 1965. Good information and many historic photographs of old newspaper operations.

Miller, Ronald Dean. *Shady Ladies of the West.* Tucson, Ariz.: Westernlore Press, 1985.

Mothershead, Harmon Ross. *The Swan Land and Cattle Company, LTD.* Norman: University of Oklahoma Press, 1971.

Moulton, Candy. *The Grand Encampment: Settling the High Country.* Glendo, Wyo.: High Plains Press, 1997. Good information about tie hacks and copper mining.

Petrick, Paula. *No Step Backward.* Helena: Montana Historical Society Press, 1987. An excellent resource dealing with prostitution in Helena.

Pinkerton, Joan Trego. *Knights of the Broadax: The Story of the Wyoming Tie Hack.* Caldwell, Idaho: The Caxton Printers, 1981.

Seagraves, Ann. *Soiled Doves: Prostitution in the Early West.* Hayden, Idaho: Wesanne Publications, 1994. A good general source with information about specific prostitutes.

Seymour, John. *The Forgotten Crafts: A Practical Guide to Traditional Skills.* New York: Portland House, 1984. An excellent resource.

Slatta, Richard W. *Comparing Cowboys and Frontiers.* Norman: University of Oklahoma Press, 1997.

Stanley, Henry. *My Early Travels and Adventures in America and Asia.* New York: Charles Scribner's Sons, 1905.

Van Dorn, Perry. *Flickering Lights in Vacant Windows: A History of the J.W. Hugus & Co.* Grand Junction, Colo.: Pyramid Printing, 1992.

Voynick, Stephen M. *Colorado Gold: From the Pike's Peak Rush to the Present.* Missoula, Mont.: Mountain Press Publishing Co., 1992.

———. *Leadville: A Miner's Epic.* Rev. ed. Missoula, Mont.: Mountain Press Publishing Co., 1988.

Ward, Fay E. *The Cowboy at Work: All About His Job and How He Does It.* Norman: University of Oklahoma Press, 1987.

Warp, Harold. *A History of Man's Progress from 1830 to the Present.* Minden, Nebr.: The Harold Warp Pioneer Village, 1978. An excellent resource for its photographs, even if the text is weak.

West, Elliot. *The Saloon on the Rocky Mountain Mining Frontier.* Lincoln: University of Nebraska Press, 1979. An excellent resource.

Wheeler, Keith, and the Editors of Time-Life Books. *The Chroniclers.* Alexandria, Va.: Time-Life Books, 1976. A good reference book.

———. *The Townsmen.* Alexandria, Va.: Time-Life Books, 1975. A good reference book.

Williams, Richard L., and the Editors of Time-Life Books. *The Loggers.* Alexandria, Va.: Time-Life Books, 1976. A good reference book.

CHAPTER FOURTEEN

ENTERTAINMENT

usic, ranging from sharing of songs played on a piano, accordion, fiddle or mouth harp; reading newspapers, periodicals, novels and the Bible; storytelling; and visiting were primary entertainment for people throughout the West during the period.

Book peddlers traveled throughout the West, but most residents obtained reading material through mail order from newspaper and periodical advertisements. Many people also received reading materials from family or friends in more settled areas. Not all people engaged in reading as many were illiterate.

Most households had a Bible, but westerners also read classics by authors like Charles Dickens, Shakespeare, Byron and Sir Walter Scott. Many periodicals had weekly serials. Among the most popular periodicals and newspapers were *Frank Leslie's Illustrated Newspaper, Harper's Weekly, Harper's Monthly, Scribner's Monthly, Atlantic Monthly, Scientific American, Ladies Home Journal* and *Godey's Lady's Book*. People read what they could find ranging from catalogs to almanacs and religious tracts.

Social events ranged from horseback riding across the prairie to hunting, fishing and sporting contests involving both men and women; ice skating or sleigh riding; taffy pulls; spelling bees; and masquerade parties or balls. Westerners also found "entertainment" in the courthouse, where they attended criminal trials, and even at lynchings or legal hangings. Practical jokes were common, such as snipe hunting, where locals took a gullible newcomer out after dark to a secluded area and left the new snipe hunter holding a bag at a "snipe run." The experienced snipe hunters said they would scatter out and spook the snipes down the run and into the bag. They left their new companion with his bag and scattered, making noise as they went to scare up fresh snipe. Then they headed back to town or to a local home where they likely waited for their initiate to return (once he caught on to the fact that no snipe would run into his bag). It was a common practical joke that remains effective today.

It took little encouragement for people to gather for a dance at a home or perhaps the schoolhouse, and in such cases the dancing generally lasted throughout the night, with a dinner at midnight or a breakfast at dawn before people returned to their homes to do chores and work. In almost all cases the entertainment involved the entire family. As early as 1850, California had theaters which hosted traveling companies of performers presenting both plays and operas, and motion pictures could be viewed by 1897.

MUSIC AND DANCES

Whenever people gathered, those who were musically inclined found themselves recruited to provide entertainment. They played fiddles, accordions, mouth or Jew's harps, mandolins, guitars, banjos and organs or pianos when available. Hispanic residents in California and the Southwest hosted fandangos, which were lavish parties involving traditional dances, food and music.

Music played an important role in entertainment for westerners and was provided by many instruments such as this square grand piano, now located at the Gand Encampment Museum, Encampment, Wyoming. Residents often had paintings done of themselves to display in their homes, such as the wedding portrait of Charles and Emma Vyvey, shown at right.

Settlers passed word throughout a region of a dance that could be reached by horse and wagon within a reasonable period of time, and then gathered at a central location such as a ranch house or the school-house. If no building was available, and the weather cooperated, dances took place out-of-doors on the lawn or bare piece of ground. At most dances the men had a bottle of whiskey or other alcoholic beverage which they freely shared, and they may have danced even while smoking their long-stemmed pipes.

When it came time for the dance, residents moved furniture outside or pushed it against the walls. They rolled up the rugs, and the activity started. All members of the family attended a dance, from the eldest to the youngest. As infants and young children grew tired, their parents placed them on coats or blankets out of the way and the adults continued dancing (and visiting) until dawn. Sometimes pranksters changed the babies' clothing and parents actually returned home with the wrong child. In one instance in southern Wyoming in the 1890s, cowboys swapped teams on wagons, and ranchers driving home in the predawn darkness didn't realize that they had their neighbor's team until they arrived home and it got light.

Banjos, guitars and fiddles were among the instruments used to provide music at western dances and Mexican fandangos. These banjos are part of the Grand Encampment Museum collection.

Dances at military posts were also routine entertainment for the people stationed there. In areas where men heavily outnumbered women, some of the men tied a handkerchief on their arm and took the part of women for dancing purposes.

For a dance in Grand Encampment, Wyoming, in 1898, the women wore calico dresses or skirts and took with them a tie of similar material. The men picked a tie as they arrived, and then spent the evening as a partner to the female wearing a matching dress.

While some religious groups, like the Methodists and German Baptist Brethren, opposed dancing, the Mormons endorsed it as an entertainment, holding regular dances when they migrated from Illinois to Utah in 1846-47, and after they settled in Utah.

By the 1850s dancing schools had been established in California; at these schools people could learn to properly do the polkas, waltzes, square dances, the Virginia reel, quadrilles, and schottisches that were the common Anglo dances of the period. At military balls near Hays, Kansas, during the 1860s, men either wore white gloves or placed a handkerchief between their hand and their partner's dress, as it wasn't considered appropriate for a man to place his hot hands directly on a woman's back. Because there were approximately ten men to every woman, a special committee, comprised of Catherine Cavender and two other girls whose fathers served at the fort, had the assignment of finding more female dancing partners. The girls from the surrounding area were contacted to attend the ball. They were chaperoned by wives of company lieutenants and transported from their homes in military ambulances.

Dances were social outings for young people as well as for matrons and elderly men. If those individuals didn't participate in every dance, they did take the opportunity to visit with neighbors, catching up on news from outlying homesteads and ranches and sharing information about books they'd read, clothing styles, recipes and the like.

In some western cities, and at military forts, dances often became grand balls with music provided by multiple-piece orchestras and participants wearing their finest suits or ball gowns. At a grand ball given at Fort Hays, Kansas, by Company C, Sixth Cavalry in 1874, the elaborate ballroom had flags covering the ceiling with chains of evergreens adding to the decorations.

> The walls were ornamented with pictures, quaint designs in sabres, pistols, and carbines, and occasionally a helmet was displayed midst a profuse ornamentation of rosettes and evergreens, the music stand, an elaborate platform, tastefully decorated with flags and evergreens, from which the Sixth band discoursed elaborate strains of music. Hays City turned out in en masse, and, in fact, the crowd was immense, and good will pervaded the entire affair, and not an ill word was spoken nor an intoxicated person seen or known to be around the premises.—*Junction City, Kansas,* Union, *April 4, 1874*

Many communities, as soon as they had adequate population, formed brass bands or orchestras.

THEATER

Public theater performances in the West date to the earliest part of the period; these performances were sometimes provided by local actors, but often by traveling troupes of professional stage actors. They performed in whatever venue was available, ranging from the elaborate playhouses in mining boomtowns (such as San Francisco, California; Leadville, Colorado; or Virginia City, Montana) to canvas-sided, tentlike structures. The theater companies performed often in the mining boomtowns of the West where they knew men had money for such entertainment. In certain cases miners would pay a $100 to attend the opening-night performance. Following a popular play, the miners threw coins onto the stage for the actresses, covering the stage with their offerings that might also include small buckskin sacks of gold dust.

The actresses had talent and wore flamboyant—often flimsy—costumes that many "proper women" abhorred. Sarah Lippencott in *New Life in New Lands* noted that actresses in Denver in 1871 were "in horrible undress, swinging and tumbling, and plunging heals over head out of their sphere." And she added, "actresses coming to Colorado have been compelled, at a painful sacrifice to their modesty to 'shed the light frivolity of dress' in great measure."

Not all communities had a hall or venue capable of hosting a traveling theater group, nor the population to command such performances. However,

---

SONGS

Some popular Anglo songs in the West were these:
Old Dan Tucker (1843)
My Old Aunt Sally (1843)
Buffalo Gals (1844)
Jimmy Crack Corn, or The Blue Tail Fly (1846)
Seein' the Elephant (1849)
Sweet Betsy From Pike (1849)
Old Folks at Home, or Swanee River
Carry Me Back to Old Virginny (particularly popular in California mining regions)
Ol' Susannah (particularly sung by travelers on the California Trail)
Old Zip Coon
Tassels on My Boots

Cowboys sang to the cattle when on the trails to keep them calm. Many of the cowboy songs were tunes adapted from popular ballads or lullabies and verses were often added by singers as they made their way around the herd at night. Among the favorite cowboy songs were:
Cotton-Eyed Joe
Dinah Had a Wooden Leg
Black Jack Grove
Doney Gal
Billy on the Low Ground
The Old Chisholm Trail
Give the Fiddler a Dram
The Devil's Dream
Arkansas Traveler
Good-bye Old Paint
Saddle Ole Spike
The Unfortunate Pup
Git Along Little Dogies
Hell Among the Yearlin's
Sally Gooden

---

those areas didn't forsake the possibility of theatrical entertainment, and melodrama was the most common form. Variety shows presented at local businesses, such as saloons or hurdy-gurdy houses (dance halls), also were popular, with entertainment ranging from singing and dancing to lectures, short plays, speeches and poetry readings.

Hurdy-gurdy houses got their name from the wheezy-sounding pump organ used at the earliest establishments of their ilk. Some dance halls employed girls as taxi dancers, or partners for male customers, with the $.25 fee charged per dance going directly to the dance hall proprietor, who in turn paid the girls.

A variety of patent medicine shows traveled the region, usually comprised of a limited company involving the "doctor" or medicine man, a woman (generally buxom to entice male customers) and perhaps an assistant or two to help with sales and promotions as well as standing in when another performer was necessary. The medicine shows played on a vacant lot or in a small local hall. They were often free and involved musical entertainment, some variety acts, the singing of popular ballads and other songs and then the selling of patent medicines. The routine of having some entertainment followed by a period to sell medicine might be repeated several times during the course of one show, or until the audience had dwindled to a point where it was not profitable to continue.

CHAUTAUQUA

After 1865 tent shows started touring the West providing such entertainment as music and dramatic performances. They were followed by lyceums, organized in communities in order to discuss or debate interesting topics of timely importance, and Chautauquas, in which poets, visiting lecturers and musicians not only entertained, but also educated people. At Chautauquas in Beatrice, Nebraska, from 1889 through 1916, activities involved discussions, lectures and lessons in the fine arts and domestic sciences. The community built a pavilion in 1889 just for the Chautauqua, and special railroad rates and reduced lodging prices at local establishments all contributed to the growth of the event.

"The entire Chautauqua interest of the state is centered on the Beatrice assembly. It is surely destined to be the most popular assembly in the state," the *Beatrice Daily Express* reported in 1889. Among the programs were musical entertainment and a lecture on "The Bedouins of Arabia," showing the diversity of interest.

The Chautauqua took its name from Lake Chautauqua, New York, where in 1874 a group of 142 Methodist Sunday School teachers gathered for training. Soon the Chautauqua format spread throughout the country. The Interstate Chautauqua Assembly formed to serve Kansas, Colorado, Iowa and Missouri.

Other entertainment involved debating societies, poetry readings and the like. In Brownville, Nebraska, the Brownville Lyceum, Library and Literary Association debated topical issues such as the Missouri Compromise. Other communities throughout the West had similar activities.

> A few days ago, in Liberty township, Ohio, a young woman was so much affected while reading a piece of poetry entitled 'Do they miss me at home,' that she fainted. Her mother, supposing that she was dying, became terribly excited, causing the rupture of a blood vessel, and she died in less than an hour. The daughter was insensible for about fifteen minutes, and then recovered.
> —FLIN, *July 25, 1857, 126-3*

GAMES AND SOCIALS

When they didn't have musical instruments, people provided their own music by chanting or singing rhythmic verses to such songs as "Old Dan Tucker" or "Skip to My Lou." At some gatherings people engaged in games such as charades, cribbage and checkers or running contests like "Run, Sheepie, Run"; "Flying Dutchman"; "Ring-around-the-Rosy"; and "Forfeits."

Party games included "Blind-Man's-Bluff," sometimes called "Boston" or "Quack," where a blindfolded contestant had to catch someone else, and "Old Mother Wobble," where participants mimicked each other doing silly things (like standing on their head). Those who couldn't do the mimicking had to forfeit a personal item such as a shoe, and penalties were assessed, such as allowing the men to "pick three cherries" where all the men gave three kisses to the girl who had failed in a stunt. In "Clap-in, Clap-out" the young men left the room while the young girls selected a partner from the absent men. Then as each man entered the room he had to sit beside whomever he thought had chosen him. The girls clapped if he sat in the wrong seat, and then he had to go back outside the room and wait for another chance to try to determine which girl had selected him. The game lasted until everyone had a partner.

Many of the socials involved games that allowed (and encouraged) kissing or hugging. As the June 28, 1878, *Dickinson County Chronicle* in Abilene, Kansas, reported, "Hug socials are now the rage. It costs ten cents to hug any one between fifteen and twenty [years old], five cents from twenty to thirty, one dollar to hug another man's wife, old maids two for a nickel, while female lecturers are free with a chromo [colored picture] thrown in. At these prices it is said that the old maids are most productive, because they can stand so much of it without getting tired."

Box socials became popular in the latter part of the period, with funding from sale of boxes often used to support schools or churches. For such socials, women made a meal and placed it in a decorated box which they took to the social. There the box was sold to male bidders and the high bidder for each box then ate the meal with the woman who had prepared it.

Another type of social—one involving work—was popular throughout the period. Known as a "bee," the social involved such activities as making quilts or building houses and barns. At quilting bees, neighborhood women gathered to help with the quilting of a comforter that in most cases had been pieced together by the woman hosting the "bee." The men also gathered for activities such as barn raisings or house bees. The combined efforts of several men meant a house or barn could be built fairly quickly. Cornhusking bees occurred during harvest season in regions where corn was a primary crop, and in most cases they turned into contests to determine who could husk the most ears of corn the quickest. If a man happened to husk an ear of uncommon red corn, he might be rewarded with a kiss from his choice of girls.

Socials might also involve simple get-togethers with storytelling and family suppers.

Millponds were the recreational hubs of many communities, a place for picnics, fishing and skating during the winter. Few bodies of water existed in southwestern Nebraska so the Champion Townsite Company actively promoted the Champion millpond, holding the first county fair near it in 1886. Other fairs took place west of the pond and a horse racing track went in as well.

Cowboys liked to play poker, wrestle, tell stories and sing songs. In some communities baseball became a popular pastime, and during the latter portion of the period, urban dwellers or those who had a more leisurely lifestyle played croquet or tennis.

> The West is famous for doing things in a thorough way; even in their amusements the same qualities are evinced. The present rage for base-ball has taken such hold on them that the Board of Trade of Chicago has challenged the Common Council of that city to a match game. The next novelty will be the judges and the parsons contending in the same spirit of friendly emulation.
> —FLIN, *September 7, 1867, 387-3*

Tenpins (which replaced ninepins when it was declared illegal in Connecticut in 1841) also was a popular game, played in California and other parts of the West after 1850. Other general entertainment included bare-fisted fighting, bearbaiting, wrestling matches, drinking or shooting contests and contests pitting various types of animals against each other—such as bulls and bears, or cocks, dogs and cougars. Asians enjoyed time in opium dens.

In mining communities, like those in Nevada, the activities were broad in scope. As Mark Twain put it in *Roughing It:* "There were military companies, fire companies, brass bands, hotels, theatres, 'hurdy-gurdy houses,' wide-open gambling places, political pow-wows, civic processions, streetfights, murders, inquests, riots, a whisky mill every fifteen steps . . . and some talk of building a church!"

Children's games included hopscotch, skipping rope, "Drop the Handkerchief," "Duck on Rock," "Ante Over," "Pom Pom Pull Away," "Run Sheep Run," "Single Hole" (a game involving marbles), "Blindman's Bluff," "Fly Away, Pigeon" and various games involving balls.

CLUBS AND ORGANIZATIONS

Wealthy cattle ranchers or business owners often established private clubs where they could gather. At places such as the Cactus Club (later the Cheyenne Club) in Cheyenne, Wyoming; the Montana Club in Helena; and the Denver Club in Colorado; cattle barons and businessmen routinely ate fine food, drank the best wines, whiskeys and other liquors and engaged in entertainment ranging from dances and social gatherings to gambling. Some of those establishments restricted participation to men.

Other westerners joined together in a variety of organizations such as the Independent Order of Odd Fellows (IOOF), Woodmen of the World, Knights of Pythias, AF&AM (Masonic lodges), Good Templars, Sons of Malta and Sons of Temperance. Women were involved in groups such as the Relief Society and Ladies Aid. A number of agrarian organizations, which had both male and female members, became popular during the period after 1867, including the as National Grange of the Order of Patrons of Husbandry, Farmer's Alliances, and the Grange. Bohemian immigrants in Kansas and Nebraska organized into unions such as the Western Bohemian Fraternal Association and Zapadni Cesko Bratrske Jednota (ZCBJ), building union halls in numerous towns.

HOLIDAYS

Probably the biggest Anglo celebration of the year took place on Independence Day when residents of nearly all communities gathered for parades, dances, picnics, horse races, speeches and other celebratory activities. As overland travelers headed toward Oregon and California, they considered it important— almost mandatory—to reach Independence Rock in present central Wyoming by the Fourth of July, so they could be sure to be over the western mountains before snow closed the passes. And when they reached Independence Rock, or wherever they happened to be on July 4th, travelers often celebrated. An 1853 wagon train celebration included a menu that had cake, pies, preserves, butter, rice, biscuits, sausage, tea and coffee along with a "fruit cake baked back home in Illinois and saved for the celebration."

> This morning about one o'clock the gards commenced to welcom in the glorious fourth aday sacred to every American by discharging their revolvers which was soon answered from camp this was the onley way we could celabrate but we thought of the sturing times at home the Orations the boom of Canon, bands of martial music pleasure rides prety Girls & Ball Rooms. The imagination had to take the place of the realaty.
> —*Edwin Bird, 1853 diary; typescript copy at Wyoming State Museum; original in Ayer Collection, Newberry Library, Chicago, Ill.*

At a Fourth of July celebration in Fort Stockton, Texas, the soldiers held contests with a greased pole and a greased pig, and they competed with neighboring ranchers and cowboys in wheelbarrow and sack races.

Most Hispanic and Anglo westerners made some attempt to celebrate Christmas. Among the "nearly essential" elements of a Christmas celebration were a tree—often a piece of sagebrush, a cottonwood or even a tumbleweed in plains areas where there were few evergreen trees—and some gifts. Holiday tree decorations included cranberries and popcorn strung together, pieces of colored paper or ribbon and candles. The candles were placed in tin holders and only lit under constant supervision as they could easily start a fire. Practical, homemade items like knitted socks, scarves and mittens found their way into Christmas packages or onto tree branches, as did food items such as apples, oranges, canned fruits and candy like taffy or popcorn balls. Little girls received rag dolls and miniature quilts, while little boys got tops or toys carved from locally available wood.

Because Christmas represented the only time all year when some people, both adults and children, received presents, the holiday had an important place in the minds of each. Some settlers seldom went to town, but they usually made at least one trip in anticipation of Christmas, buying new shoes, coats or other clothing, necessities that also served as presents.

Western businessmen, therefore, catered to the demand, such as those in Georgetown, Colorado, where the *Miner* reported in 1872:

> Monti & Guanella, agents of Santa Claus in Georgetown, are preparing to fill all orders for Christmas goods promptly, and to the entire satisfaction of their customers. The innery old gentleman flashing over the country with his capacious freight teams, has cramed [*sic*] the large store of his favorite agents with turkies and chickens, gobbling and crackling, to grace Christmas feasts. And then such quantities of vegetables, fruit confectionary, cake and toys for little girls, blushing maidens, stately dames, little boys and old boys, as the jolly old elf has on exhibition at his headquarters at Monti & Guanella's is a sight entertaining and highly satisfactory to the inhabitants of the "Silver Queen."

Asians in the West traditionally celebrated the Chinese New Year with a parade, fireworks and gifts. In Rock Springs, Wyoming, China Town residents had a thirty-foot-long silk dragon with a huge head, red and green eyes and a forked tongue. Between thirty and forty men carried the dragon by placing it over their heads as they paraded through town, stopping before each Chinese business and bowing several times.

CIRCUSES

The earliest circuses played in California prior to 1846. After 1869 when Dan Castello took his circus across country by rail to perform at large and small communities, circuses were a common and popular form of entertainment throughout the West. Though some circuses traveled by wagon, railroad transportation made it easier for the big shows to play in a variety of areas. The circus acts involved wild animals, acrobats, brass bands, clowns and high-wire artists.

WILD WEST SHOWS

The first clearly recognized Wild West show started in 1881 in Columbus, Nebraska, when William F. "Buffalo Bill" Cody, with his friends Luther and Frank North, former leaders of the Pawnee Scouts, held the first rehearsal for the Buffalo Bill Wild West. In 1882 Cody advertised for cowboys to participate in the July 4 "Old Glory Blow Out," which led to the Buffalo Bill Wild West and Congress of Rough Riders. Cody's show continued throughout the period, performing not only in the United States but also in Europe, and featuring acts ranging from shooting by Annie Oakley to re-creations of attacks on the Cheyenne-Deadwood stage line, various events depicting conflicts between the frontier army and Native Americans, and exhibitions of cowboy activities. Cody employed many Native Americans as well as former Indian fighters and cowboys. Many other Wild West shows organized during the latter portion of the period.

RODEOS

The first competitions among cowboys occurred out on the range where they challenged each other in roping and riding contests to determine who were the best hands. Though cowboys participated in Wild West exhibitions such as those operated by Buffalo Bill or Pawnee Bill, they didn't consider those shows to be true rodeos. The sport of rodeo, from the Spanish *rodear*, involved contests for bronco riding, horse racing and roping. Some competitions, known as *charreadas*, also occurred among Mexican equestrians. A rodeo likely took place in Deer Trail, Colorado, on Independence Day in 1869. On July 4, 1883, the "West of the Pecos" competition occurred in Pecos, Texas, and on July 4, 1888, Prescott, Arizona Territory, had a competition of rodeo events, charging admission for such an activity for the first time. In September 1897, Cheyenne, Wyoming, sponsored its first Frontier Day. Cheyenne had sponsored a limited competition back in 1872, but not until the 1890s did large rodeos organize. Contests involved both men and women.

Newspapers strongly criticized the first Cheyenne Frontier Day as a "roughneck show seeking to perpetuate the spirit of western rowdyism through which the West is passing." The *Cheyenne Daily Leader* added this comment: "Horses jumped fences, men were knocked down, and were thought killed, but we are happy to announce that no death resulted. The influence of Frontier Day is not elevating in character. . . . And it is a curious and inexplicable thing, the unaccountable desire of dozens of ladies to stand in the race track totally oblivious to the extreme novelty and danger of their position, and while it was a relief to see them grab their petticoats and get away safely from the deadly feet of the wild and crazy horses, the spectacle was not edifying and should be dispensed with next year."

FAIRS

In farming areas a common entertainment during the latter portion of the period involved fairs where judges could determine who had raised the best produce or livestock. Fairs often included horse races and other contests and almost always involved a picnic, with participants spreading blankets on the ground and pulling from baskets various homemade treats ranging from fried chicken and ham to bread, preserves, pickles, vegetables, cake and pie.

GAMBLING

Many professional gamblers plied their trade on steamboats traveling along the Mississippi River, and a lesser number also worked on steamboats on the Missouri River. In later years gamblers sought action in communities throughout the West, particularly in mining boomtowns where prospective players had more funds with which to gamble.

Games included poker, faro, roulette, monte, red and black, euchre, whist (a forerunner to bridge), twenty-one or blackjack, Kansas lottery, Diana (played on a limited basis and never extremely popular in the West), brag (similar to poker), lanterloo or loo (with players contributing stakes to a pool), keno (similar to bingo), high dice, and chuck-a-luck (or chucker luck or sweat, because players often did that when they were unlucky) played with dice, a piece of cloth with the numbers one through six and cups. Particularly popular was billiards.

In Auraria (which became Denver, Colorado) in 1859, newspaperman Libeus Barney wrote of games at the Denver Hall:

> Upon the first table as we entered, "Lasconette" was the game under consideration; on the next two *Rouge-et-Noire,* or "Red and Black," was being played; "Spanish Monte" occupied the next three; "French Monte" drew its worshippers around the seventh table; "Over and Under Seven," occupied two; "Chuck-a-Luck," three; "High Dice," one; "Van Tauma," three; "Roulette," one; and "Kansas Lottery," the balance. The tables rent from three to five dollars a night, and seldom a night passes but all are engaged.

Overland travelers found various gambling opportunities, often managed by French Canadian traders at strategic points on the trails, such as near river crossings where people were likely to stop for a while to rest and repair equipment. Some emigrants referred to those establishments as "Gambling Hell."

Although gambling was outlawed on military posts, it commonly occurred, particularly at nearby hog ranches, which were developed almost solely to cater to the pleasures of soldiers.

Native Americans engaged in many forms of gambling. As the Santa Rosa, California, *Times* reported in 1875:

The Digger is an inveterate gambler, and his principal game is very simple, consisting of holding both hands behind him, in one of which is a stick, while another [Indian] bets he can tell in which hand he holds it. It is stated that they scorn cheating, and, after the bets are made, never change the stick from one hand to the other. Their money consists of little round shells with a hole in the centre, which one of their number is selected to manufacture. No counterfeiting is ever attempted. Each shell represents about half a cent of American money, and is taken by their tribe as greedily as gold.—FLIN, *August 7, 1875, 386-3*

Cowboys generally played poker, or more likely monte or pike monte because any number of them could participate in the latter with only a single deck of cards. The monte banker set the limit for "pikers" which usually didn't exceed a dime when played by cowboys. Cowboys also commonly played dominoes using markers made of ivory or bone.

Professional gamblers and dealers often used tactics to give them an advantage in play. Decks were marked by trimming the edges of certain cards, by rounding corners of cards differently or even by using a small machine to depress a spot on the cards marking them similarly to the use of Braille. Dice could be shaved, weighted or in some cases even magnetized so they would consistently roll a certain way. Some card players used holdouts to keep a certain card or series of cards in reserve. Holdouts fit up coat sleeves, inside pant legs, around waists, under tables or inside coat or vest fronts. Most had some type of spring-loaded mechanism to put the card into the gambler's hand when he needed it. The non-mechanized Kleppinger holdout extended from a man's forearm, past his shoulder, down his back and to his knees, and was constructed with a series of cords, pulleys and telescoping tubes. P.J. Kleppinger invented his device in 1886.

In 1879 the Dodge City, Kansas, *Globe*, reported the differences between amateur and professional gamblers:

> The old professional takes off his coat, arranges it on the back of his chair, and sits down in front of the faro table with as much of an air of business and composure as a bookkeeper commencing his daily labor. He bets his 'system' without variation, and his countenance remains calm and immovable whether he wins or loses.

> The other class of gamblers are men who have other means of earning money, but who think they are just as liable to win as those more familiar with the game. They stand around the table until they think they see a card that is lucky, and immediately deposit their spare change on that card, and excitedly await developments.

It is only a matter of time when their money is gone and they are left with their hands in their empty pockets, staring vacantly at the board.

St. Louis arrests its gamblers for vagrancy and fines them $500.
—FLIN, *October 8, 1870, 59-4*

Gambling Terms

Blacklegs: Another name for gamblers.

Dominoes: A game commonly played by cowboys. The faces of the bone or ivory pieces were divided into two sections with a number of spots on each (or sometimes no spot at all). The game could involve two or four players and there were several variations such as Block and Draw (players draw seven pieces), Bergen (six pieces per player) and Muggins (players draw five pieces). Players chose the appropriate number of pieces then the player with the highest-numbered double piece played it by laying it on a table or flat surface. Other players then played, matching their pieces to the same number of dots until all pieces were played or until no one could play. The players then counted their spots. The person with the lowest number added it to the numbers held by other players. The game winner was the person who first gets one hundred points.

Fan Tan: A popular game among the Chinese. Counters of brass or porcelain tokens were spread on a table. Then a dealer placed some of them under a cover. The players then attempted to guess what number of markers would be left when all the markers were divided by four. After bets were placed, the dealer uncovered the markers and counted them by fours to get a remainder of one, two, three or none. Those who bet correctly were paid four times the amount of money they had bet.

Faro: Introduced to New Orleans by the French, the game gave players an almost even break. The chips and layout were decorated with a Bengal tiger. Also called pharo, pharon or pharoah, it was the most popular game in the West. Bets were placed on any card by putting chips next to the replica of the card that lay upon the playing table. The dealer then laid out two cards. The person who had bet on the first card selected by the dealer lost, but the second card selected was a winner. The loser of course forfeited his or her bet. Other players who had either bet on the winning card or any other card could pick up their bets, or let them lay for the next play. In the event the dealer laid out a pair, he or she took half the winning money, so many crooked dealers put lots of pairs in each deck they used. Bets were placed on top of the card, or if someone wanted to bet on two adjacent cards, the bet could be placed between them. Originally bets were made with pennies, but later gamblers used six-sided red-and-black tokens, known as coppers, or multicolored oblong chips. The dealer used a device similar to an abacus to show how many of each card had been dealt during a game so players could have a better chance to bet on a winning card. It generally took three people to operate a faro game: the dealer, the casekeeper who managed the abacus and a lookout.

Gulls or Coneys: Names given to neophytes to the games.

Hazard: A game using three dice, hazard had odds highly in favor of the house ranging from 180 to 1 to the more common 215 to 1 chances to win. Dice were usually dropped through a dice horn constructed like two funnels placed together at the narrow ends. Sometimes the dealers used a tin hazard horn which led to the term "tinhorn gambler." Other hazard dealers used a rotating wheel (like a roulette wheel) with various dice symbols marked on it. When the wheel stopped revolving at a certain combination of dice markers, that was the same as a roll of actual dice.

Monte: Commonly played throughout the West in a variety of versions, many based on Spanish influences in the game. Monte was the most common game among cowboys because a large number could participate without the need for several decks of cards. A variant of a three-card shell game.

Poker: Commonly played throughout the West, and particularly by cowboys. A card game in which players were dealt five cards and bet based on the cards they held in their hand (or expected to draw from a dealer). By 1877, rules showed that a flush (all cards in the same suit) beat any straight of consecutive cards; however, a straight flush (five consecutive cards all in the same suit) had not yet been declared the top hand in any poker game so that four of a kind—say four eights—could beat a flush or a straight flush. Two unbeatable hands were four aces (and any other card) or four kings and one ace. A hand of two black aces and two black eights (plus a jack of diamonds) became known as the Deadman's Hand, because that is suppos- edly what gambler Wild Bill Hickok was holding when he was shot in the back and killed by Jack McCall in Deadwood, Dakota Territory, on August 2, 1876. It's not clear, however, exactly which cards Hickok had, whether they even were aces and eights or what suits were involved. The fifth card, believed by some to be a jack of diamonds, also is not certain. Even so, anyone who later drew aces and eights was holding a "Deadman's Hand."

Roulette: A game using a revolving wheel with numbered compartments and a ball. Players bet on which compartment the ball would rest in when the wheel came to a stop. The gambler who had bet on that particular num- ber was a winner and all others lost. Early American roulette wheels had thirty-one numbered slots in alternating red and black; later wheels had thirty-six slots.

NATIVE AMERICAN GAMES AND ENTERTAINMENT

Native Americans engaged in many forms of entertainment with actual games varying from tribe to tribe. Some entertainment, however, was universally popular, such as dancing and storytelling.

Because most Indian history is preserved through oral means, storytelling is not only entertainment but also education and tradition. In all tribes storytelling had a prominent role, particularly during long winter months when people were more closely confined to their homes, lodges or tipis.

Native Americans also engaged in musical entertainment, though for them much of the music, whether the playing of drums or flutes, also had religious and symbolic meaning. Dancing, likewise, was most often done for ceremonial purposes. The southwestern tribes, such as the Hopis, had annual dances related to planting and harvesting of corn or dances to honor and recognize the sacred beings known as *kachinas*.

Other games and entertainment involved races, wrestling, throwing sticks or shooting contests, as well as swimming in the summer or sliding down snow-covered hills by riding on a buffalo hide in the winter.

ADDITIONAL READING

Barney, Libeus. *Early-Days Letters from Auraria*. Bennington, Vt.: Bennington *Banner*, 1858-1860.

Brown, Dee. *The Gentle Tamers*. Lincoln: University of Nebraska Press, 1981. An excellent general resource with much detail about western entertainment.

——. *Wondrous Times on the Frontier*. New York: August House, 1991. Reprint, HarperPerennials, HarperCollins, 1992. An excellent resource.

Dary, David. *Seeking Pleasure in the Old West*. New York: Alfred A. Knopf, 1995. An excellent resource.

Lippencott, Sarah. *New Life in New Lands*. London: n.p., 1873.

Monnett, John H. *A Rocky Mountain Christmas*. Boulder, Colo.: Pruett Publishing, 1992. Good information about early Christmas in the West.

Paul, Lori Cox. *Frontier Christmas*. Lincoln: Nebraska State Historical Society, 1997. An excellent resource, particularly about frontier military Christmas traditions.

Thorp, N. Howard. *Songs of the Cowboys*. Estancia, N. Mex.: News Print Shop, 1908. An excellent resource on cowboy music.

The Editors of Time-Life Books. *The Gamblers*. Alexandria, Va.: Time-Life Books, 1978. A good resource for information about western gambling.

Twain, Mark. *Roughing It*. New York: Harper & Row, 1899.

CHAPTER FIFTEEN

LANGUAGE

The words, and particularly the phrases, used in the West are very often unique, and extensive. There are far too many to list them in this space, but a random sampling is included to give the flavor of speech and language in the West during the period.

To capture the way westerners spoke and wrote, read their journals, diaries and newspapers. The references listed under "additional reading" are detailed compendiums of western language.

Ace high: A winning hand in poker, and a term given to a top hand on the range.

"When it came to keeping the tallow on 'em, Johnny Stringfellow was ace high."—Teddy Blue Abbott

Alcalde: A Spanish term for a mayor, judge or officer of the court.

Alias: A name used by someone when he or she didn't want to use his or her real name. Someone using an alias could be "under a flag," or using a "summer name." Aliases were common in the West. It was generally considered rude, and often not prudent, to ask someone his name. If he wanted you to know, he'd tell you.

Argonaut: Someone who sought gold in California in 1849-50.

Bang Juice: What miners called nitroglycerin and what loggers called dynamite.

Box Rustlers: A term for females who provided entertainment in boxed enclosures at theaters.

Brigham: What people in Arizona called gravy; also a name for a tea made of ephedra, a low, wiry bush used by Brigham Young for his version of a healthy tea.

Brush Popper: A cowboy from the Texas or New Mexico brasada or brush country.

Buckaroo: A cowboy from the desert country of Oregon, Nevada, California or Idaho.

Cackleberries: The loggers' name for eggs.

Chuck: Food to a cowboy, prepared at a chuck wagon by a chuck tender with supplies taken from a chuck box. Those eating it might be called chuck eaters when the cook called "Chuck away." At a ranch or mining camp the food might be prepared in the chuck house, while chuck-line riders were out-of-work cowboys, also known as grub liners, or men who were riding the grub line.

Cibola: An Indian word for buffalo. The Spanish called the ancient golden cities the Seven Cities of Cibola.

Ciboleras: An Indian word for buffalo hunters.

Cocinero: A Spanish term for a camp cook, also known as a coosie; cocinera when female.

Comancheros: Traders (Pueblo and white) who traded with the Comanches.

Cookie: A term for a range cook; others were bean master, biscuit roller, dough puncher, grub spoiler, hash slinger and pot rustler.

Count Coup or Counting the Coup: An act by Indians to show their bravery, by touching an enemy.

> [The Sioux] consider the greatest act of valor to be the striking of their enemy with some hand instrument while alive, and whether alive or dead, it is the first one that strikes the fallen foe that 'counts the coup,' and not the one that shoots him.
> —FLIN, *July 29, 1876, 339-3*

Cowpuncher: A name for a cowboy which came from the practice of men using a prod pole to "punch" cattle up loading ramps and onto trains for shipment to markets. In use after about 1875.

Dally Welter: A cowboy who wraps the end of his rope around the saddle horn, rather than tying it hard and fast as some California and all Texas cowboys do. Most dally welters rode on the northern ranges or in California.

G.T.T.: Gone To Texas. A common expression in use following the Civil War.

Galvanized Yankees: Former Confederate soldiers who served in the U.S. Army in the West following the Civil War, and primarily during the Indian Wars.

Gobacks: The name given to people who left Denver City when the first mineral strike in the area didn't last; also used to refer to others who'd ventured into the West and then returned to the East.

> We hope that this class are all again safely at home with their Pa's and Ma's, their sweethearts, or 'Nancy and the babies . . .' Farewell to these 'gobacks.'—*William Byers,* Rocky Mountain News, *1859*

Gravy: Made from pan drippings after cooking meat; also called Texas butter or sop.

Henskins: Thin blankets used by Texas cowboys.

Nebraska Marble (or Brick): Sod used in building houses; also Kansas marble/brick.

Nigger: A term used by mountain men to refer to themselves or their friends. On the frontier it might refer to anything bad such as a nigger brand (a saddle sore). Not necessarily an offensive word. Commonly in use during the period.

Orphan Elixir: An oil and mining region synonym for nitro glycerine. —FLIN, *February 24, 1872*

P.I.'s: The term used by cowboys for men who managed affairs of prostitutes.

> "As for the P.I.s, the rest of the word is m, p, s."—*Teddy Blue Abbott.*

Prairie Feathers: Wild hay or slough grass cut and placed into ticks for beds or pillows.

Rawhides: A derogatory term for Texas cowboys used by northern cowboys. It came from the practice of Texans repairing equipment with rawhide strips.

Regale: A drinking bout common among mountain men prior to starting on expeditions.

Skunk Eggs: The loggers' name for onions.

Smoked Yankees: The name given to African-American soldiers by Spaniards during the Spanish-American War of 1898.

Thundermug: Chamber pot.

Out from under the box would come—what in those days we called a 'thundermug'—you know what I mean; one of those things we used to conceal under the bed in the daytime, before we had sewers and such."—*Will E. Stoke*, Episodes of the Early Days, 19

War Bag: What cowboys carried their gear in.

I had my bed and my war bag and stuff up in the hayloft and I packed them on a horse that night and I drifted.—*Teddy Blue Abbott*

ADDITIONAL READING

Abbott, Teddy Blue, and Helen Huntington Smith. *We Pointed 'em North.* New York: Farrer and Rinehart, Inc., 1939. An excellent reference about cowboying in the 1880s.

Adams, Ramon F. *Cowboy Dictionary: The Chin Jaw Words and Whing-Ding Ways of the American West.* New York: Perigee Books, Putnam Publishing Group, 1993. Previously published as *Western Words.* Norman: University of Oklahoma Press, 1968. An excellent reference.

Blevins, Winfred. *Dictionary of the American West.* New York: Facts on File, 1993. A good reference.

Lamar, Howard. R., ed. *The Reader's Encyclopedia of the American West.* New York: Crowell, 1977.

McCullough, Water F. *Woods Words: A Comprehensive Dictionary of Loggers Terms.* Portland: Oregon Historical Society, 1958.

McCutcheon, Marc. *The Writers Guide to Everyday Life in the 1800s.* Cincinnati: Writer's Digest Books, 1993. A good reference.

Potter, Edgar. *Cowboy Slang.* Seattle: Hangman Press, 1971.

Slatta, Richard W. *The Cowboy Encyclopedia.* New York: W.W. Norton, 1994.

Stoke, Will E. *Episodes of the Early Days.* Great Bend, Kans. Press: Published by the author, 1926.

Stoutenburgh, John Jr. *Dictionary of the American Indian.* New York: Wings Books, 1990. A good reference to Indian terms.

Watts, Peter. *A Dictionary of the Old West.* New York: Wings Books, 1977.

CHAPTER SIXTEEN

TRAVEL AND COMMUNICATIONS

T
he West is comprised of hundreds of thousands of acres that in 1840 had only a series of limited trails mostly used by Native Americans or buffalo, though a few had been developed by pioneering explorers, trappers and traders. During the period 1840 to 1890 travelers and government explorers forged routes that provided access to land in Oregon and Utah, to gold and silver fields in Montana, California, the Dakotas, Colorado, Wyoming, Nevada and Alaska, and to commercial areas in the Southwest.

Nearly all the eventual western overland roads started by following Native American or buffalo trails, in part because those trails were located in logical places—over or through mountain passes, along streams and rivers and near forests. From 1840 until 1869 travel in the West was mostly by horse-, mule- or oxen-drawn wagons or stagecoaches. Some people rode horses or mules, and many simply walked wherever they needed to go. In 1869 completion of the nation's first transcontinental railroad changed long-distance transportation in the West, as people gave up their wagons for a seat in a railroad car. Following completion of the transcontinental line, other railroads established routes spreading generally from east to west and providing transportation opportunities for travelers and freight services for farmers. Wagon use continued throughout the latter half of the nineteenth century, however, as horses were the main motive power in the West.

The West had several primary transportation routes such as the Santa Fe, Oregon, Mormon, California and Overland Trails, and there were transcontinental railroad, mail, stage and telegraph services as well. The region also had

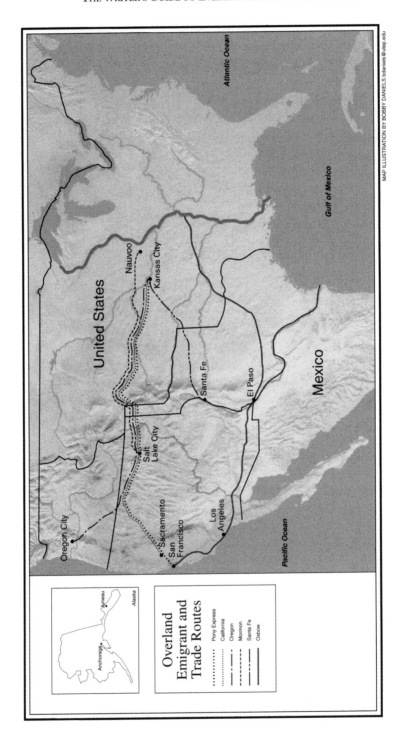

many stage, mail and telegraph services, roads and routes serving more localized areas. Few rivers in the West were navigable by large craft, although the Missouri River did serve as a major transportation route.

SANTA FE TRAIL

Pioneered in 1821 by William Becknell as a trade route from Franklin, Missouri, the Santa Fe Trail went to the Spanish provinces at Santa Fe. A Missouri River flood in 1828 destroyed Franklin, and the starting point for the Santa Fe Trail began moving westward to places like Independence and Westport Landing (Kansas City). One version of the trail started at Fort Atkinson (north of present Omaha, Nebraska). It was used primarily as a freighting route between 1821 and 1880. During the period of September 1843 until the summer of 1844, the trail closed under provisions of a decree issued by Mexican authorities. In May 1846 when the United States declared war on Mexico, the Santa Fe Trail became a military road used by the Army of the West.

The Route: Starting in Franklin, Missouri, the trail extended nearly due west to Council Grove and the Arkansas River. The mountain branch then followed the Arkansas to Bent's Fort (in central Colorado) before turning south over Raton Pass to Santa Fe, New Mexico. The Cimarron Cutoff extended southwest from the Arkansas River to follow the Cimarron River. That route was drier, with one fifty-five mile stretch where there was no water for people or animals.

Explorations: William Becknell launched his first crossing of the trail on September 1, 1821, in Franklin, Missouri, with the men accompanying him riding and packing mules. On May 22, 1822, he left Franklin with mules and three wagons full of trade goods. Becknell and other traders took a variety of goods to Santa Fe which they traded for gold, mules, donkeys, woolen blankets and furs. The United States Congress funded an 1825 survey of the route. Funding included $10,000 for the survey and $20,000 allocated to buy gifts for Indians through whose lands the Santa Fe Trail passed. As U.S. Senator Thomas Hart Benton, author of the bill authorizing the funding, said, "It is not a County or State road which they have to mark out but a highway between Nations."

Freighting: The earliest trading caravans used mule pack trains, but by 1825 travel on the Santa Fe Trail involved freighting companies. The earliest freight wagons were conestogas. The traders hauled such goods as cloth, needles, thread and other sewing notions; axes, nails, shovels, log chains; clothing items; and household goods.

EL CAMINO REAL

The Royal Road, or the King's Highway, linked Santa Fe, New Mexico, with El Paso, Texas, and Cuidad Juarez, Chihuahua and Mexico City, Mexico. It served as a major trade route and as an extension of the Santa Fe Trail. Travel over the route began in about 1540 and continued through 1890.

CHEROKEE TRAIL OF TEARS

In 1838 the first Cherokees began a journey from their homelands in Georgia to Indian Country (Oklahoma). The overland route became the Trail of Tears. It extended from Georgia and Alabama across Tennessee, the southwestern corner of Kentucky, and Missouri, then across Arkansas. Some Cherokees made the trek over a water route that went up the Tennessee River, then down the Mississippi River before traveling up the Arkansas River to Fort Smith.

CHEROKEE TRAIL TO CALIFORNIA

After prospectors found gold in California in 1848, many Cherokees traveled from Indian Territory to California where they worked in the mining industry, having learned that trade when they lived in Georgia. The Cherokee Trail crossed out of Indian Territory to Julesburg (Colorado) and then followed the same route as the Overland Trail. One branch went up the Cache la Poudre (near Fort Collins, Colorado) into North Park, and through the upper North Platte River Valley along the eastern edge of the Sierra Madre to join the main Cherokee Trail near Bridger's Pass (southwest of present Rawlins, Wyoming).

OREGON-CALIFORNIA TRAIL

The first emigrant wagon train over what became the Oregon-California Trail was the Bidwell-Bartleson Train in 1841, which reached California that fall. The first emigrant party to reach the New Helvetia settlement, started by John Sutter at present Sacramento, California, arrived in 1844. Emigration to Oregon started with a company led by Daniel Waldo, James Nesmith and Jesse Applegate in 1843, arriving at Oregon City on November 6, 1843. During the period from 1843 until 1873 at least 400,000 people followed the Oregon-California Trail.

The Route: The route to Oregon and California started in Independence, Missouri, at the southwest corner of Courthouse Square. Nearby was a large open area known as the Breaking Ground, where men could drive new teams in anticipation of purchasing them and using them on the trail. The main route proceeded west from Independence, Missouri, along the south bank of the Kansas River crossing into present Nebraska at Odell. It then followed the Blue River northwest toward Fort Kearny where the trail reached the

Platte River, which it followed west sticking to the south bank of the North Platte River until reaching the site of Platte Bridge Station (Casper, Wyoming). There the trail crossed the river and headed northwest toward the Sweetwater River Valley and over South Pass. Then it continued west to Fort Hall (Idaho) and the Snake River, which it followed until reaching the Columbia that served as a guide to Oregon City and the Willamette Valley (Oregon).

The route of the Oregon Trail and the California Trail is essentially the same from the Missouri River west past South Pass. In what is now western Wyoming the trails began to diverge. Some California travelers after 1846 headed south on the Hastings Cutoff to Fort Bridger, traveled over the Wasatch mountain range, through the Great Salt Lake valley, and then rejoined the main trail along the Humboldt River. Most California-bound travelers continued along the primary Oregon route to Soda Springs (Idaho) where they then forked toward the southwest to the Humboldt River, which they followed to the Sierra Nevada.

For both trails many routes existed in the region east of Fort Kearny (Nebraska) with primary beginning—or jumping-off—points at Independence, Missouri; St. Joseph, Missouri; and Council Bluffs, Iowa. West of Fort Kearny the trails were along virtually the same road, with some major shortcuts developed during the years of emigration.

Major Shortcuts

Goodale Cutoff: Pioneered as an emigrant route by Tim Goodale. The route went north of Massacre Rocks (in Idaho) on the main branch of the Oregon Trail. Also heavily used by Nathan Hall, founder of Fort Hall, as a supply line to the Columbia River, it was in use after 1862. The first documented crossing over the route was by Nathaniel Wyeth in 1834.

Greenwood Cutoff: Pioneered in 1844 by the California-bound Stevens-Townsend-Murphy wagon train that was guided by Isaac Hitchcock and Caleb Greenwood, for whom it is named. A primary route used by Forty-niners headed to California. The cutoff extended almost due west from the Green River to the Bear River, bypassing Fort Bridger to the south. The trail divided at Parting of the Ways (Wyoming).

Hastings Cutoff: In 1846 Lansford Hastings headed west from Fort Bridger turning over the Wasatch Mountains toward the Great Salt Lake Valley and then west across present Utah and Nevada to California. Although he made the trip without undue delay, the Donner-Reed party, which traveled a few days behind Hastings and upon his recommendation, had significant difficulties in crossing the Wasatch Range. It took them sixteen days to travel thirty-five miles (much longer than the Hastings crossing), the last day carving a crossing up and over a mountain since known as Donner Hill. They had to use almost every team to pull each wagon up and over the hill. The effort significantly affected the spirit of the animals and resulted in additional delays as the party continued west. Heavy snows ultimately stranded the Donner-Reed party in the Sierra Nevada (on Donner Pass) where some members resorted to cannibalism as a way to survive.

Lander Road: Explorations of the route began at South Pass on July 15, 1857, under the direction of Frederick West Lander. The route extended northwest from South Pass along the Sandy and Green Rivers and over the Salt Range (Wyoming) and to Fort Hall (Idaho). The road opened in 1859 and had 13,000 travelers that year—people headed toward Oregon. It remained in use until 1912. The official name was the Fort Kearny, South Pass and Honey Lake Road.

Nebraska City to Fort Kearny: A more direct route than the Oxbow Trail providing access from Nebraska City to Fort Kearny.

Oxbow Trail: Used by freighters primarily, although Mormons also traveled the route on church trains leaving from the town of Wyoming, Nebraska, and following a zigzag pathway to Fort Kearny.

Sublette Cutoff: Another (more common) name for the Greenwood Cutoff (Wyoming) which came into use after its inclusion in the 1849 guidebook prepared by Joseph E. Ware.

MORMON TRAIL

By 1840 the Church of Jesus Christ of Latter-day Saints (the Mormons) had its primary headquarters in Nauvoo, Illinois, having been earlier located in Kirkland, Ohio, and at various sites in Missouri. Joseph Smith had founded the Mormon Church in 1829, served as the church president, and was recognized as its prophet as well. In 1844 Hyrum Smith and Joseph Smith were killed while incarcerated at the jail in Carthage, Illinois. Previous to his death, Joseph Smith had advocated moving the Mormon people from Illinois to an unspecified location farther west.

Following Smith's death, Brigham Young became the leader—ultimately the president—of the LDS Church, and in January 1846 he started the exodus from Illinois. The Mormons constructed more than twelve thousand wagons for the journey. The first leg of the trail, traversed in 1846, led from Nauvoo across Iowa to Kanesville (Council Bluffs), and subsequently ended on the west bank of the Missouri at Winter Quarters (Florence, Nebraska). The migration called itself the Camp of Israel. Once at the Missouri River, having had difficult travel in rainy, muddy conditions, the Mormons weren't prepared to continue heading west in 1846.

Brigham Young negotiated with envoys from President James Polk to raise a 500-member Mormon Battalion, which participated in the Mexican War (see chapter five.) That provided funds—from the uniform allowances provided to the individual soldiers—to feed Mormon families during the winter of 1846-47. And it gave Young a bargaining chip to negotiate a place on Omaha Indian lands for the Mormons to use during the winter. That location—Winter Quarters—soon had a large number of roughly built log houses and cabins for the Mormons to use. Some 10,000 Mormons made the trek from Nauvoo to Winter Quarters in 1846; about 600 died at Winter Quarters during the late summer, fall and winter, primarily from cholera. In 1847 a pioneer company consisting of 144 men, 3 women and 2 children left Winter Quarters en route to Utah, building a road for others to follow. The pioneer party left Winter Quarters in April 1847 and arrived in the Great Salt Lake Valley between July 22 and 24, 1847.

The Route: The trail followed the north bank of the Platte River from Winter Quarters to Fort Laramie, then crossed to the south river bank, following it to a crossing that became Platte Bridge Station (later Fort Caspar, now Casper, Wyoming). Then the route paralleled the Oregon Trail west to Independence Rock, up the Sweetwater River Valley, over South Pass, southwest to Fort Bridger, then west to Utah. The final course routed the Mormons down Emigration Canyon and into the Salt Lake Valley. Between 1847 and 1869, approximately 70,000 LDS members followed the Mormon Trail. Later parties traveled from points farther south on the Missouri River. One main starting point was at the town of Wyoming, Nebraska (now a ghost town located north of Nebraska City, Nebraska).

Mormon Ferries: The Mormons operated several ferries on the route, including those over the Missouri River near Bellevue and Plattsmouth, and one over the Elk Horn River (in Nebraska); one over the Platte River (at Casper, Wyoming); and the Lombard Ferry over the Green River (in western Wyoming). They allowed Mormon parties to cross without paying but charged other travelers.

Church Trains: Because the Mormons forged their trail west with the goal of moving their entire church membership, the pioneer party members, and some members of the Mormon Battalion who had made their way to Great Salt Lake Valley from California, immediately returned to Winter Quarters to bring their families to the valley. In subsequent years church leadership organized trains, called "church trains" or "down and back trains," which left Utah in the spring (about April), traveled east over the trail with wagons loaded with freight such as grain, stockpiling some supplies at way stations on the trail. At the Missouri River they sold the remaining supplies they'd brought from Utah and loaded the wagons with Mormons and new supplies of goods unavailable in Utah before they headed to Zion. The church trains operated through the mid-1850s, when the church ran short on funds for the program. Most church trains followed the Mormon Trail; some after 1862 used the Overland Trail.

Perpetual Emigration Fund: Brigham Young started the Perpetual Emigration Fund (P.E.F.) to bring additional Mormon converts to Zion, particularly those from England, Scandinavia and other European countries. The fund was designed to pay costs associated with immigration. Those who benefited from the fund were then expected to help pay for other converts to make the journey.

Handcart Experiment: In 1856 Brigham Young launched a new method of transporting people to Zion. The P.E.F. (see above) hadn't been able to sustain itself when church trains consisted of wagons drawn by horses, mules or oxen. Young said the people could walk to Zion, pushing and pulling small handcarts filled with their belongings. The use of handcarts by three thousand immigrants, primarily from England and European countries, occurred between 1856 and 1860.

Handcart Companies: First Company, Edmund Ellsworth, Captain, 1856—274 members crossed the Atlantic on the *S. Curling* and the *Enoch Train*.

Second Company, Daniel D. McArthur, Captain, 1856—497 members crossed the Atlantic on the *S. Curling*.

Third Company, Edward Bunker, Captain, 1856—320 members known as the Welsh Company crossed the Atlantic on the *S. Curling*; most were Welshmen and women.

Fourth Company, James Grey Willie, Captain, 1856—764 members crossed the Atlantic on the *Thornton*. This company became stranded on South Pass in October, had to be rescued and reached Salt Lake City, November 9, 1856; between 62 and 67 company members died.

Fifth Company, Edward Martin, Captain, 1856—856 members crossed the Atlantic on the *Horizon*. This company became stranded in the Sweetwater River Valley in October, had to be rescued and reached Salt Lake City late in November; between 135 and 150 company members died.

Sixth Company, Israel Evans, Captain, 1857—803 members and 14 returning missionaries crossed the Atlantic on the *George Washington*; no complete roster available.

Seventh Company, Christian Christiansen, Captain, 1857—504 members and 4 missionaries crossed the Atlantic on the *Westmoreland*.

Eighth Company, George Rowley, Captain, 1859—725 members crossed the Atlantic on the *William Tapscott*.

Ninth Company, Daniel Robinson, Captain, 1860—594 members crossed the Atlantic on the *Underwriter*.

Tenth Company, Oscar O. Stoddard, Captain, 1860—730 members crossed the Atlantic on the *Underwriter*.

OVERLAND TRAIL

Ben Holladay bought the Central Overland and California and Pikes Peak Express Company on March 7, 1859, from William Russell, James Waddell and

Alexander Majors. Holladay had been their creditor. In 1862 Holladay started a mail-delivery operation over the route known as the Overland Trail, replacing stations along the Oregon-California Trail that had been used by Russell, Majors and Waddell. Stations were established along the Overland route, situated roughly ten to twelve miles apart. Travel to Oregon and California shifted south from the Oregon-California Trail as Holladay established a stagecoach line over the route, and to avoid difficulties with Native Americans on the route farther to the north, though the trouble followed the travelers to the southern route. The Overland Trail saw only limited emigrant travel; by 1862 emigration had slowed considerably. It did serve as a main conduit for the mail and for freighting and stagecoach travel. The U.S. Army established posts along the route to provide protection to travelers. People using the Overland had many confrontations with Native Americans, particularly in the section between Virginia Dale Station (on the Colorado-Wyoming state line) and Bitter Creek just east of Fort Bridger. Travelers in that area became known as those "running the gauntlet." Ben Holladay sold the line to Wells, Fargo, and Company on November 1, 1866, and the route generally ceased stagecoach travel after May 1869, when the Union Pacific and Central Pacific railroads linked at Promontory, Utah.

The Route: The Overland branched from the Oregon Trail at the junction of the North Platte and South Platte Rivers in Nebraska, crossing to the southwest to Fort Sedgwick near Julesburg, Colorado, and toward Denver. It then turned north crossing into present-day Wyoming at Virginia Dale and then extended west on a line parallel with the present Wyoming-Colorado border, generally about fifty miles north of that border.

STAGE AND MAIL ROUTES

The trails that served as conduits for people and commerce, such as the Santa Fe, Oregon-California and Overland (Central Overland California and Pikes Peak), also served as stage and mail routes. The delivery of goods and mail over the various routes between 1849 and 1869 kept hundreds of men and women using thousands of animals busy. They hauled everything from letters and newspapers to people, food, clothing, household items and farm implements, as well as gold, currency and government documents.

Few roads and routes existed that connected the East, or The States as westerners referred to that region, with the West Coast. California mail and freight in 1850 went via ship around the tip of South America, or used the Panama route. It took six months for the South American sailing and about a month via Panama. The earliest overland freighting occurred on the Santa Fe Trail and over the Oregon-California-Mormon Trail route.

Mail delivery occurred under government contracts approved by the Postmaster General. Payments involved $290,000 annually for mail delivered between the Atlantic and Pacific coasts and $.12 per pound of mail that was hauled across Panama.

In the Far West, where the settlements are thin, it is not possible to establish regular Post Offices, and therefore a box is affixed to an upright post in the prairie near the traveled road. The post-boy, as he rides along, drops into this box the mail matter for settlers ten miles or more in every direction.
—FLIN, *October 26, 1867, 92-1*

A variety of smaller, more regionally based stage and mail routes developed with deliveries by teamsters or in some cases horseback-riding young men in local versions of the Pony Express (see page 251).

Some of the primary stage and mail routes were these:

Butterfield Overland Mail Route: Separate legs of the trail started in St. Louis, Missouri, and in Memphis, Tennessee, joining at Fort Smith, Arkansas, then extending southwest to Fort Belknap, Fort Chadbourne, and El Paso, Texas, then continuing west to Tucson and Fort Yuma, Arizona Territory, before turning north to Los Angeles, Visalia and San Francisco, California. It made such an arc that it became known as the Oxbow Route. Some also called it The Horseshoe or The Sideline. The Butterfield stages, operated under the American Express Company owned by John Butterfield, covered the route in twenty-four days, averaging four and one-half miles per hour. The Butterfield operated until the start of the Civil War, delivering more mail than all the ships that had similar government contracts for the region in the same period. There were 139 relay stations. Mail deliveries started on September 15, 1858.

California Mail Operators: The first mail delivery network in California started in 1849 under the management of Alexander Todd. He provided mail service in the gold camps at these rates: $2.50 to carry a letter from the goldfields to the post office in San Francisco; $1 to put a man's name on a subscription list in order to check if the miner had any incoming mail; and one ounce of gold (about $16) to deliver incoming letters from San Francisco to the miner in a gold camp. Todd also carried other items—including gold dust—taking a five percent commission on the value of the dust as his fee. Todd's primary route extended from near Sutter's Mill (Sacramento) to San Francisco.

Cheyenne-Deadwood: A stage route serving the gold rush to the Black Hills, the Cheyenne-Deadwood was in use after 1875 from Cheyenne to Fort Laramie where it crossed an iron bridge built by the U.S. Army in 1875, then north and east to Deadwood.

El Camino Real: The road between San Diego and San Francisco (The Royal Road). By 1850 a network of routes linked northern and southern California.

Leavenworth and Pikes Peak: A stage and mail route from Leavenworth, Kansas, to Fort Riley, then swinging north and due west to Denver.

Horse snowshoes from the Grand Encampment Museum collection.

Overland mail deliveries: The earliest official overland mail delivery route followed the Oregon-California-Mormon emigrant trail corridor with a terminus at Fort Smith, Arkansas. Contractor William Bayard initially said he would carry the mail and passengers in stagecoaches from Fort Smith to San Francisco; he ultimately barely made it with the mail to Salt Lake City. A separate contract extended from Salt Lake City to San Francisco, operated by Absalom Woodward and George Chorpenning who used pack mules. Throughout the 1850s mail delivery between eastern and western points continued in a haphazard fashion. Travelers who were headed east carried letters in that direction, while those en route west also carried mail to various points, such as Fort Bridger or Great Salt Lake City.

San Antonio and San Diego Mail: Known as the Jackass Mail. The trail extended from San Antonio through El Paso, Texas, Tucson and Ft. Yuma, Arizona, to San Diego, California. Travel started in 1858 and the pathway followed the Oxbow route.

Sidney-Deadwood: A route in use during the gold rush to the Black Hills; not as popular as the Cheyenne to Deadwood route.

Smoky Hill Trail: (Butterfield Overland Despatch) from Atchison, Kansas, to Fort Riley, along the Smoky Hill River and to Denver. The Butterfield Overland Despatch, owned by David Butterfield challenged the operations of Ben Holladay's Overland Stage Company. David Butterfield was no relation to John Butterfield of the southern Butterfield Route. David Butterfield sold the line in 1866 to Holladay.

MAJOR EXPRESS COMPANIES

Freighting occurred over the same routes as did mail deliveries. The season started in mid-March and mid-April when ice went off the Missouri River, enabling boats to transport goods to landings where freighters collected it for the trip overland. Freighting companies received about $1.80 per one hundred pounds of merchandise for each one hundred miles it was hauled.

Freighters used both oxen and mules. A mule skinner sometimes walked beside the left mule closest to the wagon, but just as often he rode that animal.

A bullwhacker walked beside the left ox leading the team. The two animals in front were the lead team. Those teams in the middle of a multiple-animal hitch were the swing teams or swingers, while the two closest to the wagon were the wheel team or wheelers and were always the biggest, heaviest animals in the hitch. Mules traveled faster than oxen but had to be grain fed, and the grain itself needed to be hauled as freight. Oxen lived better from eating natural grasses, but they didn't move as quickly (only about two miles per hour as compared with three miles per hour by mules). Indians were more likely to steal mules than oxen. Mules required a harness, while oxen only needed a yoke, which was generally less expensive. The oxen were all steers but were referred to as bulls. The man who handled them did so using a bullwhip, and he became known as a bullwhacker. Freight teams ranged from four or six animals to as many as twenty.

> As an evidence of the extent of the transportation of goods across the Western plains, the Atchison correspondent of the St. Louis *Republican* gives a table, showing that from Atchison alone no less than 1651 men, 1338 wagons, 1192 mules, 14,312 oxen were employed in transporting the enormous amount of nearly 7,000,000 pounds of merchandise across the plains during the present season. This in addition to the thousands of private teams, which are incessantly crossing the vast thoroughfare in every direction.
> —FLIN, *October 6, 1860, 313-2*

American Camel Company: The first use of camels as draft animals occurred in 1855 by the military at Camp Verde, Texas. The American Camel Company used Asian camels to transport cargo in the area around Virginia City, Nevada, after 1860. The camels ate sagebrush, thistles and creosote bushes. They swam rivers and ignored rattlesnake bites. They sneezed, vomited and spit, caused dogs to bark and mules and oxen to stampede.

American Express Company: Organized in 1850. This company and the Butterfield Overland Mail Company were both owned and operated in California by John Butterfield.

California Stage Company: Organized as a collaborative venture by several smaller stage and express delivery outfits. The consolidation came at the behest of James Birch in 1854.

Holladay Overland Mail & Express Company: Owned by Ben Holladay, the "Stagecoach King." Also known as the Overland Stage Line. (See Overland Trail page 246 for more about Holladay).

Russell, Majors and Waddell: Headquartered first at Leavenworth, Kansas, and later at Nebraska City, Nebraska, and owned by William Russell, Alexander Majors and William B. Waddell, the company—comprised of individual companies owned by the three men—formally merged in December 1854.

It won the government mail contract at Fort Leavenworth on March 27, 1855. The company had 500 wagons, 1,700 teamsters and 7,500 oxen when it began hauling the first 2.5 million pounds of freight under the contract. It was the biggest company of its kind and in 1858 negotiated a new contract to haul 25 million pounds of freight. That venture would require 3,500 wagons and 40,000 head of oxen. The wagons burned during the 1857 Mormon War during a raid by Mormons. They belonged to Russell, Majors and Waddell, and were hauling government supplies.

Wells, Fargo & Company: Henry Wells and William G. Fargo owned the firm that dominated express deliveries in California and the West. (William Harnden had been involved with the company in its infancy, but died before it became a successful enterprise.) Wells started in the delivery business in New York and by 1843 expanded to take in Fargo as his partner. They then expanded operations to Cincinnati and Chicago. Wells, Fargo & Company organized March 18, 1852, in New York City at the Astor House Hotel. It opened its first office in San Francisco that year. The company trademark was its green color. Iron shutters at Wells, Fargo offices were painted green; each stage carried a green strongbox; in California the company had green mailboxes. Wells, Fargo provided a variety of services including delivering relief aid following a major fire in Sacramento in 1852, and distributing eastern newspapers at no charge to western editors who gleaned information for their own publications. The company prided itself on making deliveries of luxury items: German cigars, grapevine cuttings from Switzerland, fresh butter from Vermont and French wines.

Wells, Fargo used a variety of transportation methods including freight and light express wagons, mule trains, stagecoaches, men on snowshoes, steamers around the southern tip of South America, and boats on the Sacramento River and boats and mules to cross Panama. After 1860 the company carried mail over the Oxbow route and during the Civil War served as the primary stage service on the western side of the transcontinental route. In 1866 Wells, Fargo had 196 branch offices and by 1868 the company dominated travel and deliveries in the West. That year the company purchased thirty Abbot and Downing coaches from the Concord, New Hampshire, company (the largest shipment of coaches ever made at one time to one company). Wells, Fargo by 1893 had 37,766 miles of express routes and operated 2,829 branch offices.

PONY EXPRESS

Organized as a mail delivery service by the freighting firm of William Russell, Alexander Majors and William Waddell, the Pony Express started on April 3, 1860, and ceased on November 20, 1861. It was operated under the auspices of a Russell, Majors and Waddell company, the Central Overland California and Pike's Peak Express Company, nicknamed the "Clean Out of Cash and Poor Pay." The need for the company and its rapid mail delivery service was negated when the transcontinental telegraph went into service in October 1861.

The Route: The Pony Express started in St. Joseph, Missouri, and followed the basic corridor of the Oregon-California Trail to Fort Kearny, Fort Laramie and Fort Bridger. It then took the route similar to the Hastings Cutoff by crossing the Wasatch Range to Great Salt Lake City before continuing west across present Utah and Nevada to Carson City (Nevada), Sacramento and San Francisco, California.

The Operation: The Pony Express delivered mail efficiently by having relay riders carry it between various points. There were 190 relay stations between St. Joseph, Missouri, and San Francisco. Riders were hired after the firm placed this ad:

WANTED: YOUNG SKINNY WIRY FELLOWS not over eighteen. Must be expert riders willing to risk death daily. Orphans preferred. WAGES $25 per week. Apply, *Central Overland Express, Alta Bldg., Montgomery St.*

In its eighteen months of existence, probably 180 riders worked for the Pony Express.

Home stations were located about seventy-five miles apart and served as home base for the riders. At each home station a rider received the mail and began his own ride along the line. Any individual rider generally traveled over his section of the route, delivered the mail to the next rider on the line, then waited for the return mail when he rode back to his home station.

Relay stations, also called swing stations, where riders changed horses, were located about ten or fifteen miles apart. To save time and ensure security for the mail, letters were placed into a leather *mochila,* which the riders then shifted each time they began using a new horse. The mochila was designed to fit over the saddle with a slit in the leather so the mochila could be placed over the saddle horn. The mochila had four pockets for the mail, which were kept locked during a ride. The mochila and saddle together weighed around fifteen pounds without mail and about twice that with letters and newspapers.

Though called the Pony Express, the riders used horses—primarily thoroughbreds, mustangs and Morgans—all selected for their endurance. The riders, called Pony Boys, initially carried a rifle, but soon discarded it as being too heavy. They did wear two Navy Colt .36 caliber revolvers and generally carried a small horn, which they blew as they approached a station to alert attendants.

Generally speaking it took about ten days to cover the two-thousand-mile route. The service started with weekly deliveries, but later changed to semi-weekly deliveries. Initially it cost $5 per half-ounce. Later the charge was $1 per half-ounce.

RAILROADS

Several major east-west surveys considered routes for a transcontinental railroad line. From north to south, they were:

Dodge and Judah Surveys: The Dodge Survey went from Omaha, Nebraska, along the Platte River route to north of Salt Lake City, then along the Humboldt River to the Sierra Nevada where it met the Judah Survey that extended from Sacramento east to the Sierra Nevada. The combined surveys ultimately became the route of the Union Pacific and Central Pacific railroad lines.

Gunnison and Beckwith Survey: From St. Louis west across Missouri, Kansas, present Colorado, then along the Wasatch mountain range north to Salt Lake City and then west across Utah, along the Humboldt River to near Fort Reading (California).

Pope and Parke Surveys: The Pope Survey headed west from Preston, Texas, across Texas to a point in present New Mexico; the Parke Survey headed east from San Diego across southern California and Arizona in the area of the Gadsden Purchase.

Stevens, Saxton, McClellan Survey: From St. Paul (Minnesota), across a route primarily north of the Missouri River, over the Bitterroot Mountains in present-day Montana then along the Columbia River to Oregon, with a loop northeast into present British Columbia, Canada.

Whipple Survey: From Fort Smith (Arkansas) due west across present Oklahoma, New Mexico, Arizona and California to Los Angeles.

Another survey, the California and Oregon Survey, provided a connecting survey to link potential routes in Oregon with those in California.

The route selected for the transcontinental railroad under the Pacific Railway Act of 1862 followed the Judah and Dodge Surveys, and became the Central Pacific and Union Pacific railway lines. In consideration for construction, the Central Pacific, being built eastward from California, received ten miles of land in alternative sections on each side of the right-of-way for each track mile laid and subsidies of $16,000 for each mile of plains track, $32,000 per mile for track laid through the Great Basin, and $48,000 per mile for track laid through the Rockies and the Sierra Nevadas. The same general conditions applied to construction on the Union Pacific, being built westward from Nebraska; there the land sections were increased to twenty miles of land in alternating sections along the line. The land grants were in a checkerboard pattern extending either ten or twenty miles both north and south of the railroad lines.

Between 1850 and 1872, Congress and state governments granted 116 million acres of free land to various railroads for construction projects; at the end of that period only one line operated in the West (the Central and Union Pacific between Sacramento and Omaha).

Railroad builders included Irish and German immigrants, Chinese, Civil War veterans, Mormons, Shoshones, Paiutes and Washoes. In 1865 the West had thirty-two hundred miles of short-line railroad track, by 1890 it had seventy thousand miles of track. Semiskilled Irishmen and Chinese workers, called Celestials, earned about $35 per month. The white workers also received free bed and board; the Chinese lived in dugouts and tents and had their food shipped in from San Francisco's Chinatown, at their own cost.

Rails weighed five hundred pounds and were held in place with twenty-eight to thirty spikes. It generally took three blows to drive a spike; there were four hundred rails per mile, and two pairs of rail were laid each minute. Ties for the line came from native timber chopped in forests, sometimes located hundreds of miles away, by workers known as tie hacks (see chapter thirteen).

Railroad Construction Completion Dates: Union Pacific and Central Pacific, Promontory, Utah Territory, May 10, 1869; Southern Pacific, 1883; Northern Pacific, 1883; Atchison, Topeka, and Santa Fe, 1885; Great Northern, 1893.

Passenger Service: The Union Pacific/Central Pacific line started passenger service on May 15, 1869. The fare was $100 for first class service from Omaha to Sacramento; for an extra $4 first-class passengers could obtain meal service on the train; otherwise they ate at stops along the way. Second-class passengers rode and slept in day coaches and paid $80 for a ticket from Omaha to Sacramento. Third-class passengers, primarily emigrants, traveled in cars fitted with narrow wooden benches in rows. They paid $40 for an Omaha-to-Sacramento ticket. The cars with emigrants were often attached to freight trains and were stopped for other trains to pass; therefore, it might take an emigrant ten days to make the same trip a first-class passenger could make in four days.

In 1864 George Mortimer Pullman constructed improvements to his railroad cars including hinged seats and seat backs that could be laid flat for night travel, and the Pullman sleeping car with hinged upper berths that could be folded up to the ceiling of the car. The Pullman dining cars were not in wide use until after 1880; prior to that most travelers ate at stations when the train stopped. The Pullman dining cars provided luxury meals consisting of such items as antelope steaks, boiled ham and tongue, broiled chicken, roast beef, corn on the cob, fresh fruit, and trout on trains in the Rockies.

Union Pacific

Organized under the Pacific Railway Act of 1862, the Union Pacific groundbreaking occurred in Omaha on December 2, 1863. No track was laid for a year. Primary organizers were Oakes Ames, financier; Thomas C. Durant, promoter; and Major General Grenville M. Dodge, builder.

The Route: Along the Platte River route from Omaha to Fort Kearny, then west to Julesburg, Colorado, and Cheyenne, across southern Wyoming Territory, and over the Uintah mountains to Promontory, Utah Territory. Workers laid about three miles of track a day across the plains.

Hell-on-Wheels Towns: These tent-city communities sprang up periodically at the end of the Union Pacific railroad construction line. Places like Julesburg, Colorado, and Cheyenne, Laramie, Benton, Bear River City and Evanston, Wyoming Territory, all started as hell-on-wheels towns. Although some achieved permanent status, most faded as they were replaced by another on down the line.

Central Pacific

Groundbreaking for the Central Pacific occurred on January 8, 1863, in Sacramento, California. Principal organizers were Charles Crocker, Mark Hopkins, Collis P. Huntington and Leland Stanford. Facing the potential of crippling labor strikes, the Central Pacific turned to Chinese laborers. The Central Pacific waged a race with the Union Pacific to complete the most miles of track on the transcontinental line. The two joined at Promontory, Utah Territory, May 10, 1869.

CATTLE TRAILS

Although cattle went to markets in Missouri from Texas as early as the 1840s over the Shawnee Trail, by far the majority of cattle on the various routes were gathered and moved following the Civil War. In 1867, 35,000 cattle went up the trails. That figure increased tenfold by 1869 when 350,000 animals followed the trails to the railroads. The peak year was 1871 when cowboys moved 600,000 cattle over the trails. In 1881, the last year of major trail travel, 250,000 animals moved north from Texas.

Trail herds had a certain order they maintained. The trail boss led the way, followed by a lead animal—often a steer that had been over the trail before. The best known of all lead animals was Old Blue, a steer owned by Charles Goodnight. At the right and left of the lead animals were the point riders, followed midway back in the line of cattle by the swing riders and then the flank riders. The drag riders brought up the rear. The wrangler with the horse herd, or remuda, rode to the side of the herd, and the cook with his chuck wagon generally went out in front to set up camp and prepare for meals.

Cattle had a road brand placed on them for the trip so trail riders knew to which herd they belonged, since many herds followed the same trail during peak periods of migration from 1871 to 1881. At the end of the trail, cattle owners rebranded cattle with a permanent brand.

Travel on the cattle trails ceased for several reasons including economic conditions, overpopulation on northern ranges, quarantine laws that prohibited movement of Texas cattle, which had a tick that caused a fever in northern animals, homesteading across trail corridors, and fencing.

The primary cattle trails were these:

Chisholm: The southernmost point of the Chisholm Trail, pioneered by Jesse Chisholm, was Brownsville, Texas, but several other starting points existed in Texas ranging from Corpus Christi, Victoria and Houston to San Antonio and various places in West Texas to near the Rio Grande and the Pecos River. The trail collected itself at Fort Worth, Texas, and again at Red River Station, Texas, then proceeded north to the Kansas cow towns of Dodge City, Caldwell, Wichita, Newton, Ellsworth and Abilene. More than half the cattle trailed north on all the trails followed the Chisholm route.

Goodnight-Loving: Developed by Charles Goodnight and Oliver Loving, the trail bearing their surnames started in central Texas, headed due west across the Pecos River, then followed that watercourse north through New Mexico Territory and across Colorado before slipping into Wyoming at Cheyenne. The first herds over the trail to Wyoming reached Cheyenne in 1860, brought in by John Wesley Iliff, a Colorado cattle buyer who agreed to purchase Goodnight's herd if it would be delivered to Cheyenne. In 1861 Goodnight took cattle as far north as Chugwater, about fifty miles beyond Cheyenne.

Shawnee: The first cattle trail in the West extended from Brownsville, Texas, to Missouri ending at Kansas City, Sedalia and St. Louis. It was in use in the 1840s and continued in use until the Civil War.

Texas/Western: Starting in San Antonio, the Western Trail headed due north through Texas and Indian Territory (Oklahoma) to Dodge City, Kansas, and eventually to Ogallala, Nebraska. There it split into the Texas Trail with one branch continuing directly north to Fort Buford, Dakota Territory, and the other extending west to Cheyenne, before turning north again and continuing past Fort Laramie through the Powder River Basin and on to Miles City, Montana Territory.

METHODS OF TRANSPORTATION

River Transportation

Only a handful of the West's rivers and streams were navigable by steamboats and other large watercraft. Steamboats were introduced on the Mississippi River in 1811, and by 1820 paddle wheelers were in use on the Mississippi as well. The Missouri River did serve as a main conduit for travelers, with steamboats providing transportation as far north and west as Fort Benton, established in 1850 in what later became Montana Territory. At Fort Benton people left the steamboats and proceeded to destinations via overland means including horseback, stagecoach or wagon train, while cargo was offloaded and transfered to freight wagons. The Missouri River also provided access to the West, with various river towns developing all along its length that served as starting points for travelers or freighting companies interested in western journeys. Some steamboat travel occurred on the Sacramento River, while the Columbia River had significant numbers of travelers. Emigrants headed to the Willamette Valley in Oregon used a variety of craft ranging from flat boats and canoes to rafts to transport themselves and their goods on the river.

Native Americans, trappers and some early explorers used homemade canoes, dugouts made from a hollowed-out tree, and bull boats made from hides stretched over a willow frame and usually round or oval in shape. Other watercraft included flatboats or mackinaws, up to seventy feet long, made of whipsawed lumber, propelled with oars and a small sail and steered by a man wielding a big oar at the stern. Mackinaws were used to haul large amounts of cargo downstream but never to make upstream journeys.

Keelboats were also up to seventy feet long and were used to haul cargo both upstream and downstream. They had a cabin at the center of the boat with a narrow walkway along each side. The walkway had cleats to give the men—who used poles to maneuver the vessel upstream—traction as they walked. The six to twelve oarsmen for each keelboat had seats for use when rowing was possible. Often poling or rowing was not practical, and in such cases the keelboats were moved up the river by men who pulled them with heavy ropes.

The two primary steamboats in use during the period were side-wheelers and stern-wheelers. The first true Missouri riverboat, a stern-wheeler capable of carrying 350 tons of cargo, went into use in 1859.

The St. Louis *Democrat* contains a list of the disasters in the western rivers during the six months ending on the 30th of June last. The number of steamers lost is forty-six, as follows: by fire ten; by collision, ice, snags &c, thirty-six; total forty-six. The number of lives lost was forty-three. During the same period there were two explosions. The total amount of property destroyed was $1,200,000.
—FLIN, *July 26, 1856, 103-3*

On the 27th of June a steamer arrived at St. Louis from a point one hundred and eighty miles beyond Fort Union, at the mouth of the Yellow Stone, two thousand five hundred miles above St. Louis! Thus is the Missouri river, which joins the Father of Waters fifteen hundred miles from the Gulf navigable for twenty-five hundred miles by steamboats, so that there is in all four thousand miles of unbroken steamboat navigation.—FLIN, *August 1, 1857, 142-3*

Overland Transportation

Covered Wagon: Covered wagons all had some similar elements of construction, though wagons of different shapes and sizes were used in the West. The common elements are these: The *running gear* or *undercarriage* consisting of an axle assembly of both the front and back wheels, which generally were wooden wheels bound with iron rims. The two *axle units* were held together by the *reach* of the wagon (a part that often broke in rough country). The *tongue* of the wagon was used to attach the draft animals that pulled the wagon, and the *hounds* fastened the rear axle to the reach and the front axle to the wagon tongue. Atop the running gear was the *bolster*, a basic frame with four upright supports which held the *wagon bed* in place. Though the running gears and bolster were similar on all wagons, the wagon bed varied in size and shape. The front of each wagon generally had a tool box or *jockey box*. A number of curved wooden pieces called *bows* fit through sprockets on the side of the wagon bed and a cover of heavy canvas, often treated with linseed oil to make it water-resistant, was stretched over the bows and tied in the back and front.

With all wagons it was necessary to slow or brake them when descending hills. The wagons each had a brake for the rear wheels that could be engaged by the forward movement of a brake handle, which a teamster could set either with his hand or foot or by pulling a rope. Generally, the brake was on the right rear wheel, though some were on both rear wheels. In mountain country additional braking was necessary. Teamsters placed shoe brakes (called skid shoes) onto the wheel. Sometimes they stopped the wheels from turning by putting chains on them in a process known as "roughlocking" or by tying a tree to the back of the wagon to provide a drag. The Mormon brake, named for its inventors, involved jacking up the rear of the wagon and placing a tree under the rear axle then chaining or tying the tree to the center pole above the axle before letting the rear wagon wheels down onto it. This served as a drag going down the hill. Once at the bottom of the hill, the tree could be discarded. Occasionally in steep areas travelers poured sand over the brakes to increase resistance on the wheels.

Construction Materials: Wagonmakers used hardwoods such as oak, maple and hickory. They reinforced wheels and parts that sustained the most pressure with iron.

Primary Wagon Builders: The J. Murphy Company of St. Louis, the Studebaker Brothers Manufacturing Company of South Bend, Indiana, and Peter Schuttler of Chicago.

Draft Animals: At various times oxen, mules and horses pulled wagons. Oxen traveled more slowly than mules or horses, and subsisted primarily from grazing. Two oxen hitched together were a yoke. Mules had more endurance than horses and were faster than oxen. Used by some freighting companies, and by most travelers to California and other gold-rush destinations, two mules hitched together were a span. Horses generally traveled more quickly than oxen and about the same speed as mules, but they didn't have the stamina of mules making them less desirable; however, horses cost less. Both mules and horses needed grain as a feed supplement.

Types of Wagons

Buckboards and Buggies: A variety of lightweight vehicles ranging from two-wheeled carts to surreys, some with coverings and others without.

Celerity Wagons: These were light stagecoaches with roller flaps on the side so the canvas coverings could be moved out of the way to provide views for passengers.

Wagons served a variety of purposes from hauling people and freight to serving as transportation means in mining camps and during construction projects. This wagon has an unusual bottom-dump bed. It could have been used to haul ore from copper mines near Grand Encampment, Wyoming.

Replica of an 1880s model chuck wagon, owned by Ben Kern.

Chuck Wagon: The first chuck wagons were placed in use along the cattle trails and on ranches after 1866 when Charles Goodnight rebuilt an Army surplus wagon to serve his trail crew. The chuck wagon was similar to other covered wagons, but had added features such as a water barrel, a tool box, coffee grinder, and the all-important chuck box. The chuck box sat in the back of the wagon and was stationary. It had a back panel that folded down with a swinging leg to form a table. The box itself had various cubby holes and drawers where the cook could store pots, pans, utensils, food items and miscellaneous goods. One box, known as the "possibles" drawer, held everything from sewing needles, buttons and thread to a bottle of whiskey, administered as medicine by the cook. The Studebaker Company eventually built chuck boxes, charging from $75 to $100 for one. Besides holding the cook's supplies, the chuck wagon served as a freight wagon for cowboy gear holding bedrolls, lanterns, kerosene, slickers, rope, guns and ammunition, axle grease, grain for the team and extra wagon wheels. The boot, a boxed-in area at the back of the wagon under the chuck box, served as a storage area for the cook's frying pans and dutch ovens. The coffeepot had its own cubbyhole in the chuck box.

Conestoga Wagons: Used as freight wagons primarily and seldom by emigrants or in the West. The large, canvas-topped Conestoga wagons could haul large loads. The canvas covers were called osnaburg covers for Osnabrück, Germany, where that type of cloth was made. Some Conestoga wagons could carry up to six thousand pounds of goods.

Freight Wagons: Generally freight wagons cost less than $200. They varied from a capacity of one to ten tons; most hauled five to seven tons of freight. The boxes were sixteen to eighteen feet long and four and one-half feet wide.

Handcarts: Used by Mormon immigrants between 1856 and 1860, there were two types of handcarts, both with wheels set the usual width of a wagon's running gear. The open wooden cart was constructed of hickory or oak with shafts and a wagon box made of the same materials. Axles were generally of hickory. The box was about six to seven feet long. There was a space of about three feet from the front of the cart to the front bar or singletree with which the cart could be pulled by a lead horse, or by the lead man, woman, boy or girl of the team. The covered family cart was of similar construction, but it had an iron axle. The wagon box was three or four feet long with side and end pieces about eight inches high. A handcart was generally assigned to five people.

Military Ambulance: Used to transport injured soldiers, the military ambulances were boxlike conveyances often serving as the mode of travel for officers' wives when they accompanied their husbands to various western military posts or even on field campaigns.

Stagecoaches: Abbott and Downing built the famed Concord stagecoaches in Concord, Massachusetts. Each coach weighed more than two thousand pounds and cost from $1200 to $1500. Each coach sat upon a thoroughbrace construction—two, three-inch-wide leather strips that cushioned the coach—making the ride over rough country smooth. Mark Twain called it a "cradle on wheels." Mail and a strongbox of valuables went into the front boot, while express cargo and baggage was stored in the rear boot, both made of heavy leather. Other cargo could be stored atop the coach on the box. The driver, a gun-wielding express messenger and some passengers also sat on top of the coach, exposed to the weather but having a 360-degree view of the country. Up to twenty-one passengers could ride on a single coach, with nine inside and a dozen more on the roof. The coaches had windows with leather curtains, and three leather-covered seats for passengers inside. Average speed was eight miles per hour.

Swing stations, where horses were changed, were about twelve miles apart; home stations, where people had meals and sometimes spent the night, were about forty to fifty miles apart. Beds at home stations were for drivers, conductors and express messengers; passengers slept on the floor if necessary, but generally the coaches just changed drivers at the home stations so passengers slept in the coach as they traveled. Passengers had about fifteen inches of seat space if the interior of the coach carried its capacity of nine people. There was little legroom. Those in the center seat had no back support but held onto leather straps suspended from the ceiling. Coaches stopped about forty minutes a day for passengers to eat; otherwise, they moved continuously. A stage trip from Atchison, Kansas, to Denver took six days, as compared with a trek of five weeks by wagon.

Steam Engine or Steam Wagon: In 1861 Thomas L. Fortune of Mount Pleasant, Kansas, built a steam engine designed to pull twenty-five freight wagons. The 60-horsepower engine had eight-foot-high wheels and the vehicle weighed ten tons. It was difficult to maneuver, became mired in mud and never pulled a single wagon. A similar vehicle was built in Nebraska City, Nebraska, and it too failed to work as designed, though the road on which it was tested received the name Steam Engine Road.

Travois: This method of hauling goods or people involved lashing two poles or sticks to a harness attached to the draft animal—either a horse or a dog. A hide or other covering was placed over the poles making a platform for the material or person. Some travois had woven basket or cage-like areas on them, in which small children could ride. In common use among Native Americans, and sometimes used by Euro-Americans, travois were used particularly to transport an injured person when a wagon wasn't available.

Windwagon: Constructed in 1853 in Nebraska, the windwagon involved placement of a twenty-foot mast on a wagon onto which was placed a sail. The man who built the conveyance is known only as Windwagon Thomas. Some other versions of windwagons were developed in the West, though none were produced commercially.

CREIGHTON TELEGRAPH

Started as a communications system that would quickly relay information across the West, the transcontinental telegraph was built in 1861. The Telegraph Act of 1860 authorized construction of a line from Missouri to California and on January 11, 1861, Nebraska chartered the Pacific Telegraph Company. On June 17, 1861, Edward Creighton and the Pacific Telegraph crews started construction from Omaha, Nebraska. Construction crews averaged three to eight miles a day; they had to ship in poles for the line for the treeless section between Fort Kearny and Salt Lake City. On October 18, 1861, officials sent the first test message between Salt Lake City and Omaha.

The Route: Omaha to San Francisco over a route close to the Oregon-California Trail corridor. The telegraph linked Omaha with Fort Kearny and Plum Creek, Nebraska; Julesburg, Colorado Territory; Fort Laramie and Fort Bridger, Wyoming; Salt Lake City, Utah; Ruby Valley, Idaho; Fort Churchill and Canon City, Nevada; Sacramento, San Jose and San Francisco, California. There were other stations along the route as well.

Problems on the line: Lightning, wind, blizzards that buried poles and lines, bison (which scratched on the poles), emigrants (who chopped down the

---

THE PACIFIC TELEGRAPH

The telegraphic line to the Pacific is being carried rapidly westward. It already reaches to the city of the Mormons in the Great Salt Lake Valley. The first message which came over it was a despatch from Brigham Young to Hon. J. H. Wade, President of the Company constructing it, and was received in Cleveland on the 18th of October, dated on the morning of the same day. It is as follows:

Sir—Permit me to congratulate you on the completion of the over land telegraph line west to this city; to commend the energy displayed by yourself and associates in the rapid and successful prosecution of a work so beneficial, and to express the wish that its use may ever tend to promote the true interest of the dwellers on both the Atlantic and Pacific slopes of our continent.

Utah has not seceded, but is firm for the Constitution and laws of our once happy country, and is warmly interested in successful enterprises like the one so far completed.

Brigham Young

—FLIN, *November 2, 1861, 371-2*

---

poles to use as firewood and for wire to use in wagon repairs), and Indian sabotage, primarily after 1864.

Costs: Initially $1 per word, later $7 per ten words. Both rates were above limits set in the Telegraph Act of 1860 which established fees at $3 for ten words.

ADDITIONAL READING

Cattle Trails

Gard, Wayne. *The Chisholm Trail.* Norman: University of Oklahoma Press, 1954.

Tinsley, Jim Bob. *He Was Singin' This Song.* Gainesville: University Presses of Florida, 1981.

Mormon Trail

Bartholomew, Rebecca, and Leonard J. Arrington. *Rescue of the 1856 Handcart Companies.* Provo, Utah: Brigham Young University, Charles Redd Center for Western Studies, 1993.

Brown, Joseph. *The Mormon Trek West.* Garden City, New York: Doubleday & Company, 1980.

Hafen, Leroy R., and Ann W. Hafen. *Handcarts to Zion.* Lincoln: University of Nebraska Press, 1992. The best reference to the Mormon handcart experiment.

Schlinder, Harold. *Orrin Porter Rockwell: Man of God/Son of Thunder.* Salt

Lake City: University of Utah Press, 1966. Good information about the Mormon migration.

Stegner, Wallace. *Gathering of Zion: The Story of the Mormon Trail.* Lincoln: University of Nebraska Press, 1992. An excellent reference.

Oregon-California Trail

Butruille, Susan. *Women's Voices From the Oregon Trail.* Boise: Tamarack Books, 1993. A good reference for women's issues, but be careful of details about Native Americans.

Haines, Aubrey. *Historic Sites Along the Oregon Trail.* St. Louis: The Patrice Press, 1981. An excellent reference.

Mattes, Merrill. *The Great Platte River Road.* Lincoln: University of Nebraska, 1981. The best reference related to the Oregon Trail in Nebraska Press.

———. *Platte River Road Narratives.* Urbana, Ill.: University of Illinois Press, 1988. An excellent reference as it provides direction to find other sources.

Moulton, Candy, and Ben Kern. *Wagon Wheels: A Contemporary Journey on the Oregon Trail.* Glendo, Wyo.: High Plains Press, 1996.

Parkman, Francis. *The Oregon Trail.* 1872. Harrisburg, Pa: The National Historical Society, 1993.

Schlissel, Lillian. *Women's Diaries of the Westward Journey.* New York: Schocken Books, 1982. An excellent reference to women on the trail.

Pony Express

Bradley, Glenn Danford. *The Story of the Pony Express.* Edited by Waddell F. Smith. San Francisco: Hesperia House, 1960.

Settle Raymonda W., and Mary Lund Settle. *Saddles and Spurs: The Pony Express Saga.* Harrisburg, Pa.: Stackpole Company, 1955. The best reference to the Pony Express.

Smith, Waddell F., ed. *The Story of the Pony Express.* San Rafael, Calif.: Pony Express History and Art Gallery, Post Centennial edition, 1964.

Railroads

Athearn, Robert G. *Union Pacific Country.* Lincoln: University of Nebraska Press, 1976. A good reference about the Union Pacific Railroad.

Bartlett, Richard A. *Great Surveys of the American West.* Norman: University of Oklahoma Press, 1926.

Bebe, Lucius, and Charles Clegg. *Narrow Gauge in the Rockies.* Berkeley, Calif.: Howell-North, 1958.

Griswold, Wesley. *A Work of Giants.* New York: McGraw-Hill, 1962.

Kraus, George. *High Road to Promontory.* Palo Alto, Calif.: American West Pub. Co., 1969.

Painter, Gerald Leroy. *The Tie that Binds: Grenville M. Dodge and the Building of the First Transcontinental Railroad.* Northfield, Vt.: Norwich University Press, 1985.

Santa Fe Trail

Beacham, Larry M. *William Becknell—Father of the Santa Fe Trail.* El Paso: Texas Western Press, 1982.

Brown, William E. *The Santa Fe Trail.* St. Louis: The Patrice Press, 1988.

Crutchfield, James A. *The Santa Fe Trail.* Plano, Tex.: Republic of Texas Press, 1996. An excellent reference.

Gregg, Josiah. *Commerce of the Prairies.* New York: Henry G. Langley, 1844. Reprint, Ann Arbor, Mich.: University Microfilms Inc., 1966. A valuable reference.

Lavender, David. *The Trail to Santa Fe.* Santa Fe: Trails West Publishing, 1989.

Telegraph

Ault, Phil. *Wires West.* New York: Dodd, Mead, and Co.,1974.

Thompson, Robert L. *Wiring a Continent.* Princeton, N.J.: Princeton University Press, 1947.

Unrau, William. *Tending the Talking Wire.* Salt Lake City: University of Utah Press, 1979. An excellent reference including letters from a soldier working along the transcontinental telegraph in 1865 Wyoming.

Other General Sources

Frederick, J.V. *Ben Holladay: The Stagecoach King.* Glendale, Calif.: Arthur H. Clark, 1940. Reprint, Lincoln: University of Nebraska Press, 1989.

Haites, Erik F. *Western River Transportation.* Baltimore: Johns Hopkins University Press, 1975.

Hoffman, H. Wilbur. *Sagas of Old Western Travel and Transport.* San Diego: Howell-North Books, 1980.

Holmes, Kenneth L., ed. *Covered Wagon Women.* Ten volumes of diaries and letters from the western trails. Glendale, Calif.: Arthur H. Clark and Company, 1983. Reprint, Lincoln: University of Nebraska Bison Books, publication started in 1996 and continues. An essential reference series when writing about trail travel.

Peters, Arthur King. *Seven Trails West.* New York: Abbeville Press, 1996. A good overview book to western trails.

Petsche, Jerome E. *The Steamboat Bertrand: History, Excavation and Architecture.* Washington, DC: National Park Service, 1974.

Schlissel, Lillian. *Women's Diaries of the Westward Migration.* New York: Schocken Books Inc., 1982. An excellent reference.

Spring, Agnes Wright. *The Cheyenne and Black Hills Stage and Express Routes.*

Lincoln: University of Nebraska Press, 1948. The best reference to the Cheyenne and Black Hills stage route.

Strahorn, Carrie Adell. *Fifteen Thousand Miles by Stage, Vol. 1.* New York: Knickerbocker Press, 1911. Reprint, Lincoln: University of Nebraska Press, 1988.

Webber, Bert. *Indians Along the Oregon Trail.* Medford, Ore.: Webb Research Group, 1989.

Worcester, Don, ed. *Pioneer Trails West.* Caldwell, Idaho: The Caxton Printers, 1985. An excellent reference with details about most western trails.

Chapter Seventeen

CRIME AND PUNISHMENT

L aw in the West evolved throughout the period with several major types of law practices as well as enforcers. Early law in the region came in the form of rules and regulations imposed by the various fur companies as they established trading networks that were in place from the 1820s until the early 1840s. Known as the "law for the beaver," the fur company regulations were formal and generally based upon accepted British and American law practices. For the most part, by the time our era begins, the fur trade had withered so new forms of organization and law were needed. They came as law developed in the borderlands, by Mormons, in mining camps, on cattle drives, in military jurisdictions and in towns (courthouse law). Finally, an independent style of law, known as vigilante law, developed and played a significant role in the West throughout the period.

Borderlands law involved principles developed in Canada, where the Hudson's Bay Company had dominated early legal actions, as well as principles from Spanish Louisiana, or Spanish Mexico. In all cases those types of formal law were manipulated into a form of American common law and applied during the era.

Mormon law in Utah superseded American judicial practices; if the leaders of the Church of Jesus Christ of Latter-day Saints decreed a punishment on a member, it was carried out regardless of adherence to or conflict with other laws of the land. The leadership in Utah was a theocracy, and life there did not function on general democratic principles of the period.

Law as it related to the cowboy era, and particularly to the cattle-drive period 1865-90, also was singular in application. The cowboys fell under authority of various marshals, sheriffs and the like when in cow towns, but on the trail and on the range they adhered to the law of the range: the decisions of the cow boss or the foreman. One interesting element of range law related to men riding the grubline. Though he might have been fired by the range foreman or cow boss during the spring, summer or fall, if a man rode into a cattle ranch in winter, he was generally allowed to stay for a few days or longer; it was unacceptable to refuse hospitality in such cases. Grubline or chuckline riders were out-of-work cowboys who moved from ranch to ranch seeking a free meal—or free grub or chuck (food). They knew they'd need to move once the weather cleared or spring work became available.

In regions near military outposts or forts, law enforcement often rested with soldiers and officers. Soldiers assisted in finding and arresting suspected criminals, who were sometimes held in military jails or other facilities pending trial, or if convicted, held there as a part of their punishment. Military courts also dealt with infractions committed by soldiers.

Miners' law originated with the placer diggings in California in 1848 as miners organized courts or tribunals to hear petitions related to claims and claim jumping. The miners' law spread throughout the western mining camps; in 1872 Congress adopted some of its provisions, which remained in effect in the 1990s.

A common issue in mining camps related to race. In California, for example, crimes against Chinese, Mexican, Spanish-American or California-Indian miners were seldom given any credence. Shooting local Indians, for example, was not considered a crime. Foreigners suspected of crimes were subjected to quick trials and speedy enforcement of punishment, as in the case in California in January 1849 of two Frenchmen and one Chilean who were suspected of thievery, sentenced to whippings, then subsequently charged for an earlier murder and attempted robbery on the Stansilaus River. Without benefit of an interpreter and within the space of a half hour, the three were tried, convicted by a jury of some two hundred miners and hanged. Though Spanish-Americans had been in California long before the gold discovery of 1848, they, too, were often considered "foreigners" and subjected to punishment meted out by miners' courts, which disallowed claims staked by such individuals. In 1848 on the American River, for example, Spanish-Americans had only three hours' notice before they were required to vacate their claims.

A common factor in many western legal cases was the speed with which "justice" was carried out. Often lawbreakers were captured, tried and punished in short time spans. By the end of the era, criminal law in the West was more organized as lawyers used various legal maneuvers on behalf of—or in prosecution of—individuals charged with crimes.

Law generally revolved around a limited number of situations: collecting debts, crimes and property transactions. As areas became recognized territories, U.S. district judges were appointed. They generally had jurisdiction in large areas, making their jobs difficult. Both judges and lawyers had routine areas to which they traveled, known as circuits, and they became circuit-riders. They would arrive in a town and clients would then approach the lawyers and the judge for decisions concerning various issues. Once the issues had been decided, the judge and lawyers would leave for the next town. Most often trials took place on Saturday. The court sessions occurred in a variety of locations, often in stores or saloons. Defendants had the right to a jury trial, but it wasn't always easy to find a jury, particularly in sparsely populated regions.

Counties or towns also selected judges and justices of the peace, who heard cases involving local laws and misdemeanors. Federal, state and county courthouses were eventually built so judges no longer needed to ride around their district to hear cases. Instead they presided over hearings and trials in one location.

The laws applied in the Indian Territory were particularly difficult to enforce due to vast distances lawmen needed to travel to find, arrest and return suspects to a court. The Creek, Choctaw, Cherokee, Chickasaw and Seminole tribes had their own laws with courts and a police force which they used for tribal disputes. However, crimes committed by Indians when accompanied by Anglos, against Anglos, or crimes which Anglos themselves committed, could not be handled by the Indian courts. Those cases instead were handled in the federal court system for the Western District of Arkansas.

It was a difficult assignment for a district judge. Isaac Charles Parker took the position in 1875, quickly showing a tough style. Sitting in his courtroom in Fort Smith, Arkansas, Judge Parker became known as "The Hanging Judge" for his tendency to sentence men convicted of serious crime to death by hanging. A gallows capable of hanging a dozen men at a time was constructed near the courthouse and routinely used. During most of his tenure on the bench, Judge Parker's decisions about crimes committed in Indian Territory were final; there was no opportunity to appeal. The sentences often were carried out soon after the rulings. In 1889 Congress changed the nature of the court's jurisdiction, allowing convicted felons to appeal their cases to the U.S. Supreme Court, which many did, winning reversal of some of Judge Parker's decisions.

On nearly all fronts throughout the period, the West was a violent place. Almost all people carried weapons—primarily guns—which they were ready and willing to use as a means to prove a point, protect their property or lives, or sometimes for ill-gotten gains.

Outlaws raided towns, rustled cattle, destroyed sheep herds and robbed trains and stagecoaches. They burglarized homes or businesses, raped women and assaulted or murdered people.

> The highwaymen of Sacramento, Cal., have taken to garroting and 'choloroforming.'—FLIN, *October 29, 1870, 103-4*

In a region where people's very existence often depended upon transportation by horse or horse-drawn vehicle, the crime of horse theft was particularly heinous, though amongst Native Americans it was considered an act of bravery—not necessarily a crime—to capture horses; Indians of the period seldom referred to taking enemy horses as stealing. For Crows, known for their prowess at obtaining horses from their enemies, to sneak into a rival camp and slip away with horses showed bravery and was a true sign of being a warrior. The more horses a Crow captured, the greater his wealth and subsequently the greater his status in the tribe. Horse raids were prevalent, the most common form of action taken by one tribe against another. Likely more Indians died during or as a result of horse raids than from any other Indian-against-Indian conflict, according to John C. Ewers in *Plains Indian History & Culture.*

Among Euro-Americans, however, horse theft was the one crime likely to land the perpetrator up a tree with a rope around his or her neck.

> Western journalism is concise: 'Mr. Jim Clementon, equine abductor, of Minnesota, was lately the victim of a neck-tie sociable.'
> —FLIN, *February 24, 1872, 379-4*

NATIVE AMERICANS

When crime occurred in any part of the West, locals generally dealt with it. Among Native Americans, tribal leaders responded to inappropriate activities with various methods, making it necessary to research specific tribes for the measures employed. Cheyennes, for example, heard complaints in a general council where public opinion determined action to be taken. If someone had killed a fellow tribal member, he or she might be ordered to pay the relatives of the deceased person.

Other Cheyenne punishment included whippings, destruction of property such as lodges or lodge poles, or even the killing of horses. A killer also might be prevented from eating or drinking from any but his or her own cup. And if the killer did use someone else's cup or other eating utensil, it had to be purified before further use. To purify the utensil, a person rubbed his or her hand on the ground then over the dish four different times. Murderers were shunned in other ways as well. People refused to talk to them, told them to shut up and, in some instances, murderers were banished from the tribe, which often lead to death because people could not survive alone without shelter and sometimes without food. With such penalties imposed, murder amongst the Cheyennes was rare throughout the period.

After tribes had been placed on reservations, other types of legal remedies might be imposed as Indian Police units organized.

The Five Civilized tribes had an extensive network for dealing with crime and punishment after they had settled in Indian Territory. They had courts, sheriffs, juries and process servers long before many western communities had similarly functioning positions, and it was a law developed for and by the tribes themselves.

THE LAWMEN

Aside from Indian territory and reservations, lawmen from various jurisdictions generally dealt with criminal activities and the perpetrators.

The most important position of all the law officers rested with the U.S. marshal, who was appointed by the President with the consent of the Senate. A U.S. marshal had broad powers and influence, particularly when selecting and hiring deputy marshals. The jobs were highly coveted. In New Mexico in 1882 the Albuquerque newspaper reported on the selection of a new U.S. marshal for the region: "The President is still holding off the appointment of a U.S. marshal. It is understood there are fifty-one applications, with sixty-four bushels of petitions and seventy-three barrels of recommendations on hand."

Some U.S. marshals worked more on paperwork than they did in pursuing criminals, but others took their enforcement jobs seriously, riding long hours and distances to capture criminals and return them to courtrooms to face the consequences of their crimes. U.S. marshals could appoint deputies or organize posses if needed.

Deputies charged with arresting and bringing in criminals from Indian Territory to face Judge Parker in Fort Smith, Arkansas, often traveled in groups of four or five men, making sweeping forays through the region and then bringing large numbers of suspects at the same time to appear in court. The deputies received a stipend of two dollars per arrest. They got nothing if they brought someone in dead—unless a "dead-or-alive" reward had been posted. The prisoners walked, or rode in a wagon if they were injured.

Three of the most well-known marshals involved with capturing criminals in Indian Territory were Bill Tilghman, Heck Thomas and Chris Madsen, who became known as The Three Guardsmen.

In an early case at Koyukuk camp in 1897, Frank Canton, who had a career as an outlaw in Oklahoma before becoming a sheriff in Wyoming and the first U.S. deputy marshal in the Alaska Interior, "swore in twenty special deputies, organized a trial, and as self-appointed judge, fined the three thieves a total of two thousand dollars."

County sheriffs generally had responsibility for less territory than U.S. marshals; however, they too played a vital role in law enforcement, often tracking and capturing outlaws, thieves, murderers and the like. Sheriffs also maintained the county jail, sold property tax delinquents, served court orders, and in some states they inspected livestock brands, operated dog pounds and looked for strayed livestock.

Texan street-car conductors are made Deputy-Sheriffs by a law of the State.—FLIN, *December 23, 1871, 235-4*

Town marshals had the smallest territory to deal with, but they, too, had difficult responsibilities, particularly in the sometimes out-of-control cow towns or mining camps. In addition to maintaining order, marshals collected

Jail, Bannack, Montana, circa 1860s. Heavy bars across the windows and huge timbers forming the walls and roof make it unlikely a prisoner could escape.

business license fees and taxes; served as health, fire or sanitation inspectors; maintained records and the town jail; served subpoenas; and provided evidence as needed at court hearings.

In almost all cases the lawmen exhibited top physical condition. They were quick with their guns, using them to control lawlessness by often shooting and wounding or killing suspects, though some lawmen seldom resorted to using weapons as a way to maintain order.

There were other organized law enforcement groups, most notably the mounted police or rangers of Texas, Arizona and New Mexico, who had broad powers and reputations for tracking down evildoers in the vast open spaces of the Southwest.

As Captain Burt Mossman of Arizona's Rangers noted, dealing with criminals often required a tough stance:

> If they come along easy, everything will be all right. If they don't, well, I guess we can make pretty short work of them. I know most of them and the life those fellows are leading in the mesquite shrub to keep out of reach of the law is a dog's life. They ought to thank me for giving them a chance to come in and take their medicine. Some of them will object, of course. They'll probably try a little gunplay as a bluff, but I shoot fairly well myself, and the boys who back me up are handy enough with their guns. Any rustler who wants to yank on the rope and kick up trouble will find he's up against it.

Because of its remoteness from the remainder of the United States, justice in Alaska was particularly difficult. The territory's few law enforcement officers and judges were spread over a vast geographic region where weather conditions often made it impractical or nearly impossible to hold or try suspected criminals. On the eve of the 1896 gold rush, the Klondike, in Yukon Territory (Canada), Alaska Territory, which had been a part of the United States for nearly thirty years, had one judge, one marshal, ten deputy marshals and twenty Indian police commissioners. Those who headed toward Yukon Territory traveled through Alaska Territory, creating some difficulties because of a lack of law-enforcement officers in the huge region. Once in the Yukon, however, law enforcement was provided by the Canadian Mounted Police and was strict, available and consistent.

Assisting lawmen in bringing criminals to justice were bounty hunters and detectives, the most well-known being those who worked for the Pinkerton Detective Agency. Allen Pinkerton started his detective agency in 1850. The Pinkertons trailed individual criminals or outlaw gangs, provided security on railroad trains in an effort to stop robbings, and even set up a secret service for the Union Army in 1861. Pinkerton detectives had a reputation for doggedly pursuing suspects, though they didn't always get their man. They failed to break up the James Gang, but their pursuit of Butch Cassidy and the Sundance Kid forced the two outlaws into exile in South America.

VIGILANTES

Sometimes, organized, official law wasn't available in a region or community, or it failed to act. In such cases groups of citizens banded together to enforce and uphold their own version of the law. Known as vigilantes, such bands generally became empowered as a city first sprang into being, although sometimes they grew in already established towns and cities. And they also had a role in rural areas, particularly on the open range. Though vigilantes generally had no "legal" authority, they did usually operate within accepted bounds. For instance, they usually told an individual the charge against him, often allowed the prisoner to present a defense, sometimes even allowing him representation by an attorney and usually had some form of jury (which might have been the vigilantes themselves); then they determined guilt or innocence and almost immediately carried out the punishment. Vigilantes didn't always convict the prisoner, though that was most often the result of such "trials." Punishment ranged from whippings and banishment (particularly in the case of violations of rules applied in mining districts) to death, most often by hanging.

As the Union Pacific Railroad laid its tracks west across Nebraska, northeastern Colorado, and Wyoming in 1868-69, vigilante bands became the first, and only, law and order around. The Hell-on-Wheels towns grew quickly and most often were temporary. Cheyenne, Wyoming Territory, from the beginning appeared to have a chance at permanence. When the town showed no signs of control, a quasi-secret vigilance committee organized. Though the committee didn't advertise its membership, town officials gave it at least tacit approval. The committee of some two hundred men began to patrol Cheyenne's streets, first tying together three drunken thieves who had been arrested but then released. A sign left with the drunks said, "$90 stole . . . 500 recovered. City authorities please not interfere. Next case goes up a tree. Beware of the Vigilance Committee." Subsequently; the vigilantes, who wore gunnysack masks with slits cut to form eyeholes, sometimes needed only to make their presence known as an inducement for criminals—or those contemplating criminal activities—to find another locale.

Vigilantes should not be confused with lynch mobs—which were individuals who banded together to take action against a suspected or convicted criminal. Lynch mobs seldom allowed the suspect the opportunity to present any defense. Some vigilantes had extensive operations that lasted weeks or even months, while lynch mobs generally organized on the spur-of-the-moment and just as quickly dispersed.

Examples of a lynch mob include the group that gathered in Carbon, Wyoming, in the early 1880s upon hearing that "Dutch" Charley Burris was being transported by train from Laramie City to Rawlins to stand trial for the murder of two lawmen. The mob boarded the train when it stopped in Carbon, found Burris and took him to a telegraph pole in the town. There they asked him to confess his part in the killings. He refused, so they threw a rope over the telegraph pole and placed it around his neck. They asked again, he refused. They pulled the rope and held him for a while, then put him down and again requested a confession. Burris continued to refuse and ultimately died from hanging on the pole.

In 1881, when "Big Nose" George Parrott was returned to Rawlins to stand trial on the same charges as Burris, a similar mob organized at Carbon, dragging him from the train. Parrott, unlike Burris, made a full confession and was allowed to continue in the custody of the local sheriff to Rawlins where he was subsequently tried and sentenced to hang. Not long before his scheduled execution, however, Parrott attempted to escape from the Carbon County jail. He was recaptured and returned to his cell. During the night another lynch mob visited the jail, took Parrott from the custody of the sheriff and his deputy and subsequently hanged him.

Although vigilantes generally operated outside the purview of town officials, sometimes they had the tacit approval of those same officials. In Aurora, Nevada, in 1864, for example, when a gang of outlaws and horse thieves murdered thirty settlers, the vigilantes captured the gang and prepared for a hanging. One citizen sent an urgent message to the governor, who in turn contacted U.S. Marshal Bob Howland in Aurora. The marshal responded to the governor's concerns this way: "Everything quiet in Aurora. Four men to be hanged in fifteen minutes."

Flagrant vigilante activity occurred in San Francisco where the Vigilance

Committee controlled the city in the 1850s, maintaining a grip on activities for a decade. Vigilantes there organized when the police failed to enforce laws against criminals such as the organized mob group, the Sydney Ducks. Skagway, Alaska, also had an active vigilante confrontation in 1898 when the vigilante Committee of One Hundred and One, backed by city leaders, engaged in a power play against a gang led by Soapy Smith and known as The Law and Order Committee of Three Hundred and Three. Smith was shot and subsequently many from his group were arrested, as members of the Committee of One Hundred and One blocked the trail between Skagway and Bennett, and watched the wharf and other nearby areas. Several of the Smith vigilante members eventually were tried and convicted of various crimes.

At one time or another almost all areas of the West had some involvement with vigilantes. Vigilantes in Montana in 1864 spread a reign of terror in the region near Bannack and Virginia City.

> The Vigilance Committee example is spreading. The people of St. Paul, Minnesota, held a public meeting recently, with the view to the adoption of summary measures for the extirpation of gamblers, cut-throats and thieves who infest that city.
> —FLIN, *September 6, 1856, 195-3*

Vigilante or lynch-mob actions involved punishment meted out to both men and women, though instances against the latter were uncommon. Two well-known cases include the hangings of Elizabeth Taylor near Nebraska's Blue River in 1885 and Ellen Watson in Wyoming's Sweetwater country in July 1889. Both women died for suspected cattle rustling. And Josefa, a Mexican dance hall girl, was hanged in Downieville, California, on the Fourth of July in 1851 after she stabbed and killed a miner.

RANGE DETECTIVES

Hired gunmen protected the interests of stagecoach and express companies, and railroads authorized employees to protect each line's interests, giving them power to make arrests or inspections. The best known of the vigilante groups involved various organizations of stockgrowers, homesteaders and range associations. Those groups included gunmen such as Billy the Kid, who worked with cattlemen in New Mexico in an organization calling themselves The Regulators. Range detectives went by such names as stock inspectors and cattle detectives, but no matter the title, their job was to protect the interests of their employers and they did so in all regions of the West. No matter what they were called, those men were fast with their guns, daring, confident and deadly. They often were either "reformed" criminals or on their way to becoming criminals.

Particularly active in the period 1880-1900, range detectives threatened real or would-be rustlers and other ne'er-do-wells with their very presence. They might work in groups or alone, and they seldom announced to the general public exactly who they were and what they did. They depended on the wealth and position of their employers to protect them from prosecution for any actions they took that were outside the accepted laws of the times and region.

Range detectives earned top pay—$100 to $150 per month and sometimes as high as $250 each month. Men with reputations for gunplay drew the most pay and had their choice of jobs. They included such people as Pat Garrett, former Texas Ranger John Armstrong, and Tom Horn, likely the best known of all the range detectives.

GUNFIGHTERS AND OUTLAWS

Gunfighters and outlaws routinely plied their trade in the West during the era, and particularly in the period after the Civil War. There were shoot-outs in dusty streets and even more during bank robberies, train robberies, and as outlaws attempted to elude pursuers.

A brief chronology of some of the activities of the West's best-known gunfighters and outlaws is as follows:

1866: February 13—Robbers hold up the Clay County Savings and Loan in Liberty, Missouri, taking $15,000 in gold and $45,000 in securities. Credit for the robbery goes to Frank and Jesse James, though Jesse may not have been present.

1867: Jesse James kills three people while robbing the bank in Richmond, Missouri.

1868: Jesse and Frank James, joined by Cole Younger and his brothers, rob the Southern Bank of Kentucky in Russellville. Robberies by the James Gang or the James-Younger Gang continue at least annually through 1872.

1868: November—John Wesley Hardin, age 15, kills his first man, an African-American man named Mage. He subseqently killed between thirty and fifty other men, primarily in Texas.

1873: The James-Younger Gang derail a Rock Island train in Adair, Iowa, effecting their first train robbery and killing several passengers and an engineer in the process.

1875: Pinkerton Detective agents firebomb the home of Frank and Jesse James's mother, Zerelda; she looses an arm and a younger half-brother is killed.

1876: September 7—Jesse and Frank James; Jim, Bob and Cole Younger; Charlie Pitts, Clell Miller and Bill Chadwell attempt a bank robbery in Northfield, Minnesota, that goes awry. Before the day has ended Chadwell and Miller are dead; Cole Younger, Frank James and Jim Younger are shot. In a subsequent conflict Pitts is killed, the Youngers are arrested. The Youngers

TOM HORN: RANGE DETECTIVE

Tom Horn worked as a scout for the U.S. Army in the Southwest, where he participated in the final surrender of Geronimo, and he was a packer for the Army. He served a stint as a detective for the Pinkerton Detective Agency and by 1894 had made his way to Wyoming. There he obtained work as a range detective for the Swan Land and Cattle Company, living at Iron Mountain Ranch owned by John Coble, for whom he also later worked.

Over the next seven years Horn patrolled the range, watching for rustling or other illegal activities. He was suspected of a number of murders in Wyoming, including those of William Lewis, a Mill Creek rancher, and Horse Creek settler Fred Powell, and Colorado cowboys Matt Rash and Isom Dart.

Once Wyoming Governor W.A. Richards met with Horn about the possibility of the range detective working for Richards on his ranch in the Big Horn mountains. At a meeting held at the state capitol, Horn outlined his terms: $350 in advance to purchase two horses and a pack outfit plus $5,000 when he had successfully handled Richards's business, placing no limit on the number of men he would kill in order to do just that. As Horn told the governor, "Whenever everything else fails, I have a system which never does."

The governor balked before consummating the deal, but Horn continued to work in Wyoming. Horn once said: "Killing men is my specialty. I look at it as a business proposition, and I think I have a corner on the market." The fee for each killing varied, though Horn often received $500. In order to be paid, he had a signal for his employers—placing a rock under the dead man's head.

Horn, like other range detectives, could be counted on to do his job and to keep his mouth shut. As one rancher noted, "Tom Horn had the honorable trait never to peach on accomplices or employers. He classed cattle thieves with wolves and coyotes, and looked upon himself as a benefactor of a society in destroying them, killing without feeling or compunction when certain he was after a guilty man."

The range detective finally made a mistake, however, when he bragged to U.S. Marshal Les E. Snow about killing fourteen-year-old Willie Nickell on Iron Mountain in 1901. A court stenographer recorded the confession, which landed Horn first in court, and later at the end of a rope, on November 29, 1903.

Some involved with the case at the time, and certainly since, questioned Horn's actual role in the Nickell killing, believing he did not fire the fatal shot, but had confessed while drunk and as a part of his general braggadocio. Whether truly guilty or not, Horn died without commenting on the roles his employers had played in that incident or others: the true sign of a good range detective.

are later convicted and sent to jail; the James brothers escape to Tennessee where they hide out under assumed names.

1878: April 1—Billy the Kid (a.k.a. William Bonney, William Antrim, Henry McCarty) and five companions in Lincoln, New Mexico, kill Sheriff Bill Brady, Deputy George Hindman and three other men, believing the authorities were on their way to assassinate A.A. McSween, for whom Billy the Kid and his companions had worked.

1878: July 19—Billy the Kid and several companions are involved in a showdown at the A.A. McSween compound in Lincoln, New Mexico. McSween and several others are killed in the fight.

1878: December 22—Billy the Kid surrenders to Lincoln County authorities. He subsequently escapes from jail.

1879: March—Billy the Kid discusses amnesty with New Mexico Governor Lew Wallace, and the Kid and Josiah "Doc" Scurlock subsequently surrender to Lincoln County sheriff George Kimball, but the Kid's "amnesty" deal later falls through and in May he escapes.

1879: Frank and Jesse James reorganize and rob a bank in Riverton, Iowa, and trains near Winston, Missouri, and Glendale, Missouri.

1879: Black Bart robs stagecoaches in California.

1880: The *Santa Fe Weekly New Mexican* is the first publication to refer to Billy the Kid by the name Bonney.

1880: December—A $500 reward is offered for the arrest of Billy the Kid. A posse led by Pat Garrett attacks the Kid and his pals at Stinking Spring, New Mexico, December 23, killing Charlie Bowdrie and apprehending Billy Willson, Dave Rudabaugh and The Kid, subsequently putting them in jail at Las Vegas, New Mexico.

1881: April 6—Billy the Kid goes on trial in Mesilla, New Mexico. On April 28 he escapes from the jail there.

1881: June 28—Virgil Earp becomes police chief of Tombstone, Arizona.

1881: July 14—Pat Garrett shoots and kills Billy the Kid, who is twenty-one years old.

1881: October 26—Wyatt, Virgil and Morgan Earp and their friend Doc Holliday have a shoot-out near the OK Corral in Tombstone, Arizona, with Frank and Tom McLaury and Ike and Billy Clanton. The McLaurys and Billy Clanton are killed; Ike Clanton escapes. The fight lasts about thirty seconds.

1881: December 1—A Tombstone justice of the peace rules the Earps had been acting as peace officers at the time of the gunfight at the OK Corral. Doc Holliday is subsequently acquitted for firing a pistol in the city limits.

1882: One-time gang member Bob Ford shoots Jesse James in the back and kills him; Frank James subsequently surrenders to authorities and is acquitted of his crimes.

1882: Robert Leroy Parker, who will become better known as Butch Cassidy, begins rustling along with Utah bandit Mike Cassidy.

1882: Black Bart continues to rob stagecoaches in California.

1889: Robert Leroy Parker holds up a bank in Telluride, Colorado, and rides to a hideout in Hole-in-the-Wall country in Wyoming Territory.

1891: The Dalton gang robs the Santa Fe Limited in the Cherokee Strip (Oklahoma).

1892: Robert Leroy Parker earns the nickname Butch while working for a Rock Springs, Wyoming, butcher.

1892: October—The Dalton gang attempts to rob two banks simultaneously in Coffeyville, Kansas, and most of the gang is killed. Emmet Dalton survives but subsequently serves fourteen years in prison.

1894: Robert Leroy Parker (Butch Cassidy) begins serving a prison term at the Wyoming Territorial Prison in Laramie for horse theft.

1895: August 19—John Selman shoots and kills John Wesley Hardin.

1896: Butch Cassidy (Robert Leroy Parker) meets Harry Longabaugh (The Sundance Kid) and they organize the Wild Bunch, which engages in a five-year crime spree, primarily robbing trains.

1897: February 6—The last members of the Dalton Gang are captured by a posse in Texas.

1899: The Wild Bunch stops a train near Wilcox, Wyoming, and blows up the freight car and safe.

1902: Butch Cassidy and the Sundance Kid leave with Etta Place for South America.

PUNISHMENT

Sometimes enforcing the law meant immediate retribution and some criminals died with no chance to present their case in court. Lynchings and gun battles took the majority of criminal lives as vigilantes and lawmen took action. Gun battles occurred in downtown business districts and out on the range. Those suspected of criminal activity sometimes found themselves staring at the business end of a noose. Having an opportunity to explain or plead their case wasn't necessarily allowed.

In situations where formal charges resulted, criminals were held in jails until a trial could be held, perhaps before a circuit-riding judge and sometimes in front of a local justice of the peace or judge.

Jails varied considerably, but generally were small, stoutly built facilities with limited amenities. When sentenced, prisoners might be transferred to frontier or territorial prisons, where they found themselves involved in labor-camp situations. The Wyoming Territorial Prison in Laramie City required prisoners to raise gardens for food, and it had various industries including a broom factory. Constructed in 1873, that prison was an imposing stone structure with small iron cells, furnished with tiny cots.

> The rioters in San Francisco, who attacked and beat the Chinese mercilessly, have been dealt with in the most summary way, being promptly arrested, tried and sentenced to considerable terms of imprisonment—FLIN, *April 27, 1867, 83-4*

Though many lawbreakers received justice without benefit of legal trials, some did appear before judges and in such cases they usually had defense attorneys, either hired by themselves, their families or friends, or appointed by the court. If found guilty, punishment ranged from a stint in prison to death—which was most often accomplished by hanging.

Legal hangings occurred near jails or prisons, often in enclosed courtyards specifically built for the activity. Though crowds often gathered for a hanging, witnesses were generally limited to small numbers of people including friends and acquaintances of the condemned person, law officers, reporters and a religious advocate for the prisoner. Other individuals jockeyed for position outside the enclosed hanging area, looking through knotholes and cracks in board walls to catch a glimpse of the gallows' trapdoor springing.

For legal hangings, officials took care to do the job efficiently. When the prisoner was atop the gallows, officials allowed a final statement or prayer by a religious advocate, and they gave the prisoner a chance to make comments. They bound the prisoner's feet or legs and usually the hands and arms, too; then they placed the noose tightly around the prisoner's neck, positioning the knot under the ear (usually the left ear) so when the prisoner fell the impact would break the neck. A black hood then went over the prisoner's head, and the hangman gave a signal to release the trapdoor on the gallows, allowing the prisoner to fall.

In the latter half of the period, Wyoming prisoners sentenced to death by hanging could invite friends and relatives to their executions; many sent formal invitations.

> Dear Sir:—You are respectfully invited to attend my execution December 15, A.D. 1884, at 11 o'clock A.M. at the Court House in the City of Laramie. Yours, Respectfully. . . .
>
> George Cooke

By far the majority of hangings in the West occurred independent of formal court proceedings—particularly during the early part of the era—as noted by *Frank Leslie's Illustrated Newspaper* on March 1, 1856:

There were forty-eight lynch-law executions in California during last year, and only nineteen legal ones.

Under the headline "Another Chinese Enterprise," the *Denver News* reported on a crime in Montana Territory. In 1873 two Chinamen, You and Lung, were indicted for the theft of a Mr. Mellen's safe. In a subsequent trial Lung was acquitted, but You was convicted and sentenced on April 25, 1873, to three years in the Montana Territorial penitentiary in Deer Lodge, where as a dishwasher he "attended strictly to the business of being a prisoner." However, as the paper reported, there was more to You's story:

But it now turns out that You is innocent, and with fixed and contented purpose has become the scapegoat of the guilty parties, whom he knew,—for a consideration. How it was fixed up, or where, is not communicated to the writer, but not improbably during the trial. As stated, You was guiltless, of the deed, but knew the guilty parties. He accepted the sentence, and is serving out the time on condition that the guilty parties shall pay to a person designated by him $3 per day for each and every day of his sentence, aggregating in the three years $3,385. He has now served two years, and over $2,100 has been placed to his credit as directed—$21 each week—with a punctuality that would be amazing in hard times, were not the circumstances calculated to induce it. The theory of You is, probably, that he could not earn $21 per week more easily, and the humiliation of penitentiary service sits easily on his conscience. When his time is out he will have sufficient capital to invest in the washee business, a store, or a visit to China, and he hasn't had a very hard time or had to spend his earnings for gumboots or stone-fence whisky either. It would hardly strike an American as a good speculation, but a Chinaman may look at it angularly, and take a different view of the project. Anyhow, You seems to be content, and the real thieves are probably more punished by the constant drain upon their exchequer and the apprehension of future revelations and punishment than they would be if in his place.—Denver News *as reported in* FLIN, *January 29, 1876, 342-1*

Military law involved soldiers who faced harsh discipline if they disobeyed or violated a wide variety of rules and regulations. Military courts—comprised of officers—had broad powers to decide cases and determine punishment. Among the penalties that could be imposed were whippings, confinement, wearing a ball and chain or neck collar with spikes on it that made it impossible for a man to sit or recline, hanging from the thumbs, or participation in forced marches, occasionally with heavy packs. For desertion a soldier could be sentenced to death, though that seldom, if ever, happened.

The common thing with frontier justice was the speed under which actions occurred. Though court proceedings could sometimes last several days, with subsequent events occasionally lasting weeks or months, many times justice took place within days or even hours of an incident.

> A young man was detected last week on a Mississippi steamboat with the watch of the captain in his possession. The passengers at once tried, convicted him, and then put him on shore.
> —FLIN, *February 25, 1860, 201-3*

Hamilton Scott traveled the Oregon-California trail in 1862 with a wagon train. On July 6 he wrote in his diary of a murder:

> July 6. . . . Two men quarreled about a team, one shot the other, took his team and money. . . .

> July 7. Started at sunrise, traveled four or five miles and found grass on river bottom. Several trains were camped here so we drove in and camped too. We are informed that the murderer is camped here. By request of some men from another camp, Captain Kennedy of our train ordered out twenty men, well armed to surround and take him, which they did. With court organized and a jury of twelve men selected, he was given a fair trial and a twelve to one verdict, [*sic*] guilty of willful murder. The prisoner kept under guard, we hitched up at two p.m. and drove eight miles. . . . Captain Kennedy called their whole company together and laid the case before them. They decided that the prisoner be executed tomorrow morning.

> July 8. Gave prisoner his choice to be shot or hanged. He preferred to be shot. Twenty five armed men marched him one-half mile to where his grave had been prepared. Fourteen of the guns were loaded with bullets and the rest were blanks. When the signal was given they all fired, the prisoner falling backwards and dying within one minute. It was a sad sight to look upon. We immediately laid him in his grave without even a rough box. As soon as our work was completed, we moved on toward the setting of the sun. Drove twelve miles and camped on the river.

ADDITIONAL READING

Bakken, Gordon Morris. *Practicing Law in Frontier California*. Lincoln: University of Nebraska Press, 1991. A good reference about early law practices.

Gard, Wayne. *Frontier Justice*. Norman: University of Oklahoma Press, 1949.

Grover, David H. *Diamondfield Jack: A Study in Frontier Justice*. Reno: University of Nevada Press, 1968.

Horan, James D. *Desperate Men: The James Gang and the Wild Bunch*. New York: Doubleday, 1949. Reprint, Lincoln: University of Nebraska Press, 1997.

Hunt, William R. *Distant Justice: Policing the Alaskan Frontier*. Norman: University of Oklahoma Press, 1987.

Hutton, Harold. *Vigilante Days: Frontier Justice Along the Niobrara*. Chicago: Swallow Press, 1978. A good reference for vigilante activities.

Jameson, W.C., and Frederic Bean. *The Return of the Outlaw Billy the Kid*. Plano, Tex.: Republic of Texas Press, 1998.

Johnson, William Weber, and the Editors of Time-Life Books. *The Forty-Niners*. Alexandria, Va.: Time-Life Books, 1974.

Krakel, Dean F. *The Saga of Tom Horn, The Story of A Cattleman's War*. Lincoln: University of Nebraska Press, 1954.

McLaren, John, Hamar Foster, and Chet Orloff, eds. *Law For The Elephant, Law For The Beaver*. Pasadena, Calif.: Ninth Judicial Circuit Historical Society, 1992.

Metz, Leon. *John Wesley Hardin: Dark Angel of Texas*. El Paso, Tex.: Mangan Books, 1996.

Miller, M. Catherine. *Flooding the Courtrooms: Law and Water in the Far West*. Lincoln: University of Nebraska Press, 1993.

Monaghan, Jay. *The Legend of Tom Horn Last of the Bad Men*. New York City: Bobbs-Merrill, 1946.

Shirley, Glenn. *Law West of Fort Smith: A History of Frontier Justice in the Indian Territory, 1834-1896*. Lincoln: University of Nebraska Press, 1968.

Trachtman, Paul, and the Editors of Time-Life Books. *The Gunfighters*. Alexandria, Va.: Time-Life Books, 1974. A good reference for information about gunfighters.

Wheeler, Keith, and the Editors of Time-Life Books. *The Townsmen*. Alexandria, Va.: Time-Life Books, 1975.

CHAPTER EIGHTEEN

COINS/MONEY AND
HOW MUCH THINGS COST

btaining goods and services in the West throughout most of the period involved a combination of methods including bartering or exchanging products, credit and paying outright with paper money or with gold or silver coins, nuggets or dust.

A few mountain men still worked beaver streams at the beginning of the period, and they no doubt continued to exchange pelts, known as plews, for necessary items such as ammunition, tobacco, clothing and food. They made their trades at posts that had first been opened by fur trading companies, but which increasingly were falling into ownership and jurisdiction of the United States government.

Native Americans, likewise, had long-established trading practices and trade routes that connected northern tribes with southern tribes and allowed them to barter for items ranging from jewelry to horses.

Early Anglo settlers often had little cash, so they also relied on barter or trading to obtain food, clothing and goods. Men and women exchanged labor to build houses, barns and the like, and a family with extra hogs might trade meat for crops such as wheat or potatoes. Two of the most universal products traded in the West were milk and eggs as people could share excess from their cows and chickens in order to obtain products they needed. In some cases such trading occurred among neighbors, but more often it involved a town merchant as people took their extra supplies to the mercantile owner exchanging them for credit at the store, which they then used to buy products. In many cases no actual money exchanged hands; the transaction was on paper, kept by the merchant in his record book.

Miners likewise earned credit at stores, often those owned by the company for which they worked. In such cases the amount of their wages was provided as a credit figure, and the miner, or a family member, could then purchase goods with costs deducted from the account balance. Since the company paid the miners and owned the stores, in many situations there was little excess income beyond what a miner and his family needed for basic survival because the company stores charged fluctuating prices that related to a miner's wage.

Independent miners often paid for goods by using nuggets, or more likely, dust, found in their mining efforts. They carried the minerals, usually gold, but sometimes silver, in small leather bags and businesses had scales to use in weighing the proper amount of each mineral.

In the late 1850s Kansas and Nebraska lawmakers authorized banks to print money. Wildcat banks quickly started in many communities, printing scrip for public projects, loans and real estate deals. But the lawmakers had failed to require the banks to have adequate capital to cover the amount of scrip they issued. In some cases wildcat banks had virtually no assets. A financial panic occurred leading to failure of most of the wildcat banks in 1857 and subsequently leaving the paper money as worthless scraps. Private companies also produced money in some locations, such as in Colorado during the period from 1859 until 1863. This private company then sold its opertion to the United States which opened the Denver Mint.

Economic downturns affected the United States several times during the period, including the panics of 1857, 1873 and 1893.

Coins available during the period included the Spanish real, commonly used throughout the United States, known as a "bit" in the West, and worth $.12½. Two "bits," of course, became a quarter. The half-bit (worth $.06¼ and known as the medio, fip, or picayune) was also widely used, particularly in Louisiana. Those Spanish coins were popular in the West particularly, but like all other foreign coins were banned by the U.S. government in 1857.

Some other common coins used in the West throughout the period included the "eagle," a gold piece worth $10 which had a Liberty head with coronet on the front and a heraldic eagle on the back. The "double eagle" was worth $20 and also had a Liberty head on the obverse and a heraldic eagle on the reverse. The "half eagle," worth $5, had a Grecian head with a coronet on the obverse from 1839 to 1866 and had a heraldic eagle from 1866 to 1908. The "quarter eagle," valued at $2.50, was a gold piece featuring a Liberty head with coronet.

The silver dollar, featuring a heraldic eagle or flying eagle on the reverse and a seated Liberty on the obverse, was in use throughout the period. The words "In God We Trust" were added in 1872, and during the period 1873-85, the silver dollar became known as the trade dollar, when it was used to meet export demands in the Orient. The "slug," a gold piece worth $50, was used most widely in California, though available throughout the United States.

During the 1850s the gold dollar became available, featuring a Liberty head

Silver dollars circa 1880-1885, from author's collection.

on the obverse and a wreath surrounding the numeral 1 on the reverse. The design changed to an Indian wearing a feathered headdress on the obverse during the period 1854-56, and a different, larger Indian head during the period 1856-89, with both coins still featuring the numeral 1 and the wreath on the reverse.

Prices for goods and services varied throughout the era and from region to region. A sampling of costs for a selection of items is as follows:

Accommodations

1860: "For a comfortable house, within a few minutes of the City Hall, San Francisco, 25 by 100 feet, from $800 to $1,000 is charged."
—FLIN, *February 25, 1860*

Late 1870s: Straw mattresses sell for $2.50 on railroad trains for use by passengers.

Clothing

1847: Costs at Fort John, June 2: Sheeting, shirting, calico and cotton, $1 per yard; butcher knife, $1; robes from $3 to $5; buckskins $2 to $5; moccasins, $1.

1847: Costs at Fort John, September 25: Robes $1.25 to $2; antelope skins, $.75 to $1.50.

1863: Buffalo robes $7 undressed.

1886: An anti-dude club in Newton, Kansas, assesses these fines: carrying a cane, $5; wearing a plug hat and kid gloves, $10; parting a man's hair in the middle, $20.

Entertainment

1838: Tickets to an exhibition of George Catlin's artwork are $.50.

1869: Admission to a concert and festival in Lincoln, Nebraska, is $.50.

1882: Tickets to a lecture by Oscar Wilde at the Tabor Opera House in Denver are $1.50.

Food

1806: "A California paper mentions a drove of over 200 turkeys en route for San Francisco which had been over a hundred miles, and averaged ten pounds each, and was contracted for 'on foot' at twenty-three cents a pound."—FLIN, *August 11, 1806*

1847: Costs at Fort John, June 2: Flour $.25 per pound.

1847: Costs at Fort Hall, August 23: Flour $20 per 100 pounds; beef $.10 per pound.

1847: Costs at Fort John, September 25: Tea, $4 per pound, flour, $.25 per pound.

1847: Costs at Richard (trading post), October 1: $.10 per pound for dried buffalo meat; robes $2 to $8.

COMPARISON OF FOOD PRICES			
Article	*1860*	*1864*	*1878*
Wheat, per bu.	$ 8.60	$ 1.53	$ 1.08
Flour, per bbl (barrel)	$ 5.25	$ 8.00	$ 4.00
Corn, per bu.	$ .88	$ 1.27	$ .50
Molasses, gal.	$ .33	$ .50	$ .25
Mess pork bbl.	$16.12	$19.75	$ 9.25
Mess beef bbl.	$ 5.00	$ 5.80	$ 8.50
Lard, per lb.	$ .10	$ .12	$ .07
Butter, per lb.	$ .15	$ .27	$ .18
Sugar, per lb.	$ .06	$ .13	$ .075
Cheese, per lb.	$ .09	$ .12	$ .07
Rice, per lb.	$ .035	$ .085	$ .06

1849: Breakfast in Sonora: $5 for sardines, $1 for sea biscuits, $8 for a bottle of English ale, and $12 for barley for the horse.

1863: "Provisions are very cheap in Missouri, The Macon *Gazette* quotes turkeys 25 cents, chickens 75 cents a dozen, butter 9 cents a pound, flour $3.75 per 100 pounds. Groceries however, are dear—coffee, 50 cents, sugar 16 cents, and tea $2 a pound."—FLIN, *February 14, 1863*

1865: "Congress has agreed to levy $2 a gallon on all distilled spirits after the 1st of January."—FLIN, *January 7, 1865*

1865: December—Sugar is $1 a pound and flour is $28 a sack in Bannack, Montana Territory.

1867: "Out in Minnesota, the principal products of which are wheat and wood, flour is $12 a barrel, and wood is $10 a cord, while three families have, during the winter, starved to death.—FLIN, *April 27, 1867*

1870: "Most of the salt used in California is imported from Mexico, and is sold at an average price of $9 per ton."—FLIN, *September 24, 1870*

1871: "Strawberries in San Francisco are from four to six cents per pound."—FLIN, *May 27, 1871*

1875:
Boston and San Francisco

The following shows the difference between prices for restaurant food in Boston and in San Francisco; For green turtle soup, Boston charges 50 cents; San Francisco, 15 cents—for bouilion, 20 cents; San Francisco, 15 cents; and so on in proportion. Boston always keeping 5 to 35 cents ahead. Now for the fish: Boston, for fried smelts, demands 40 cents; San Francisco, 25 cents; for fried cod, 40 cents, San Francisco, 25 cents. Next we have the *entrees*: Boston, for a porter-house steak demands $1; San Francisco, 50 cents— for kidneys with wine sauce, 50 cents; San Francisco, 25 cents— for mallard ducks $2; San Francisco, 40 cents. . . . calf's liver Boston considers worth 40 cents; San Francisco 25 cents—boiled ham, Boston rates at 40 cents; San Francisco, 40 cents—venison steak, $1; San Francisco, 25 cents. Cold roast beef, 50 cents; San Francisco, 25 cents—tea, 20 cents; San Francisco, 15 cents. For the matter of eggs, bread and vegetables the charges are even.
—FLIN, *January 2, 1875*

1886: In Topeka, Kansas, butter costs $.20 a pound, eggs are $.20 a dozen, prunes cost $1 for 18 pounds, sugar is $1 for 14 pounds, and coffee costs $1 for 8 pounds.

Gold

1869: $162 per ounce.

1871: "While gold is worth $17 an ounce, fine blonde hair readily commands $25 [per ounce]."—FLIN, *February 4, 1871*

Land

1856: "The *Nebraska City News* says that a land fever is raging there. Claims of one hundred sixty acres, within two and a half miles of that city, are selling from $500 to $800. For one farm joining the city on the West, the owner has been offered $6,000 in gold, which was refused."—FLIN, *March 15, 1856*

1867: City lots sell for $400 to $1,200 in Cheyenne, Wyoming Territory.

1870: "Farm lands in the vicinity of Fort Scott, Kansas, may be bought for from $12 to $20 per acre. Unimproved lands within twelve miles, may be bought for from $3 to $7 per acre."—FLIN, *February 5, 1870*

1870: Land involved in the development of Greeley, Colorado Territory, sells for $1 per acre.

1873: "NEBRASKA—Improved farm-lands are selling from $10 to $30 per acre, and unimproved from $4.00 to $10."—FLIN, *July 12, 1873*

1874: "Land cost $20 to $80 per acre in Sutter County, California." —FLIN, *August 22, 1874*

Laundry

1874: "Cost to have a dozen collars washed in San Francisco, $2." —FLIN, *August 8, 1874*

Livestock

1847: Fort John, June 2, 1847: Cows $15 to $25.

1850s: A pair of oxen cost $40 to $160; a team of mules cost $200 to $400.

1860: "Americans are purchasing largely of horses of Canada West, and prices ranging from one to three hundred dollars."—FLIN, *February 25, 1860*

1866: Range cattle sell for $3 or $4 per head in Texas; or for $30 or $40 per head in northern and eastern markets.

1879: Cattle prices in Texas: yearlings, $3 to $5; two-year-olds, $6 to $7; three-year-olds, $7 to $8; and beeves, $8 to $10.

1880: Cattle prices in Texas: yearlings, $7 to $8.50; two-year-olds, $9 to $10; three-year-olds and older, $12 to $13.

1881: Cattle prices in Texas: $10 for yearlings, $12.50 for two-year-olds, and $15 to $16 for three-year-olds and beeves. Female cattle are scarcely to be purchased at any price.

Medical Fees

1874: Doc Holliday charges $3 for each tooth he extracts in his Dallas, Texas, dental practice.

1880: Standard price for an infant delivery (confinement) in Madison, Nebraska, in 1880 was $10 with a $1 fee for a doctor's visit in town either day or night.

Military Pay

1840s: Privates earn $5 per month prior to the Mexican War in 1846 when their pay increased to $8 per month. A second lieutenant earns $42 per month in 1842. Often troops are not paid for months.

1865: "One thousand dollars are now paid to all persons enlisting for three years or the war."—FLIN, *January 21, 1865*

1898: Mustering-out pay for Rough Riders following Spanish-American War of 1898, $77.

Postal

1848: The California Star Express carries letters from San Francisco headed to Independence, Missouri, for $.50 each.

1860: Cost to send a half-ounce letter by Pony Express is $5.

1862: The Postmaster General is authorized in 1862 to establish a uniform money order system. For orders of $10 to $20 the charge is $.10 with a charge of another $.05 for each additional $10. "Roots, cuttings and seeds could be sent by mail at one cent per ounce."—FLIN, *March 15, 1862*

1870: "The new postage-stamps will be the size of the old stamps, and consist entirely of profile busts taken from standard original marbles, executed by artists of acknowledged reputation. They will comprise the heads of the following distinguished Americans: one cent, Franklin, by Burton; two cents, Jackson, by Powers; three cents, Washington, by Houdin; six cents, Lincoln, by Volk; ten cents, Jefferson, by Powers; twelve cents, Clay, by Hart; fifteen cents, Webster, by Clarenged; twenty-four cents, Scott by Coffee; thirty cents, Hamilton, family bust; forty cents, O.H. Perry, by Wolcutt."
—FLIN, *January 1, 1870*

Taxes

1870: "A Kansas County Treasurer recently made a tour of his county to collect the taxes, and succeeded in raising $3.60. He will send out his deputy next time."—FLIN, *January 22, 1870*

1872: "Salt Lake City taxes billiard and drinking saloons $300 a month." —FLIN, *July 13, 1872*

1872: "Wolf-scalps are legal tender with which to pay taxes in Arkansas." —FLIN, *July 20, 1872*

1872: "Brigham Young proposes to tax his Saints $1 a head on their wives, for the benefit of the poor."—FLIN, *July 27, 1872*

1873: "The San Francisco *Bulletin* says that the taxes in California—State, County, and Municipal—range from 3 to 4 per cent. on the value of property."—FLIN, *April 5, 1873*

Transportation

1847: Mormon Ferry costs at the Platte River: Mormons ferried 24 wagons over the river at $1.50 each, receiving pay in the form of supplies at these values: flour $2.50 per 10 pounds, meal $.50 per bushel, and bacon $.06 per pound.

1854: Alexander Majors and William H. Russell haul military freight between Fort Leavenworth and Albuquerque, charging the army $10.83 per 100 pounds.

1860s: Stage fare from Denver to Central City: $6 on a feeder stage operated by the sheriff; $2 on a competing stage operated by Ben Holladay. After the sheriff closes his line Holladay raises his rate to $12.

1863: "The price of passage in the steamers from San Francisco to New York is now $265, $185, and $135."—FLIN, *October 31, 1863*

1864: Stage fare from Atchison, Kansas, to California costs up to $600.

1864: Stage fare from Salt Lake City to Virginia City, Montana, cost $150— on lines operated by Oliver, Peabody and Caldwell in 1862-63; $25 on Ben Holladay's line.

1865: Stage fare from Atchison, Kansas, to Salt Lake City, Utah: $150 on Ben Holladay's Overland Stage Line. Fare rises to $350 if there was a threat of Indian attack; after 1866 Holladay charges $350 for the fare, with or without threat of Indians.

1865: Steamboat fare from St. Louis to Fort Benton, Montana Territory, ranges from $150 and $200.

1869: Railroad First Class fare coast to coast, $250 to $300, round-trip, plus meals.

1869: Railroad Coach fare Omaha to San Francisco, $32.20.

1870: Train fare from Denver to Golden, Colorado, $1.50.

1872: Freight from San Francisco to Omaha: $350, but the cost to ship freight from San Francisco to New York City is only $325.

1874: "San Francisco hackney carriages cost $1.25 per mile per person."
—FLIN, *August 8, 1874*

1886: Rail fare between Kansas and California is $12, first class, or $7, second class.

Banking

1873: Wall Street has a financial crash in October.

> "A slight run having been made on the banks of St. Louis, it was decided to suspend the payment of checks or drafts, either in currency or exchange, until the excitement in the East subsides and the former condition of the markets is restored."
> —FLIN, *October 11, 1873*

> "California Street [San Francisco] is the Wall Street of the Pacific Coast."—FLIN, *June 20, 1874*

Barter

The Ames Old Colony Shovel (built by the Oakes Ames Company) has a fine reputation and is used as barter in lieu of money.

Coins

1857: "The Mint began on the 25th of May to pay out the new coin in exchange for Spanish and Mexican coins at their nominal value, or in exchange for the old cent now in circulation. The silver and copper coins must be presented in even sums of not less than five, and not exceeding fifty dollars."—FLIN, *June 6, 1857*

1861: "A change has been made in the ten cent pieces that bear date this year from those heretofore coined. The figure of Liberty, instead of being surrounded by stars, is encircled by the words, 'United States of America,' which formerly were placed on the reverse of the piece."
—FLIN, *November 2, 1861*

1865: "The new 50 cent currency has been issued, although not generally distributed. It is much larger than the present, being four inches long and nearly two inches wide."—FLIN, *January 7, 1865*

COMPARISON OF THE PURCHASING POWER OF MONEY

Year	Value of $100 in paper as compared to $100 in gold for each year
1862	$86.20
1864	$45.24
1866	$68.56
1868	$70.42
1870	$85.47
1872	$89.20
1874	$89.28
1876	$89.28

1876: There is a proposal for two new silver coins to be available as legal tender. And on April 29, 1876, silver exchange for currency is allowed. "Silver dollars have not been in circulation since 1837, and with the exception of trade dollars, they have not been coined since 1853. . . . In 1873 the silver dollar was abolished, and under existing laws no piece of silver is legal-tender for a greater sum in one payment than five dollars."
—FLIN, *May 13, 1876*

Salary/Wages

1849: Carpenters in San Francisco earn $16 per day.

1857: "Rev. Dr. Scott, pastor of a Presbyterian church in San Francisco, receives for his services the handsome salary of $12,000 per year."
—FLIN, *August 1, 1857*

Wagon masters earned $125 per month. Teamsters earn $20 to $25 per month plus food.

1861: San Francisco carpenters earn $4 per day.

1867: Buffalo Bill Cody receives $500 per month to kill twelve buffalo each day along the Kansas Pacific Railroad route.

1869: U.S. Army privates earn $16 per month. Deductions include $1 for pay at the end of service and $.125 for the Soldier's Home, leaving a net paycheck of $14.875

1870: "San Francisco school teacher salary, $13,000 per year."
—FLIN, *August 20, 1870*

1871: Wild Bill Hickok earns $150 per month in salary as marshal of Abilene, Kansas.

1875: Wyatt Earp earns $60 per month as a police officer in Wichita, Kansas.

1876: Elizabeth Custer receives $30 per month as an army pension following the death in battle of her husband, George Armstrong Custer.

1878: Wages per month in Dodge City, Kansas: marshal, $100; assistant marshal and policeman, $75 each.

1880: "California averages higher rates for farm labor than any State in the Union, at $41 a month without board, and $2.27 a day for transient help in harvest times."—FLIN, *February 28, 1880, 471-4*

1880: Pat Garrett earns $10 per day as a special deputy U.S. marshal.

1880s: Santa Fe prostitutes: $1 to $2 per trick in about 1880.

1897: Frank Canton earns $750 per year as U.S. deputy marshal in Alaska.

Wages Strikes

1873: "MONTANA—An exchange gravely asserts that the servant girls of Helena have struck for sixty dollars a month, two silk dresses, and the privilege of the parlor every Sunday."—FLIN, *July 5, 1873*

ADDITIONAL READING

Bowers, Q. David. *The History of United States Coinage as Illustrated by the Garrett Collection*. Los Angeles: Bowers & Ruddy Galleries, 1979.

Coffin, Joseph. *Our American Money*. New York: Coward-McCann, 1940.

———. *The Complete Book of Coin Collecting*. 1938. Reprint, New York: Coward-McCann, 1967.

Davis, Norman. *The Complete Book of United States Coin Collecting*. New York: Macmillan Publishing, 1976.

Evans, George Greenlief. *Illustrated History of the United States Mint With a Complete Description of American Coinage from the Earliest Period to the Present Time*. Philadelphia: G.G. Evans, 1888.

Nugent, Walter T.K. *Money and American Society 1865-1880*. New York: Free Press, 1968.

Nussbaum, Arthur. *A History of the Dollar*. New York: Columbia University Press, 1957.

Ritter, Gretchen. *Goldbugs and Greenbucks: The Antimonopoly Tradition and the Politics of Finances in America*. New York: Cambridge University Press, 1997.

Taxay, Don. *The United States Mint and Coinage; An Illustrated History from 1776 to the Present*. New York: Arco Publishing Co., 1966.

———. *Money of the American Indians and Other Primitive Currencies of the Americas*. New York: Mummus Press, 1970.

Yeoman, R.S. *A Guide Book of United States Coins*. Racine, Wisc.: Western Publishing, 1988.

WRITER'S RESOURCE GUIDE

The following listings of research institutions, historic sites and organizations are meant as a start to help you begin doing further research about the West. At least one site is listed for each of the western states. Often those listed can direct you to additional resources for your particular topic. If you need specific information about a topic or region, it is also a good idea to contact the Tourism Division in each state. Those offices are generally located in the state capital. On the Internet you can obtain state information for Alaska at this address: http://www.state.ak.us/. Insert the proper two-letter state code in the place of the "ak" to reach other states.

ALASKA
Alaska State Archives
141 Willoughby Ave., Juneau, AK 99801-1720
Tel.: 907/465-2270, Fax: 907/465-2465
E-mail: archives@educ.state.ak.us
http://www.educ.state.ak.us/lam/home.html

ARKANSAS
Arkansas History Commission
One Capitol Mall, Little Rock, AR 72201
Tel.: 501/682-6900, Fax: 501/682-1364
http://www.state.ar.us/ahc/archives.htm

ARIZONA
Arizona Historical Society
949 E. Second St., Tucson, AZ 85719
Tel: 520/628-5774, Fax: 520/628-5695
E-mail: ahsaadmin@rtd.com
E-mail Southern Arizona district: azhist@azstarnet.com
http://www.azstarnet.com/
Arizona Historical Foundation Manuscript Collection
http://www.public.asu.edu/%7Ewabbit/collect.htm

CALIFORNIA
California Historical Society
678 Mission St., San Francisco, CA 94105
Tel.: 415/357-1848, Fax: 415/357-1850
E-mail: info@calhist.org
E-mail requests or comments: loren@calhist.org
http://www.calhist.org/

COLORADO

Colorado State Archives
1313 Sherman St., Room 1B-20, Denver, CO 80203
Tel: 303/866-2055
Research and Reference Services
Tel.: 303/866-2358 or 303/866-2390, Fax: 303/866-2257
E-mail: comments@www.state.co.us
http://www.state.co.us/gov_dir/gss/archives/arctext.html
Denver Public Library
10 W. 14th Avenue Parkway, Denver, CO 80204
Western History/Genealogy Dept.
Tel.: 303/640-6291, Fax: 303/640-6298
E-mail: webmaster@denver.lib.co.us
http://www.denver.lib.co.us/
Bent's Old Fort National Historic Site
35110 Highway 194 East, La Junta, CO 81050-9523
Tel: 719/383-5010, Fax: 719/384-2615
http://www.nps.gov/beol/
An authentic reconstruction of the southern Great Plains's most notable fur post.
Center of the American West
University of Colorado
Campus Box 234, Boulder, CO 80309
Tel.: 303/492-4879, Fax: 303/492-1671
E-mail: centerwest@colorado.edu

IDAHO

Idaho Historical Society
450 N. Fourth St., Boise, ID 83702-6027
Tel.: 208/334-3356, Fax: 208/334-3198
http://www.state.id.us/ishs/index.htm

IOWA

State Archives of Iowa
600 E. Locust, Des Moines, IA 50319
Tel.: 515/281-6200 (library), Tel.: 515/281-8875 (archives)
Fax: 515/281-0502
State Library of Iowa
1112 E. Grand, Des Moines, IA 50319
Tel.: 515/281-4105

KANSAS
Kansas State Historical Society
6425 S.W. Sixth St., Topeka, KS 66615-1099
Tel.: 785/272-8681, Fax: 785/272-8682
TTY: 785/272-8683
E-mail: archives@hspo.wpo.state.ks.us
http://history.cc.ukans.edu/heritage/kshs/

LOUISIANA
Louisiana State Museum
751 Chartres St., New Orleans, LA 70116, Tel.: 504/568-6976
Fax: 504/568-4995
E-mail: lsefcik@crt.state.la.us
http://www.crt.state.la.us/crt/museum/lsmnet3.htm

MINNESOTA
Minnesota Historical Society
Library and Archives Division
345 Kellogg Blvd., St. Paul, MN 55102-1906
Tel.: 612/296-6980, Fax: 612/296-9961
http://www.mnhs.org/

MISSOURI
Jefferson National Expansion Memorial
11 N. 4th St., St. Louis, MO 63102
Tel.: 314/425-4465, Fax: 314/425-4570
http://www.nps.gov/jess/arch-home
    Museum of Westward Expansion, St. Louis Gateway Arch, Old Court-
house and Museum.

MONTANA
Montana State Historical Society
225 N. Roberts, Helena, MT 59620
Tel.: 406/444-2694, Fax: 406/444-2696
Photo archives: 406/444-4739
    Extensive photo collections of northern plains, Montana, Northern
Pacific Railroad; manuscript resources on vigilante records, homestead-
ing, mining, medicine.
Montana Ghost Town Preservation Society
P.O. Box 1861, Bozeman, MT 59715

NEBRASKA
Nebraska State Historical Society
P.O. Box 82554, Lincoln, NE 68501
Tel.: 402/471-3270, Fax: 402/471-3100 or 471-3314
E-mail: nshs@nebraskahistory.org
http://www.nebraskahistory.org
  Extensive collections, particularly photographs by Solomon Butcher of sod houses/prairie life circa 1885. Photography collection and index available on microfiche.
Harold Warp's Pioneer Village
P.O. Box 68, Minden, NE 68959
Tel.: 308/832-1181, Fax: 308/832-1181
  Collection of buildings and artifacts tracing man's progress since 1830.
Little Bat's Trading Post
Robert Rybolt
123 Main St., Crawford, NE 69339
Tel.: 308/665-1900, Fax: 308/665-1448
E-mail: littlebats@cuqk06a.com

NEVADA
Nevada State Department of Museums, Library and Arts
100 N. Stewart St., Carson City, NV 89701
Tel.: 702/687-5160, Fax: 702/687-8330
http://www.clan.lib.nv/us/

NEW MEXICO
New Mexico State Library
325 Don Gaspar, Santa Fe, NM 87501-2777
Tel.: 505/827-3800, Fax: 505/827-3888
Indian Pueblo Cultural Center
2401 12th St. NW, Albuquerque, NM 87102
Tel.: 505/843-7270 or 800/766-4405 (outside New Mexico)
Pueblo of Acoma—Sky City
P.O. Box 309, Acoma, New Mexico 87034
Tel.: 505/470-4966
Lincoln County Heritage Trust
P.O. Box 90, Lincoln, NM 88338
Tel.: 505/653-4025, Fax: 505/653-4627
  General and specific information dealing with the Lincoln County War, Billy the Kid, Selman's Scouts, Seven Rivers settlement, Fort Stanton, and even Smokey Bear. Holds the complete Philip J. Rasch collection, and the only verified tintype of Billy the Kid.

Fort Union National Monument
P.O. Box 127, Watrous, NM 87753
Tel.: 505/425-8025, Fax: 505/454-1155
E-mail: foun_administration@nps.gov
Remains of the largest post-Civil War military installation in the Southwest.

NORTH DAKOTA

North Dakota State Historical Society
612 E. Boulevard Ave., Bismarck, ND 58505-0830
Tel.: 701/328-2666, Fax: 701/328-3710
E-mail: ccmail.histsoc@ranch.state.nd.us
http://www.state.nd.us/hist/index.html

OKLAHOMA

Fort Sill Museum
Bldg. 437, Fort Sill, OK 73503
Tel.: 580/442-5123

The Five Civilized Tribes Museum
Agency Hill, Honor Heights Dr., Muskogee, OK 74401
Tel.: 918/683-1701, Fax: 918/683-3070

Western Publications
205 W. 7th, Suite 201-C, Stillwater, OK 74074
E-mail: Western@cowboy.net
Home of *True West* and *Old West* magazines. Has one of the largest research libraries dealing with outlaw-lawman research, including a comprehensive database of all articles and photos appearing in the forty-five years of *True West*. Research may be done on-site, or by mail for a slight fee. Contact Marcus Huff, editor.

Oklahoma Historical Society
2100 N. Lincoln Blvd., Oklahoma City, OK 73105
Tel.: 405/521-2491, Fax: 405/521-2492
E-mail: webmaster@ok-history.mus.ok.us
http://www.ok-history.mus.ok.us/

University of Oklahoma Western History Collection
630 Parrington Oval, Room 452, Norman, OK 73019
Tel.: 405/325-3641, Fax: 405/325-2943
http://www.ou.edu/

Thomas Gilcrease Institute
1400 N. 25th, Tulsa, OK 74127
Tel.: 918/581-5311
Archives, library, manuscripts and Gilcrease collection of artifacts, weapons and art.

National Cowboy Hall of Fame
1700 NE 63rd St., Oklahoma City, OK 73111
Tel.: 405/478-2250, Fax: 405/478-4714
http://www.cowboyhalloffame.org/

OREGON
Oregon State Archives
800 Summer St. NE, Salem, OR 97310
Tel.: 503/373-0701, Fax: 503/373-0953
E-mail: reference.archives@state.or.us
http://arcweb.sos.state.or.us/
Oregon Historical Society
1200 S.W. Park Ave., Portland, OR 97205
Tel.: 503/306-5247, Fax: 503/221-2035
E-mail: orghist@ohs.org
http://www.ohs.org/

SOUTH DAKOTA
South Dakota State Historical Society
900 Governors Dr., Pierre, SD 57501-2271
Tel.: 605/773-3458, Fax: 605/773-6041
E-mail: archref@chc.state.sd.us
http://www.state.sd.us/state/executive/deca/cultural/sdshs.htm
http://www.state.sd.us/state/executive/deca/cultural/archives.htm

TEXAS
Institute of Texan Culture
801 S. Bowie St., San Antonio, TX 78294
Texas State Library and Archives Commission
P.O. Box 12927, Austin, TX 78711-2927
Tel.: 512/463-5455
    Information, documents and photos dealing with Texas history and prison system. Holds all old Texas prison records and mug shots.

UTAH
Utah State Archives
P.O. Box 141021, Salt Lake City, UT 84114-1021
Tel.: 801/538-3013, Fax: 801/538-3354
E-mail: research@state.ut.us
http://www.archives.state.ut.us/
Family History Center
35 North West Temple, Salt Lake City, UT 84150
Tel.: 801/240-2331, Fax: 801/240-5551
    With more than 270 million names in the ancestral files, this is the most extensive genealogical collection in the world. Available on CD-ROM at history research centers operated by the Church of Jesus Christ

of Latter-day Saints throughout the world. Contact local LDS Church officials for information about the site nearest you. Records date from 1550 to 1920.

Outlaw Trail History Association & Center
155 E. Main St., Vernal, UT 84078

WASHINGTON

Washington State Historical Society
Heritage Resource Center
211 W. 21st Ave., Olympia, WA 98501
Tel.: 360/586-0219, Fax: 360/586-8322
E-mail: mwarner@wshs.wa.gov
http://www.wshs.org/

University of Washington
Special Collections and Preservation Division
Gary Menges, Head
482 Allen Library, P.O. Box 352900, Seattle, WA 98195

University of Washington
Manuscripts and University Archives
Karyl Winn, Head
482 Allen Library, P.O. Box 352900, Seattle, WA 98195

Fort Vancouver National Historic Site
612 E. Reserve St., Vancouver, WA 98661-3897
Tel.: 360/696-7655
http://www.nps.gov/fova/
Reconstructed headquarters of the Hudson's Bay Company's Columbia Department Headquarters

WYOMING

Wyoming State Museum and Archives
2301 Central Ave.
Cheyenne, WY 82002
Tel.: 307/777-7826, Fax: 307/777-7044
E-mail: wyarchive@missc.state.wy.us
http://-commerce.state.wy.us/cr/archives

American Heritage Center
University of Wyoming
P.O. Box 3924, University Station, Laramie, WY 82071
Tel.: 307/766-4114, Fax: 307/766-5511
E-mail: ahcref@uwyo.edu
http://www.uwyo.edu/ahc/ahcinfo.htm

Buffalo Bill Historical Center
720 Sheridan Ave., Cody, WY 82414
Tel.: 307/587-4771, Fax: 307/587-5714
E-mail: bbhc@wave.park.wy.us

http://www.TrueWest.com/BBHC
Four museums dedicated to Buffalo Bill Cody, Cody Firearms Museum, Winchester Gallery of Western Art, and Plains Indian Museum; Mc-Cracken Research Library. Extensive information on Buffalo Bill, Wild West shows, firearms, cowboy photography, including the Charles Belden collection.

Fort Laramie National Historic Site
HC 72, Box 389, Fort Laramie, WY 82212
Tel.: 307/837-2221, Fax: 307/837-2120
E-mail: fola_info_requests@nps.gov
http://www.nps.gov/fola
Fur-trading fort and military fort located on the route of the Oregon, California, Mormon and Pony Express Trails. Many original trail ruts in nearby vicinity.

Grand Encampment Museum
P.O. Box 43, Encampment, WY 82325
Tel.: 307/327-5308 (Memorial Day-Labor Day, open daily 1-5 p.m.)
Historical site includes original buildings: one-room school, homestead house, tie-hack cabin, stage station. The museum is a national repository for U.S. Forest Service items.

OTHER REGIONS

Museum of the Cherokee Indian
Cherokee, NC 28719
Tel.: 704/497-3481

Olin Library
Cornell University
David Corson, Director
Ithaca, NY 14853
Tel.: 607/255-4144
http://urisref.library.cornell.edu/olinfer.htm

ORGANIZATIONS

Western Writers of America
1012 Fair St., Franklin, TN 37064-2718
http://www.imt.net/~gedison/wwahome.html
An organization for professional writers about the historic and contemporary West, both fiction and nonfiction. Annual awards for published work. Annual conference, June.

Roundup Magazine

Box 29 Star Route, Encampment, WY 82325

http://www.imt.net/~gedison/wwa.html

The official publication of Western Writers of America, available with WWA membership, or by subscription.

Women Writing the West

P.O. Box 2199, Evergreen, CO 80437

http://www.sni.net/www-writers/

A marketing organization to promote fiction and nonfiction books about the women's West. Annual conference, fall.

Western History Association

Paul Andrew Hutton, Director

Department of History

University of New Mexico

Albuquerque, NM 87131-1181

Tel.: 505/277-5234, Fax: 505/277-6023

E-Mail: wha@unm.edu

http://www.unm.edu/~wha

An organization of individuals interested in the history of the American West; primarily educators. Annual conference, fall.

WestWeb

http://www.library.csi.cuny.edu/westweb/

An on-line research site created by Catherine Lavender, City College of New York. This is an extensive site with primary and secondary documents, bibliographical and biographical resources as well as hot links to diverse sites related to the historic and contemporary West. If you are not sure where to start, this is the place.

CHRONOLOGY

1836	Texas declares its independence.
1837-40	Between 100,000 and 300,000 Native Americans die of smallpox.
1841	Chartran's trading post opens to trade with Brulé Sioux on Chadron Creek in present-day Nebraska. It remains open for about three years.
1841-72	James Bordeaux operates a trading post on Chadron Creek in present-day Nebraska.
1841	The Bidwell-Bartleson wagon train crosses the plains; the first emigrants on the Oregon Trail.
1841	Congress approves Preemption Act giving settlers the right to claim land and purchase it at a cost of $1.25 per acre.
1842	John C. Frémont explores the West.
1842	Congress approves Donation Acts, encouraging settlers to claim land in areas like Oregon and New Mexico.
1842	Willamette University opens in Oregon, the first in the West.
1842	James Beckworth starts a trading post at Fort Pueblo (Colorado); the Bent Brothers had operated a fort in eastern Colorado since 1826.
1843	Oregon migration begins. During the next thirty years more than 400,000 emigrants cross Nebraska en route to Oregon and California.
1843	March 25—The "Black Bean Affair" occurs in Texas.
1844	June 27—A mob executes Mormon Church Founder Joseph Smith and his brother Hyrum in Illinois.
1844	December 3—President James Tyler appeals to Congress to annex Texas.
1845	March 1—The United States annexes Texas.
1845	March 28—Mexico breaks diplomatic ties with the United States.
1845	May 28—President James Polk sends troops to Texas to defend the border against Mexico.
1845	The U.S. Army builds the first Fort Kearny at Nebraska City (originally called Camp Kearny).
1846	Brigham Young and the first of the Mormons leave Nauvoo, Illinois, headed west. They cross the Missouri River and establish Winter Quarters near present-day Omaha, Nebraska.
1846	June 14—Homesteaders William B. Ide and Capt. John C. Frémont declare California independent, raising a flag with a bear on it in an incident known as the Bear Flag Revolt.
1846	June 15—The United States and Great Britain sign the Oregon Treaty, establishing the dividing line in the Pacific Northwest at the 49th parallel.

1846 August 17—Commodore John Sloat announces the annexation of California and declares himself governor.

1846 Colonel Stephen Watts Kearny captures Santa Fe without shooting and claims New Mexico for the United States.

1846 December—Yerba Buena is renamed San Francisco.

1846-47 Winter—The Donner emigrant party fails to cross the Sierra Nevada mountains before heavy snows close the passes, stranding the party and leading to cannibalism before the survivors are rescued in February.

1847 January 10—Fighting ends in California.

1847 January 20—Taos Indians and revolutionists launch the Taos Revolt, killing Governor Charles Bent.

1847 Mormon migration to Utah begins from Winter Quarters.

1847 September 13-14—Major General Winfield Scott captures the Chapultepec Palace outside Mexico City, bringing the Mexican-American War to an end.

1848 January 24—James Marshall discovers gold in California on the south fork of the American River.

1848 February 2—The United States claims upper California, New Mexico, Utah, Nevada, most of Arizona and some of Colorado under terms of the Treaty of Guadalupe Hidalgo with Mexico.

1848 June—Construction begins on a new Fort Kearny, located in central Nebraska as a fort to protect travelers on the Oregon-California Trail.

1848 November 29—Cayuse Indians attack the Whitman Mission, killing eleven men, one woman (Narcissa Whitman), two children, and taking an additional forty-seven people as hostages.

1849 Thousands of gold seekers follow the California Trail, even more travel to the gold fields via ship around Cape Horn, or via ship to Central America and canoe to Panama and then by land across the Isthmus of Panama to catch another ship to California.

1849 The American Fur Company sells Fort John/Fort Laramie in present-day Wyoming; it becomes a military post.

1849 Cholera spreads throughout the West.

1849 August 20-21—William Bent, unable to receive compensation for Bent's Fort from the United States Government, removes his belongings and then destroys the fort in present-day Colorado.

1850 Census
   Arkansas 210,000
   California 92,497
   Iowa 192,000
   Kansas 107,000
   Louisiana 518,000
   Minnesota 6,000

             Missouri 682,000

             New Mexico 61,547

             Oregon 12,093

             Texas 212,592

             Utah 11,380

             Washington 1,000

1850   The Compromise of 1850 proposes admission of California as a free state, organization of the territories of Utah and New Mexico (with no reference to slavery) and changes in the boundaries of Texas.

1850   Overland mail service in the West begins with a monthly route between Independence, Missouri, and Salt Lake City, Utah Territory.

1850   Sioux call the winter "the big smallpox winter."

1851   May 3—The fifth and largest fire in San Francisco since the beginning of the Gold Rush destroys 70 percent of the city and kills thirty people.

1851   May 7—Cherokees establish seminaries near Tahlequah (Oklahoma).

1851   May—Indian Agent W.P. Richardson orders vaccination of 1,700 Sac and Fox Indians for smallpox.

1852   March—Wells, Fargo & Company organizes. Offices are subsequently established at 114 Montgomery Street in San Francisco, California.

1852   August 29—Brigham Young publishes the revelation on celestial marriage, openly admitting that the Mormons practice polygamy.

1853   February 21—The Coinage Act authorizes $3 gold pieces.

1853   December 30—The Gadsden Purchase is signed in Mexico City, expanding the United States by enlarging Arizona to allow for a railroad right-of-way through the Rocky Mountains.

1854   April 3—Private coinage of gold is no longer allowed due to establishment of a branch mint in San Francisco.

1854   May 30—Congress approves the Kansas-Nebraska Act, establishing Nebraska and Kansas Territories. The Kansas-Nebraska Act repeals the 1820 Missouri Compromise.

1854   August 19—Sioux and the U.S. military clash near Fort Laramie after a Miniconjou kills a cow belonging to some Mormons. Though the Indians try to make restitution, the military refuses and a fight ensues between the Sioux under Conquering Bear (The Bear) and the military under the leadership of Lt. John Grattan. The military force is destroyed in the first armed confrontation between the Sioux and the U.S. Army. It becomes known as the Grattan Massacre.

1854   Smith and Wesson invent their revolver.

1855   William Russell, Alexander Majors and William Waddell start freight-
        ing from Nebraska City; their freighters subsequently forge the
        Oxbow Trail from Nebraska City to Fort Kearny, Nebraska
        Territory.

1855   September 3—As retaliation for the Grattan Massacre, Brig. Gen.
        William S. Harney attacks Little Thunder's band of Brulé Sioux
        at Blue Water Creek, western Nebraska Territory, killing between
        85 and 135 Indians, many of them women and children.

1855   December 15—*Frank Leslie's Illustrated Newspaper* begins publication
        in New York, providing readers with the first illustrations of the
        West. It changes its name to *Frank Leslie's Illustrated Weekly* on De-
        cember 5, 1891 and publishes under that name until January 1895.

1856   October—The fourth and fifth handcart companies organized by
        the Mormons to cross the plains become stranded in central Wyo-
        ming. Hundreds die before rescue parties from Salt Lake reach
        them and provide assistance. The first three handcart companies
        had crossed the plains without incident earlier in the year.

1856   A Vigilance Committee maintains order in San Francisco.

1857   A financial panic hits the country as "wildcat" banks, which had
        issued money with no security, fail.

1857   September 7-11—The Mountain Meadows Massacre occurs in
        present-day Utah.

1858   Green Russell discovers gold near the confluence of the South Platte
        River and Cherry Creek, precipitating the Pikes Peak Gold Rush.
        Further strikes of both gold and silver occur in the Colorado re-
        gion in 1859 and 1860.

1859   The *Rocky Mountain News* begins publication.

1860   Census
        Arkansas 435,450
        California 379,994 (San Francisco, 56,802)
        Colorado 34,277 (Denver, 4,749)
        Dakota 4,837
        Iowa 674,913
        Kansas 107,206 (Kansas City, 7,000)
        Louisiana 708,002
        Minnesota 172,000
        Missouri 1,182,012
        Nebraska 28,841
        Nevada 6,857
        New Mexico 93,516
        Oregon 52,000
        Texas 604,215
        Utah 40,273
        Washington 11,594

1860   April 3—Russell, Majors and Waddell, of Nebraska City, start the
        Pony Express. It continues through mid-October 1861.

1860   Congress approves a subsidy for development of a telegraph line from
        western Missouri to San Francisco.

1860   The Winchester repeating rifle goes into production as does the
        M1844 rifle which has a .44 caliber rimfire cartridge.

1861   The Civil War starts. Mississippi, Alabama, Florida and Georgia se-
        cede from the Union in January, Virginia secedes in April, North
        Carolina secedes in May and Tennessee secedes in June.

1861   May 9—Gov. Algernon S. Paddock calls for volunteers to serve the
        Union in the Second Nebraska Cavalry.

1861   October 24—Transcontinental Telegraph begins operation; the
        Pony Express ceases.

1862   July 1—President Abraham Lincoln signs the Pacific Railway Act.

1862   Congress approves Homestead Act; it becomes effective January 1,
        1863.

1862   July 28—William Eads makes the first really big gold strike in what
        will become Montana Territory; Bannack springs up almost over-
        night and is soon named the first territorial capital.

1862   First troops stationed at Fort Omaha, Military District of Nebraska.

1863   January 1—The Homestead Act goes into effect.

1863   January 1—President Abraham Lincoln signs the Emancipation
        Proclamation.

1863   May 26—Bill Fairweather and associates find gold in Alder Gulch,
        Idaho Territory, which becomes Virginia City, Montana Territory.
        Virginia City soon replaces Bannack as Montana's territorial
        capital.

1863   July—John Jacobs and John Bozeman locate the route of what will
        become the Bozeman Trail, known as the Bloody Bozeman. The
        Bozeman Trail extended from present-day central Wyoming,
        through the Powder River Basin to Montana Territory southeast
        of present-day Billings, and to Virginia City, Montana Territory.

1863   August 21—William Clarke Quantrill leads a raid on Lawrence, Kan-
        sas, one of the atrocities of the Civil War in the West.

1863   September—The Denver Mint begins operations.

1863   October 10—The first telegraph line to Denver is strung from Jules-
        burg, Colorado Territory.

1863   December—Montana vigilantes organize at Bannack.

1864   November 29—The Sand Creek Massacre occurs in Colorado
        Territory.

1864   The U.S. military establishes Fort Sedgwick near Julesburg, and Fort
        Collins, both in Colorado Territory.

1865   Indians retaliate for the unprovoked attack at Sand Creek, raiding thoroughout 1865 on the Overland Trail and other areas as 1865 becomes known as the Bloody Year on the Plains.

1865   The United States military establishes Fort Morgan, Colorado Territory.

1865   Union Pacific Railroad construction starts from Omaha.

1865   The U.S. Army organizes the Pawnee Scouts under Capt. Frank North.

1865   April 9—Lee surrenders to Grant, leading to the end of the Civil War; the final surrender by Confederate troops occurs May 20 when General E. Kirby Smith surrenders the troops in the West. The last Confederate general to surrender is Cherokee chief Stand Watie, in June.

1865   December 18—Congress ratifies the Thirteenth Amendment abolishing slavery.

1866   February 13—The James gang robs its first bank, in Liberty, Missouri.

1866   Hostilities break out in the Powder River Basin as the Sioux object to military forts Reno, Phil Kearny, and C.F. Smith.

1866   November 1—Wells, Fargo assumes control of the Holloday Overland Mail and Express Company, establishing Wells, Fargo and Company in a deal known as the "Great Consolidation."

1866   December 21—The Fetterman Fight (sometimes called the Fetterman Massacre) occurs near Fort Phil Kearny.

1867   April 9—The United States purchases Alaska for $7 million.

1867   November 25—Lt. Col. George Armstrong Custer is court-martialed for ordering deserters to be shot and being absent from his command. He is to be suspended from rank and pay for one year.

1867   Los Angeles installs gaslights and iron water mains.

1868   Nathaniel Hill erects the first smelter at Blackhawk, Colorado Territory, changing mining from placer to hardrock methods.

1868   June—Mail service operated by Wells, Fargo begins between Cheyenne, Wyoming Territory, and Virginia City, Montana Territory.

1868   July 28—Secretary of State William Seward signs a treaty allowing unrestricted emigration by Chinese.

1869   First Texas cattle ship to market on Union Pacific from Schuyler, Nebraska.

1869   May 10—The Union Pacific and Central Pacific Railroads meet at Promontory, Utah Territory, where officials drive in a golden spike symbolizing the linking of the country.

1869   December 10—Wyoming Territorial Governor John Campbell signs the law granting equal suffrage to women, giving them not only the right to vote, but also the right to hold public office and serve on juries.

1870   Census
        Arizona 9,658
        Arkansas 484,471
        California 560,247 (Los Angeles, 5,614; San Francisco, 149,473)
        Colorado 39,864 (Denver, 4,759)
        Dakota Territory 14,000
        Idaho 15,000
        Iowa 1,194,000
        Kansas 364,000
        Louisiana 727,000
        Minnesota 440,000
        Missouri 1,721,000
        Montana 20,595
        Nebraska 123,000
        Nevada 42,000
        New Mexico 91,874
        Oregon 91,000
        Texas 818,579
        Utah 87,780
        Washington 23,955
        Wyoming 9,000
1870   February 15—Construction starts on a second transcontinencal railroad, the Northern Pacific; it is not completed for fifteen years.
1870   Ghost Dancing begins in the Mason Valley of Nevada when a Paiute shaman predicts the return from the dead of fallen warriors, and that white people will fall into great holes in the ground.
1870   The Denver Pacific Railroad reaches Denver in June and the Kansas Pacific arrives in August, signaling an end to ox-powered freighting and stagecoaches as primary means of transportation.
1870   August 1—Women vote in Utah Territory, the first in the nation to do so.
1870   September 6—Louisa Swain casts the first woman's ballot in Wyoming Territory.
1872   The first Grange in Nebraska organizes in Orleans. The Nebraska State Grange and other granges throughout the plains states organize this year as well.
1872   March 1—Yellowstone becomes the first national park.
1872   The Nebraska State Department of Agriculture approves Arbor Day as a new state holiday.
1872   Russian Grand Duke Alexis visits the West, guided by George Armstrong Custer.
1873   Dr. Brewster M. Higley writes the words to "Home On The Range." The music is later written by Dan Kelley. Both were living in Kansas at the time.

1873   Grasshoppers ravage crops throughout the plains.
1873   March 3—Congress approves the Timber Culture Act, which makes it possible to make a homestead claim based upon the planting of trees. The Coal Lands Act allows claims of coal-bearing public domain land at a price of $10 to $20 per acre, with up to 160 acres available to individuals and as much as 320 acres available to groups.
1873   Barbed wire is developed by Joseph Glidden, who will receive a patent in 1874. Some forms of wire with barbs had been developed as early as 1867, and numerous similar types of wire followed Glidden's product.
1873   Levi Strauss patents jeans which have copper rivets at stress points. They become "501 Double X" overalls.
1873   Winchester Arms Company manufactures a new repeating rifle which fires a .44-40 centerfire ammunition from a magazine that holds fifteen rounds.
1874   Adolph Coors begins brewing beer in Golden, Colorado.
1874   British Lord Dunraven begins a land-purchasing scheme in Estes Park, Colorado Territory, when he pays out-of-work cowboys and others from the Denver region to file on homestead land. They then transfer the land to Dunraven. Before authorities stop Dunraven from the fraudulent practice, he gains control of 15,000 acres.
1874   February—The first men arrive and establish a tent camp on the White River in northwestern Nebraska, initially called Camp Robinson, and which in 1877 becomes Fort Robinson, named for Lt. Levi Robinson.
1874   Lt. Col. George A. Custer leads an exploration of the Black Hills that confirms gold in the region.
1874   September 5—The Army establishes Fort Hartsuff, Nebraska.
1875   Grasshoppers ravage the plains.
1875   May 2—Isaac Parker, who will become known as The Hanging Judge, arrives in Fort Smith, Arkansas, to serve as the federal judge for Indian Territory.
1875   Coal miners strike in Rock Springs, Wyoming Territory.
1875   The Cheyenne-Deadwood Stage Route opens.
1876   Spring—Henry T. Clarke builds a toll bridge across the North Platte River in Nebraska to serve traffic on the Sidney to Deadwood Trail. The government responds by establishing Camp Clark to protect the bridge.
1876   June 25—Battle of the Little Bighorn occurs in Montana Territory.
1876   August 2—Jack McCall shoots Wild Bill Hickok as the latter played poker in Deadwood, Dakota Territory.
1876   September 7—The James-Younger gang launches a raid on the First National Bank of Northfield, Minnesota. They meet resistance

leading to penitentiary sentences for Cole, Jim and Bob Younger. Frank and Jesse James escape and hide out in Tennessee.

1877   May 6—Crazy Horse and his Lakota people surrender at Fort Robinson, Nebraska.

1877   September 5—Crazy Horse is stabbed and killed at Fort Robinson.

1878   Cowboys and cattlemen become involved in a conflict in Lincoln County, New Mexico. Among those involved: William Bonney, alias Billy the Kid, and companions known as the Regulators.

1879   June 18—The first ice plant opens in Phoenix, Arizona.

1879   June 23—Congress appropriates $50,000 to establish Fort Niobrara, Nebraska.

1879   The San Francisco California Electrical Company begins selling electrical service, the first company in the world to do so.

1880   Census

       Arizona 40,440

       Arkansas 802,525

       California 864,694 (San Diego, 11,183; San Francisco, 233,959)

       Colorado 194,327 (Denver, 35,959)

       Idaho 32,610

       Iowa 1,624,615

       Kansas 996,096

       Louisiana 939,946

       Minnesota 780,773

       Missouri 2,168,380

       Montana 39,159

       Nebraska 452,402

       Nevada 62,266

       New Mexico 119,565

       North Dakota 39,909

       Oregon 174,768

       South Dakota 98,268

       Texas 1,591,749 (San Antonio, 20,550)

       Utah 143,963 (Salt Lake City, 20,768)

       Washington 75,116

       Wyoming 20,789

1880   The Farmer's Alliance organizes near Filley, Nebraska; within two years 65,000 members belong to 2,000 alliances in Nebraska.

1880   Plattsmouth, Nebraska, has its first railroad bridge built across the Missouri.

1880   May 1—The *Tombstone Epitaph* begins publication in Tombstone, Arizona.

1880   July—Wyatt Earp is appointed a Deputy Sheriff by Pima County Sheriff Charlie Shibell in Tombstone, Arizona.

1880	The Cactus Club, forerunner to the Cheyenne Club, opens in Cheyenne, Wyoming, as an exclusive club for wealthy cattlemen.
1880	October 30—A riot erupts over Chinese-white relations in Denver's Hop Alley.
1880s	Omaha becomes a center of livestock shipping and production processing centers.
1881	July—Late the night of July 13 or early the morning of July 14, Pat Garrett kills Billy the Kid, who asks *"Quien es?"* ("Who is it?"). The actual time of the killing is uncertain.
1881	September—The Tabor Opera House opens in Denver with a performance of *Maritana*, featuring Emma Abbott and her Grand English Opera Company.
1881	October 26—Wyatt, Virgil and Morgan Earp, backed by friend Doc Holliday, have a shoot-out at the OK Corral in Tombstone, Arizona, with Ike and Billy Clanton and Tom and Frank McLaury. Both McLaurys and Billy Clanton are killed.
1882	March 22—The Edmunds Act, outlawing polygamy, passes.
1882	William F. Cody organizes his first Wild West exhibition.
1882	April 3—Jesse James dies of a gunshot in the back fired by Robert Ford.
1882	October 5—Frank James surrenders to Missouri Governor Thomas Crittenden.
1883	Cheyenne, Wyoming, has electric lights.
1883	Denver gets its first electric lights.
1883	The Buffalo Bill Wild West and Congress of Rough Riders of the World makes its debut in North Platte, Nebraska, as the "Old Glory Blowout."
1884	Prairie fires burn millions of acres in North Dakota.
1884	The first windmills are installed in Texas.
1885	April 3—U.S. Land Commissioner W.A.J. Sparks opens some 2.75 million acres of land in Oklahoma, Kansas and Dakota Territory; much of the land had already been taken by railroads, cattlemen and claim jumpers.
1885	April 22—This day becomes Arbor Day as the holiday spreads nationwide
1885	John B. Stetson begins making hats.
1885-86	
1886-87	The winters known as "The Great Die-Up" during which hundreds of thousands of cattle die from Canada to Texas.
1886	Geronimo surrenders and is removed to Florida.
1887	February 8—Congress passes the Dawes Severalty Act, which will divide Indian lands.
1887	March 3—The Edmunds-Tucker Act expands actions against Mormons practicing polygamy.

1887   September 5—Oregon is the first state to recognize Labor Day as a legal holiday; it spreads to thirty-two other states by 1894.

1888   January 12—The School Children's Blizzard sweeps the plains, killing hundreds of people.

1888   October 1—President Grover Cleveland signs the Scott Act, which prohibits Chinese workers from indefininte work periods and which also prohibits Chinese who have left the United States from returning.

1889   January 1—An eclipse leads Paiute shaman Wovoka to claim it is time to begin the Ghost Dance, which will lead to the Indians' ancestors return from the dead, and to the disappearance of whites from the West. Tribes throughout the West practiced the Ghost Dance and the Lakota wore Ghost Dance Shirts—white muslin shirts they believed would protect them from bullets fired by soldiers.

1889   April 22—The first Oklahoma Land Run occurs when some 50,000 to 60,000 people rush into former Indian Territory to claim 1.92 million acres.

1889   July 20—Cattlemen lynch James Averell and Ellen Watson, who is subseqently better known as Cattle Kate, the only woman ever hanged in Wyoming. No one was ever tried in the case.

1890   Census
        Arizona 88,243
        Arkansas 1,128,179
        California 1,213,398 (Los Angeles, 50,395; San Francisco, 298,997)
        Colorado 413,249
        Idaho 88,548
        Iowa 1,912,297
        Kansas 1,428,108
        Louisiana 1,118,588
        Minnesota 1,310,283
        Missouri 2,679,185
        Montana 142,924
        Nebraska 1,062,656
        Nevada 47,355
        New Mexico 160,282
        North Dakota 190,983
        Oklahoma 258,657
        Oregon 317,704
        South Dakota 348,600
        Texas 2,235,527
        Utah 210,779
        Washington 357,323
        Wyoming 62,555

1890   Fort Laramie is abandoned as a military post.

1890   July—North Dakota backs prohibition.

1890   September 25—The Mormon Church denounces polygamy, which had been effectively abolished under terms of the Edmunds-Tucker Act (upheld by the U.S. Supreme Court on May 19). Church President Willford Woodruff tells Mormons to obey federal law as he outlaws plural marriages. Not all church members comply.

1890   December 29—Soldiers open fire on Sioux at Wounded Knee, South Dakota, when troops under Colonel James W. Forsyth attempt to disarm the Indians. As many as 150 Indian men, women and children died in the Massacre at Wounded Knee.

1892   April 5-12—An antirustling cattleman's group dubbed the Regulators kills two homesteaders before the group falls under siege themselves in the Johnson County Invasion in Wyoming.

1892   April 19—A second land run occurs in Oklahoma on the "Cherokee Strip."

1893   Drought results in financial panic; grasshoppers eat the few crops that do grow.

1893   September 16—The third and largest of the Oklahoma land runs occurs.

1893   November 1—Congress repeals the Sherman Silver Purchase Act, leading to closures of silver mines in Colorado and the subsequent Panic of 1893.

1893   Katharine Lee Bates writes "America The Beautiful" after being inspired by a trip to Pikes Peak, Colorado.

1894   William Jennings Bryan of Lincoln, Nebraska, proposes free silver to solve the nation's economic woes.

1894   Mormons in Utah, who were disenfranchised due to antipolygamy laws, have their civil rights restored and President Grover Cleveland pardons them.

1895   Sears, Roebuck and Co. begins operation.

1895   Bannock Indians have a conflict with settlers and officials over hunting rights near Jackson Hole, Wyoming.

1896   August 12—Prospectors discover gold in the Klondike, traveling through Alaska to reach the Canadian Yukon.

1896   Lincoln, Nebraska resident William Jennings Bryan, "The Great Commoner," is the Democratic candidate for U.S. President.

1897   Union Pacific Railroad Company organizes as a group of investors led by Edward H. Harriman purchases the railroad when the line goes bankrupt.

1897   June—Three companies of Buffalo Soldiers use bicycles as transportation en route from Montana to St. Louis.

1897	The Dawes Commission and the Chickasaw and Choctaw Nations reach an agreement that abolishes the tribal governments and divides their lands.
1898	June 1- October 31—Omaha hosts Trans-Mississippi and International Exhibition.
1898	The Spanish-American War breaks out; western troops include the Rough Riders organized by Theodore Roosevelt, who see action in Cuba; and Torrey's Rough Riders and Griggsby's Cowboys, who don't make it to the fighting.
1899	May 10—David Brunton obtains the first automobile in Denver.
1899	June 2—Butch Cassidy and the Sundance Kid (or their cohorts) rob a Union Pacific Train at Wilcox, Wyoming.

ADDITIONAL READING

Flanagan, Mike. *The Old West Day By Day.* New York: Facts on File, 1995. A good resource though there are some minor errors on location and dates.

Roadside History Series. Missoula, Mont.: Mountain Press Publishing Co. Each book in the series has a chronology for the state.

BIBLIOGRAPHY

Aadland, Dan. *Women and Warriors of the Plains: The Pioneer Photography of Julia E. Tuell*. New York: Macmillan, 1996.

Alcorn, Gay. *Tough Country*. Saratoga, Wyo.: Legacy Press, 1984.

Armitage, Susan and Elizabeth Jameson, eds. *The Women's West*. Norman: University of Oklahoma Press, 1987.

Bird, Isabella. *A Lady's Life in the Rocky Mountains*. Sausalito, Calif.: Comstock, 1960.

Bratt, John. *Trails of Yesterday*. Lincoln, Nebr.: University Publishing, Co. 1921.

Brown, Dee. *The Gentle Tamers*. New York: Bantam, 1958. An excellent general resource.

————. *Wondrous Times on the Frontier*. Little Rock: August House, 1991. An excellent general reource.

Butcher, Solomon D. *Pioneer History of Custer County Nebraska*. Denver, Colo.: Sage Books, 1965.

Cleland, Robert Glass, ed. *Apron Full of Gold*. San Marino, Calif.: The Huntington Library, 1949.

Crabb, Richard. *Empire on the Platte*. Cleveland, Ohio: The World Publishing Company, 1967

Dary, David. *Buffalo Book: Full Saga of the American Animal*. Athens, Ohio: Swallow Press/University of Ohio Press, 1989.

DeGraf, Anna, *Pioneering on the Yukon, 1892-1917*. Edited by Roger S. Brown. Hamden, Conn.: Archon Books, 1992.

Dick, Everett. *The Sod-House Frontier*. Lincoln, Nebr.: Johnson Publishing, 1954.

Exley, Jo Ella Powell. *Texas Tears and Texas Sunshine*. College Station: Texas A&M University Press, 1985.

Foote, Cheryl J. *Women of the New Mexico Frontier, 1846-1912*. Niwot: University Press of Colorado, 1990.

Greeley, Horace. *An Overland Journey*. New York: Knopf, 1969.

Haines, Francis. *The Buffalo: The Story of American Bison and Their Hunters from Prehistoric Times to the Present*. Norman: University of Oklahoma Press, 1970.

Holmes, Kenneth L. *Covered Wagon Women*. Lincoln, Nebr.: University of Nebraska Press, 1995-1998. A series of ten books being reprinted from their earlier editions which are out of print. A vital resource for anyone writing about western migration.

Irwin, Henry, and William F. Cody. *The Great Salt Lake Trail*. Reprint, Topeka, Kans.: Crane, 1913. Williamstown, Mass.: Corner House Publishers, 1978.

Juster, Norton. *A Woman's Place: Yesterday's Women in Rural America.* Golden, Colo.: Fulcrum Publishing, 1996.

Karolevitz, Robert F. *Old Time Agriculture in the Ads.* Aberdeen, S. Dak.: North Plains Press, 1970.

Lavender, David. *Bent's Fort.* Lincoln: University of Nebraska Press, 1954.

Lecompte, Janet. *Pueblo, Hardscrabble, Greenhorn: The Upper Arkansas: 1832-1856.* Norman: University of Oklahoma Press, 1978.

Lee, Wayne C. *Trails of the Smoky Hill.* Caldwell, Idaho: The Caxton Printers Ltd., 1980.

Lindgren, H. Elaine. *Land In her Own Name.* Norman: University of Oklahoma, Press, 1996. An excellent resource about women's homesteading; much of the information, however, is from the period after 1900.

Luchetti, Cathy, and Carol Olwell. *Women of the West.* New York: Orion Books, 1982. An excellent general resource.

Mayer, Melanie J. *Klondike Women.* Athens, Ohio: Swallow Press/Ohio University Press, 1989.

Moulton, Candy. *Legacy of the Tetons: Homesteading in Jackson Hole.* Boise: Tamarack Books, 1994.

Moynihan, Ruth B., Susan Armitage, and Christiane Fischer Dischamp, eds. *So Much to Be Done: Women Settlers on the Mining and Ranching Frontier.* Lincoln: University of Nebraska Press, 1990.

Myers, Lois E. *Letters by Lamplight: A Woman's View of Everyday Life in South Texas, 1873-1883.* Waco, Tex.: Baylor University Press, 1991.

Neiderman, Sharon. *A Quilt of Words.* Boulder, Colo.: Johnston Books, 1988. An excellent resource, though some information is from the period after 1900.

Peavy, Linda, and Ursula Smith. *Women in Waiting in the Westward Movement.* Norman: University of Oklahoma Press, 1994.

Petrick, Paula. *No Step Backward: Women and Family on the Rocky Mountain Mining Frontier, Helena, Montana, 1865-1900.* Helena: Montana Historical Society Press, 1987.

Pound, Louise. *Nebraska Folklore.* Lincoln: University of Nebraska Press, 1989.

Reedstrom, Ernest L. *Scrapbook of the American West.* Caldwell, Idaho: The Caxton Printers Ltd., 1991. An excellent general reference, includes much detail about military clothing, weapons and language references related to gamblers, miners, cowboys, members of the militory.

Reiter, Joan Swallow, and the Editors of Time-Life Books. *The Women.* Alexandria, Va.: Time-Life Books, 1978

Riley, Glenda. *The Female Frontier: A Comparative View of Women on the Prairie and the Plains.* Lawrence: University of Kansas, 1988. An excellent resource.

————. *Frontierswomen: The Iowa Experience.* Ames: The Iowa State University Press, 1981.

————. *A Place to Grow: Women in the American West.* Arlington Heights, Ill.: Harlan Davidson, Inc., 1992.

————. *Women and Indians on the Frontier, 1825-1915.* Albuquerque: University of New Mexico, 1984.

————. *Women in the West.* Manhattan, Kans.: Sunflower University Press, 1982.

Russell, Don. *The Lives and Legends of Buffalo Bill.* Norman: University of Oklahoma Press, 1960.

Sage, Rufus G. *Rocky Mountain Life.* 1846. Reprint, Lincoln: University of Nebraska Press, 1989.

Sheldon, Addison Erwin. *History and Stories of Nebraska.* 1846. Reprint, Lincoln, Nebr.: University Publishing Co., 1919.

————. *Nebraska Old and New History, Stories, Folklore.* Lincoln, Nebr.: University Publishing Co., 1937.

Thrapp, Dan. L. *Encyclopedia of Frontier Biography.* Glendale, Calif.: Arthur H. Clark and Company, 1990. Lincoln: University of Nebraska Press, three volumes and CD-Rom, 1994. A vital resource for anyone writing about the people of the West. Because of its ease of conducting subject searches, the CD-Rom is highly recommended.

The Editors of Time-Life Books. *The Spanish West.* Alexandria, Va.: Time-Life Books, 1976.

Twain, Mark. *Roughing It.* Hartford, Conn.: American Publishing Co., 1872.

Welsch, Roger. *It's Not the End of the Earth, But You Can See It from Here: Tales of the Great Plains.* New York: Fawcett. 1991.

————. *Shingling the Fog and Other Plains Lies.* Lincoln: University of Nebraska Press, 1972.

Wheeler, Keith, and the Editors of Time-Life books. *The Alaskans.* Alexandria, Va.: Time-Life Books, 1977.

INDEX